NETHERWORLD

NETHERWORLD

ROBERT TEMPLE

www.robert-temple.com

CENTURY · LONDON

First published in the United Kingdom in 2002 by Century

Random House Group Limited
20 Vauxhall Bridge Road, London SW1V 2SA

Random House Australia (Pty) Limited
20 Alfred Street, Milsons Point, Sydney,
New South Wales 2061, Australia

Random House New Zealand Limited
18 Poland Road, Glenfield, Auckland 10, New Zealand

Random House (Pty) Limited
Endulini, 5A Jubilee Road, Parktown 2193, South Africa

The Random House Group Limited Reg. No. 954009
www.randomhouse.co.uk

A CIP record for this book is available from the British Library

Papers used by Random House UK Limited are natural,
recyclable products made from wood grown in sustainable forests.
The manufacturing processes conform to the environmental
regulations of the country of origin.

ISBN 0 7126 8404 2

Typeset by MATS, Southend-on-Sea, Essex
Printed and bound in Great Britain by
Mackays of Chatham PLC, Chatham, Kent

For my wife, Olivia,
partner in all my writings,
companion in all my journey,
sharer in all my travail,
fellow of all my feelings,
unique in this world.

CONTENTS

Every effort has been made to trace the ownership of all illustrative material reproduced in this book, and written material quoted. Should any error or omission in acknowledgement have been made, the author offers his apologies and will make the necessary correction in future editions. The author would be obliged to learn of any means by which he may contact the estate or executors of the late Robert F. Paget, whose publishers, agents and even acquaintances were unable to help him to do so.

ILLUSTRATIONS

Figures

ACKNOWLEDGEMENTS

First, I wish to thank my wife, Olivia, for her unfailing support and encouragement, and particularly for her invaluable editorial comments at all stages of the writing of this book.

For help with the Oracle of the Dead, I wish to acknowledge the years of discussions and correspondence with the late Colin Hardie, who encouraged me to persevere in its investigation. I wish to thank my friends Michael and Jane Baigent for accompanying me and Olivia into the Oracle, and to acknowledge Michael's splendid photographic achievements such as the photo on the cover of the jacket for this book. I wish to thank Dr Paola Miniero and Professor Stephano de Caro for facilitating the access to the Oracle, and the British School at Rome for their help over the years.

I wish to thank Paul Griffiths of Ashcott, Somerset, for his good-humoured assistance in the investigation of extispicy, which involved trouble and delay to his usual work. I also wish to acknowledge the late Dr Ulla Jeyes for her considerable help in the consideration of Babylonian and Assyrian extispicy. Her premature death was a great loss to her friends.

My chief editor, Mark Booth, is solely responsible for this book seeing the light of day, and I am grateful as usual for his support, encouragement, and friendship. I wish also to thank my editor Anna Cherrett, and am grateful also for the editorial assistance of Hannah Black. My literary agent Bill Hamilton of A. M. Heath is uniquely supportive at all times and I am grateful for his encouragement and friendship, and I wish to thank also Sara Fisher of A. M. Heath for her assistance.

I am also grateful to the following for help of various kinds, personal or scholarly, which contributed towards the completion of this book: Warwick Bray, Gavin Bridson, the late Schuyler Cammann, Sylvia Cave, Robert Costa, Du Xiansheng, Mrs Jack Gates, Robert Gilbert, Murray Groves, Professor John R. Hale, John Hurt, Raimundo Irace, Stephen Karcher, Isabella (You-hsien) Lewis, Professor Ioannis Liritzis, the late Lu Gwei-djen, David N. Menton, Adriana Natcheva, the late Joseph Needham, Tom Rees, Rudolf Ritsema, Ehud Sperling, Henry Spiller, John Stubbs, Rima Stubbs, Professor Kenzi Tamaru, Nigel Unwin, Edward J. Voso, Professor Chandra Wickramasinghe, the late Professor Hellmut Wilhelm, Frances Wood, the late Arthur M. Young.

In addition, the staffs of the Department of Western Asiatic Antiquites of the British Museum, of Dr Williams's Library in London, of the London Library, of the Library for the Promotion of Hellenic Studies in London, of the Library of the School of Oriental and African Studies of the University of London, and of the British Library have all been helpful at various times.

'There might even be a science of expectation,
as some say there is of divination.'

Aristotle,
'On Memory and Recollection',
Parva Naturalia, 499b, 12–13

INTRODUCTION

We do not know who we are; we do not know why we are here, and we do not know what will happen to us. In the midst of all this uncertainty it is not surprising that, during our history as an intelligent species, we have tried in various ways to escape from the suffocating helplessness of our ignorance. Today, most of our hopes rest on science. But before there was science, a branch of religion or philosophy existed for the purpose of helping man to step outside the confines of the present and to catch glimpses of the future.

Prophecy offered some comfort. We might not have any more idea of who we were and why we were here, but we could at least have some idea of what would happen to us. The terrifying uncertainty of events in the next few days, or the next few years, or even the next few centuries, could be diminished. We were not complete prisoners in time, for liberation was possible, if erratically and briefly.

That, at least, is what our ancestors believed. Nor would I be so presumptuous as to say that they were entirely wrong. We are sometimes tempted to think of our predecessors as fools, possessing less wisdom than we do today. But in charity to ourselves, who will doubtless be thought fools in the future, we should extend a more tolerant attitude towards our forebears and seriously question whether they were as foolish as we like to think. Let us more often try to see things from their point of view, and judge them for what they accomplished within the situations in which they found themselves.

In the history of humanity, there is little which is as fascinating and incredible as the story of mankind's institution and practice of forms of divination and prophecy to enable him to see into the future.

In this book I shall be considering this 'underside' of man's history and surveying four major forms of institutionalized prophecy. Astrology is not among them. It was always of lesser importance than the other forms discussed here, though it was by no means negligible. In any case, so much has been written about astrology that the reader may forgive me for omitting a consideration of it from this book; it is the form of divination or prophecy least in need of further attention in comparison to its neglected sister disciplines.

I have chosen to call this book *Netherworld*. I survey prophetic arts and divination not only from the traditional Western heartland of the Mediterranean area, but also from the East. In fact, the main institutionalized forms of divination break down neatly into two Western disciplines and two Eastern disciplines: oracles and divination by entrails in the West, and Oracle-Bone-cracking and the *Book of Change* in China. I believe I have found the connecting link between the latter two which has escaped previous investigators. As for the two former, although there is much in print on the subject of oracles, there has been until now no popular account in English of divination by entrails. With regard to oracles, I think the reader will discover that most of what is presented to him here is entirely new and somewhat surprising.

I should mention that there were countless lesser forms of divination, which perhaps took over as the chief forms from time to time in particular areas. I have accumulated enormous amounts of information about these lesser forms and it is not from lack of interest that I omit their description here, but because I feel that the subject of man's attempts to know the future is best dealt with by concentrating on the most notable techniques.

Let us now turn our ears to some ancient murmurs. It may be possible to overhear something, to catch some phrases, to achieve some insights into the minds of our ancestors as they speak. They are asking questions. The settings are strange, but the questions are familiar . . .

PART ONE

The Western Tradition

ONE

DISCOVERY OF THE UNDERWORLD

The most terrifying and dangerous of all ancient rituals for foretelling the future was undertaken by means of the descent into Hell. This took place at the Oracle of the Dead at Baia, in southern Italy. It was not just a poetical or mythological allegory: it *actually happened,* and the description of how it occurred is one of the most bizarre stories of ancient history, and one which has been known by archaeologists only since 1962.

It was in May 2001 that I finally managed to gain access to this amazing place, after twenty years of trying. It was one of the strangest experiences I have ever had. The entrance is all but invisible, and you have to descend on a ladder. Then, with great trepidation, you step into another world entirely.

Entering the Oracle of the Dead is like a scene from a film where the camera plunges down the bloodstream towards a pulsating heart. The only element missing is the sound effect of the 'thump thump thump'. In fact, as you move down the entrance tunnel you are struck by its eerie silence. It pierces directly into the heart of the earth for a great distance that seems endless. The tunnel goes on and on in a narrow needle-corridor, and my shoulders rubbed on both sides most of the time. You not only have to stoop slightly, you have to twist like a liquorice stick as well.

But what is this place? Why does it go onwards so relentlessly? Why are these tunnels so narrow and so carefully and elegantly arched at the top? And there – what is that dark cloud moving up ahead? As we get closer I see it is a cloud of insects which had been clinging to the wall, but are now in angry mood, disoriented by our lights. What is that *creature*? It looks like a cockroach on stilts. There's another one . . . and another! There's one on my arm. They're everywhere – clumps of thousands upon thousands of giant mosquitoes, hurtling into my eyes, mesmerized by the miner's light on my hard hat.

The smell is otherworldly, unlike anything I have ever experienced before. It smells like *dead soil, earth which has died.* I am wearing a dust mask now, but later, when I have to remove it, I will get a horrible choking sensation, as if mud is being stuffed down my throat. I walk into another cloud of the giant mosquitoes. Why don't they bite? The Italian workmen tell me that these creatures are presently in a state they call *morbido*. I don't know whether that means they have just been born or are dying, are too young to have learned how to bite, or are too exhausted to continue, but they are the largest mosquitoes I have ever seen, and tens of thousands of them move in endless swarms all the way along the tunnel until we reach the Styx. They hang like tiny bats in clusters from the roof and walls, and then, as we go deeper and further into the tunnels they fade away, too far from the entrance for their comfort.

It is a great relief that, despite the stern warnings from the Italian authorities, the sulphurous fumes and the poison gas do not exist after all. We put our gas mask adapters away and just use the dust filters. It was a phantom scare, a case of hysterical imagination. The discoverer Robert Paget never encountered poison gas either. I am convinced that it has never existed, that it is all part of the paranoid fear of the powers of Hell and a superstition of the Church: if Satan lives surrounded by fumes of sulphur, then the ancient Greek Underworld must be the same – a case of reverse-reasoning.

The tunnel goes on and on; we have gone hundreds of feet. But now it is coming to a point where it bends to the right, going down and out of sight. Our endless journey now becomes a descent as well.

No one has been here in the thirty years since Paget died. In fact, there is no one alive who has ever entered this gloomy underground Oracle. This amazing place is now coming alive for a new generation as we pierce the earth and descend towards – what? The artificial River Styx, the underground river along which enquirers at this eerie oracle were rowed by a man dressed as Charon the Underworld ferryman, to disembark at the far side and ascend to the séance, which was staged there for enquirers who wished to speak to the spirits of the dead.

And there it is. The river is choked with mud and the water level has risen, preventing a boat from passing along it. It would have to be dredged and cleared if it was to function again as the Styx. But we call it the Styx. The water is crystal clear, except for a calcareous mineral scum which floats on the top. It is just like the scum I saw floating on the water in the channels surrounding the sarcophagus in the 'Chamber of Osiris' beneath the Chephren Causeway on the Giza Plateau in Egypt just a few months earlier. But the Giza Plateau is limestone, and this Oracle is cut out of tufa stone. Maybe the limestone in the water comes from the rubble and sludge thrown into the River by the Romans, and later by Robert Paget, as I shall describe. I half expect to see a ghostly albino fish swimming through the water, but it does not contain any life. In the 1960s the water was boiling hot, but when we put a thermometer into it it reads only 28°C, a mere degree hotter than the air temperature throughout the central complex of the Oracle. Although I say 'air temperature', there is so little air in the central and further parts of the Oracle that it might be more accurate to speak of the 'temperature of the vacuum'. In those remote parts of the structure we have to move slowly, like men in space, conserving our energy, breathing steadily but laboriously, struggling to perform the increasingly futile gestures of inhalation and exhalation. Our lungs become bellows, but they seem to get emptier and emptier. We get increasingly confused and begin to forget things. I was going to take a photo of that feature – where is it? What was it? I forget. What am I doing in this place?

I am with my friend, the writer Michael Baigent, an expert at tunnel exploration who in the past spent months in the caves at Qmran looking for additional Dead Sea Scrolls. He has also brought special photographic apparatus to get shots of the dark tunnels. He crouches at one end with his camera and the main flash and I have to set off two additional flashes within one second, a test of my physical coordination. Was that his flash? Missed it! Try again. Pop, Pop. This time it worked. See Plate 8 for the result.

We have been accompanied by Gino and Pepe, two Italian workmen attached to the archaeological authorities for the area. They speak no English and we speak no Italian, but it doesn't matter: 'Ciao Gino! Ciao Pepe!' and that is all it takes in Italy to be friends. They have brought a generator to power large lights for us, and put it at the entrance. The cables run with us for hundreds of feet but are eventually too short, the Styx being 600 feet from the entrance. There are no snakes, which is a relief, because our wives waiting outside see a fat one slithering into a hole near our tunnel.

I am streaming with so much sweat that inside my dust mask my mouth and nose feel as if they are inside a fish bowl, and drops fall repeatedly from one lip to the other. I want to scratch the drops off the tip of my nose but I can't. I try and scrunch my nose against the mask instead, but it won't reach. My shirt is so soaked that it feels as if I've been in a pool with my clothes on.

We struggled up what Paget named 'the Rise', the dog-leg tunnel that curves upwards from the bank of the Styx. This was hard going because it is largely filled with loose earth and stone rubble. As you step on it, your foot slides back again, starting a mini-avalanche. When first encountered by Paget, the Rise was completely filled with earth and not only impassable but impenetrable as well. In 1962, the complex thus stopped at the Styx in an apparent dead end. The passage which leads into the inner Oracle is now passable only because of Paget's clearing efforts. At the time, he and his friends could only stay at the Styx for fifteen minutes without passing out because of the lack of air and intense heat. So, in order to study the Oracle, they took colour snapshots of everything and projected the slides on to the walls of Paget's house in the evenings.

It was only by close scrutiny of the photos that Paget and his team eventually noticed a large tile positioned over the bank of the Styx, so they went back into the Oracle and managed to remove it. Paget's small friend, Keith Jones, squeezed through the narrow opening we now call 'the Chimney', and found himself inside the concealed central portions of the complex. Over a period of months, Jones threw enough of the soil that blocked the Rise down the Chimney into the Styx, clearing it sufficiently to allow scrambling access. Paget discovered that underneath the remaining earth in the Rise stairs had been cut in the rock. If fully cleared, its true height would be six or seven feet, although its current height is about three feet, which forced us to travel up it on our hands and knees.

Much of the additional mud and rubble that now silts up the bottom of the Styx was created by Jones's clearing process. Although this extra soil raised the level of the Styx, the subsidences of the Vesuvius region had already done the same thing in the two thousand years before. But this had gone undiscovered, as no one had entered the Oracle of the Dead at Baia since the reign of the Roman Emperor Augustus when General Agrippa tried to block up the whole complex to ensure that its use again as an oracle could be prevented forever.

As we went up the Rise we passed the remains of an ancient door, which can be seen in Plate 11. At the top of the Rise you can now look down upon the bank of the Styx through the vertical Chimney which is constructed of tufa bricks. Beside this chimney is a flat perch, which may be where they kept the hound that we believe howled in imitation of Cerberus, the hound of Hell, as clients were ferried across the Styx on the way to the ceremonies.

At the top of the Rise, we reached a point where three tunnels run off in various directions and you encounter the bricked-up doorways of the Inner Sanctuary. If you go up and along a narrow ledge to the left, you enter the tunnel named '120' after its compass orientation, which then divides again by sending a side-branch off to the left. If you continue round to the left of that there is a strange elevated platform, the purpose of which is not clear. But if you go round to the right you find 'North 120', which runs parallel to 'South 120' for approximately 150 feet. Unfortunately Agrippa was so determined to render the Oracle ineffective that it is mostly blocked by soil and rubble and cannot even be crawled over after a short distance; its termination, however, can be seen at the other end.

'South 120' is partially filled with soil at the beginning but you can get along some of its distance if you crouch. However, you then have to crawl on your belly through a space perhaps a foot and a half high. Michael and I crawled along for thirty or forty feet to a point where the soil becomes less deep and you can almost stand. Michael then continued for the entire 150 feet length of the tunnel on his stomach, pushing his cameras through the dust ahead of his face and repeatedly scraping his head along the ceiling. When he got to the end he was unable to turn around and had to crawl backwards for part of the 120 feet. Without his dust mask he would have choked to death. We had debated whether we should do this together, so that if he got stuck or passed out I could try and pull him out. But we finally decided it was a worse danger that I might block his retreat entirely in an emergency, and we could not communicate because we dare not remove our masks, so that his only form of communication to me would be to kick me in the face, a mode of signalling somewhat counterproductive.

When Robert Paget discovered this oracle complex, he was 72 years old, and never crawled along South 120 because he was not up to it. Keith Jones, his much younger colleague, did that for him. Both Paget and Jones and Michael and I performed a little experiment at the end of this tunnel which I shall describe later. We also discovered some curious features there which were not noticed or reported by Paget, and we believe we have found another tunnel there as well, concealed below, running north-wards beneath the entrance tunnel of the Oracle, leading to some yet undiscovered part of the structure. Excavation would be necessary to clear this.

If at the top of the Rise you go up and round to the right, you go along another tunnel which leads down to the other end of the River Styx, which is mostly blocked now. At the end of the passable portion of this tunnel we saw a small bat which seems to live alone on the ceiling, poor thing. Gino and Pepe spoke of it affectionately as *uno pipistrello solo* ('a single pipistrel bat'). Far along 'South 120' we had seen a semi-mummified body of a hare that must have become lost in the tunnels and died there of starvation.

Beside one of the blocked doors of the sanctuary is the prominent niche that Paget believed was where the client placed a small branch of golden mistletoe as an offering to Persephone, as described in Book Six of the *Aeneid*. In this scene, Aeneas goes down into this very oracle: 'Aeneas springs forward to the entry [to the Sanctuary, since he is already deep inside 'Hades'], sprinkles his body with fresh water, and fixes the bough in the fronting portal.' (Davidson's translation) Since we had no idea where to find any mistletoe, I made Persephone an offering of myrtle sprigs, which Olivia had bound for me with grass. This may be seen in Plate 18. It seemed only polite to show respect for a goddess who had been sadly neglected for so long. I hardly need add this was purely symbolical.

I noticed two small animal bones at the foot of the door beside this niche. I suspected that when Paget last left this place, he may have made some symbolical offering of his own, or perhaps it was the remains of a subterranean picnic. Somehow I couldn't believe in the picnic, however, as any food eaten in such a place would taste so foul.

We found the general atmosphere of the Oracle surprisingly friendly. There was no sense of an evil presence, no brooding doom. Despite the two and half millennia of the Oracle's existence, the drastic eruptions of nearby Vesuvius and the many earthquakes and subsidences, not a single hairline crack of any kind can be seen anywhere in the tunnels. The only evidence of all these upheavals is the rise in the water level of the River Styx. In fact, Paget recorded a sudden two-foot drop in level in a single day in May 1965, and since his time it has risen higher while the nearby city of Pozzuoli has been sinking into the sea due to seismic reasons.

Where were all the sulphurous vapours of which we had been warned? I had been trying to get in here for twenty years and all the efforts on my behalf over many years by the British School at Rome had met with total failure. In 1999, in one of their many communications to me over the years they wrote: 'The underground passage at Baia is absolutely not accessible for safety reasons.' In 2000 I was informed by the Italians that sulphur fumes had been detected near the entrance and that the passages were full of poisonous gas. I was then told that the entrance was blocked by stones and rubble placed there in the 1970s to prevent entry. In fact, when we did finally gain admittance, I had to sign documents absolving the Italian authorities of any responsibility or liability regarding my safety, which I was happy to do.

We only managed to enter the Oracle because of the spirited attitude and keen interest of the Italian archaeologist Dr Paola Miniero, who accompanied us for part of our first day of exploration and facilitated the work in every way that she could. We are very grateful to her for everything she did. She went in for the first time with us, and was the first living Italian archaeologist to enter the place. She had imagined that the tunnels were simply for some sort of water supply, but when she saw the complexity of the construction she realized that this theory would not hold up. She said that as she could not understand what she had seen, she would have to think about it. I leave it to her to express her own views when she arrives at them. Dr Miniero deserves much of the credit for making it possible for the Oracle to be rediscovered in our own time, and her superior, the Superintendent of Antiquities for Campania, Professor Stephano de Caro, must be congratulated for being enlightened enough to grant the official permissions and allowing the study to go ahead. Our exploration in May 2001, as I have just described, was a first step, and will be followed later by dating work, the subsequent processing of the dating samples for which will take many months. The results will be reported by myself and another colleague in a subsequent book, along with results from Egypt and other cultures. The appearance of this present account of our exploration occurs before it is possible to have any firm evidence to resolve the true date of this mysterious Oracle of the Dead. It is one of the greatest and most completely preserved archaeological remains in the world, already old when the Romans conquered the area for its grain, its olives, and its vines, and when their empire was only just beginning to take shape.

Let us now consider the work of Paget, who inspired me in my twenty years of effort to try to get access to this Oracle. I never knew him, as he died in the 1970s and although he was married to an Italian opera singer, they had no children. He was born in 1890 and spent most of his life as a chemical engineer. He retired in 1958 and settled at Baia, where he took a keen interest in the local antiquities. After countless vicissitudes, he discovered the Oracle of the Dead in 1962, after being ridiculed by all the authorities and experts for years, all of whom insisted it was only a myth. But then amateur archaeologist Heinrich Schliemann had experienced similar scoffing, and went on to discover Troy. Paget was in the same mould, but he was not really an amateur. Apart from the book recording the discovery of the Oracle of the Dead (to be quoted at length in what follows), not long before his death he brought out an impressive work entitled *Central Italy: an Archaeological Guide; The Prehistoric, Vilanovan, Etruscan, Samnite, Italiote and Roman Remains of the Ancient Road Systems.*[1] It seems that Paget realized late in life that he should never have been an engineer at all, but rather an archaeologist, and he must often have wondered why he had once held the incongruous official job of Petroleum Officer for North-Eastern England!

We will now consider the amazing discovery he made, which we have at last reopened to the world, and which must now be more thoroughly studied and explored, and cleared of the obstructions placed there two thousand years ago. For it is time that we have a more thorough understanding of this amazing place. My old friend Colin Hardie, classics don from Magdalen College, Oxford, died in 1998, the last surviving person to have entered the Oracle before myself. He always used to say to me:

'Robert, whatever you do, whatever it takes, you *must* enter the Oracle. Going in there was the most amazing experience in my life. It is quite frankly the most incredible place on earth.' How I wish Colin were still alive so that he and I could sit and chat and compare our experiences, so that he could know that after two decades of trying I finally made it. But perhaps he does, for who can say? – he may have been present in ghostly form so that he didn't really miss the adventure!

Many people know the story of Orpheus and Eurydice: that Orpheus descended into the Underworld in an attempt to see his wife Eurydice, who had died. In Homer's *Odyssey*, Odysseus also

Figure 1: Dante and Vergil entering the Gate to Hell, as imagined by Gustave Doré – an illustration for Cary's English translation of Dante's Inferno of 1903. The text of Canto III says woefully: 'Abandon all hope, you who enter here.' (Collection of Robert Temple)

*This spelling is preferred to the more common 'Virgil'. His name in Latin was Publius Vergilius Maro.

descends into Hades and invokes the shade of the dead seer Teiresias. In the *Aeneid* of Vergil,* Aeneas too descends into Hell, which is minutely described. What is not widely appreciated is that *these episodes were based on an actual physical location.*

Robert Paget's collaborator was an American naval officer, Keith W. Jones. Together these two men did what seemed impossible: they discovered the Underworld.

Paget had settled on his retirement in 1958 at Baia, on the coast a few miles northwest of Naples. Jones had been posted to the Naples headquarters of NATO's Southern Flank. The two men met and discovered that they shared an enthusiasm for exploring the antiquities of the area. There had been some professional local excavations, but anyone who has spent any time in Italy knows that there is always far more underfoot than has ever been discovered. The Italian government, aware that it would take centuries to excavate every site professionally, has an enlightened policy of encouraging responsible amateur archaeological exploration. So Paget and Jones arranged to get official sanction for just such a purpose.

Paget and Jones began looking for the ancient Oracle of the Dead, said in ancient tradition to be near the Crater Avernus in the area of Baia. Orthodox opinion was that it never existed, that it was no more than a myth. Archaeologists insisted that Baia was only the site of some Roman baths, and had no connection with any ancient oracle. So Paget and Jones began their search at nearby Cuma, which was known to be a very ancient settlement, and the earliest Greek city established in Italy. Also it had in antiquity had a famous prophesying Sibyl. They began to explore holes in the ground wherever they could find them – and they were not difficult to find in that volcanic area which has eighty-seven craters within a five-mile radius of Avernus.

They crawled into well over a hundred such holes in their fruitless search. Paget says of them: 'Some were damp and smelly, some dry and smelly, but all more or less charged with sulphurous and other volcanic gases, the homes of scorpions, poisonous snakes and huge black spiders with bodies as big as nuts and legs three inches long, barring the way with their sticky webs and poisonous bites ... fitting guardians to the Gates of Hell.'[2] This went on for two whole years, but they found no Oracle of the Dead. They began to wonder whether, after all, the ancient accounts might not have been referring to Cuma, but instead to Baia a few miles away.

Professor Amadeo Maiuri had made a sensational rediscovery (see Appendix 1) when he excavated the famous site of the Oracle of Cuma in 1932. Paget says of it:

> It is, indeed, a fearsome cavern 150 yards long ... it conforms in a truly eerie manner with the description given by Vergil. Here, Aeneas came to consult his father in the Underworld. He was informed by the priests of the temple that the Sibyl would assist him in his desire, if he complied with the rites and sacrifices that such a tremendous project required. After the funeral of Misenus the Sibyl conducted Aeneas to a place where there was another 'fearful cavern', down which she would guide him to the Underworld.[3]

So it seemed that the elusive Oracle of the Dead must indeed be somewhere else, although nearby. It had been connected with, but was physically separate from, the Sibyl's cave at Cuma.

The Sybil of Cuma holds a special place in accounts of ancient prophetesses. Christian commentators have maintained that she prophesied the birth of Christ. She was supposed to have been known personally to the poet Vergil, who, as we shall see later, was intimately acquainted with the Cuma region and who lived nearby for some years. In his 'Fourth Eclogue', which is supposed to repeat the Sibyl's prophecy, he says:

> We have reached the last era in Sibylline song. Time has conceived and the great Sequence of the Ages starts afresh. Justice, the Virgin, comes back to dwell with us ... The First-born of the New Age is already on his way from high heaven down to earth. With him, the Iron Race shall end and Golden Man inherit all the world. Smile on the Baby's birth ... this glorious Age will dawn ... the ox will not be

frightened of the lion [this is reminiscent of the New Testament's later prophecy that the lamb shall lie down beside the lion] ... Your very cradle will adorn itself with blossoms to caress you ... Enter – for the hour is close at hand – on your illustrious career, dear child of the gods ... See how the whole creation rejoices in the age that is to be! ... Begin, then, little boy, to greet your mother with a smile ...[4]

The Emperor Constantine, who in the fourth century established Christianity as the Roman Empire's state religion, identified the Child of Vergil's prophecy with Christ.[5] St Augustine, Arnobius, St Anthony and other Church Fathers said that Vergil had taken this prophecy from the Sybil of Cuma. And Justin Martyr, who wrote before any of them, said of this Sibyl that 'she used to ascend to some high place and teach the people ... and she left, written in verse, the coming of God to the world, and the miracles He was to work.'[6]

The great Spanish Renaissance philosopher Luis Vives wrote a lengthy commentary to St Augustine's *City of God* in which he discusses the Sibyls. An English translation of Vives's work published in 1620 under the initials 'J.H.' tells us in quaint language of the Sibyl of Cuma: 'Her chappell was to bee seene at Cumae ... Dionysius saith it was to her that Aeneas went ... Even this is she whom Virgil called Cumaea; for she prophesied at Cumae in Italy, saith [Martianus] Capella, and so thinke I. There is Cumae in Ionia by Erythraea, but Aristotle saith directly, there is a cave in Cumae a city of Italy, in which Sibylla dwelt.'[7] It should be added that a succession of these Sibyls delivered the oracles of Cuma over the centuries, and references to 'the Sibyl' at various times in history are to the office, not to a single person. Servius Honoratus, an early commentator on Vergil who lived in the fourth century AD, actually stated that the subject matter of Vergil's 'Fourth Eclogue' came directly from the Sibyl of Cuma of Vergil's own day, and that she had written 'the age of Iron would follow the age of Gold, with the birth of the new Prince',[8] but it is also thought that Vergil was an expert astrologer and

Figure 2: The Sibyl of Cuma placing a leaf, on which she has written a prophecy, on the floor of her cavern. Her prophetic messages would be blown into disorder by the wind when the enquirer opened the door of the cavern. Thus, he would never know the full content of her prophecy, but only grasp at fragments – an accurate reflection of the state of human knowledge. (Engraving by Romain de Hooghe, 1688)

that the 'New Age' was meant to represent the vernal equinox shifting, by the precession of the equinoxes, into a new sign of the Zodiac: Pisces. However, this does not explain the references to the Holy Child. Augustine, who enthusiastically believed in the prophecy, rather uncritically adds of her, she 'hath not one word in all her verses tending to idolatry, but all against the false gods and their worshippers, so that she seemes to me to have beene a citizen of the City of God'.[9]

Vergil tells us that the Sibyl would write her prophecies on leaves, and arrange them on the floor of her cavern, in order to form a message. Then she would depart. The enquirer would then be allowed to enter the cavern, but as he did so the draught from the door would blow the leaves around the cavern so that the message could never, for certain, be properly reconstructed in its entirety.

This may however be Vergil's way of concealing a deeper meaning. The story may be a veiled reference to a secret technique of concealing messages in ancient Sibylline verses by means of acrostics or anagrams. This is attested explicitly by Cicero, who tells us in his fascinating treatise *On Divination:*

> We Romans preserve with solicitude the verses which the Sibyl is reported to have uttered . . . For, whoever was the author of these Sibylline oracles, they are very ingeniously composed . . . It is evident, however, that they are not a song composed by any one in a prophetic ecstasy, as the poem itself evinces, being far less remarkable for enthusiasm than for technicality and labour; and as is especially proved by that arrangement which the Greeks call acrostics – where, from the first letter of each verse in order, words are formed which express some particular meaning; as is the case with some of Ennius's verses, the initial letters of which make, 'Which Ennius wrote'.[10]

This sort of hidden message in a text giving the name of the author was very common in ancient times, and gave a certain protection to an author against plagiarism, or forged writings being put forward in his name. The Pythagorean philosopher Epicharmus of Syracuse adopted such a technique in his treatises,[11] and the Greek tragic playwrights, who were members of a fraternal guild, used a secret technique of recording their names in anagrams in the opening lines of their plays. Their opening lines therefore often appear strained or oddly worded. For instance, the first couplet of *Seven Against Thebes,* if treated as an anagram, reads in translation: 'Say to yourself, shifting the letters of the topmost couplet: This is evidently the poetry of the Athenian Aeschylus.'[12] The same lines, if not unscrambled, read in translation:

> Citizens, sons of Cadmus! The man who holds the helm
> Of State, and from the bridge pilots with sleepless eyes.[13]

Cicero tells us further:

> Now, in the verses of the Sibyl, the whole of the paragraph on each subject is contained in the initial letters of every verse of that same paragraph. This is evidently the artifice of a practised writer, not of one in a frenzy; and rather of a diligent mind than of an insane one. Therefore, let us consider the Sibyl as so distinct and isolated a character, that, according to the ordinance of our ancestors, the Sibylline books shall not even be read except by decree of the senate, and be used rather for the putting down than the taking up of religious fancies.[14]

It should be added that Cicero held the position of Augur at Rome, which was the highest priestly office and entitled him to access to the Sibylline books. Many readers of Cicero's political writings are unaware of this side of his life.

A remarkable – and presumably forged – Sibylline acrostic verse is preserved by the Church Father Eusebius. The first letters of the lines spell out the message 'Jesus Christ Son of God the Saviour'. Vives comments on this at length in his commentary on Augustine's *City of God,* and 'J.H.' gives an ingenious English translation which preserves the acrostic. To show how it is done, I give here the first verse, which spells the name 'Jesus' in its initial letters:

In signe of Doomes-day the whole earth shall sweate.
Ever to reigne, a King, in heavenly seate,
Shall come to judge all flesh. The faithfull, and
Unfaithfull too, before this God shall stand,
Seeing him high with Saints in times last end.[15]

The Emperor Constantine quoted this very verse when he addressed the First Council of Nicaea. He said to the assembled bishops: 'Truly filled with the divine Breath, this Sibyl predicted in verse that which should happen concerning the coming of the Son of God, and declared clearly the coming of Jesus Christ, by the order of the first letter of each line placed in the form of an acrostic – *Jesus Christ, Son of God, Saviour, Cross*.'[16] He claimed that this verse had actually been written either by the Sibyl of Cuma in Italy or by the Sibyl of Cuma at Erythrea in Asia Minor, the two often being confused (or possibly even being the same Sibyl). Justin Martyr had much earlier, about AD 150, visited Cuma in Italy and had inspected the Sibyl's chamber and enquired after her. He enthusiastically claimed that 'she predicts, under the clearest evidence, the future coming of Jesus Christ, our Lord, and all the details of His Life'.[17] He specifically says that she was the Sibyl of 'a certain city called Cuma, six miles from Baiae, the place of the Campanian baths'.[18] We may thus conclude that either the later Sibyls of Cuma, if they continued, were favourably disposed to early Christianity, or were even themselves secret Christians, and produced Sibylline verses for Christian propaganda purposes, or that the attribution of the Sibyl of Cuma was fraudulently attached by the early Christians to verses fabricated by themselves. But whichever was the case, it says a lot about the importance with which the Sibyl was viewed by both pagans and Christians alike.

Be that as it may, we are more concerned with the times before Christianity existed. And it was the Sibyl of Cuma of a much earlier day who was supposed to have said to Aeneas that she would take him to the Underworld. Paget says, 'Cuma stands isolated from the crater of Avernus, by a wide stretch of what was then, probably, marshy jungle. We noted that at Cuma itself there is nothing that suggests an Entrance to the Underworld, nothing with any connection with the Avernus beliefs.'[19]

Cuma is one of the most magical and delightful ancient sites I have ever visited. The archaeological park there is well kept by the Italian authorities and has few visitors, so is quiet and peaceful. It is pleasant to sit there outside the Sibyl's Grotto, enjoying the wild flowers and listening to the roar of the waves on the beach below. Seas of wild vetch surge like foam round the site in late spring, and groups of stately acanthus spot the landscape like clusters of statuary. A wonderfully preserved Roman road winds lazily up the hill and we took our shoes off and walked barefoot on the smooth, warm stones. In the acropolis portions, some of the old Greek stone paving survives, but the Romans replaced most of it with their own patchwork of flagstone blotches which remind me of inkspots hurled down by someone hurrying along.

A local woman came herb-hunting with her jolly smiling dog she had rescued from being a stray. She was collecting her daily bunches of wild rocket leaves for her salad and said she knew where all the bunches grew. At one point, when she approached the seas of wild vetch, her fiercely devoted dog put its back up and growled savagely to protect her.

'Serpenti,' she explained languidly, avoiding the clump, not at all surprised that the snakes seemed to like wild rocket as much as she did.

Most of our attention was taken up by the Sibyl's Grotto, of course. Cuma was founded in the eighth century BC by Greek immigrants from Chalcis in Euboea (today called 'Avia'). It is often said to be the oldest Greek city in Italy. People unfamiliar with ancient history may think that Italy was always a country dominated by the Romans. However, the Romans were Johnny-come-latelies, pampered and spoilt militaristic hedonists with no taste, whose art was largely poor copies of Greek originals, even though they had some good poets. But they did manage excellent engineering, because it was needed for conquest. Unfortunately this local tribe from the region of Rome took over the whole of Italy in the end, and these days few realize that they were only a minority group who, like the Bolsheviks, seized an entire country because they were ruthless enough to be prepared to slit everyone else's throats. If you don't care whom you kill, or how many, you can generally seize power anywhere. And the series of such incidents constitutes what is generally referred to as 'the history of the world'.

The Sibyl of Cuma was the chief prophetess for the whole of Greek Italy. Cuma was thus the Delphi of the West. As Vergil makes clear in the *Aeneid*, anyone wishing to consult the Oracle of the Dead at nearby Baia first went to Cuma and consulted her. She would answer normal oracular enquiries, but if the matter were more serious, she would make the arrangements for Baia and take the visitor there in person. In the *Aeneid* it is she who actually escorts Aeneas into the underground Baian Oracle. Her own grotto, which is a kind of semi-cave, is fairly impressive in its own right. It is approached on ground level, at the base of a small hill which then rises above it. It consists of a very long tunnel carved out of the rock, running adjacent to the side of the hill. All along that side are a series of openings onto the outside, thus conveying no underworld aspect at all. It can be seen clearly in Plate 20, which shows the curious trapezoidal shape of the tunnel. The effect of the design is enhanced by the repeated openings, so that one goes through a succession of doorways.

The description in the *Aeneid* fits the actual site (discovered by Maiuri in 1932) very well. At the beginning of Book VI of the *Aeneid*, Aeneas arrives at Cuma by ship. (The later, Roman, port of Cuma was actually discovered in 1967 by none other than Robert Paget.) Vergil describes 'the Euboean coast of Cuma' in line 1, not because it was in Euboea in Greece but because it had been settled by Euboeans from Greece. Soon after arrival, Aeneas goes to 'the spacious cave, the cell of the Sibyl'. Vergil later says:

'The huge side of an Euboean rock is cut out into a cave,

whither a hundred broad avenues lead, a hundred doors; whence rush forth as many voices, the responses of the Sibyl . . . the prophetess, as yet not suffering the influence of Phoebus [the god Apollo], raves with wild outrage in the cave, struggling if possible to disburden her soul of the mighty god: so much the more he wearies her foaming lips, subduing her ferocious heart, and by bearing down her opposition, moulds her to his will. And now the hundred spacious gates of the abode were opened of their own accord, and pour forth the responses of the prophetess into the open air . . .'[20]

If we accept the figure of 'one hundred' as poetic exaggeration, everything else fits the site perfectly. The grotto is indeed a 'huge side of a rock cut out into a cave', and it does have many broad doors with entrances which could be considered 'avenues'. The Sibyl's responses could indeed very easily 'pour forth into the open air' through these, as her chamber (see Plate 21) is directly opposite one of these openings to the outside. If instead of one hundred we set the number of doors more conservatively at twenty or thirty, we might be correct. But of course if they were folding doors like those ossified at Pompeii, each door would easily consist of several panels, and by that means one could easily reach a total of one hundred door *panels* for the Oracle, so that even that detail might be a correct one. It is very picturesque to envisage all of these doors flung open dramatically by the attendants to accentuate the moment of the Sibyl's prophetic utterance. Certainly all visitors' hair would stand on end at such showmanship, and they would be most impressed by the dramatic event.

At the very end of the long trapezoidal tunnel of the Sibyl's Grotto, one comes to three chambers, the inner one on the left being the chamber where the Sibyl delivered her oracles against the back wall. On either side are prominent dog-ties carved into the stone, suggesting she sat flanked by ferocious hounds. One of these dog-ties may be seen in Plate 22. We have certain evidence that infernal hounds were officially associated with Cuma because they are depicted on the coins of the city. Cerberus, the three-headed Hound of Hell, is a common motif on Cumaean coins, as reproduced in Fiego's book of 1927 entitled *Cumae and the Phlegraean Fields*.[21] There we see a coin with the Sibyl's head on the obverse and a three-headed Cerberus hound on the reverse, over the name of the city. We can be certain that ferocious hounds were not limited to Cuma alone, but were employed within the nearby Oracle of the Dead as genuine Hounds of Hell.

The central chamber at the very back of the tunnel appears to have been blocked by a partition, and was where the Sybil would have rested and made herself ready to come forth into her prophetic chamber. The chamber on the right, which opens to the outside, would have held the waiting colleagues of the client, and its doors would have been flung dramatically open behind them at the moment of the Sibyl's frenzied prophetic outburst.

As I gazed at the place where it appears the Sibyl once sat, I seemed to see in my mind's eye two female faces as clearly as if I were really looking at them face-to-face. The one prophesying had odd eyes – one blue and one green. She was young and beautiful, with a good soul, but looked tormented. She was aged about 30 and had an olive complexion and dark hair. Nearby hovered an older woman with fairer hair, apparently the former Sibyl who had now retired. She was a scheming and dangerous woman, a master-manipulator, and wished to dominate the young Sibyl. Of course, all this may all be pure fantasy, and quite likely it is. But it was a fascinating scene nevertheless, so I hope the reader will not mind my wasting his or her time with it. The ancient incident I fancy I sensed in some telepathic manner was a moment of high drama when some crucial prophecy was about to be delivered, and many important people were awaiting it. But alas, I haven't the faintest idea what the occasion may have been. It was just one of those powerful moments of imprinted energy in a scene appearing to erupt. I can only say that it seemed to be well before Roman times, and the dress appeared distinctly Greek. I continually recur to this image, charged with desperate tragedy and extraordinarily intense drama (I had the feeling that it involved the fate of Cuma at that time), as if I should somehow understand it, but I cannot. But I am unable to get the vision of the Sibyl with one green eye and one blue eye out of my mind. I also saw her before her seizure came on, when I gazed deeply into her eyes and she into mine. She did not recognize me, so we were not personal friends, but I remember thinking she was one of the strangest and most utterly fascinating women I had ever 'set eyes on'. I would not normally mention this kind of experience, but as I am haunted by it and it seems so powerfully imprinted into the grotto by someone's overwhelming emotional trauma, I thought perhaps I should record it. If I were to come across that Sibyl today, I would certainly recognize her.

Also off to the side of the trapezoidal tunnel are two large pits with steps descending into them. One of these is clearly a bath, in which clients purified themselves before consulting the Sibyl. The other may have been a 'pit of ordeal'. It has a circular hole above it in the nearside corner in the form of a chute, through which someone could have been lowered. This has been described by the ancient author Pausanius in his account of his consultation of the Oracle of Trophonios in Greece, which I give in a later chapter. In Pausanius's account, he slides down a chute into a pit full of serpents. I suspect that this pit at Cuma served a similar purpose. However, that is merely one possible explanation based on Pausanius.

Some Italian archaeologists, who seem as concerned with 'suppressing oracles' in their minds as the early Christians were at suppressing them on the ground in the early years of the Church, like to suggest that the Sibyl's Grotto as a whole is merely a military facility of the Romans. Nothing about the grotto suggests such a use. The large number of unfortified entrances makes any security impossible, and the work involved in the construction would have been wholly pointless for any other than a ceremonial purpose. A large naval tunnel nearby, known to have been constructed by the Romans, seems to have led certain people astray into thinking that every tunnel must be military.

Two years of exploration demonstrated to Paget and Jones

that Cuma was not the locality of the Oracle of the Dead. Where, then, was the Sibyl intending to take Aeneas? It was not at Cuma, but was nevertheless nearby. The traditions were that it was near the Crater of Avernus. Aeneas says to the Sibyl in the *Aeneid:*

> Virgin Divine, nothing remains in this life, that can tire me or frighten me. Nothing will be new to me, or that I have not foreseen. I am prepared for every kind of suffering. All I ask of you, since it is here, it is said, that the Entrance to the Underworld and the Lake of Acheron begins, let me come to see my beloved Father. Here is the Gate if you will show me the Road and be my Guide.[22]

Let us turn for enlightenment to the ancient geographer Strabo (who lived from about 63 BC to about AD 25). He first describes the city of Cuma as 'the oldest of all [the Greek cities] in Sicily or Italy'.[23] Strabo, according to his custom, then moves along to the next place and gives the following interesting information:

> Near to Cumae is the promontory of Misenum [now Punta di Miseno], and between them is the Acherusian Lake [now Lago di Fusaro], which is a muddy estuary of the sea. Having doubled Misenum [gone round it by ship], you now come to a harbour at the very foot of the promontory. After this the shore runs inland, forming a deeply indented bay, on which are Baiae and the hot springs, much used, both as a fashionable watering-place, and for the cure of diseases. . . . Former writers, mingling fable with history, have applied to Avernus the expressions of Homer in his Invocation of Departed Spirits, and relate that here formerly was an oracle of the dead, and that it was to this place that Ulysses came. . . . The Avernus is surrounded with steep hills which encompass the whole of it, with the exception of the entrance. These hills, now so beautifully cultivated, were formerly covered with wild forests, gigantic and impenetrable, which overshadowed the gulf, imparting a feeling of superstitious awe. The inhabitants affirm that birds, flying

over the lake, fall into the water, being stifled by the vapours rising from it, a phenomenon of all Plutonian localities. They believed, in fact, that this place was a Plutonium, around which the Kimmerians used to dwell, and those who sailed into the place made sacrifice and propitiatory offerings to the infernal deities, as they were instructed by the priests who ministered at the place. There is here a spring of water near to the sea fit for drinking, from which, however, everyone abstained, as they supposed it to be water from the Styx. They thought likewise that the oracle of the dead was situated somewhere here. ... Ephorus [an earlier historian, a contemporary and enemy of Aristotle, who had come from Cuma at Erythrea in Asia Minor and was thus interested in this other Cuma], peopling this place

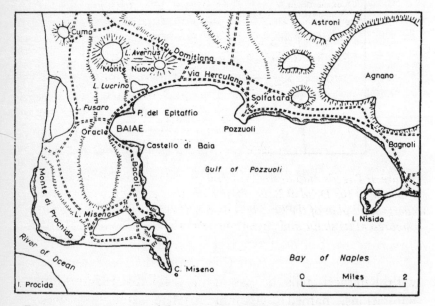

Figure 3: Paget's map of the general area of the Bay of Naples. At the extreme top left is Cuma, the site of the oracular cavern where the Sibyl of Cuma was consulted. The Crater of Avernus is to the right of Cuma, towards the top centre of the map. Below these sites along the peninsula is the area of Baia, and the site of the underground Oracle of the Dead is marked 'Oracle'

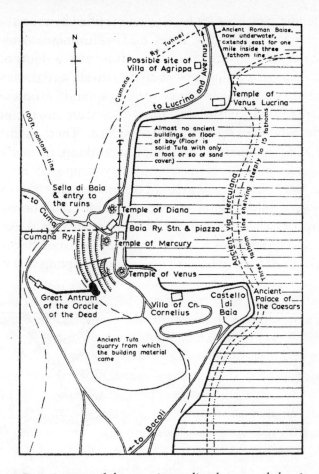

Figure 4: Paget's map of the area immediately around the site of the Oracle of the Dead at Baia. To the left and centre of the map the underground plan of the Oracle is drawn as if it were a surface feature, to represent its shape and extent in relation to the surrounding terrain

with Kimmeri, tells us that they dwell in underground habitations, named by them Argillae, and that these communicate with one another by means of certain subterranean passages; and that they conduct strangers through them to the oracle, which is built far below the surface of the earth. . . . It was a traditional custom for the servants of the oracle never to behold the sun, and only to

quit their caverns at night. It was on this account that the
poet [Homer] said, 'On them the Sun/Deigns not to look
with his beam-darting eye.' . . . Such were the myths related
by our ancestors. But now that the wood surrounding the
Avernus has been cut down by Agrippa, the lands built
upon, and a subterranean passage cut from Avernus to
Cumae, all these appear fables. . . . The whole district . . . to
Baiae and Cumae [is] full of sulphur, fire, and hot springs.[24]

So Paget and Jones turned their attentions back to Baia. In doing
so, they were following the information in the ancient texts, such
as Strabo, which archaeologists had belittled. Paget and Jones
felt that surely Ephorus was right – there *had* been an Oracle of
the Dead at Baia to which the Sibyl of Cuma had taken very
special enquirers.

At first they lost even more time, because the most promising
opening in the ground, under the site of an ancient temple, was
said to be unsafe by an archaeologist who insisted that when he
had stepped into it briefly it was full of poisonous gases and must
be avoided at all costs. But they did find the *argillae* mentioned
by Strabo and the 'subterranean passages' connecting these cells
in which ancient custodians of the Oracle had lived. They
crawled through some of these. When they found that the
passages actually did link up, they knew that they had made a
major discovery, and that the account given by Strabo was
turning out to be true. But where was the Oracle itself? It must
be in the immediate vicinity. In desperation, they finally
descended into the cavern which had been said to be unsafe
because of its poisonous fumes. One of them went in on a rope,
and the other prepared to haul him out by it if he fainted. But
there were no poisonous fumes after all. And what is more, this
was indeed the entrance or *antrum* – to the Oracle!

To their amazement, they found that this led into an ancient
tunnel 200 yards long and perfectly preserved. It sloped gently
downwards to reach eventually a depth of 140 feet below the
surface. This fully confirmed Strabo's information, taken from
the historian Ephorus, that the Oracle was 'built far below the

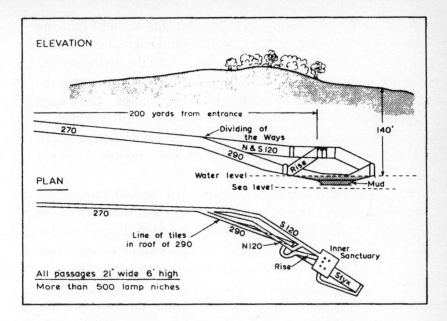

ELEVATION

200 yards from entrance

270

Dividing of
the Ways

140'

N & S 120

290

Water level

Rise

PLAN

Sea level

Mud

270

Line of tiles
in roof of 290

290

S 120

N 120

Inner
Sanctuary

Rise

Styx

All passages 21' wide 6' high
More than 500 lamp niches

*Figure 5: Paget's drawing showing the elevation and plan of the Oracle
of the Dead at Baia, the results of his surveying of the site over
many months. As an engineer, he was well qualified
to do this highly technical task*

surface of the earth'. What had sounded like a fanciful tale
turned out to be absolutely true.

To appreciate the magnitude of this find in purely physical
terms, imagine yourself standing on a 140-foot cliff looking
down at the sea. This is the depth of the tunnel beneath the
surface; and the extent of the tunnel, carved out of solid rock, is
just short of an eighth of a mile.

Although the extent of the penetration of the complex into the
rock is about 200 yards, the total length of all the tunnels in this
single complex (not counting the separate tunnels where the
priests lived) is 880 feet – nearly a sixth of a mile.[25]

As Paget and Jones explored this extraordinary tunnel complex, they noticed that a niche in the tunnel wall had a stain, like
an oil stain, running down from it. In Paget's vivid words:

Keith said, 'That looks uncommonly like an oil stain,' and then I realized we were looking at a lamp niche. Examination of others confirmed this. In some cases the imprint of the shape of the bottom of the lamp could be clearly seen. We counted the niches and found that in total there were more than 500.

At this moment I realized we had found the Oracle of the Dead.[26]

The Inner Sanctuary at Baia is oriented towards the sunset of the summer solstice.[27] And the long entrance tunnel is absolutely accurate in its construction, the first 408 feet being oriented towards the point of sunrise of the same day, the summer solstice (which is Midsummer's Day, the longest day of the year).[28] As the engineer Paget says in a masterpiece of understatement: 'There are several engineering problems that call for a little discussion. . . . [They] testify to an engineering skill of a high order.'[29] How were the unknown builders of this remarkable underground complex able to construct it with such precise orientations, and with no deviations, 140 feet beneath the earth's surface? The whole complex was quite obviously planned as a single unit. A close study of the slight deviation of the orientation from the present-day solstice points might, considering the slow precession of the equinoxes, provide a date for construction of the tunnel complex. This has apparently not been attempted and would require extremely precise measurements. It is to be hoped that someone will undertake this interesting task one day.

The Baian oracle cult was suppressed by the Roman admiral Marcus Agrippa during the reign of Augustus in the first century BC. He cut down the sacred groves which surrounded the area and used the trees to build ships for his fleet. He had a special hatred of the Oracle of the Dead for some reason which we do not know. He blocked up some of the passages and the Inner Sanctum, though not the long entrance tunnel. But even the limited blocking-up for which he was responsible was a gigantic undertaking.

Paget did calculations for the operation as follows: 'All this filling material was carried in from the surface in baskets. Calculation shows that some 700 cubic yards of earth were required for the work. The basket [based on what we know of Roman baskets] would hold about 40–50 pounds. No fewer than 30,000 man journeys were involved in the transport of all this material.'[30] And the tunnel would not allow anyone to pass anyone else except at one point where it divided, so a man with an empty basket could not pass a man with a full basket in the tunnel but would have to wait for him to emerge before entering. Bearing this in mind, the 30,000 man-journeys cannot have been work done by gangs of men working side by side, but would have had to be nearly the equivalent of a single man making 30,000 journeys of a quarter or a third of a mile dragging for half of that distance a fifty-pound load. If we allow for a ten-hour working day with no breaks at all and allot for each journey a time of fifteen minutes (which is highly optimistic in such a tunnel and assumes constant and frantic activity) this means 750 days, or over two years without a break! As Paget says, although he did not work out these further calculations, 'Why did [Agrippa] not just block the entrance . . . ? It seems certain that there was some psychological reason for doing the job the way he did.'[31] This is Paget's tactful way of suggesting that any admiral who would waste years of his sailors' time blocking up an underground oracle complex had to be not only obsessed but perhaps a little insane as well. Tacitus tells us of this Marcus Agrippa that he was 'a commoner but a first-rate soldier' singled out by Augustus as his personal henchman, and that later he married Augustus's daughter Julia.[32] Agrippa's grandson was the notorious Emperor Nero, who was not noted for his mental stability. We know that Agrippa was capable of emotional tantrums on a grand scale: Suetonius in his *Life of Augustus* tells us that Agrippa was piqued that Augustus 'was not behaving as warmly towards him as he should', and that he 'resigned all his offices, and went off to Mytilene in Asia Minor'.[33] This is certainly not the behaviour of a man with an even temper.

Even Agrippa's determined effort over some years did not achieve the blocking of all the inner tunnels, let alone the entrance tunnel. So we may imagine what a colossal operation the *construction* of the tunnel complex must have been. The process of removing the rubble alone would have represented at least a dozen years' work, without taking any account of the far more laborious actual digging through the rock with primitive tools, the making of stairs and doorways, the 500 lamp niches, and so on. In short, we have here a tunnel complex which could almost certainly not have been constructed within the active lifetime of any of the individuals who initiated it.

But the most extraordinary feature of all has yet to be mentioned. This is the so-called River Styx, which is at the core of the whole plan. The Styx is an underground stretch of water fed by a pair of hot springs (named by Paget, drawing on ancient accounts, the River Acheron and the River Phlegethon – these 'rivers' being of course underground ones). The Styx maintains a constant level by means which have not been discovered. In the ceremonies, to be described in the next chapter, it provided a small 'river' along which a boat could take a visitor from a descending tunnel to an opposite ascending tunnel. This boat journey was an enactment of the crossing of the mythical River Styx, with the ferryman Charon at the helm. But the question is this: *How did the constructors of the tunnel complex know in advance of the existence of this supply of water 140 feet beneath the surface of the earth?* The entire complex is constructed around it, so clearly they must have intended this. The water temperature is well in excess of 120° Fahrenheit as it emerges from the springs, and in 1965 two divers, Lieutenant-Colonel David Lewis of the US Army and his son, discovered that the water was coming from passages or fissures which could not be probed for more than twenty or thirty feet because of the intense heat.[34] But the water is drinkable, its level is fifteen feet above sea level, and it appears to have no connection either with the sea or with the many sulphurous springs in this generally volcanic area. The entire water system is an engineering mystery. Did the ancient engineers actually spend even more years constructing the two-foot-wide passages of the spring sources to let this hot water into their 'River Styx'? If so, where did the water come

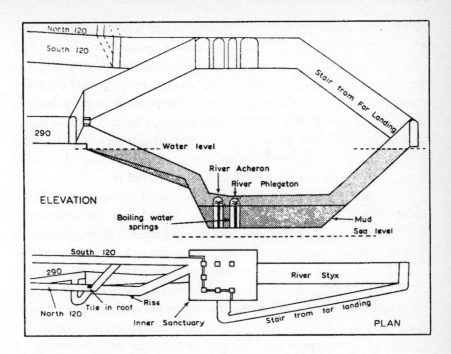

Figure 6: Paget's elevation and plan of the River Styx, in the underground Oracle of the Dead at Baia. The present water level is far too high, because of the rubble and earth deposited in the river bed both by the Roman admiral Agrippa, who wished to destroy the Oracle forever and render its use impossible and by Paget and Jones in their clearance work. However, Lieutenant-Colonel Lewis of the US Army was able to explore the full extent of the Styx underwater and find the two hot spring inlets, which were named Acheron and Phlegethon. The bottom of the Styx cannot be reached because of the rubble and mud, though it appears to be at more of an angle than is shown in this elevation (the part below mud level is imagined). If the rubble and mud could be cleared from the Styx, it would presumably be possible to re-enact the ride in Charon's boat and experience the Oracle as it was in its heyday. At the moment, the Styx can only be seen from its two ends, and the water level is too high to allow a boat to pass over it

from? How did they control it so that its rate of flow did not exceed the desired level in the already constructed Styx bed? How did they make the underground passages (for they are clearly man-made and not natural) for the leading-in of the springs when these are too narrow for a man to dig?

A clue to the solution of this problem may be a secret connecting tunnel discovered by Paget and Jones in the underground living quarters, the *argillae,* prior to their discovery of the oracle complex They found there a tunnel which was blocked, having been filled to the roof with loose earth for the first twenty feet of its length. Paget says:

> We made ourselves a pair of steel scoops, which we could slip over our hands. With these we scraped the earth away, burrowing like rabbits. We had not the slightest idea what we might find on the other side of the block . . . At the end of 48 feet, we found a massive rectangular doorway. The side posts and lintel were of hard dark grey lava . . . Passing through this, we found ourselves in a large vaulted room 21 feet long by 9 feet wide by 15 feet high. One half of the floor, longitudinally, was raised to form a bench 4 feet above the floor. Opposite the entrance door was a small door in the bench giving access to a tunnel. This tunnel traversed the whole length of the room and passed through the walls at either side. The dimensions of the tunnel were 18 inches wide by 30 inches high.[35]

Paget and Jones crawled along the tunnel for fifty yards until they suddenly realized that they did not know where they would come out – if anywhere – and that 'the dimensions of the tunnel would not permit us to turn round. Backing out, in that confined space for 50 knee-scraping yards, very nearly cured us of tunnel exploration.'[36] It is important to realize that this tunnel was not even as wide as the distance from elbow to fingertip of a grown man. The height was only thirty inches. Yet it had been laboriously carved out of the rock as a connecting passage which ran for an undetermined distance, but certainly for more than fifty yards, to a destination which remains unknown.

We must entertain the notion that tiny tunnels such as this may have been made and used by young boys. Boy slaves were common in ancient times. Might they have excavated the two-foot-wide tunnels to let the springs feed the River Styx? It is at least a possibility, though when the source was reached the boy tunnelling would certainly have been drowned by the inrush of water.

Even by interpolating boy slaves, however, the whole thing seems wildly improbable. For the same question recurs: how did they know which way to dig to find the springs? The springs would have been no more visible from the surface than the Styx itself. Even if they were the most brilliant water-diviners in history, how could they have known not merely the location of water beneath certain points, but also its precise depth, course, and rate of flow in order to achieve the level required for Charon's ferry and no higher? But if they exploited existing tunnels, as seems more likely, they still needed to know all these same factors in order to build the complex around the water, and drive a straight tunnel towards it without deviation from a precise point on the surface which was in a line with the solstice sunrise point. There are no traces of exploratory or random passages, or of false starts. The solid tufa rock into which this is all cut does not appear to have natural caverns, tunnels or channels, which would allow exploratory access or naturally occurring streams of water. There was no way in without cutting. But the cutting was perfect. The constructors of this underground complex knew exactly what they were doing before they started. Everything was fully conceived in advance. The complex is a single, planned entity. *And we do not know who built it.*

In the summer of 2000 I visited and photographed the other major Oracle of the Dead from the classical world, the one in Greece. It has been thoroughly excavated and is open to any tourist, though it is in Thesprotia, a region where relatively few tourists go. The Greek Oracle of the Dead is often called the Thesprotian Oracle, after the name of the region. It is also known as the Nekromanteion, which is simply the Greek word meaning 'Oracle of the Dead'. In ancient times it was reachable by river from the sea. The name of the river, on which one can now take pleasure boat journeys, is the River Acheron. Strangely, there is a River Acheron near Baia as well, and indeed there are several 'underworld' names common to the locales of both ancient Oracles of the Dead. It seems that the Oracle on the west coast of Italy and the one near the west coast of Greece were intended to be complementary. It is likely that one was modelled after the other, and it appears that the Greek one was a copy of the Italian one, rather than the other way around, for there is no evidence that the Nekromanteion is nearly as old as the Oracle of the Dead at Baia. As for the actual name 'Baia', it is extremely old. According to the ancient geographer Strabo, whom we have previously quoted: 'They say that Baia took its name from Baius, one of the companions of Odysseus . . .'[37] This ancient tradition is doubtless associated with the visit of Odysseus to the Baian Oracle which is recounted in the *Odyssey*.

The Nekromanteion was destroyed by the Romans, who burnt it down in 167 BC during a war. The excavated ruins stand on an outcrop of rock rising from a plain, and near the meeting point of three small rivers, of which the Acheron is the largest. An eighteenth-century Greek monastic church perches on top of the site, straddling a 'polygonal-style' stone wall of the Oracle.

The Nekromanteion appears to have commenced functioning as an Oracle of the Dead in the eighth century BC, too late for the visit of Odysseus and also subsequent to the actual composition of the *Odyssey*. There is every reason to suspect that the Oracle of the Dead at Baia, which is a much more spectacular and eerie structure underground, was the original such oracle, and that the Thesprotian Oracle was a copy of it. The underground séance crypt of the Thesprotian Oracle has been fully excavated, and may be seen in Plates 27 and 28. From these we may clearly see that it is far less impressive than the tunnels and chambers at Baia, which extend a fifth of a mile into the solid rock and incorporate an underground 'river'. The crypt of the Greek Oracle, reached by a ladder, rope, or perhaps just ordinary stairs, would have been evident to any visitor as a chamber built specially for purposes of consultation, whereas the Baian complex could have been conceived of as true entrances to Hades, particularly by drugged and stupefied visitors. And the small 'labyrinth' constructed in stone at the entrance to the Nekromanteion was too small to be particularly impressive. There is really no comparison betwen the two sites. In short, the Nekromanteion could never have inspired a sense of overwhelming awe, whereas the Baian Oracle would have made people's hair stand on end with genuine terror.

I do not wish to imply that the Greek Oracle of the Dead would not have had an eerie atmosphere. It was, after all, in a suitably remote and rather wild area. That in itself would have enhanced its impact on visitors. It is perched on a craggy rock which would have been far more striking in ancient times than it is today, now that the surrounding area has been drained and turned into harmless and well-tamed farmland.

For something of a flavour of the wild surroundings of antiquity, it is only necessary for a modern tourist to take the boat journey up the Acheron. If you look closely, you will see an extraordinary collection of wildlife perched on every log, draped from overhanging tree branches, and squatting along the length of the river bank. Snakes, frogs, turtles, brightly coloured birds, turquoise dragonflies, herons, buzzards, hawks and small mammals are creeping and circling everywhere. This is practically within walking distance of the Oracle. It doesn't take a lot of imagination to realize that these critters were on the doorstep of the Oracle in ancient times, and that visitors would almost have had to step over them to get in. The area was a massive swamp, teeming with creepie-crawlies, out of which – as one approached in a boat – rose a dark craggy rock with ancient trees and a sombre, sinister stone structure. It would have been impressive enough on the approach alone to have earned its fees.

The Nekromanteion was excavated by the Athenian Archaeological Society between 1958 and 1977, under the direction of the distinguished Greek archaeologist Sotirios I. Dakaris. The excavations of the subterranean consultation chamber were taken down to the bedrock. There are no entrances to any further tunnels from that chamber. You can see the two views of it, facing each way, in Plates 27 and 28. In Plate 27 you can see the metal descending stairway by which tourists enter the chamber today. The opening above is quite narrow, and the descent is straight down, as may be seen in Plate 25, where my wife Olivia is seen 'ascending from Hades'. If you stand in the chamber today you can admire it and imagine what must have gone on there, but the site is curiously devoid of atmosphere, as if all the demons had fled long ago and left a dry husk. One doesn't get any shivers down one's spine. It is as if someone had sucked all the psychic energy out of it. Perhaps this is because it is the remnant of a fire. When the Romans made their very determined effort to destroy the Oracle in 167 BC, they were thorough, and it was never revived. It may well be that destruction by fire takes away something which means the 'atmosphere' is destroyed. For otherwise it is strange that the place does not evoke much awe.

By contrast, the high mountains that loom behind certainly are atmospheric, and as you wind up them, gaping gorges are encountered, and long stretches where not a soul can be seen for miles. When you penetrate such terrain, you enter the real Greece. That was the land in which in ancient times one encountered such bizarre foci of cult activity as the Oracle of the Dead, which would have made one tremble from head to toe, and where contact not only with the spirits but with the deities of the Underworld was imminent if one made the right sacrifices and paid the priests the correct fees. And of course, there was the very real danger that one might enter the Underworld and get stuck there and never return to the light. It was therefore a perilous undertaking.

The excavator Dakaris has given an interesting description of what it would have been like to enter the Thesprotian Oracle. After ritual bathing in a special room with a bath, he says:

From there, passing through the northeast doorway, one came to the east corridor and then to the southern one, which was a dark labyrinth with three arched doorways barred with iron. This strange arrangement obliged the visitor to follow a complex path through murky corridors which gave him the impression of wandering through the gloom of Hades.

Investigation up to now has established the following facts. After incubation (sleeping) in one of the rooms of the north corridor and a purifying bath, each visitor, before passing [through the] gate, apparently cast down a stone in order to protect himself from the evil influence of the spirits, for a large heap of stones was found to the right of the entrance.

In room *thēta*, the east wall of which has now fallen away, the pilgrims' final preparation presumably took place. Through the gate of this room they came to the east corridor (where the outer passage has also crumbled away). On the floor of this corridor were found several small pits full of coals, ashes, and the burned bones of sheep and cattle. Here, presumably, burnt sacrifices were offered. In the labyrinth on the south there was a continuous layer of broken basins, datable to the third and second centuries BC, which had served for the offering of white barley described by Homer [Homer's description was doubtless of an offering of barley at Baia, just as the same was done here later]. Next, one entered the central hall. Here we found another layer of broken pottery, especially cups and amphoras, and a second heap of pebbles. Here, it seems, the visitor cast a second apotropaic stone [for protection against the dead] and poured a libation from one of the narrow-necked vessels, which he then broke. It was the intention that libations should seep through the natural openings in the stone floor into the subterranean hall, to the palace of Hades and Persephone, the divine couple of the nether world. This was the final purpose, and it was here that the ghosts of the dead appeared, 'the strengthless forms of men outworn', in the words of Homer. These, when they had drunk the liquid offerings and eaten the white barley, gained consciousness and could converse with the living. How the spirits became visible is not known. Undoubtedly faith contributed greatly, aided by the physical and psychological preparation and the

vivid suggestions to which the visitors had been exposed
during their wanderings in the dark corridors of the
sanctuary before coming to the sombre realm of Hades.[38]

Some of the traditions associated with the Oracle of the Dead
survive into contemporary times. Dakaris says:

> The recurrence even in our own times of the place name
> *Aidonati* suggests that memories of the ancient worship of
> Aidoneus, king of Ephyra [the nearest ancient town to this
> Oracle, which was sometimes called the Ephyran Oracle of
> the Dead] and god of the lower world, have persisted. Today
> in Thesprotia, furthermore, when travellers pass the place
> where a murder has been committed, they cast down a stone
> to protect themselves against the dead, as did visitors at the
> sanctuary some twenty-two centuries ago.[39]

A further description of the process of consulting the Oracle,
incorporating excavation findings by way of confirmation, was
published by Dakaris several years later:

> When at last the critical moment arrived for communicating
> with the dead, the pilgrim entered the east passage bearing
> the prescribed offerings for the libations and the sacrifice. In
> the passage he sacrificed a sheep in a pit; these pits were
> discovered during the excavations, still containing the
> remains of charcoal and burnt animal bones. Next he passed
> through the labyrinth, a meandering passage that induced
> the illusion that he was wandering through the dark,
> crooked streets of Hades. The labyrinth had three arched,
> ironbound doors, the same number as the doors of Hades,
> with large iron nails, many of which were found in the
> excavations. The middle and last of these doors leading to
> the central hall are well preserved. It seems that there in the
> labyrinth, he offered the barley meal (ancient alphita),
> because on its floor a large number of wide-mouthed vessels
> were found, chiefly bowls suitable for holding solid

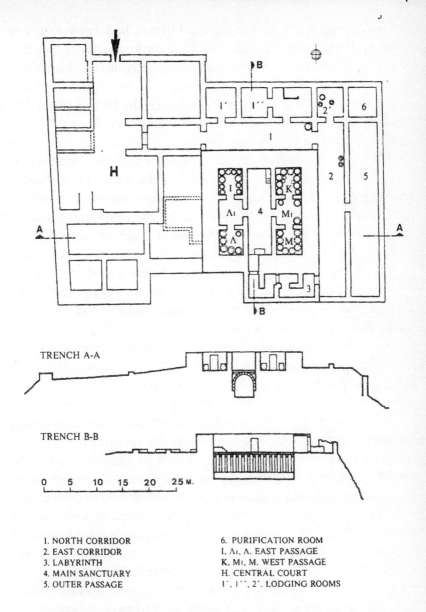

TRENCH A-A

TRENCH B-B

0 5 10 15 20 25 M.

1. NORTH CORRIDOR	6. PURIFICATION ROOM
2. EAST CORRIDOR	Ι, Λι, Λ. EAST PASSAGE
3. LABYRINTH	K, Mι, M. WEST PASSAGE
4. MAIN SANCTUARY	H. CENTRAL COURT
5. OUTER PASSAGE	Ι΄, Ι΄΄, 2΄. LODGING ROOMS

Figure 7: Top: the plan of the Greek Oracle of the Dead, the Nekromanteion. Below: section views of the underground séance chamber, or crypt, at the Oracle. The first view shows it end-on, and the second shows it sideways. These are taken from Sotirios Dakaris, The Nekyomanteion of the Acheron, *3rd edition, Athens, 1998, p.15. (Note: Nekyomanteion is an alternative name for Nekromanteion.)*

offerings and a clay lamp dating to the 3rd or 2nd c. BC.
Lastly, after going through the third doorway, now closed
by a modern iron door imitating the ancient one, he came to
the central hall. There he cast another apotropaic stone, and
onto the stone floor poured libations to the gods of the
underworld, Aidoneus and Persephone, who dwelt in the
underground hall. There his progress ended.

Throughout his passage the priest-guide never ceased to
invoke the spirits of the dead, according to Lucian
(Menippus 9 ff.) 'nocturnal Hecate and dread Persephone',
muttering different outlandish and meaningless names and
polysyllabic words. The progression ended there in the hall,
where the images of the dead communicated with the
consultants.

The physical and spiritual trials during the sojourn, which
lasted for many days in the dark chambers of the Necro-
manteion, together with the isolation, the magic rituals,
prayers and invocations, the perambulation through the
dark passages and the common belief in the manifestation of
the dead spirits created the proper psychological state of
mind in the pilgrim. This was greatly assisted by the special
diet he was given. In the course of the excavations large jars
full of carbonised fruits, wheat, barley and broadbeans were
found, of a small variety similar to the Egyptian 'fool' (*Vicia
faba equina*) and quantities of lupine seeds. Broadbeans
possess toxic properties, and when eaten green cause wind,
indigestion and a relaxation of the senses to the point
of giddiness and hallucination and allergic syndromes
(cyamiasis). The same effects are produced by lupines (the
ancient thermoi), when they are eaten green (lathyrism).
Thus, with the relaxation of the senses, often approaching
the point of vertigo and loss of understanding, the necessary
condition of mind was achieved for communication with the
spirits of the dead.[40]

Figure 7 shows the plan of the Oracle of the Dead and below
it, the sections from the front and from the side of the top of the

hill. These show the extraordinary underground crypt where the actual séances with the spirits of the dead took place. I have already mentioned the two photos, Plates 27 and 28, which I took to show either end of the crypt as it is today. The bedrock base of the room is rough and uneven, and must once have been covered with a smooth surface or floor of some kind; as it is, one trips easily just trying to take a step in any direction. It would not have made a good impression to have dignified priests and priestesses tripping in their ceremonies as they carried their incense. We therefore presume the presence of a floor which was destroyed in the fire of 167 BC, along with any other perishable trappings not already looted by the Roman soldiers. It is not impossible that before firing the place, the soldiers stripped out any good floor planks for more practical use. After all, Roman soldiers were billeted on the local population in rather poor conditions and in hovels, and the floor of an oracle sanctuary would have made an excellent base for an officer's tent or mess tent. The same is true for any panelling that might have adorned the walls between the ribbed arches. We may also imagine some impressive and stately chairs and tables were once used in the crypt, along with screens to conceal whatever was happening to create the illusions of spirit apparitions, if that is what was done there.

The excavator describes the crypt as follows:

Beneath the central hall is an underground hall of the same size, hewn out of the rock, probably on the site of the original prehistoric cult cave ... The ceiling of the crypt and the floor of the overlying hall is supported by fifteen arches of poros stone. These were hewn with great care: each arch-stone of a course is the same width as the arch-stone of the next course, so that the joints of the fifteen arches are all aligned, emphasizing the depth of the underground hall. This is the dark palace of Persephone and Hades.[41]

However impressive all this was, it does not in any way rival the size and design of the truly extraordinary Oracle of the Dead at Baia. It is likely that, by the seventh century BC, the Greeks thought it best to have a grand Oracle of the Dead of their own (for there were several smaller, less impressive ones scattered round Greece which lacked grandeur) situated in Greece itself instead of far away on the other side of Italy in a remote and dismal region which could only be reached after a long sea journey. This was certainly considered desirable by the local potentates of Greece who didn't want to have to drag themselves or their envoys all the way to the west coast of Italy. We know of the use of the Thesprotian Oracle by King Periander of Corinth at the end of the seventh century BC, as it is well documented by Herodotus (V, 92). King Periander wanted to interrogate the spirit of his dead wife Melissa to ask her where she had concealed some treasure.[42] Other oracles such as Delphi and Dodona would have scorned such an enquiry, as they did not deal in the business of communication with dead spirits.

As mentioned above, there are some place names in common between the Italian and Greek Oracles of the Dead. With regard to both River Acherons, it is a definite puzzle as to which was named first. But because the Greek site of the Oracle is not early enough to have inspired Homer, and as there seems little doubt that the Italian Oracle was older, we are left to presume that the River Acheron in Thesprotia got its name from the one in Italy in the seventh century BC. The word is Greek, and means 'woe'. It comes from the early word for 'white poplar' (*acherōis*) used by Homer; in later times the white poplar was called *leukē*. A legend said that Herakles had brought the white poplar up from Hades, so the river was therefore given a name with a suitable archaic reference to the Underworld. A small stream that joins the Acheron near the Greek Oracle was given the grand name of the River Kōkytos ('wailing'), from a very old word related to the Sanskrit verb root *kū*, which means 'to cry out or moan'. This was either because spirits wailed and moaned or because women wailed and moaned at funerals. Another small stream which joins the Acheron near the Greek Oracle was given the even more impressive name of the River Pyriphlegethōn, which means 'fire-blazing'. It is clear from these grand names for the two trickling brooks, which joined the small River Acheron, that a great deal of showmanship was involved in setting up the Greek Oracle. An air of mystery and magic was supposed to be created by advertising the location as being at the confluence of the Rivers of Woe, Wailing, and Blazing Fire. The site is actually quite small, but by the time a pilgrim consulted the spirits, he was well and truly drugged and stupefied. As a result, the impression made by the séance was certain not to disappoint him, as he was already hallucinating before he entered the crypt.

According to the ancient geographer Strabo (first century BC), there was a River Pyriphlegethōn at Baia as well as a River Acheron.[43] It makes more sense for a river whose name means 'Blazing Fire' to be there than in Thesprotia in Greece, because the region near Baia was a volcanic one, with many steam geysers and hot springs emitting boiling water. Thesprotia did not have anything similar, so it is therefore likely that the river name was transferred to Greece from the original source in Italy.

Strabo's descriptions of the Oracle of the Dead at Baia are so precise that there cannot be any doubt that Baia was the main oracle of its kind. Nothing could be clearer than this passage from Strabo: '... they conduct strangers through them [subterranean passages] to the oracle, which is built far below the surface of the earth.'[44]

The replica of Hades, 'far below the surface of the earth', was at Baia. It was sufficiently awe-inspiring to create a demand for a substitute Hades which could be reached much more easily. So the Nekromanteion, the Thesprotian Oracle of the Dead, came into being, and many people made do with that. But for the real experience, people had to go to Baia. Let us now see something of the fantastic things that actually went on there.

TWO

THE DESCENT INTO HELL

It should be emphasized that the main purpose of the Baian Oracle of the Dead was to allow a man the privilege of going through the entrance to Hell, of consulting there the dead spirit of a friend or relation, and of returning alive to the surface. The enquirer might wish merely to see again a lost loved one, or, more commonly, he might wish to pose some particular question or set of questions to the spirit in order to obtain its advice. Since Homer describes Odysseus as consulting the spirit of the seer Teiresias, apparently at Baia, the antiquity of the place must be considerable. It seems to have been in use for hundreds of years.

Consultation was so immensely expensive that the ordinary person could probably never have afforded it. But those rich and powerful enough to consult the Oracle certainly got their money's worth. The Sibyl of Cuma and her priests and assistants who arranged the event with their Baian colleagues got first share of the largesse. In the *Aeneid,* Aeneas has to provide seven bullocks and seven ewes for the Cumaean Sibyl. Since only small portions of these sacrifices were actually made as offerings to the deities, these beasts would provide enough meat, fat, offal, hides and even wool to make life comfortable for the religious officials of Cuma for a considerable period. In addition, the beasts would have been purchased by the visiting enquirer from the very same officials, thus filling the priests' pockets with ready money at the same time. Vast quantities of the best olive oil also had to be purchased to pour over the carcasses as they roasted, and we can be sure that many jars were left over for the priests' use afterwards. It was also necessary to purchase an expensive bronze tripod, yet more olive oil, wine and barley cakes as offerings to the Sibyl herself. Naturally the more eager the enquirer, the more lavish he would be in what he gave her.

The enquirer would be directed or led to Baia, where another set of officials conducted the actual consultation of the Oracle of the Dead. In the *Aeneid,* Aeneas here has to purchase and sacrifice four bullocks, a lamb, a ram, a cow, and several gigantic bull oxen, all to be basted with more of the expensive olive oil as they roasted. Additional sums of money were probably charged as consulting fees. The officials were meanwhile running up considerable expenses on their own part. They were filling more than 500 lamps with oil and wicks and preparing large numbers of torches, costumes and assorted props. But these background activities were not known to the enquirer. He himself would most likely be in great awe and apprehension of his forthcoming ordeal, and entirely preoccupied with what had brought him to the Oracle in the first place – most likely a dilemma he hoped the Oracle would resolve.

Having been brought to the temple precincts outside the entrance to the Baian tunnel complex (these outer precincts being now mostly gone), the enquirer was detached from his friends and associates and led alone into a room which Paget and Jones have named the 'Painted Room'. Vergil refers to it as being 'Before the vestibule itself and in the first jaws of hell'. He describes the paintings and the enquirer's (Aeneas's) jumpiness, 'disconcerted with sudden fear', pointing his sword at the painted images.[1] On the walls were horrifying paintings which portrayed various Diseases, Old Age, Fear, War, Poverty, Sleep, 'Joy of Sinning', Hunger, Strife, Insanity, and 'the Counsellor of Evil'. The enquirer would have plenty of time to dwell on these sobering and graphic pictures, for he seems to have stayed alone in the Painted Room for three whole days with no other amusement. He would come to know every detail of the gruesome visages before him in his isolated room, and how marked would be their effects on his narrowed attention! Three days of isolation in these surroundings were a necessary part of putting the enquirer into the right frame of mind. We can imagine him jumping at the slightest noise, and expecting almost anything to happen.

Modern studies of military brainwashing and psychological manipulation stress the need for preliminaries such as this. One recent author sums up this aspect of captivity as a condition 'as a result of which the soldier has to live usually in cramped circumstances, undergoing physical hardship and a boring routine existence, always surrounded by the uncertainty of his fate and having to obey the superior position of his captor(s)'.[2] All these conditions were effectively fulfilled by the enquirer's stay in the Painted Room, for he was entirely under the control of the priests and officials of the Oracle during this time.

A psychiatrist who studied the initial shock reactions of Jews entering a German prison camp in 1941 made some discoveries which are especially relevant to our considerations. He found the predictable immediate reactions of 'depression and retardation, loss of initiative (even for washing and eating), and . . . sleeplessness, constipation . . . Suicide and panic, however, were *not* observed.' Then comes the surprising and particularly relevant further observation: 'Many experienced feelings of unreality, as if surrounded by ghosts.'[3] This occurred only during the first two weeks or so, and then receded. But it is important for us to have such modern scientific evidence of the heightened morbid suggestibility of someone in the initial stages of captive isolation in a deprived environment. For it helps us to understand the possible state of mind of our enquirer at Baia. We must remember that the ancient peoples had little or no exposure to powerful and horrifying visual images. Today we see so many images of all kinds on television, in newspapers, magazines and films, that our senses are to some extent deadened and jaded by overexposure to horror. But this was not the case with the ancients. They would have been far more susceptible to the suggestiveness of the Painted Room. By the third day ghostly hallucinations would almost certainly have begun to assail the enquirer.

In recent years, a psychological experimental study of such SD (sensory deprivation) was undertaken for a four-day period. 'Several [subjects] became fearful that something terrible might happen to them or that they might be affected adversely . . . Still others were bothered because they could picture clearly what they were thinking in front of them and some reported later that they had been unable at times to distinguish wakefulness from sleep, feeling that the room was closing in on them or that their bodies were different from normal.'[4] And the average weight loss of the subjects over these four days was 4.5 pounds! They found that they were unable to eat, although they were hungry. Feelings of fear built up, no accurate perception of time remained, and their thinking became confused.

But just as interesting as the effects during the confinement were those just after release: 'On release, after ninety-six hours in the dark and quiet, ordinary visual objects were seen as exceptionally rich in detail and saturated in hue, with more sounds apparently crowding in on them . . . these effects lasted for no more than a few hours.'[5] We shall see that it was at just about this point of maximum suggestibility and grossly heightened perception of colour and sound that our enquirer 'descended into Hell'. Before these effects could abate, and when he was in a debilitated state of maximum confusion, unable to summon any inner resources or pull himself together, he was rushed down into the Baian tunnels for his experience of the Underworld. By the time he could come to himself once again, the descent into 'Hell' would be over. Let us consider, however, what else went on before the enquirer was led into the tunnel complex.

Very early every morning, while it was still dark, two young boys brought the enquirer out of the Painted Room to sacrifice a black ewe in the forecourt. The entrails of the ewes were examined, presumably by torch-light, by a priest-diviner, who would pronounce as to whether they were favourable for the projected consultation. This would increase the anxiety and tension for the enquirer, since each of these sessions might yield unfavourable omens, in which case the consultation would be called off because the gods were not pleased. This served to remind him once every twenty-four hours how important it was for him to do everything that was expected of him, in order not to displease the gods. But it also provided a convenient excuse for

the priests to cancel any proposed consultation in the caverns if
the subject appeared for any reason to be unsuitable, or if he
were seen to be resisting the effects of his treatment. The
practised eye of the priest could spot trouble-makers or sceptics
at these pre-dawn sacrifices, where the possibility of 'angry gods'
was built into the ceremonies as their very *raison d'être*.

If the enquirer were the right sort of person, if he were well-
meaning, moderately credulous, entirely sincere and unsus-
pecting – in short, an ordinary human being participating in a
ritual of his own, officially sanctioned religion, which fostered a
belief in infernal powers – the readings of the entrails would
presumably always be favourable.

After the third day's pre-dawn sacrifice, the enquirer was
asked to bathe in the (still surviving) bath near the Painted Room
which contained what was called 'the Water of Forgetfulness'.
(Later we shall see that somewhat similar practices occurred at
the underground Oracle of Trophonios in Greece, the site of
which has not yet been discovered in ancient times, and were
related at length by one who personally went through it all.)
After this bath, further fasting and, presumably, prayer in the
Painted Room were required until noon, when another
immersion took place in a separate, smaller bath containing 'the
Water of Memory'.[6]

What were these baths for? These and the water from them
which the enquirer drank before entering the Underworld were a
most important part of the procedure, and one not sufficiently
appreciated without an acquaintance with the use of powerful
drugs at the ancient oracle centres. For these 'waters', by bathing,
by breathing of their fumes, and especially by drinking, put the
enquirer into his final and necessary state of mind before
descending into Hell. For the waters were drugged. They ensured
that the enquirer was a pliant, hallucinating subject in just the
proper state of awe and suggestibility; but also that he was
sufficiently conscious to remember what had happened to him
and be terrified by the recollection of it for the rest of his life. But
above all, he must in future remain *convinced* that what had
happened to him in Hell was real. (In Chapter 3 we shall examine

the drugs and their methods of use in this and other instances at ancient oracle centres.)

Our enquirer in all probability believed that Baia really did have an entrance to the Underworld. He presumably believed in the physical existence of such an Underworld, and that he was about to be given the rare opportunity to descend into the bowels of the earth and consult, at the very doors of Hell itself, the pale and mournful spirit of a departed relative or friend. He had been reduced to a state of mind in which there is every likelihood that he would really believe whatever the priests of the Oracle wanted him to believe. Let us see what that was.

At sunset on the third day, the enquirer offered a sacrifice of a black lamb to 'the Mother of the Fates, Dread Night, and her Sister the Earth'.[7] He was then 'dressed in a white linen tunic reaching to mid-thigh. His hair [was] bound with white ribbons and he [wore] sandals on his feet. Around his waist [was] a belt with a bronze sword.'[8]

Dressed in this manner, and carrying in his hand a 'golden' branch of mistletoe, he joined the scarlet-robed Sibyl of Cuma, who was to act as his guide. They descended by a ladder through a narrow hole down a bottleneck, twenty-one inches wide and eight feet in depth, into a round chamber.[9] This arrangement, known as a *tholos,* will be described more fully when we consider the remarkable descent to the Oracle of Trophonios. But the *tholos* seems to have represented the cervix, and the passage through it the return to the womb of Mother Earth. Surviving ancient structures of this kind should perhaps be viewed in this light: *tholos* tombs may be meant to represent a dead person's return to the Great Mother. But such ideas seem to go back at least to Minoan times, and are of a stratum of ancient Greek belief hundreds or even thousands of years earlier than the age of classical Greece at the time of Pericles, Socrates, Plato, and Aristotle.

At this point the enquirer, led by the Sibyl, entered the long passageway leading into the Baian tunnel complex. From another of the three separate entrances appeared the priests of the temple. They would be dressed in black overalls with pointed headdresses and only slits for eyes,[10] and bearing branches of

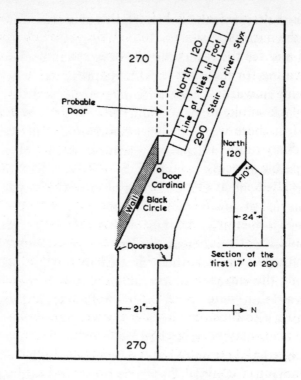

Figure 8: Paget's plan diagram of 'The Dividing of the Ways', a crucial junction in the underground tunnel complex of the Oracle of the Dead. The entrance tunnel may be seen here leading upwards from the bottom of the page; at the junction, a swinging door blocked either of the two possible directions. If one went straight ahead, one was led directly into the Inner Sanctum of the tunnel complex. However, enquirers to the Oracle were never taken this way; instead, they were led to the right, down the stairway to the River Styx, where they embarked on Charon's boat. At the far end of the Styx, they disembarked and reached the Inner Sanctum through an ascending stairway behind. Then, after the consultation, they were brought back from the Inner Sanctum to the Dividing of the Ways where the swinging door had swung shut the other way, and they progressed back through the entrance tunnel, unaware of how this miraculous return to the entrance had occurred.

black cypress. They would go before the Sibyl and the enquirer down the entrance tunnel, chanting and singing an eerie, mysterious dirge. The sacrificial animal which was to be offered to the infernal powers would be brought in from the third entrance, and dragged along behind the enquirer. Paget says: 'Owing to the narrowness of the tunnel, the suppliant could not turn round and see the sacrifice following, but he could hear its frenzied bleating (or its terrified screams), and feel a nasty cold wind blowing inwards round his legs. Overhead the rolling clouds of black smoke told him they were on their way to Hell. Every few feet there was a flickering smoking oil lamp illuminating the dusty tunnel for a short distance ahead.'[11]

The single-file procession eventually reached the end of the long entrance tunnel, at the point known as 'the Dividing of the Ways'. This is an ingeniously designed intersection of three tunnels which was entirely disguised to the enquirer when he first passed it, and Paget's drawings of this may be seen in Figures 9 and 11. On the left was a concealed door which would have been closed during the entrance of the enquirer. The Romans sealed this doorway shut with a very thin cemented partition and plastered over it to hide the fact that it ever existed. This sealed plastered surface may be seen to the left of the photo in Plate 8. Michael Baigent and I tested this by standing on either side of the door and having a conversation with one another through it. Robert Paget was never able to get to the other side because it requires crawling nearly 150 feet on your stomach, with no air and in clouds of dust. He therefore sent his younger friend, Keith Jones, on that errand and they communicated by knocking. Michael and I, however, were able to converse quite freely through the apparent 'wall', even though the total roundabout distance from one location to another is about 400 feet. Eventually this door should be reopened, restoring the full air circulation to the Oracle. It would also facilitate the clearing of the thousands of tons of soil from the interior passages.

Because Paget never saw the other side of the door, he was unaware of the strange feature seen in Plate 15, where one of the tunnels suddenly splits into two before bending round to this door and joining a third passage. Technically speaking, therefore, the 'Dividing of the Ways' is really a fourfold junction, though the reason for this remains obscure. Michael and I also detected simultaneously, unknown to one another until later, on

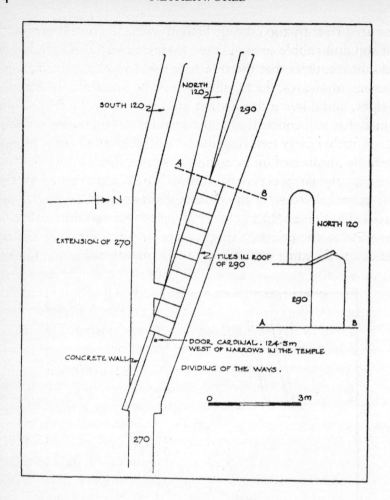

Figure 9. Paget's other drawing of the crucial 'dividing of the ways', where he shows the 'concrete wall' (actually probably just cement over a partition, as it is not thick or strong enough to be concrete) by which the Romans sealed the doorway. Michael Baigent and I were able to converse with each other in a normal voice through this thin partition which should be removed as past of an archaeological clearance programme.

our two sides of the door apparent evidence of a tunnel running underneath the spot at right angles to the entrance tunnel, leading northwards to some unknown further destination. The entrance to this deeper tunnel is still concealed, and the inner areas are presently too cramped for movement and heavily filled with soil and rubble to enable us to locate it. However, there is no doubt whatever that the Oracle still has secrets left to reveal.

Passing unawares, the enquirer would be led along the fork to the right, and down a descending tunnel towards the River Styx – which was still concealed by an S-bend. The tunnel, which descends a further forty feet, is about six feet high; along its 150-foot length the number of oil lamp niches suddenly increases, so that there was one lamp every three feet or so. Within this relatively short tunnel there were more than one hundred lamps, which created an intense light in preparation for the experience ahead.

As soon as the priests, the Sibyl, and the enquirer had forked right at the Dividing of the Ways, the concealed door would be

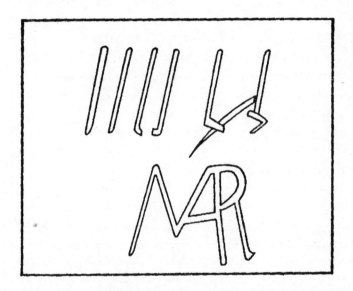

Figure 10: This strange graffiti occurs on the wall of the traverse between the two 120 tunnels at the west end, where photography is difficult. The letters are a foot high and an inch wide on the east wall, and appear to say 'Illius' (a reference to Troy). The bottom sign is apparently a traditional shorthand sign for a prayer to the goddess Hera. Beside this graffiti is one of the many lamp niches cut into the walls, and Paget found a mason's lead plumb bob resting in the niche (the present whereabouts of which is unknown). This drawing of the graffiti was done by Paget

swung across, opening the straight continuation of the entrance tunnel through into the Inner Sanctuary of the Oracle, which the enquirer would visit later by a completely different route. The sacrificial animal would now be dragged through to the altar and made ready for the sacrifice – and the enquirer would never know how it got there ahead of him, for he knew that as he had gone down into the bowels of the earth the animal had certainly

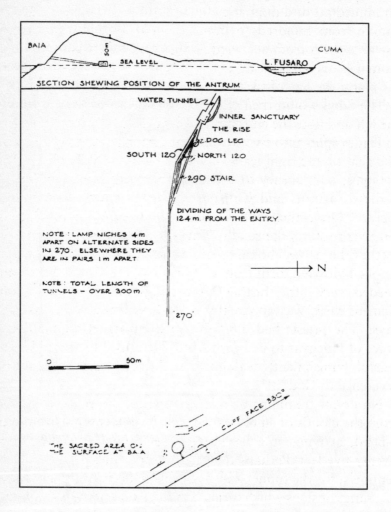

Figure 11: Paget's drawing showing what happens after the 'dividing of the ways', and also the relation to old level.

been behind him. However, this was the least of the 'miracles' which pressed on his confused and stupefied consciousness in an irresistible onrush of evidence of the supernatural.

As the passage straight through to the Inner Sanctum was opened up by the swinging of the concealed door, this same door swung shut behind the enquirer and the Sibyl, sealing off the tunnel to the Styx, down which they were descending. This had an immediate and dramatic effect on the air in the passage. The smoke from hundreds of lamps would suddenly be diverted towards them from an opening high up to their left (which the Romans covered up with tiles, and which Paget therefore calls in his plans 'the line of tiles').

The Sibyl would then stop and say to the enquirer: 'Look to the left and note the entrance to Tartarus. It is here that the road to Hades splits into two ways. That on the left goes to Tartarus, and that on the right leads on to the House of Persephone; by it we make our journey to Elysium. The other brings evil men to godless Tartarus and with never a pause exacts their punishment.'[12] Or, as the Sibyl tells Aeneas in the *Aeneid:* 'Look to the left, where starts the road to Tartarus. There in mud and murk seethes the Abyss choking forth all its sludge.'[13] With the acrid smoke billowing forth from this opening, the visitor presumably needed very little further convincing, but as an additional element there was apparently a loud, warning voice. As Paget says: 'The priests had, probably, also arranged for the doleful voice of Phlegyas to be heard from Tartarus, "Be warned by my fearful punishment, deal justly with your neighbour and do reverence to God".'[14]

No doubt trembling at this experience, the enquirer was led from the clouds of smoke down a flight of steps and around the S-bend, arriving at a level stretch of tunnel extending about twenty-five feet. Perhaps the priests stood to either side as eerie sentinels, for the tunnel widens at this point by four feet, ending in a series of steps which form a landing-stage at the water's edge. This is the bank of the River Styx. The water level is no longer stable. In Paget's account:

The height from the roof to the water is approximately 5
feet and waterlines on the side walls show that the level has
varied considerably in the past. In the three years that we
have known it, it remained absolutely constant until May
1965. It then suddenly dropped nearly 2 feet in level, and
has remained static. We assume that the cause is telluric, and
connected with the general recrudescence of volcanic
activity in the region, due to the predicted imminent
resumption of activity by Vesuvius. Other hot springs in the
ruins have been affected.[15]

The bottom of the Styx is now very deeply silted up with mud.
Much of it was deposited in the water by the Romans, in order
to cause the water level to rise and make passage across the Styx
by boat impossible, evidently another of Agrippa's desperate
attempts to ensure that this oracle centre would never be used
again. Only about a foot of the two boiling spring inlets, from
which the hot water still poured, extended above the mud level
when Paget found them. However, a lot of this mud is the
remains of soil which once blocked 'the Rise' and which was
shovelled down into the Styx through 'the Chimney' by Keith
Jones, since he could not carry it out of the Oracle. The water of
the Styx is quite fresh though no one knows how this can be, and
can still be drunk. Experiments by Paget and Jones using
fluorescent tracer material proved that the Styx and the many
springs outside the caverns are not connected.[16]
    At the landing-stage of the Styx, the black-hooded priests
presumably standing to either side as the extra width at this point
of the tunnel allows, the enquirer and the Sibyl would find the
dread ferryman Charon. He would be standing in his small
coracle made of basketwork and covered with skins. His
appearance was that of an ancient filthy demon, with ragged
white unkempt hair and beard, with a dirty torn garment.[17]
Charon would row the visitors slowly across the water to the far
end, where they disembarked. Here, according to tradition, the
three-headed Hound of Hell, Cerberus, was supposed to wait:
' "When he growls in all his three throats, the mountains tremble

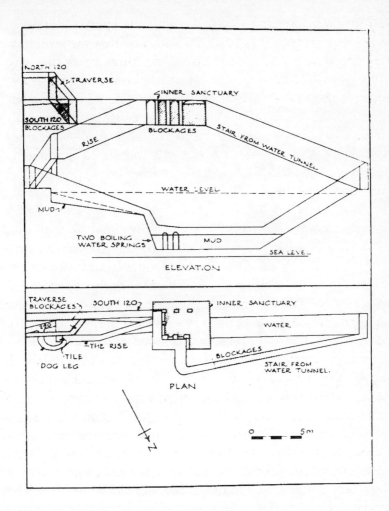

Figure 12: *The mud and blockages recorded by Paget. However, there is now much more mud in the Styx, than is shown here, thrown into it by Keith Jones when he cleared the blocked 'Rise' which leads into the inner portions of the Oracle complex.*

and the sound rumbles through the caverns of Hell", but to visitors such as the Sibyl and her guests the dog would give a friendly greeting by wagging his tail and pricking his ears.'[18] So presumably, the officials had a fierce hound of some kind on the far landing-point which barked in a terrifying manner as the

Figure 13: Gustave Doré's vision of Dante and Vergil being poled across the River Styx by the ferryman Charon, to see the shades of the dead in Canto VIII of Dante's Inferno, from Cary's English translation of 1903: ' "Who is this," they cried, "that, without death first felt, goes through the regions of the dead?" ' (Collection of Robert Temple)

coracle rowed across the Styx, but became friendly when it recognized the Sibyl as she disembarked. The drugged enquirer might very well believe the dog had three heads; at least its echoing and reverberating barking would seem more like that of a pack of hounds in the confined space.

Leaving the boat, the Sibyl and the enquirer turned to the right and walked up a long, very steep stairway through yet another tunnel, which led them back along the direction they had come over the water. At the top of the steep stairs, there was a sharp turn to the right, leading to an anteroom outside the still concealed entrance to the Inner Sanctuary. All this time the enquirer has been holding his branch of mistletoe, which he will shortly offer to Persephone, the goddess who was married to the God of the Underworld, Hades himself. In the earliest times, before going to Baia, the enquirer was instructed by the Sibyl to find his own mistletoe growing on a white poplar in the vast forests.[19] The mistletoe was apparently meant to represent the Golden Bough of myth, concerning which traditions are legion. Frazer's many volumes bearing the title *The Golden Bough* are testimony to this fact.[20] Robert Graves has pointed out a connection between mistletoe and Midsummer's Day, which, as we have already noted, was associated with the Oracle of the Dead by the orientation of the tunnels. An ancient Norse tradition stated that all the trees refused to do service as stakes with which to put out the Eye of the Year on Midsummer's Day except for the mistletoe, which was therefore used for this purpose. And according to Graves, a stake of mistletoe is 'no poetic fancy', despite the fact that we usually think of mistletoe as a soft spray of leaves and berries which we buy in the shops at Christmas, or a frothy growth high up in an apple tree. Graves seems to have found some sizeable mistletoe growths which were obviously of some age, for he says: 'its wood, by the way, is extremely hard and tough . . . I once cut [a stake of it] for myself in Britanny.'[21]

The enquirer had to deposit his mistletoe in a special niche in the rock.[22] This niche survives; Paget says: '. . . outside the door of the Inner Sanctuary, we found a large niche about a foot above the floor. It did not seem that a position so close to the floor was consistent with the idea of a niche for a torch. Was it the niche in which was placed [the mistletoe which served as the] pilgrim's passport for his return to the upper world?'[23]

As he offered his mistletoe to Persephone and sprinkled himself with holy water, the enquirer must have dreaded what was to be found at any moment in her House as he stood at its very door. Was he about to see the Queen of the Dead? 'Terror was in her name . . . For Homer she was always to be feared, a divinity only then to be called glorious when by so naming her you might forestall some dreadful harm. She could send forth, from where she ruled among the dead, that awful Gorgon's head that turned to stone all those whose eyes it met; her anger was therefore to be feared and in every way appeased.'[24]

The enquirer was now led into the House of Persephone, the Inner Sanctum of the oracle complex. There, lying bound on an altar would be the animal which, as far as he knew, had followed him into the tunnels. He would be led towards the altar, beside which a trench had been dug. 'Draw your sword and be ready to prevent any unwanted shade [ghost] from approaching,' the Sibyl or the hooded priests would warn him ominously.

At this moment he heard a shriek behind and above him, as the High Priest cut the throat of the victim on the altar. The blood poured down into the trench. At this moment a dreadful moaning was commenced and shadowy faces began to appear on the walls before his terror-stricken eyes. The High Priest called out, 'Be ready, the next Shade to appear will be your mother.' In the state of mind to which he had been reduced, he believed it. He was in fact too terrified to carry out his proposed conversation, and before he could collect his thoughts, the Shade of his 'mother' had disappeared. (This scene would have been quite within the resources of the priests, by means of wooden cut-outs and a lamp to provide the shadows.)[25]

Thus does Paget describe what may have occurred in the Inner Sanctum, based on accounts of these 'visits to Hell' in the ancient literature.

There would certainly have been cases in which supposed conversations with the dead took place. Paget has probably been too abrupt in his reconstruction. The faking of such conversations by modern spiritualists and mediums is so easy and common that it was surely not beyond the capacities of the ancient priests. Let us see what happened to Aeneas at this point. He consulted the Oracle in order to be able to meet and converse with the departed spirit of his father. Note what Vergil tells us in the *Aeneid* of the encounter. Aeneas cries out to the spirit of his father: 'Father, oh let me clasp your hand . . . do not slip from my embraces.' Vergil continues: 'As he spoke his face grew wet with the streams of tears. Three times he tried to clasp his arms about his Father's neck, but three times the clasp was in vain and the wraith escaped his hands, like airy winds or the melting of a dream.'[26]

This is the kind of scene one would expect in the Inner Sanctum – something emotionally climactic and fulfilling, even though unsatisfying and frustrating to the visitor, who cannot actually embrace the vague, simulated spirits. The highly charged emotional atmosphere is described by Vergil:

> Now Anchises, his father, . . . seeing Aeneas . . . stretched out both hands to him in his delight. Tears started down his cheeks and a cry broke from him. 'You have come at last. . . . Your father knew you would be true. So your faithfulness has overcome the hard journey. May I really look at your face, son, and hear the tones I know so well and talk with you. . . . But to think of all the vast seas and lands that you have had to traverse, and all the perils of your storm-tossed journey, before I could welcome you at last!'[27]

Addressed in this way, the enquirer would be overcome. During his three days in isolation, his companions or subordinates would have had little to do, and some of them would inevitably have remained close by, conversing in the normal course of things with officials of the temple. Much specific information about the departed spirit sought by the enquirer could doubtless be obtained from these companions, and a very good simulation attempted. What is more, a genuine medium might have been employed inside the Inner Sanctum, whose body would appear to be possessed in turn by various spirits, as with mediums of today. Changes of voice and appearance are common in such cases. These would be the throng of spirits spoken of by Vergil: 'And they all thronged round and the Sibyl spoke to them . . .' and she asked them how to find Aeneas's father.[28] The expected voice and spirit would eventually make its way through. The priests and the Sibyl might judge the correct voice from the enquirer's reaction to it. Thus, whether it emanated from a genuine medium in a state of trance or semi-trance, or was simply simulated through speaking-tubes (which we know were used in some

ancient temples to cause voices to issue forth from the mouths of
some statues of the gods), the enquirer would at last hear the
correct voice and exclaim 'Father!' or 'Mother!' And it is
significant that in the *Aeneid* the fairly lengthy conversation
which takes place between Aeneas and his dead father consists
entirely of generalities. The father goes into a complicated
account of creation, the universe, the after-life, and so on. He
pontificates: 'The body is the cause of fear and desire, of sorrow
and of joy . . . souls are ceaselessly schooled by retribution, and
pay in punishment for their old offences.'[29]

In vain might the enquirer attempt to elicit specific information
about individuals from such an elevated discourse. Perhaps he
would be assured that such-and-such was either happy among
the blessed, or had fallen among those 'without memory' and
stirring in him was 'a wish to re-enter bodily life . . .' or he would
hear of 'souls who are destined to live in the body a second
time . . .'[30] The transmigration of souls was apparently a doctrine
propagated at this Oracle. As Aeneas plaintively replies when
told of this by his father: 'O Father, am I then to believe, that of
these souls some go soaring hence, up to the world beneath our
sky and return once more into dreary matter?'[31]

After the enquirer had been given a suitable harangue
concerning the after-life, and been told that 'Each of us finds the
world of death fitted unto himself',[32] the encounter with the
spirits would be brought to a close. Other voices and presences
would begin to crowd round and exclude the glimpsed but
always elusive loved one. As Vergil says: 'Anchises finished and
now he led his son and the Sibyl into the midst of a great
gathering of souls, who were all busy in conversation.'[33] It is
quite clear that the end of the discourse was never allowed to be
followed by any substantial question-and-answer session, for the
grandeur would be diminished and suspicions might be aroused.
Predictions might be uttered of a long-range and vague nature,
such as 'You shall found a race. . . .' But the priests would now
be crowding around and ushering away the enquirer and the
Sibyl. From the Inner Sanctum they would leave by the tunnel
along which the sacrificial animal had earlier been dragged. This

would bring them back again to the Dividing of the Ways and the original entrance tunnel, but the enquirer would have no idea where he was, because the door would have swung across and concealed the original turning he had taken on entering. As Paget says: 'Its purpose was to shut off the continuation of [the main entrance tunnel], or the right fork of the tunnel at will.'[34]

Paget describes the enquirer's departure from the Inner Sanctum as follows: 'So before he could protest the priests hustled him to his feet and the procession re-formed and proceeded to leave the Inner Sanctuary. . . . At the traverse, the Smoke door was opened to allow them to pass . . . to the Dividing of the Ways in a breathable atmosphere.'[35] The spirit would be completing its last remarks. Vergil says: 'And Anchises having said his say escorted his son and the Sibyl with him on their way, and let them depart through the Gate of Ivory.'[36] Paget speculates: 'At the Dividing of the Ways, the door was covered with ivory on the west side. It opened to allow the procession to pass. At the same time, it closed the entrance to [the right fork], so there would be nothing to show the suppliant that he was back at the point where he had come in.'[37] The procession would then make its way up the long entrance tunnel back once more to the outside world. But a final and ultimate precaution was taken by the priests. As Paget puts it:

> When the procession reached the passage to the Sudatorium [another surface room – see map], we think that this was closed by a door and a ladder was standing ready for the ascent through the hole covered by the tile to enter the passage leading to the Room of Memory, behind the temple. Here the suppliant was carefully interrogated, to ensure he believed all that he had seen and heard. If there were the slightest suspicion that he did not accept it, I have not the least doubt that he would never leave the Room of Memory alive.[38]

I believe that Dr Paget's conclusions about this are correct. The enquirer might 'not survive' his journey to the Underworld. He might have 'looked back' and have to 'remain'. If he showed signs of scepticism and seemed likely to spread abroad that the Oracle was run by unscrupulous tricksters, he would have to be killed. Murder would not be suspected; the Underworld would merely have claimed another victim. It may be that Eurydice, who 'remained' and was lost to Orpheus, was a sceptic who was eliminated. We shall see that at the Oracle of Trophonios overdoses of strong drugs and poisons were administered to clients so often that it was an accepted fact among the public that permanent 'melancholy', insanity, or death within weeks was common for those who consulted the Oracle; but still they came in their hundreds, undeterred by this knowledge, so strong were their needs or their curiosity. If at all possible, however, happy and satisfied clients were what the Baian Oracle wanted. By and large, the elaborate arrangements and careful preparations would in nearly all cases result in the best possible outcome from such a competent and professional establishment: an enquirer very much dazed and awestruck, but thoroughly convinced and content.

The reconstruction of the events at the Oracle is largely conjectural, and most of it is drawn from Robert Paget. He pieced it together from his intimate knowledge of the site, combined with descriptions given in the *Aeneid,* the *Odyssey,* and certain inferences based upon the fuller documentation regarding the underground Oracle of Trophonios in Greece (see next chapter). The reader must not assume that the details of these events are certain, though I regard them as sufficiently reliable to be put forward as an idea of what happened. Their literal truth is not insisted upon by any means. There are many technical points of argument which I have passed over. For instance, Pausanius (second century AD) implied that Odysseus possibly made his descent into Hades on mainland Greece, at the Oracle of the Dead at Ephyra in Thesprotia.[39] The other Oracle of the Dead has been excavated there by the Greek archaeologist, Dr Sotirios I. Dakaris, as already described. As for the Baian Oracle of the Dead, a full clearance and selective excavation is required. I am certain that the Inner Sanctuary is more extensive than Paget believed, and if it were unblocked we would find entrances to further parts of the underground complex. Within the Inner

Sanctuary it is possible that we may find, beneath the soil heaped in by the Romans, the original wooden doors and other such organic material which could be carbon-dated, as well as the altar. I find it hard to imagine anyone actually dragging the various tunnel doors hundreds of feet out of the Oracle, and it is far more likely that they were thrown in with other such 'rubbish' and buried in the Sanctuary. It is also not unlikely that objects of archaeological interest could be excavated from the Sanctuary, such as cult objects or some small statuary. And finally, although this is gruesome speculation, it is not impossible that beneath all the soil in the Sanctuary we might even find a skeleton. It is possible that the Romans might have buried the head priest in his own Sanctuary, whether alive or dead. Certainly it is worth trying to find anything which is there. If anything was left inside the Oracle, the Sanctuary is where it would have been thrown, because the tunnels themselves are too narrow for dumping things beneath the soil the Romans carried in to seal the Oracle.

I believe there may also have been a 'back door' to the Oracle, a secret vertical ascent to the top of the hill, accessed from behind the Inner Sanctuary. It is even possible that this was used by the Romans for bringing in some of the soil, since the pattern of soil dispersal does not seem to have been from the entrance inwards but rather from the interior outwards. As I have already mentioned, the apparent tunnel running northwards beneath the entrance tunnel needs to be opened and followed to its destination, which may have been the very extensive living quarters of the Oracle attendants. We are told in ancient accounts that they only emerged into the outer air when it was dark, as it was their habit never to expose themselves to the light of the sun. They must therefore have had their own private entrance and exit to the Oracle, and the caves in which they resided must have been many, and must have been interconnected. Or there may be a much larger sanctuary down there. In short, we may yet not know the half of the Oracle of the Dead. In September 1962, when Paget located the entrance and went in for the first time in nearly 2000 years, he couldn't go further than the bank of the Styx. By unblocking the Chimney and the Rise, Paget opened up the interior and added several hundred feet of further tunnels to the known portions of the complex. By recruiting naval divers, he was able to prove that the Styx had a further landing-stage beyond, with the entrance to yet another tunnel. He also proved that the Inner Sanctuary was a room of considerable size, even though it is still largely filled with earth. Whatever lies beyond all of this must be of equal extent to that which we presently know.

Pausanius suggests that Odysseus visited the Oracle of the Dead in mainland Greece (which was founded later and described below), rather than the Baian Oracle. However, this is clearly ruled out from the mouth of Homer. Odysseus says explicitly to the spirit of his mother in Hades: 'For not yet have I drawn near to the Achaean shore [Greece] nor yet have I set foot on mine own country.'[40] Furthermore, had Odysseus been at this site in Greece, he would have been only a few hours' sailing time from Ithaca, his 'much longed-for home'. In any case, Pausanius only actually claims that Homer took the names of the rivers of Hades from Thesprotia; Pausanius was unaware that there were also a River Acheron and an Acherousian Lake in the vicinity of Baia. We are therefore justified in considering the account of Odysseus's visit to Hades as evidence probably concerning Baia, and *not* the Oracle in Thesprotia. I pass over many other matters, such as Professor Denys Page's interesting suggestion that Book XI of the *Odyssey,* describing the visit to Hades, is not by Homer at all but is an interpolation consisting of several disjointed sources unconvincingly combined.[41] Page, however, says: 'We have good reason to believe that there was once an independent poem on Odysseus' Visit to the Underworld . . . inserted into the *Odyssey,* and more or less adapted to it.'[42] And I believe that this Homeric poem was originally set at the Baian Oracle of the Dead.

Finally, I wish to explain why it is that world attention has never previously focused on the discovery of this amazing site originally described by Robert Paget. In a subsequent generation, I have at last been able to 'rediscover' the Oracle of the Dead, after twenty years of trying to obtain access to it. Sadly, during this time all the remaining people who had ever entered it have died. It is a strange tale:

November, 1963.

A large crowd of international journalists is gathering at the
British Officer's Club at Bagnoli, near Naples in Italy. An
important announcement is about to be made. This announcement has nothing to do with military affairs, although the press
conference has been called by Squadron Leader Jack Gates, RAF,
who is one of the British officers attached to the Headquarters of
NATO's Allied Forces Southern Europe. A number of the British
and American officers living in the area are friends and
supporters of a retired British engineer named Robert Paget who,
because of his scholarly inclinations, is widely called Dottore
('Doctor'). He and his Italian wife, Ada Immacolata, a retired
opera singer, are childless and live in a very modest house at
nearby Baia, where Paget pursues archaeological investigations
entirely on his own and at his personal expense, despite the fact
that he is nearly broke. But Paget has something important to
say. The world's press are very excited, because it is the occasion
when one of the greatest archaeological discoveries of the
twentieth century is about to be announced. Headlines are in the
making. The news will go round the world, Paget is within
minutes of being famous, and the rediscovery of the fabulous and
eerie underground Oracle of the Dead will soon become as well
known to everyone as the tomb of Tutankhamun.

But there is an interruption ...

Paget has not yet begun to speak. The journalists are still
assembling, readying their cameras and microphones. And
suddenly a shiver runs through the crowd as the news spreads. At
first people are paralysed by horror. Then they all grab whatever
they have and run from the building as if nearby Mount Vesuvius
were suddenly erupting. They try desperately to find phones, they
tear off in their vehicles like mad people, engines roaring. In a
very short time they are all gone, and Paget and his friends are
left forlorn and alone. Paget is never famous, he never holds his
press conference, his discovery is never announced. The entire

*event is utterly forgotten by the press because it has been eclipsed
by one of the most shocking acts of our time:*

President Kennedy has been shot!

*As if the gods of death had reached out from their cavernous
seclusion to protect their own privacy by an act peculiarly
suitable to themselves, they drew a veil around their great secret
by expunging all awareness through the assassination of the
American president, which eclipsed all other concerns.*

In England in 1967, Paget publishes his book In the Footsteps
of Orpheus, *which describes the Oracle of the Dead, but nobody
takes any notice. In 1968 or 1969 the book is remaindered by the
publisher. The young Robert Temple, a compulsive haunter of
bookshops, wanders into a small remainder bookshop in St.
Martin's Lane near the Coliseum Theatre, then a cinerama movie
theatre and today home to the English National Opera. He is
struck by the curious claim on the orange dust jacket of this last
remaining copy of a failed book: the author says it is about 'The
Discovery of the Ancient Greek Underworld'. Oh yes? How can
you discover the Greek Underworld? Surely an over-stated
claim! But worth buying nevertheless, because its original price
was thirty shillings, and it is now marked down to seventeen
shillings, and it seems to have a new angle on ancient myths.
Probably it will contain interesting material mixed in with a lot
of absurd adventures of an amateur archaeologist. There is a
rather blurred photo of some meaningless ruins along the bottom
of the jacket. It doesn't appear to be a very professional work, as
seems quite cheaply produced. Well, it's worth seventeen
shillings, but if it were still thirty, probably not. 'I'll buy it!'*

January, 2002.

We try again . . .

THREE

THE ORACULAR ESTABLISHMENTS

'It is good to speak to the future: the future
will listen.'

The Teaching of Ptahhotep, *a hieratic papyrus from
Thebes, circa 1850 BC*

When we think of ancient Greece and Rome we tend to think of
the great classical philosophers such as Plato and Aristotle, the
supremacy of the intellect and the rule of reason. It is not
generally realized that divination was an important part of
classical life and was practised on a daily basis. We could even go
so far as to say that the whole of classical civilization was based
on divination as the foundation of all its actions. No major
decision of state, such as going to war, was made without
consulting the gods through divination. Few personal under-
takings, such as financial investment, getting married or making
a journey, were embarked upon without divination. Even the
great Socrates consulted the Oracle at Delphi.

The classical civilizations had many forms of divination which
they used constantly: divination by lightning, by the flights of
birds (augury), by the chance words uttered by idiots or passers-
by (cledonism), by thunderbolts, by the manner in which
chickens pecked at corn, and so on. Divination by lightning and
augury by the flights of birds were both very complex systems.
The sky was generally divided up into 16 sections: if birds flew
from one section to another, that signified one thing; if they then
flew from that section to another, it meant something else, and

71

so on. The same applied to streaks of lightning. There were 'textbooks' to consult so that people could look these things up. In a surviving ancient dream book by Artemidorus dating from the second century AD,[1] there are hundreds of different dreams listed, with their prophetic meanings alongside, so that if you had a dream you could look it up under its type and consult its meaning. Such handbooks once existed for birds, lightning, and the other means of divination.

Inferior forms of divination, lacking in official sanction and prestige, were practised by wandering fortune-tellers. Farmers had much folklore about what they called 'omens', namely calves born with two heads or even children with webbed fingers, all of which portended various sorts of coming events and disasters. Other methods included an early form of roulette which was connected with the Oracle at Delphi and gave answers to enquiries rather than winners in a gambling game; both lots and dice were also used to consult the future. The Greeks were keen on an early form of crystal-gazing, whereby maidens gazed into pools of water or bowls of liquid and sought visions of the future. The Babylonians had voluminous Omen Books, many fragments of which survive, and much of that lore entered into folk wisdom, which probably survives in peasant societies today. There is certainly a very strong tradition in modern Greece among the country folk about fairies, the evil eye, and prophecy.

It is often assumed that the main divination system of the Greeks and Romans, as well as of the Assyrians and Babylonians, was astrology. But astrology was in fact a very late technique, and only really came to prominence well after the time of Christ. The main technique of divination for Greeks, Romans, Babylonians and Assyrians was by means of the entrails of animals, as we shall see in the next chapter. But for the Greeks, the second most important, and indeed one could almost say the 'state method' of divination, was by means of the many oracle centres. The chief of these were Dodona and Delphi. Delphi is well known to every tourist to Greece, although it has only been excavated and visible to the eye for about a century, as for many centuries since antiquity it was covered by deep layers of soil with a village on top. The French dug it out, and relocated the entire village lying above it. Those grand days when you could move a whole village are gone now, and such mammoth archaeological feats can no longer be contemplated. We are lucky that Delphi was excavated when it was, for if it were still waiting its turn, it is unlikely that it would ever see the light of day. It is one of the great archaeological sites on earth, and to visit it is like stepping back in time. Strictly speaking, the massive excavated site which tourists visit at Delphi is called Pytho (with the accent on the last vowel), and the gorge and spring at the bottom by the road (which many people miss) is called Castalia. Together they form the 'classical site' of Delphi, founded in the eighth century BC. However the origins of Delphi go back much further than that, at which time Delphi was much higher up the mountain and less accessible. In fact, evidence of the presence of Minoans from Crete no later than the twelfth century BC has been excavated at Delphi. As for the Oracle of Delos, it was reputed to have been founded 'by the son of Cecrops', the legendary Egyptian with a fish-tail who was said to have become King of Athens in 1558 BC, according to the official mythological lore.

The origins of the great oracle centres such as Delphi are matters of some complexity and uncertainty. And what is more, they may not originally have been oracles at all. The original purpose of the key sites of Delphi, Dodona, and Delos (which was once a major oracle but was no longer functioning as such after the seventh century BC) seems to have been a geodetic one – that is, connected with measuring the Earth. These three main oracles of Greece were evidently founded as sacred (or possibly only scientific) expressions of key points established by surveying techniques that marked out latitude lines. For instance, Dodona, Delphi and Delos form a descending scale of geodetic points which are each precisely one degree of latitude apart.

Lest one be tempted to say this must be a weird coincidence, some further geodetic connections render this impossible. Both Dodona and Delphi have legends associated with them regarding the Greek ark landing on their respective mountain peaks after the Great Flood (the Greek Noah was called Deucalion). As is well known, the Hebrew ark of Noah is said in the Bible to have landed on the peak of Mount Ararat. What is most extraordinary is that Mount Ararat on the Turkish/Armenian border and Mount Tomaros at Dodona are on the same latitude line. This means that the Jewish ark and the Greek ark landed at precisely the same latitude as each other. This can be no coincidence, and is the survival of some highly sophisticated ancient geodetic scientific lore deriving from surveying expeditions. Dodona has other geodetic affiliations with other sacred sites, but this is not our main subject of discussion here, and I have discussed the geodetics of the oracle centres at length in two previous books.[2]

Whatever the original purpose of the main oracle centres may have been (the minor oracle centres clearly originated in the normal way), as the centuries wore on the oracles achieved increasing prominence and the geodetic function was forgotten. After all, whatever scientific/navigational/surveying/mapping infrastructure once existed by whoever first established these sacred points, it was long before the Greeks existed as a people (it was at the very latest of Minoan date, and thus certainly prior to 1200 BC), so it is unlikely that the Greeks ever had any true knowledge of the purpose of Dodona, Delphi, or Delos. In fact, what happened under the Greeks was that the locations of both Dodona and Delphi were shifted slightly from their precise geodetic locations down the mountain sides to make them more accessible for religious purposes, while the oracle of Delos was allowed to die out altogether by the seventh century BC, although the Island of Delos retained its sacred character.

I am engaged in lengthy attempts to try and find the original sites of both Dodona and Delphi. Textual evidence about the original site of Delphi survives in fragments, and after studying this intently, I suggested to my colleague Professor Ioannis Liritzis – who grew up in the village of Delphi and knows all the local inhabitants – that we discuss the matter with some of the hunters and goatherds. They recommended a place to us higher up Mount Parnassos which they called Marmora, and despite his many boyhood picnics on the mountain, Liritzis had never actually visited this spot. When we had these discussions at

Delphi, the mountain was still covered in late snow, so we were unable to make the trip to Marmora together. After the snow melted, Liritzis at my urging went to the spot and found a curious ancient megalithic-style stone construction, which he thought must have had some marker or surveying function. I believe this was associated with the original site of Delphi, on an outlying basis. There was no ancient settlement in the immediate vicinity of this structure (which has never been published), so we will have to continue our search when we have a few days to spend at Delphi scouring the mountain peaks, which are very extensive. There is no doubt that the original Delphic village ruins are up there somewhere.

As for Dodona, Mount Tomaros is even more vast and intimidating than Mount Parnassos. To search its peaks would take many weeks, and the weather is not very favourable. Liritzis and I are attempting to use satellite photos and geodetic plotting to narrow the search, and I am convinced that the original site of Dodona is further south and higher up the slopes than the site now visited by tourists. In 1979 I made considerable efforts to raise funds for an expedition to Mount Tomaros to find the original site of Dodona, but was unsuccessful.

As far as the major Greek oracles were concerned, all Greeks were agreed that the senior oracle was that at Dodona, whose patron in classical times was Zeus. But because it was so distant and difficult to reach in the far northwest of Greece (like the Nekromanteion which we have considered already, which was not far away), the much nearer and 'user-friendly' Oracle of Delphi took on the role of the major arbiter of Greek affairs in classical times.

But how did these oracles actually function? How did they manage a continuity of reputation? Clearly it was necessary for a successful national oracle to produce prophecies on a production-line basis. They had to keep going year after year, decade after decade, century after century. But how did they manage this? A national oracle could not really afford a 'bad year', or even a 'bad month'. It is obvious that they found some reliable *system* to ensure that their reputations could be maintained over vast stretches of time. This system had to be both a trade secret and sufficiently simple that it would not suffer breakdowns through over-complexity. It had to be robust, so that it could survives the ups and downs of events and changes of personnel. If it were too complicated, a succeeding generation might not be able to manage it, and the whole edifice of sanctity might collapse ignominiously. In other words, some simple and secret system of systematic fraud was required to keep everything humming along properly. I believe I have worked out what this was. Look at the matter like this:

If the oracular establishments of the ancient world were not primarily prophetic centres, how did they get the reputation for being so? Surely they could not have survived for so many centuries if once in a while they did not make some prophecies which came true? I believe we can piece together more evidence to show how the oracle centres were able to maintain their reputations. The secret lies, I believe, in the oracular dove.

The dove is associated somehow or other, in myth or legend or through graphical representation, with all, or nearly all, the oracle centres.[3] I believe that the oracle centres were fed with information about important events, such as the outcomes of battles, by carrier pigeon. Such news would then be announced as prophecies, sometimes on the very days of the events. Some days or even weeks later, when human messengers were able to arrive, the 'news' they brought confirmed the 'prophecies'. There is a considerable amount of evidence for this.

The Roman author Pliny, discussing pigeons, gives the following explicit account of their use:

Moreover also they [pigeons] have acted as go-betweens in important affairs, when at the siege of Modena [in 44–43 BC] Decimus Brutus sent to the consuls' camp despatches tied to their feet; what use to [Mark] Antony were his rampart and watchful besieging force, and even the barriers of nets that he stretched in the river, when the message went by air? Also pigeon-fancying is carried to insane lengths by some people: they build towers on their rooves for these birds, and tell stories of the high-breeding and pedigrees of particular birds, for which there is now an old precedent: before Pompey's civil war [begun in 49 BC] Lucius Axius, Knight of Rome, advertised pigeons for sale at 400 denari per brace – so Marcus Varro relates. Moreover the largest birds, which are believed to be produced in Campania, have conferred fame on their native place.[4]

Pigeons were not the only birds used in this way. Pliny records that swallows too were carriers:

A man of knightly rank at Volterra, Caecina, who owned a racing four-in-hand, used to catch swallows and take them with him to Rome and despatch them to take the news of a win to his friends, as they returned to the same nest; they had the winning colour painted on them. Also Fabius Pictor records in his Annals that when a Roman garrison was besieged by the Ligurians a swallow taken from her nestlings was brought to him for him to indicate by knots made in a thread tied to its foot how many days later help would arrive and a sortie must be made. ... The swallow has an extremely swift and swerving flight, owing to which it is also not liable to capture by the other kinds of birds.[3]

The reference to carrier-swallows may be as surprising to the reader as it was to me, for I have never heard of this use of swallows in modern times. But carrier-swallows may have a long history extending back some millennia, and they are portrayed in ancient Egyptian papyri. Utnapishtim, the Babylonian 'Noah', is described in the ancient *Epic of Gilgamesh* in his ark which has just come to rest on a mountaintop after the deluge as follows:

When the seventh day arrived,
I sent forth and set free a dove.
The dove went forth, but came back;
Since no resting-place for it was visible, she turned round.
Then I sent forth and set free a swallow.

The swallow went forth, but came back;
Since no resting-place for it appeared, she turned round.[6]

The phrase 'turning round' may be particularly significant in the ancient Near East in an esoteric sense connected with the use of messenger birds. In ancient Egyptian, the verb 'to turn back' is *un,* which as a noun actually means 'dovecote' or 'sanctuary'. The reader may wonder what the ancient Babylonian 'Noah' of the flood story has to do with oracle centres. I have written about this at length in a previous book, and will not here recapitulate my previous discussion.[7] Carrier-birds were traditionally used not only for carrying messages but for sighting shore and navigation. In his book *Prehistoric Crete,* R. W. Hutchinson has a section on 'Navigation by Pigeons' in which he speaks of the shore-sighting birds and says 'this device must have been practised by Sumerian captains back in the third millennium BC', and refers to the passage of the *Epic of Gilgamesh* just quoted.[8] He then refers to the story of the Argonauts and says: '. . . what of the pigeon which Jason let loose to ascertain whether the Argo could pass through the clashing rocks? Was this a reminiscence of the bird that every good captain of a Minoan or Mycenaean ship would have taken with him on a long voyage?'[9]

The use of homing pigeons for naval purposes did not by any means cease with the ancient sailors. The British Admiralty had an active pigeon service until early in the twentieth century. The pigeons were used for sending signals and information between ships and shore stations before the advent of radio. And before the telegraph existed, stockbrokers and financial speculators in the last century often had their private homing-pigeon services to aid their speculations, and newspapers used them frequently. Reports of yacht races were often obtained by pigeons launched from lofts actually fitted into the yachts' rigging for the purpose. On some occasions in relatively modern times, homing pigeons have proved crucial to important military struggles. In the siege of Paris in 1870–71, the birds were used to great effect. And until the use of radio made them unnecessary, probably every major military fortress in Europe was equipped with a number of pigeons for communications when under siege.

It was customary for carrier-pigeons to carry to their home cities the names of the victors in the ancient Olympic Games. Pliny records an incident which occurred at Olympia which also can be explained in no other way than by the use of carrier-pigeons: 'There is one marvellous instance of the transmission of a spoken message: the battle that resulted in the destruction of Sybaris [fought by the Locrians, who defeated the people of Crotona at the River Sagra in South Italy in 560 BC] was heard of at Olympia on the day on which it was fought.' The pious Pliny does not suggest that birds were used; he attributes this incident, and others like it, to 'visions and warnings sent by the divine powers'.[10] We may imagine that this is exactly how they were presented: a priest would issue an announcement from the gods, or from one particular god, that a great battle had just been fought at such and such a place, and give the name of the winning army. When eventually this was confirmed, the common people would be utterly convinced that the divine powers were communicating with them directly, and issuing prophecies.

By chance, a striking confirmation of this attitude is to be found in the works of Cicero, regarding the very same incident mentioned by Pliny. In his work *On the Nature of the Gods,* Cicero presents a variety of speakers in a dialogue. The Stoic speaker, who is glorifying the gods and various miraculous events which they inspired, tells us: 'It is also recorded in history that when the Locrians won their great victory over the people of Crotona at the important battle of the River Sagra, news of the engagement was reported at the Olympic Games on the very same day. Often has the sound of the voices of the Fauns, often has the apparition of a divine form compelled anyone that is not either feeble-minded or impious to admit the real presence of the gods.'[11]

These Stoic views are precisely the conclusions the common people could be and would be expected to draw from such events. The god of Olympia was Zeus, the King of the Gods. We are expressly told by Homer in the *Odyssey* that 'the timorous doves ... bear ambrosia to father Zeus'. This sounds like a 'cover story' to explain the continual arrival and departure of

countless doves, with objects attached to their legs, at the temple
of Zeus. The common people would be quite content to believe
that the doves were indeed carrying ambrosia. The fact that the
remark by Homer is otherwise inexplicable is indicated by
comments by H. W. Parke, one of the leading scholars of oracle
centres. Parke was not able to guess at the truth, and commented
that Homer's statement 'is a puzzling passage which gave trouble
to scholars in antiquity. Why the doves should be bringing
ambrosia to Zeus is not clear.'[12] But it seems clear to us that the
doves were carrying not ambrosia, but information, to his
priests.

The ancient historian Herodotus preserves an amusing
account of how the priests of an oracular establishment reacted
with rage and consternation when their birds were interfered
with. The establishment concerned was the Oracle of Apollo
near Miletus at Didyma, also known as Branchidae:

> When they came to Branchidae, Aristodicus, speaking for
> all, put this question to the oracle: 'Oh King [he is
> addressing the god Apollo], Pactyes the Lydian hath fled to
> us for refuge to save him from a violent death at the hands
> of the Persians; and they demand him of us, bidding the men
> of Cyme to give him up. But we, for all that we fear Persian
> power, have not made bold to give up this our suppliant,
> until thy will be clearly made known to us, whether we shall
> do this or not.' Thus Aristodicus questioned; and the god
> gave again the same answer, that Pactyes should be
> delivered up to the Persians. With that Aristodicus did as he
> had already purposed; he went round about the temple, and
> stole away the sparrows and all other families of nesting
> birds that were in it. But while he so did, a voice (they say)
> came out of the inner shrine calling to Aristodicus, and
> saying, 'Thou wickedest of men, wherefore darest thou do
> this? wilt thou rob my temple of those that take refuge with
> me?' Then Aristodicus had his answer ready: 'O King,' said
> he, 'wilt thou thus save thine own suppliants, yet bid the
> men of Cyme deliver up theirs?' But the god made answer,

'Yea, I do bid them, that ye may the sooner perish for your impiety, and never again come to inquire of my oracle concerning the giving up of them that seek refuge with you.'

When this answer was brought to the hearing of the Cymaeans they sent Pactyes away to Mytilene; for they desired neither to perish for delivering him up nor be besieged for keeping him with them.[13]

It appears that Aristodicus well knew that the nesting birds in the temple precincts whom the god guarded so jealously were the means of 'instant' communication used by the priests in obtaining their international news. Herodotus does not specifically mention doves here. This could be either because he did not know about the carrier-pigeon network or because he is concealing the fact out of piety, as he frequently does with other religious subjects throughout his *History,* usually admitting so quite openly.

Herodotus records another instance regarding this same oracular establishment where carrier-pigeons were obviously used; once again, however, he is coy about it. The incident is too long to quote in full, but Herodotus specifies that he obtained first-hand accounts of it both in Delphi and in Miletus, for he travelled widely in search of his material. Alyattes, King of Lydia, was besieging Miletus, but fell seriously ill. His family had a long-standing respect for the Oracle of Delphi, and sent there 'to question the god about his sickness'. But a friend of the King of Miletus, in some mysterious way which Herodotus evades specifying, 'learnt what reply the oracle had given' and was able to give this information to the King of Miletus before Alyattes got it. Armed with the secret information the King of Miletus outwitted the besieging Lydians by a device suggested by what the Delphic Oracle had answered, still before the enquirer had even received the information from the Oracle.[14] Carrier-pigeons would seem to constitute the only possible explanation for this.

There are stories that some of the major oracular centres were actually founded by pigeons. Herodotus himself records: 'This, then, is the account I heard from the priests at Thebes; but the prophetesses at Dodona say that two black pigeons flew away from Thebes in Egypt; that one of them went to Libya, and the other to them; that this last, sitting perched on an oak tree, proclaimed in a human voice, that it was fitting an oracle should be erected there to Zeus; and that the people believed this to be a divine message to them, and did accordingly.'[15] Herodotus adds later: 'How could a dove speak with a human voice?'[16] The answer is that it carried a message tied to its leg. But, as Herodotus seems genuinely puzzled, we must presume that he really did not know the answer himself.

The late classical author Philostratus records what appears to be further evidence of the widespread use of carrier-pigeons or other messenger-birds by a variety of ancient temples and oracle centres: '. . . on the summit of the rock there is, they say, a cleft which draws into itself the birds which fly over it, as we may see at Athens also in the vestibule of the Parthenon, and in several places in Phrygia and Lydia.'[17] This is the only passage I have come across in ancient literature which mentions a cleft in the vestibule of the Parthenon at Athens which 'drew birds into it'. These would appear to be messenger-birds, and part of the international pigeon network. As for Phrygia and Lydia, they are regions of Asia Minor where a number of famous oracular establishments were located. The oracle centre of Hierapolis was in Phrygia; Lydia contained the Oracle of Colophon and, in earlier times, oracular centres at Erythrae[18] and one near Sardis at Mount Sipylus.[19]

The earliest divinity supposed to inspire the oracular centres with prophetic utterances was thought to be the earth goddess. It is at least true to say that she preceded the deities of classical times. This was the case at Delphi, where the earth goddess was ousted by Apollo about 800 BC, and the site of the Oracle was moved some miles down the mountain from Lykoreia to the present location of the main ruins of Delphi. The evidence for this is too extensive to be summarized briefly, and we shall not go into that particular subject here. But I mention it in connection with Figure 14. This drawing reproduces the design on a particularly interesting Boeotian plate of the middle of the fifth century BC, which is preserved at the National Museum in Athens. We see here an earth goddess seated on a throne in front of an oracular omphalos stone (presumably meant to be the one at nearby Delphi). In her hands she holds poppy heads, ears of wheat and a flaming torch. Behind her flutters the oracular dove, alighting after its flight. The poppy heads, sources of opium, relate to the use of drugs, a subject to which I return later.

According to Dr Sam Wide, a German scholar who has made the greatest study of the iconography of this particular plate, the goddess wears on her head a particular headdress which is often found in the Boeotian geometrical style of pottery and which is called a *polos*.[20] As mentioned earlier, the Egyptian word *un* meant both 'dovecote' and 'to turn back'. It is interesting that the word *polos* primarily means 'a hinge or pivot on which something turns round'. I believe we may have here some of the esoteric punning which the ancient priests liked so much. As for the Egyptian word *un*, we must remember the Greek tradition that the doves flew from Egypt to the oracle centre of Dodona,

Figure 14: A design on a Boetian plate from the mid-fifth century showing an earth goddess seated on a throne in front of an oracular omphalos stone, holding poppy heads, ears of wheat and a flaming torch.

mentioned above, and that *un* also means 'sanctuary'. And we have now seen that it was the sanctuaries which doubled as sacred dovecotes. So the fact that the same Egyptian word means both 'sanctuary' and 'dovecote' is presumably no accident.

The commonest representations of the sacred doves in connection with the oracular establishments show them in pairs, one on each side of an oracular omphalos. In Plate 30 we see one of the most ancient surviving representations of sacred doves, three doves on top of sacred columns from the Old Palace at Knossos, which is Minoan. There are many ancient Cretan representations of sacred doves or pigeons dating back three and a half to four thousand years. For other illustrations I refer the reader to an earlier book, in which I suggested the carrier-pigeon network and wrote: 'I am informed that carrier-pigeons could fly from Thebes to Dodona in about a day.'[21]

H. W. Parke was highly perplexed about the recurrent ancient tradition that 'in primitive times prophets connected with Dodona were regarded as capable of understanding the speech of birds'.[22] We are now in a position to see that 'the speech of birds' was written down and tied to their legs. The carrier-pigeon system is the explanation for the famous 'talking dove' of the oracles. And these doves helped the oracle centres to keep in touch with each other, to keep abreast of world events, and to operate a mutual-aid network to keep each other in business. It was a brilliant invention: 'the dove that utters the messages of Zeus.'[23]

Just before going to press I discovered that I had a predecessor in recognizing the importance of carrier-pigeons to the ancient oracle centres. In an old book of 1907 on *The Homing Pigeon*,[24] a pigeon expert named Edgar Chamberlain attempts to give a history of homing pigeons in antiquity. He wasn't much of a classical scholar, and he criticizes Aristotle for not describing the use of homing pigeons when he accompanied Alexander the Great on his journeys. This shows an appalling lack of knowledge of Greek history, since Aristotle never accompanied Alexander the Great on any journeys, although his nephew Callisthenes did, and there was a great deal of correspondence which is now lost. But although Chamberlain's grasp of history is shaky at best, when it comes to pigeons, he is – well, I almost said on firm ground, but that would be a wrong analogy, wouldn't it?

The interesting comments by Chamberlain are these:

'No doubt the priests of Ammon in Ethiopia [he means Egypt, and is referring to the Oracle of Ammon at the Oasis of Siwa], of Isis and Osiris in Egypt, of Nisroch in Assyria were assisted in their prophetic utterances and miraculous knowledge by innocent Homing Pigeons. These birds were held sacred by most of the ancients, and to kill them was a capital offence.'[25]

It is very interesting to see that an expert in carrier pigeons a century ago saw the obvious advantages to the ancient oracle centres of the use of the birds for producing the 'miraculous' messages. And it is always very comforting to find that others have shared an idea and an insight, especially when they are expert in some relevant technical details and can base their views on genuine expertise.

The effect that faked 'advance knowledge' can have on people is amusingly recounted by the physicist Richard Feynman, in a story he told about his youth. In the book *Surely You're Joking Mr. Feynman!*, he describes his early experiences with building a home radio:

I bought radios at rummage sales. I didn't have any money, but it wasn't very expensive – they were old, broken radios, and I'd buy them and try to fix them. Usually they were broken in some simple-minded way – some obvious wire was hanging loose, or a coil was broken or partly unwound – so I could get some of them going. On one of these radios one night I got WACO in Waco, Texas [more than a thousand miles away] – it was tremendously exciting!

On this same tube radio up in my lab I was able to hear a station up in Schenectady [in upper New York state] called

WGN. Now, all of us kids – my two cousins, my sister, and the neighbourhood kids – listened on the radio downstairs to a program called the Eno Crime Club – Eno effervescent salts – it was *the* thing! Well, I discovered that I could hear this program up in my lab on WGN one hour before it was broadcast in New York! So I'd discover what was going to happen, and then, when we were all sitting around the radio downstairs listening to the Eno Crime Club, I'd say, 'You know, we haven't heard from so-and-so in a long time. I betcha he comes and saves the situation.'

Two seconds later, *bup-bup*, he comes! So they all got excited about this, and I predicted a couple of other things.'[26]

This boyhood trick of knowing things one hour in advance and mystifying his friends was a perfect analogue of what occurred at the ancient oracle centres.

Perhaps the best way to approach the subject of the use of drugs and altered states of consciousness at the oracle centres is to consider first the consultation of the Oracle of Trophonios in Greece. We are fortunate in that we possess a great deal of highly specific information about this Oracle, including an elaborate account of the consultation by a man who experienced it himself: the gossipy travel writer and antiquarian Pausanius (*c.* 150 AD).[27] In addition, there are two lengthy second-hand accounts preserved by Plutarch[28] and Philostratus.[29]

Trophonios was a legendary hero who was credited with building the temple at Delphi, after finishing which, he consulted the Oracle and requested in payment 'what was best for man'. The Oracle replied that on the third day his request would be granted, and when the third day dawned Trophonios was found dead.[30] There is a more highly coloured legend that Trophonios was swallowed up by the earth at Lebadea (today's Livadia). In any case, the Oracle of Delphi is said to have ordered that a cult and an Oracle of Trophonios be founded at Lebadea. This was an underground one, bearing many striking similarities to the Oracle of the Dead at Baia.

Trophonius   Lebadius .

Figure 15: A fanciful seventeenth-century depiction of Trophonios, the
shadowy underworld personality whose name was given to the
subterranean Oracle of Trophonios at Lebadea (now called Livadia) in
Greece. He is holding a beehive, around which bees are buzzing; this is
because the bee was associated with oracular caves in prehistoric Greece,
including Delphi. A lengthy account by Pausanius of his own
consultation of this underground oracle is actually preserved, and he
describes sliding down a chute into a pit full of snakes who had to be
appeased by offering them honey cakes, which is yet another association
with the oracular bees. Pausanius also records the legend that the Oracle
of Trophonios was founded when a swarm of wild bees was followed to
its hive under the earth, and the site was discovered

Trophonios was sometimes looked on as semi-divine, or even as a god. He is known to have been identified with 'the subterranean Mercury'[31] and the semi-divine Trophonios may actually have replaced this ancient and obsolescent divinity because a 'subterranean Hermes (Mercury)' came to seem an anomaly in Greece and could no longer be understood by classical times. A 'subterranean Hermes' was probably a Minoan or Mycenaean concept connected with the spiralling labyrinth and the intestines (to be explained in Chapter 6 and Appendix 3).

Cicero preserves an amusing tale about the practical aspects of deciding whether Trophonios was divine or human. After Greece became part of the Roman Empire, the omnipresent Roman tax collectors set about collecting revenue from Greece and had to decide what to do about the considerable lands set aside from private ownership for the use of the oracular establishment and formally dedicated to the 'god' Trophonios. Being both practical and avaricious, they were frustrated by a legal ruling by the Roman censor that these 'lands belonging to the immortal gods were exempt' from taxation.[32] So they got round the regulation by insisting that Trophonios was not a god, and taxed the land under a bureaucratic regulation promulgated by themselves, and which did not require higher authority, asserting that 'nobody was immortal who had once upon a time been a human being.'[33]

The Oracle at Lebadea was so famous that it was often the subject of satire. The ancient satirist Lucian wrote a farcical 'dialogue of the dead' in which Trophonios is accosted by another ghost. When challenged for his presumption that, being but a ghost, he nevertheless thought himself worthy of a temple, Trophonios replies: 'I am a hero and prophesy if anyone comes down to me. But I don't think you've visited Lebadea at all, or you wouldn't be so sceptical.' The other ghost irreverently replies: 'What's that? Must I go to Lebadea, and make a fool of myself wearing linen and carrying a pancake in my hands, and crawl into your cave through that passage that's so low, in order to be able to tell that you're dead just like us, surpassing us only in false pretences? But, in the name of prophecy, what is a hero? I don't know.' Trophonios pompously replies: 'A compound of god and man.' The other ghost then says, 'Where's your divine half gone at present?' Trophonios replies that it is back at Lebadea, prophesying![34]

In yet another work of satire, the *Menippus, or the Descent into Hades,* Lucian makes further fun of the Oracle of Trophonios. His character Menippus is in the Underworld, and worrying about getting back to the surface of the earth again. Someone takes him aside and says:

'Never fear, Menippus; I will show you a quick and easy short cut.' And then, taking me to a place murkier than the rest of the region and pointing with his finger to a dim and slender ray of light coming in as if through a keyhole, a long way off, he said: 'That is the sanctuary of Trophonios, where the people of Boeotia come down. So go up by that route and you will be in Greece directly.' Delighted with his words, I embraced the sorcerer, very laboriously crawled up through the hole somehow, and found myself in Lebadea.[35]

What was the exact nature of this underground Oracle in Greece? We can do no better than to quote the first-hand account written by Pausanius, who consulted the Oracle himself:

This is what happens at the oracle. When a man decides to go down to Trophonios, he first lives a certain number of days in a building which is consecrated to Good Fortune and the Good Spirit. Living there he purifies himself and uses no hot water; his bath is the river Herkyna. He has abundant meat from the sacrifices, as a man going down offers sacrifice to Trophonios himself and to his sons, and to Apollo and Kronos and Zeus the King and Hera the Charioteer and the Demeter they call Europa, Trophonios's nurse. At each of these sacrifices a soothsayer comes to observe the entrails of the victim; making his observation, he foretells to the man going down whether Trophonios will receive him kindly and graciously. The entrails of most victims do not reveal Trophonios's mind very clearly, but on

the night a man is going down they slaughter a ram at a pit,
calling to Agamedes. It makes no difference that all the
earlier sacrifices have given good omens unless the entrails
of this ram carry the same meaning. But if they do agree,
every man goes down with true hope. He goes down like
this. First he is taken at night to the river Herkyna, and there
anointed with olive oil and washed by two boys of about
thirteen, who have to be children of genuine Lebadeians.
They call these boys Hermai: they wash the man who is
going down and act as his servants, like slave-boys. From
here he is taken by the priests, not straight to the oracle, but
to the water-springs, which are very close together. Here he
must drink the water of Forgetfulness, to forget everything
in his mind until then, and then the water of Memory, by
which he remembers the sights he sees in his descent. He
looks at the statue they say Daidalos made, which is never
shown by the priests except to men just going to
Trophonios; he sees it and worships it and prays, and then
goes to the oracle, wearing a linen tunic, which he ties with
ribbons, and heavy local boots. The oracle is on the
mountain-side above the sacred wood. It is surrounded by a
circular platform of white stone, of the same circumference
as a very small threshing-floor, and something less than five
feet in height. There are bronze posts standing on the
platform linked together with bronze chains: there are doors
to pass through. Inside the circle is a chasm in the earth, not
natural but most carefully constructed with skill and
architectural sense. It is shaped like a kiln with a diameter of
about ten feet, I would say, and hardly more than twenty
feet deep. There is no way down, but when a man is going
to Trophonios they bring him a light, narrow ladder. When
you get down you can see an opening between wall and floor
about two feet wide and a foot high. The man going down
lies on the ground with honey-cakes in his hands and pushes
his feet into the opening and then tries to get his knees in.
The rest of his body immediately gets dragged after his
knees, as if some extraordinarily deep, fast river was

catching a man in a current and sucking him down. From here on, inside the second place, people are not always taught the future in one and the same way: one man hears, another sees as well. Those who go down return feet first through the same mouth. They say no one has been killed going down except for one of Demetrios's bodyguard, and they say of him that he observed none of the rites of the sanctuary and went down not to consult the god but in the hope of bringing out gold and silver from the holy place. They say his dead body reappeared elsewhere; it was not thrown up through the sacred mouth. This was the most interesting of the stories I heard about the man. When a man comes up from Trophonios the priests take him over again, and sit him on the throne of Memory, which is not far from the holy place, to ask him what he saw and discovered. When they know this they turn him over to his friends, who pick him up and carry him to the building where he lived before with the Good Spirit and Fortune. He is still possessed with terror and hardly knows himself or anything around him. Later he comes to his senses, no worse than before, and can laugh again. I am not writing from hearsay, as I have consulted Trophonios and seen others do so. Everyone who goes down to Trophonios is obliged to dedicate the story of whatever he has seen or heard, written out on a wooden tablet.[36]

In the next passage, Pausanius describes how a swarm of wild bees was followed to its hive under the earth, which led to the site of the Oracle being discovered. Bees were associated also with Delphi, but a discussion of the mythology of the bee and its association with oracles in caves and holes in the ground, which is an extremely ancient tradition, and pre-classical, would involve too lengthy a digression for us.

The parallels between Lebadea and Baia are seen to be considerable. Here again we have the enquirer spending several days in isolation, the preliminary sacrifices, the drinking from springs which are presumably drugged, and the terrifying experiences underground. Some additional details may be gleaned from the two second-hand accounts mentioned earlier. In that of Philostratus, we learn that the experience underground involved contact with 'reptiles' – presumably snakes. One reason for the stark terror of the visitors may have been that they had to pass through what was essentially a snake-pit. We are told:

> Now the cavern in Lebadea is dedicated to Trophonios, the son of Apollo, and it can only be entered by those who resort thither in order to get an oracle, and it is not visible in the temple, but lies a little above it on a mound; and it is shut in by iron spits which surround it, and you descend into it as it were sitting down and being drawn down. Those who enter it are clad in white raiment, and are escorted thither with honey-cakes in their hands to appease the reptiles which assail them as they descend.[37]

The Greek word translated as 'reptiles' in the above quotation from the Loeb translation is *herpeton,* which does mean 'creeping thing' or 'reptile', but usually had the more specific meaning of 'snake', and this is almost certainly the meaning intended here.

In Figure 16 we see an engraving from 1700 of what the consultation of the Oracle of Trophonios was imagined to have been like. At the right we see a man sliding down a chute, honey-cakes in hand, while all kinds of strange events are taking place in various adjoining caverns.

The actual oracular caves at Lebadea have not yet been discovered, though the springs are a well-known tourist attraction, and the ruins of a temple are just discernable some distance away.[38] Scholars and archaeologists do not seem to be aware of Philostratus's account, and his specific statement that the oracular cave 'lies a little above the temple on a mound'. Peter Levi, who searched the area for the caves himself, says: 'On the way up to the Zoodochos Pegi, you can hear water inside the rock; there is still a system of caves in the mountain.'[39] In my opinion, a large oracular cavern complex may still exist at

Figure 16: The Oracle of Trophonios. The enquirer, holding honey-cakes, enters by the ladder (top right), and slides down the chute. In the centre the enquirer lies in a state of stupefaction, still clutching his honey-cakes, amid priests impersonating ghostly voices, blowing trumpets, and holding mirrors and pictures to make mysterious images in the torch-light. Below, to right and left, are connecting passageways and caverns; on the left, an enquirer who was unsuccessful or became suspicious is murdered by the priests; his body is being carried away on the right. Top left, a successful enquirer records his visions. (Engraving from De Oraculis *by Antonius van Dale, 1700)*

Livadia and should be worth a determined search. It is even possible that discoveries as exciting as those at Baia might well be made there. Some people interested in this subject, but who are of a pronounced sceptical turn of mind, have insisted that Lebadea never had any substantial caverns. They have no reason for this, except a personal inclination to disbelieve. All the experts scoffed at the notion that a cavern complex could exist at

Baia – and even now that it has been discovered there are many embarrassed authorities who simply ignore it.

Philostratus also says of the cavern complex at Lebadea, and those who visit it: 'But the earth brings them to the surface again, in some cases close by, but in other cases a long way off.'[40]

If this be true, there must have been a network of connecting caverns and secret entrances and exits over a great distance. Other ancient rumours and legends agreed that such extensive caverns existed, and it was even stated that the caves ran all the way to Delphi, though this was surely a wild exaggeration. Enthusiastic spelunkers, however, might make the finds of a lifetime if they were to explore the area around Livadia.

I have come upon one curious piece of information which goes far towards suggesting that there really were caverns of some significance. Dicearchus, one of the prize pupils of Aristotle, had a high reputation as a historian in the ancient world, though only fragments of his works survive today. But they still existed in Cicero's time, and Cicero speaks of them in a letter to his friend Atticus, written in May of 50 BC, which reveals something which may be of crucial importance:

> Having devoted my first page to answering your last, I will now return to your first. I relied on the maps of Dicearchus, a writer of no mean standing and an authority you accept, for the information that all the states of the Peloponnese bordered on the sea. In the account of the cave of Trophonios, which he puts into the mouth of Chaeron [probably the historical Charon who takes part in Plutarch's dialogue which contains an account of the same subject – see below – and which probably drew heavily on Dicearchus's lost work in many other ways], he blames the Greeks on many scores for sticking to the sea coast. . . . He was a very accurate historian and lived in the Peloponnese, so that his evidence seemed trustworthy.[41]

Here we learn indirectly that this scientific-minded scholar of Aristotle's Lyceum had written an account of 'the cave of

Trophonios'. He would hardly have done so unless there were some significant cave about which it was worth writing an account. We also have other evidence from Cicero that there was a substantial staff of diviners at the Oracle.[42] All the evidence indicates that there was a fair amount of room for several people to move around under the ground. Although Pausanius for pious reasons does not describe what happens after being pulled through the narrow hole, there are strong reasons for suspecting that that is where things really began to get interesting – as we shall now learn.

The longest account of a consultation of the Oracle of Trophonios is given by Plutarch, who as the High Priest of neighbouring Delphi can be presumed to have had much specialist knowledge of the subject. It is too long to be given here, and much of it is extraordinarily complicated and obscure, but we can give a few salient details to lead us to our next subject. The account concerns a man named Timarchus, possibly a fictitious character, whose consultation of the Oracle is described:

> ... he descended into the crypt of Trophonios, first performing the rites that are customary at the oracle. He remained underground two nights and a day, and most people had already given up hope, and his family were lamenting him for dead, when he came up in the morning with a radiant countenance. He did obeisance to the god, and as soon as he had escaped the crowd, began to tell us of many wonders seen and heard.[43]

Here we see that the underground complex must have been sufficient in extent to support the existence of a person there for days on end, which indicates a variety of tunnels and means of bringing in food and drink, not to mention a separate chamber for the person to stay in. In fact, the sage Apollonius of Tyana is said to have remained in the caverns for an entire week: '. . . he emerged after seven days, a longer period than it had taken anyone of those who until then had entered the oracle.'[44] This statement is almost certainly an exaggeration intended to make

Apollonius seem important, but it does probably set a reliable upper limit on the time spent in the caverns and affords some indirect evidence that a day or two might not have been unheard of. Plutarch continues his account:

> He said that on descending into the oracular crypt his first experience was of profound darkness; next, after a prayer, he lay a long time not clearly aware whether he was awake or dreaming. It did seem to him, however, that at the same moment he heard a crash and was struck on the head, and that the sutures parted and released his soul.

He then had a very long and elaborate 'mystical experience' with visions which take pages to describe, and are thus omitted here. After he had been immersed in his visions for an unknown time, an official of the Oracle appears to have addressed him in the darkness as follows:

> 'Timarchus, what would you have me explain?'
> 'Everything,' he answered; 'for what is here that is not marvellous?'
> 'Nay,' the voice replied, 'in the higher regions we others have but little part, as they belong to the gods; but you may, if you wish, inquire into the portion of Persephone, administered by ourselves; it is one of the four [regions], and marked off by the course of the Styx.'
> 'What is the Styx?' he asked. 'It is the path to Hades,' came the answer; 'it passes across from you here . . . it extends upwards, as you see, from Hades below [possibly an underground waterfall]. . . . As the Styx draws near the souls cry out in terror, for many slip off and are carried away by Hades . . .
> 'But I see nothing,' said Timarchus; 'only many stars trembling about the abyss, others sinking into it, and others again shooting up from below.'
> 'Then without knowing it,' the being replied, 'you see the daemons themselves . . .'

Hearing this, [Timarchus] attended more carefully and saw that the stars bobbed about, some more, some less, like the corks we observe riding on the sea to mark nets. . . .

When the voice ceased Timarchus desired to turn (he said) and see who the speaker was. But once more he felt a sharp pain in his head, as though it had been violently compressed, and he lost all recognition and awareness of what was going on about him; but he presently recovered and saw that he was lying in the crypt of Trophonios near the entrance, at the very spot where he had first laid himself down. . . . When he had come to Athens (afterwards) and died in the third month, as the voice had foretold, we were amazed and told Socrates the story . . .[45]

There are many features of the consultation of the Oracle of Trophonios which were peculiar, to say the least. What do modern scholars have to say of it? One of the leading experts in ancient Greek ritual and religion was the late Dr Jane Harrison, author of the massive *Prolegomena to the Study of Greek Religion*. In that book, she comments on Plutarch's account by saying: 'The whole ecstatic mystic account beginning with the sensation of a blow on the head and the sense of the soul escaping, reads like a trance-experience or like the revelation experienced under an anaesthetic.'[46] I believe this is exactly what it was – the experience of someone deeply drugged. The visitor to the Oracle ate for some days only what the priests gave him, which may have contained drugs, drank of two special 'waters' before the consultation, almost certainly drugged, and was anointed with olive oil before entering the cavern. This oil also probably contained drugs which were absorbed directly through the skin. There were thus four possible sources of hallucinogenic stimulus for the visitor, and they were probably all used.

Suspicions of the use of drugs in ancient oracular consultations began to arise particularly in the nineteenth century. The man to whom this insight may be credited is the remarkable French parliamentarian Eusebe Salverte, who, under Napoleon, 'devoted the whole period of the existence of the empire to

retirement and study. During that time he became, by per-
severing labour, one of the most learned men of our age, in
languages, science and political economy.'[47]

Salverte's importance to us is not merely in his speculation
about the use of drugs in ancient oracle centres. For that idea of
his was but one of a vast number, all of which had their origins
in his own particular way of thinking about ancient history. This
began when he wrote his introduction to a general history of
civilization, published in 1813.[48] In the course of his research,
Salverte encountered an enormous number of anomalies in the
writings of the ancient historians. As he puts it:

> The history and origin of the sciences occupied a large place
> in those researches, in which I was engaged, and I was soon
> convinced that it was impossible to have a just idea of the
> extent to which the sciences had been carried among the
> ancients without examining the kind of knowledge
> employed by the founders of those sciences, in working the
> wonders related in their annals. I discovered that much
> information was shut up in the temples, and employed
> there . . .[49]

In July 1817, Salverte published the first results of his research in
a journal.[50] Almost immediately his ideas were taken up by
others, such as Etienne Clavier, in his *Memoire sur les Oracles
des Anciens* (1818).[51] It was not until 1829 that Salverte brought
out his monumental work *The Occult Sciences: The Philosophy
of Magic, Prodigies and Miracles,* which is unquestionably one of
the most brilliant, original and fascinating works of non-fiction
of the entire nineteenth century. My copy of the English
translation of this two-volume book once belonged to Madame
Helena Blavatsky. It was translated into English and published in
1846 in London with voluminous notes by Dr Anthony Todd
Thomson, a medical doctor, scholar and religious bigot. Such
was the liberty one author could take with another's work in
those days that Thomson actually boasts in his editor's preface:
'. . . in undertaking the task of editing these volumes, I have felt

it my duty to expunge from their pages every passage referring to the sacred volume . . . from a conviction that the author had no correct idea of miracles, and, consequently, could not be supposed to regard those of the Bible as objects of belief.'[52]

Salverte's approach is philosophical and scholarly. He remarks upon humanity's permanent love for the marvellous, and he looks at the entire history of civilization from the point of view of the credulity of the majority of the people in past ages, and their continued manipulation by élite groups of priests: 'From the most ancient times, men of superior intellect, desirous of enthralling the human mind, have adduced miracles and prodigies as the certain proof of their missions.'[53] He even puts an extremely advanced question for his time in asking whether mankind's love of the marvellous springs from man's inner nature or is the result of historical conditioning: 'Is this taste natural or is it the result of that education which for so many ages the human race has received . . . ?'[54] He rightly says, 'This is a vast and unexplored field of enquiry.'[55]

For the sake of simplicity, Salverte groups all ancient manipulators of humanity under a general term of 'thaumaturgists' (from the ancient Greek word for 'wonder-workers'). He speaks of them as 'a class of men who, founding their empire upon the marvellous, are anxious that it should be recognized in everything; and as anxious to dupe the stupid multitude, who so easily consent to see the marvellous everywhere.'[56] Salverte calls their discipline 'magic'; 'We shall therefore apply the name *magic* to the *art* of working wonders; and in so doing we shall digress from received opinions. . . .'[57] But by doing so, he risked being misunderstood. Salverte's special use of the words 'magic' and 'thaumaturgists' was open to misinterpretation then and now. Salverte was not simply a sceptic and scoffer who was fanatically determined to explain every ancient wonder and prodigy by some physical means; neither was he a crabby old man trying to expose a long series of élitist conspiracies in history. It helps to understand his work if we look at it within the framework of his time and culture. He writes with something of the tone of Montesquieu, and implicit in his thinking are the then highly fashionable ideas of the mystical philosopher Louis Claude de Saint-Martin (died 1803), who proposed the ideal society as a spiritual theocracy where God's 'divine commissioners guide the common herd'.[58] We must remember also that under Napoleon the entire French nation had been deeply affected by the detailed studies made and reports published concerning ancient Egyptian civilization. These afforded more than enough occasion for a national brooding on the power of the ancient theocracies. All of these factors were taken for granted by Salverte in the way in which he wrote his book and in what he expected of his readers – a fact which is all too easy to overlook today. With occasional references also to Rousseau, Salverte was struggling as well to combat a current of thought in his own time which was taking shape in the Romantic movement, in which excessive credulity and 'love of the marvellous' was feeding the whole new movement in literature, art and philosophy.

Here is what Salverte had to say about the Oracle of Trophonios:

> . . . those who came to request prophetic dreams of the Gods were prepared by a fast, more or less prolonged, after which they partook of meals expressly prepared, and also of mysterious drinks, such as the water of *Lethe* and the water of *Mnemosyne* in the grotto of Trophonios; or of the *Ciceion* in the mysteries of the Eleusinia. Different drugs were easily mixed up with the meats or introduced into the drinks, according to the state of mind or body into which it was necessary to throw the recipient, and the nature of the visions he was desirous of procuring. . . . Before consulting the Oracle of Trophonios, the body was rubbed with oil; this preparation undoubtedly concurred in producing the desired vision. . . .
>
> Plutarch has preserved to us a description of the mysteries of Trophonios, related by a man who had passed two nights and a day in the grotto. They appear to be rather the dreams of a person intoxicated by a powerful narcotic than the description of a real spectacle. Timarchus, the name of

the initiate, experienced a violent head-ache when the apparitions commenced; that is to say, when the drugs began to affect his senses, and when the apparitions vanished and he awoke from this delirious slumber, the same pain was as keenly felt. Timarchus died three months after his visit to the grotto; the priests, no doubt, having made use of very powerful drugs. It is said that those who had once consulted the oracle acquired a melancholy which lasted all their lives, the natural consequence, no doubt, of all the serious shocks to their health from the potions administered to them.[59]

We find interesting confirmation of this last remark in the works of Athenaeus (third century AD) who tells us:

Parmeniscus of Metapontum, as Semus declares in the fifth book of his *History of Delos,* a man of the first rank in family and wealth, descended into the cave of Trophonios and on coming up was no longer able to laugh. And when he consulted the oracle [at Delphi] about this the Pythian priestess said to him: 'Thou, unrelenting one, askest me concerning relenting laughter; the Mother will give it to thee at home; her shalt thou honour exceedingly.' So he hoped that if he returned to his own land he would laugh again; but when he met with no success, he thought that he had been deceived; but he had occasion once to go to Delos, and there he admired the temple of Leto, thinking that he should find the statue of Apollo's mother something remarkable to look at; but when he discovered that it was an ugly block of wood he burst unexpectedly into laughter. And so he understood the meaning of the god's oracle, and having been cured of his defect he honoured the goddess greatly.[60]

A remarkable epilogue to this tale exists. Modern archaeologists have actually discovered an inscription on the island of Delos recording that the very man in the above story made a dedication to the goddess of a silver mixing-bowl, by way of thanks. This is all the more remarkable in that he was an obscure person otherwise unknown to history.[61]

What were the actual drugs which were used in the ancient oracular establishments? The survival of the ancient herbal of Dioscorides and a vast amount of other material, including much archaeological evidence, enables us to establish for certain which herbs were known and used in ancient times. Let us take two examples to start with: henbane and deadly nightshade *(belladonna)*. These two powerful hallucinogenic plants share a strange physical characteristic which must have added much to the awe in which they were held by early cultures. Salverte knew that the flower of deadly nightshade 'towards evening flashes like a kind of lightning'.[62] But he was unaware of the coincidence that henbane has a similar property, as we are informed by a herbal doctor of the turn of the twentieth century who states: 'The chemical constituents of Henbane are "hyoscyamine", a volatile alkaloid, with a bitter principle, "hyoscypricin" (especially just before flowering), also nitre of potash, which causes the leaves, when burnt, to sparkle with a deflagration.'[63] It is odd that two of the plants most used in ancient times for hallucinogenic and narcotic purposes share a capacity for flashing and sparking. This cannot have been lost on the ancient doctors and priests, and must have made these two plants seem all the more 'sacred'.

Henbane seems to possess a hypnotic quality, even in its superficial appearance, and a mysterious and sinister beauty. It is unwise to handle the plant much, or to breathe its bizarre and oppressive odour. Salverte records a story which well illustrates the effect the smell of henbane can have on people even when it is too faint to be perceptible to the conscious mind. He takes it from a French dictionary of medicine, and it appears to be a well-authenticated case:

... most striking is the case of a married couple who, although everywhere else they lived in perfect harmony, could not, without coming to blows, remain a few hours in their ordinary work-room. The room got credit for being bewitched, until the cause of these daily quarrels, over which the unfortunate pair were seriously concerned, was discovered; a considerable quantity of seeds of henbane were found near the stove, and with the removal of the substance, which emitted this unfortunate odour, all tendency to quarrel vanished.

This class of agents was so much the more valuable to the Thaumaturgist, that it not only eludes the eye, but it does not even affect the olfactory nerves in proportion to the violence of its effects.[64]

Henbane is a deadly poison if used carelessly. Twenty of its seeds will kill a man, if swallowed. This is not as drastic as deadly nightshade – a drop of juice from the berries of which can cause serious illness and three berries consumed mean certain death. The dead and dried leaves of plants such as henbane do not lose their properties; on the contrary, they are intensified in the dried plant. If you pull up a henbane plant and throw it on the bonfire, and then inhale the smoke, you may go insane or die, or at least become unconscious for a couple of days. Even the ashes are poisonous! And so dangerous is deadly nightshade that in the last century a gardener was actually hanged for neglecting to remove plants of it from a garden for which he was responsible and where a child died.[65]

These and other such deadly plants are also capable of producing the most extraordinary hallucinations and visions in human beings who survive their ingestion. Mrs Grieve, an English medical herbal expert, records an instance where a group of monks ate the roots of henbane by mistake: '. . . the whole of the inmates of a monastery were once poisoned by using the roots instead of chicory. The monks partaking of the roots for supper were all more or less affected during the night and following day, being attacked with a sort of delirious frenzy accompanied in many cases by such hallucinations that the establishment resembled a lunatic asylum.'[66] From another account of the same incident we learn further that: 'One monk would insist on ringing the large bell at midnight, to the alarm of the neighbourhood; whilst of those who came to prayers at the summons, several could not read at all, and others read anything but what was contained in their breviaries.'[67]

A traditional name for henbane was 'Jupiter's beans', implying a sacred connection. And Pliny gives us clear evidence that henbane was a sacred herb with oracular connections, pointing out that its official name was *apollinaris*. Apollo was the god of divination and prophecy, who presided over Delphi. Pliny was extremely apprehensive of henbane and said: '. . . the drug is, in my opinion, a dangerous medicine in any form. In fact, it is well known that even the leaves affect the brain if more than four are taken in drink; yet the ancients used to take them.'[68] That Pliny (who lived in the first century AD) refers to the 'ancients' indicates the extreme antiquity of the drug's use. It is unfortunate that in the Loeb edition of Pliny just quoted, the name 'henbane' for this plant is not mentioned by the translator, and there is no listing under 'henbane' in the index. In the margin the Latin botanical name of the plant, though given in the text, is misleadingly replaced by *apollinaris,* so that even a reader with botanical knowledge would be confused. Such difficulties are common in dealing with ancient accounts of plants, for the translators and editors of the texts understandably often had little knowledge of botany.

Another narcotic and hallucinogenic plant often used in the ancient world was hellebore. Pliny, preserving as usual much early mythological plant lore, tells us explicitly that this plant had oracular connections: 'Melampus is well known for his skill in the arts of divination. From him one kind of hellebore is called melampodion.'[69] Yet another hallucinogenic plant used to great effect was the thorn-apple, and indeed various of the *daturae* of which it is but one species. Dioscorides (first century AD) says of the thorn-apple, in the only English translation of his herbal which exists, dating from 1655: 'The root being drank with wine ye quantity of a dragm, hath ye power to effect not unpleasant fantasies. But 2 dragms being drank, make one beside himself for three days & 4 being drank kill him.'[70] Theophrastus, the chief of Aristotle's pupils and 'the father of botany', writes amusingly of the thorn-apple: 'Of this three twentieths of an ounce in weight is

Figure 17: The exploding plant, or Burning Bush! This nineteenth-century engraving shows the explosion and combustion of the trapped fumes, which have just been released, of the plant Dictamnus albus, *also known as* Dictamnus fraxinella, *which is native to Germany, France, Spain, Austria, Italy and Asia Minor. At one time a drug was prepared from the root of this plant, and used for nervous treatment and epilepsy. The plant is about two feet high, and when rubbed it smells of lemon peel. If the flowers are bruised more strongly, a smell of balsam may be detected. The chemical constituents of this plant have apparently never been fully analysed. But on a hot or dry day, the plant*  *sometimes exudes through small red glands in the flowers a vapour which is inflammable, as in this picture. If one strikes a match near the plant when it is exuding this vapour, there will be an explosion. This may be concentrated in the method shown in the engraving: placed inside a container which is then opened, a truly spectacular explosion may be produced. The common English name for this plant is, not surprisingly, 'Burning Bush', and it is also called Bastard Dittany. A phenomenon such as this may be referred to by the 'Burning Bush' in the Bible, which was supposedly seen by Moses (an initiate into the Egyptian mysteries, who changed snakes into rods and rods into snakes by animal-catalepsy, as I explained previously in my book* Open to Suggestion). *The fact that this plant is unharmed by the explosion of its own burning vapours adds to the awe which it can arouse. It has been more closely studied than the other 'miraculous' burning, sparking, or flashing plants, which include the oracular drug plants henbane, white hellebore, and belladonna. No thorough study of combustible plants ever seems to have been undertaken in modern times, so it is likely that the ancient priests knew much more about this strange subject than anyone does today*

given, if the patient is to become merely sportive and to think himself a fine fellow; twice this dose if he is to be permanently insane (and then they say that the juice of centaury is mixed with it); four times the dose is given, if the man is to be killed.'[71]

The science of poisons was well advanced in the ancient world. There were poisons which could kill a man in one month or in two, by calculation. It is doubtful whether modern botanists and toxicologists could attain to as much expertise as the ancients had in this field – and it is probably just as well. But oracular officials could get rid of a troublesome person and score a prophetic triumph at the same time, by announcing that such a man who had consulted them would die in one month or two. The prophecy would be fulfilled, the death being due to drugs administered at the Oracle.

Before leaving this subject, we must take notice of the opium poppy. In Plate 31 we see an ancient Minoan 'poppy goddess' from Gazi in Crete, wearing poppy heads in her headdress. The poppy heads are incised in just the fashion used in the collecting of opium. For those who have never seen it done, it is worthwhile to give a brief description of how opium is obtained. Just after the fall of the petals of the opium poppy flower, the Opium milk inside the poppy head is at a suitable stage for collection. Although the Indians cut horizontally, the traditional Mediterranean method is to incise the poppy heads vertically. This is done with a sharp blade. The milky white juice oozes out of the incision and forms into a drop, which hangs on the outside. Incisions are made all round the poppy head, so that each head has several exuded drops, which are then left to dry and congeal in the sun for some days. They turn from white to yellow to brown to black. When they are black, they are of the consistency of resin and may be scraped off the poppy heads and collected. This constitutes raw opium, which if improperly used is of course also a highly dangerous poison.

There is much evidence to indicate that the Minoan civilization was 'hooked' on opium, and that it was fundamental to their religion. Some of this evidence has gone unnoticed because many archaeologists are unfamiliar with botanical matters or with the

HENBANE
Solanaceae: Hyoscyamus

BLACK HELLEBORE
Ranunculaceae: Helleborus

WHITE HELLEBORE
Ranunculaceae: Helleborus

THORN APPLE
Solanaceae: Datura

Figure 18: Engravings published in 1563 by Pierandrea Mattioli showing henbane, black hellebore, white hellebore and thorn-apple

details of obtaining opium. The Minoan figurines of the snake-goddess emphasize bursting breasts which protrude through a special opening in the clothes – they are generally of a pronounced milky-white colour. But the rest of the goddess is usually yellow, brown and black. Associations with opium may have been in the minds of the Minoans; the goddess who gives milk, symbolized by full white breasts, may have been associated with poppy-milk. The fact that yellow, brown and black are the colours which appear to have been held sacred to the goddess may refer to the successive stages of congealing of the opium. This is not merely idle speculation. See Figure 19. As we have seen, the goddess with the poppies was also associated with the oracular doves and omphalos stones. There can be no doubt that opium was one of the main oracular drugs and, like the herbs mentioned earlier, was important in inducing visions and hallucinations.

Figure 19: Design from a Minoan gold signet ring found at Mycenae and dated c. 1500 BC. The goddess is seen seated beneath a tree and in one hand holding up poppy heads on their stalks, while with the other hand she squeezes her full breasts. There seems no doubt that human milk and the milky juice of the poppy heads are associated here.
The sacred Minoan symbol of the labrys, *or double-axe, floats in the sky at the centre of the scene. Preserved in the National Archaeological Museum at Athens*

PLATE 1: Looking towards Baia from the acropolis at Cuma. The sea is on the right and the Bay of Naples on the left. Directly ahead, with a small railway running down the middle, is the promontory of Miseno, at the base of which is Baia. It is here that the Sibyl of Cuma took Aeneas by sea around the promontory into the harbour at Baia to consult with the Oracle of the Dead. The land in pre-Roman times was largely impassable due to thick primaeval forests of holm oak, which made the Baian area one of dark and gloomy foreboding. The Romans cut down all the trees, turned the bay into an ancient version of Biarritz, and blocked and sealed the Oracle. (*Robert Temple*)

PLATE 2: Baia as seen from the water. At the left of the row of ruined Roman structures along the middle of the hill, the entrance to the Oracle of the Dead lies concealed in an inaccessible portion of the archaeological park. According to ancient historians, before the Romans cut down all the trees for ships' timbers, the approach through the forest of gigantic holm oaks sent a shiver down the spine. The Romans built over the whole area, but the earthquake of 63 AD destroyed most of their structures in the whole Bay of Naples, and many were never replaced. They intended to bury the Oracle of the Dead forever, keeping it blocked and concealed beneath a Roman spa. (*Robert Temple*)

PLATE 3: The present entrance to the Oracle of the Dead is concealed in a hole beneath and behind these Roman ruins. I am standing on top photographing the entrance passage and Olivia is on the left observing me. Just in front of her some old stone blocks, possibly from the Greek period, have been exposed within the more recent Roman brickwork. Little remains of the original exterior structures of the Oracle, which must have included a small temple building and other reception areas. Near where we are standing, clients of the Oracle were required to purify themselves in a bath and then remain alone in a room for three days before drinking extracts of powerful drug plants and being taken in a stupefied condition into the 'Underworld' for a terrifying séance. (*Michael Baigent*)

PLATE 4: Even the entrance to the Oracle of the Dead is forbidding, and difficult to access. Here I am back in the light, but wondering how I will return to the surface. (*Michael Baigent*)

PLATE 5: A close up of the lower entrance arch of the present entrance to the Oracle of the Dead at Baia, showing the construction. (*Robert Temple*)

PLATE 6: The entrance to the Oracle of the Dead at Baia seen from just inside. The structures beyond are the remnants of exterior buildings, on top of which were Roman constructions. (*Robert Temple*)

PLATE 7: The long entrance tunnel of the Oracle of the Dead, which extends straight in like this for 400 feet before it commences a descent. (*Michael Baigent*)

PLATE 8 (*left*): Looking down the commencement of the descent towards the River Styx from the 'Dividing of the Ways'. On the extreme left, the plastered portion of the wall conceals a very thin doorway, through which Michael Baigent and I talked to each other when he was in the two joined tunnels (North and South 120) just on the other side of it. Originally this was a doorway which opened and shut. Along the roof on the left is a long row of Roman tiles which have sealed up another feature of the Oracle, which Paget believed was used to allow smoke to billow into the tunnel along with simulated groans and screams, to impress upon the visitor that this was the entrance to 'Tartarus', where wicked souls were suffering. (*Michael Baigent*)

PLATE 10 (*left*): Looking down at the River Styx, the level of which is now too high to allow a boat to cross to the far landing. The temperature of the water is now only 28°C, whereas in the 1960s it was boiling. On one day in 1965, the water level suddenly dropped by about two feet. In the decades since the Oracle was closed by the authorities, the water level has risen again. The Chimney opens above one's head here. In the last period when the Oracle was still functioning, before its final blockage, a wooden room seems to have been constructed at this point on the bank of the Styx to receive visitors, in place of the Inner sanctuary upstairs which was no longer accessible. This suggests that there was a temporary attempt to revive the Oracle late in the reign of Augustus when only the entrance tunnel was still clear (as it is today) but this must soon have been given up and abandoned. (*Robert Temple*)

PLATE 11 (*right*): The ascent known as 'the Rise', still half-filled with soil. When Paget first discovered the oracle in 1962, this passage was completely blocked, and he cleared enough soil from it to enable one to scramble up it to reach the central portions. The remains of a doorway can be seen etched in white plaster on the walls and the roof of the passage. Paget established that beneath the remaining soil are steps, and that the original cleared height of this passage is six or even feet. (*Michael Baigent*)

PLATE 9 (*opposite centre*): Close up of the Roman tiles and heavy plastering on the left half of the ceiling of the descending tunnel going down towards the Styx, just past the 'Dividing of the Ways'. A few of the giant mosquitoes can be seen clinging to the ceiling. This lengthy stretch of sealed opening abuts the tunnel North 120 on the other side of the wall. When the Romans blocked up the Oracle, they took great pains to seal up this lengthy opening, through which one might have crawled to the blocked interior of the oracle 150 feet further along the tunnel. Paget believed that the enquirer, led in through the entrance tunnel, passed the concealed door on his left just before this point, but could then peer over here into the smoking 'entrance to Tartarus', where the souls of the dead were said to be writhing in torment, and from which moans and cries would issue with the smoke. (*Robert Temple*)

PLATE 12 (*above*): Michael Baigent looks up at me through the Chimney in the Oracle of the Dead, where he is sitting on the bank of the River Styx. The Chimney is lined on all sides with tufa bricks. When Paget discovered the Oracle, this Chimney was sealed at its base with a large tile. Paget's friend, Keith Jones, managed to dislodge the tile and squeeze up through the Chimney into the central portions of the oracle. He then shovelled much of the soil that completely blocked normal access through the Rise down this hole into the Styx, making it possible to come up through the Rise for the first time in 2000 years. (*Robert Temple*)

PLATE 13: I found evidence of the remains of another doorframe near the beginning of South 120, which Paget had not noticed. Here Michael was able to get a clear photo of it (in the wall of the left, but easily missed in the darkness) by means of his lights, which were far superior to what was available to Paget in the 1960s. (*Michael Baigent*)

PLATE 14: The author crawling out of North 120 into South 120. They join behind the concealed door of the 'Dividing of the Ways' and are presently hidden to anyone entering the Oracle. Originally one could walk along these tunnels, but now even crawling is not always possible, as North 120 (150 feet long) is completely blocked for most of its length, and only accessible from both ends like this. (*Michael Baigent*)

PLATE 15: A unique feature of the Oracle never seen or described by Paget. At the very end of tunnel South 120, it splits into these two smaller tunnels. If you crawl through these (before they were blocked by soil, you could walk upright in them) and go round to the left, you join up with North 120. They all meet behind the concealed door of the 'Dividing of the Ways'. Beneath the point of all the tunnels joining, another tunnel at a lower subterranean level seems to be concealed, which runs beneath the entrance tunnel to an unknown destination. The stone in the floor of the entrance tunnel adjoining this point rings hollow when struck with metal, but not before or behind. (*Michael Baigent*)

PLATE 16: Two of the doors to the Inner Sanctuary which were bricked up by the Romans (the one on the right is the same as that seen in plate 18). The top portion of the one on the right was entered by Paget's friend, Keith Jones, who crawled in far enough to get some further details of the Sanctuary, which was filled with earth. (*Robert Temple*)

PLATE 17: When the Romans bricked up this entrance to the Inner Sanctuary, they constructed this strange feature with tiles. The opening is 23 inches high, 21 inches wide and 11 inches deep. Beyond it we can see the soil the Romans carried in from outside to fill the Sanctuary from floor to ceiling in their fanatical determination to seal off the Oracle for all time. I thought I could detect two separate stages of bricking up inside the Oracle, and it is possible that Colin Hardie was right in believing that the oracle was first banned in 186 BC when the Roman Senate passed a law against non-Roman cults. Perhaps at that time the Inner Sanctuary was filled and sealed, but out of superstition of Persephone this opening was left as an offering shrine. Then, when the Oracle was finally sealed in the reign of Augustus, the entire interior was blocked off until Paget opened it in the 1960s. A brief revival of the Oracle late in the reign of Augustus would have resulted from a clearing of the entrance tunnel as far as the Styx, where a small room would have sufficed for religious purposes before it was taken away and the entire complex built over. In 63 AD, the great earthquake that destroyed Roman Baia would have covered the entrance to the Oracle and its location would have been forgotten. (*Robert Temple*)

PLATE 18: To the left is the main entrance to the Inner Sanctuary. In the centre of the photo may be seen the vertical niche in which the client placed the branch of golden mistletoe as an offering to Persephone before entering the chamber for the séance. My symbolic tribute 'offering' of some sprigs of myrtle tied in a grass stem may be seen resting in the niche, as there was no mistletoe available. To the right is the tunnel that leads towards the back landing of the River Styx, most of which is still blocked with soil placed there by the Romans. The back landing of the Styx was reached underwater by a naval diver in a special wetsuit in the 1960s. The landing stage commencement of this tunnel was studied but not photographed, as there was no way to get a camera through the Styx, which at that time was boiling hot, fed by water led in through artificially constructed arched channels made of stones. (*Michael Baigent*)

PLATE 19: To the left, part of the Inner sanctuary bricked up by the Romans, and straight ahead is the tunnel leading to the far landing of the Styx, which is now unreachable, even underwater. Soil, stones, bricks and rubble litter the surface at this point. This tunnel should be fully cleared, so that the construction of the artificial River Styx and its two opposite landing stages can be properly studied. The River Styx is one of the most remarkable engineering feats to survive from antiquity, and we do not know how it was accomplished. It is possibly the oldest completely surviving ancient hydraulic work in the world. Paget used tracer dyes to prove that its water was not connected to any nearby springs.

Before leaving the subject, we should perhaps note a few more ancient references. When ointments and oils are referred to, we must realize that one of the best ways to absorb certain substances into the body is through the skin. Nowadays people often forget this; if they had any idea of the power of the skin to absorb substances directly into the system, they would be more careful of lotions and creams, particularly sun-tan lotions. Experiments have been done where oil of lavender was rubbed on the scalp of a guinea pig. Half an hour later the animal was killed and its kidneys removed. Oil of lavender was found in them. How interesting it is, therefore, to read this account by Philostratus: '... and first they stripped, and then they anointed their heads with an amber-like drug, which imparted such a warmth to these Indians, that their bodies steamed and the sweat ran off them as profusely as if they were washing themselves by a fire'[72]

Pliny also records the following about an ointment of vervain, known as 'the sacred plant' (not to be confused with lemon verbena, from which 'vervain' tea is made): 'Both kinds are used by the people of Gaul in fortune-telling and in uttering prophecies, but the Magi (of Persia) especially make the maddest statements about the plant: that people who have been rubbed with it obtain their wishes, banish fevers, win friends, and cure all diseases without exception.'[73] In the Middle Ages, an ointment containing henbane and opium was used by 'witches' who then went to sleep and had vivid and convincing dreams of flying through the air to the Witches' Sabbath. Confirmation of this may be found in the records of the Inquisition. Many of the Inquisitors were well aware that the people they were burning at the stake were not sorceresses but drug addicts.

As for the connection of the herbs and drugs with oracular establishments, Philostratus explicitly tells us:

the wise sons of Asclepius [the god of medicine, his sons being the clan of doctors known as Asclepiadae] would never have attained to this branch of science [healing], if Asclepius had not been the son of Apollo; and as such had not in accordance with the latter's responses and oracles

concocted and adapted different drugs to different diseases
... [teaching] what herbs must be applied to running
wounds, and what to parched and dry wounds, and in what
doses to administer liquid drugs for drinking. . . . And who
can deprive the art of divination of the credit of discovering
simples . . . and in particular of using [poisons] as a cure for
many diseases? For ... men without the forecasts of a
prophetic wisdom would [never] have ventured to mingle
with medicines that save life these most deadly of poisons.[74]

This more or less proves that it was at the oracular establishments that knowledge and uses of the deadly poisons was
concentrated, and these drugs were just the ones which had the
hallucinogenic properties to induce visions such as those
experienced at the Oracle of Trophonios.

It is also probable that on many occasions the prophesying
priestesses inhaled the vapour of hallucinogenic substances, in
order to induce prophecies. The author Iamblichus records this
specifically of the priestess at the Oracle of Apollo at Branchidae:
'The woman also who delivers the oracles in verse at Branchidae
... receives the god by inhaling vapour from the water ...
[becoming] prepared for the reception, and partakes of him. . . .'
He mentions that before doing this, she took special baths, and
underwent 'fasting for three entire days'. He concludes:

For these things all make it manifest that there is an
invoking of the deity, and that he becomes present as though
coming from outside; and not only that the prophetess,
before she takes her position in the accustomed place,
receives an inspiration of a wonderful character, but
likewise in the very spirit that is brought up from the
fountain shows forth another divinity more ancient . . . who
is the cause or author ... of the whole technique of
divining.[75]

Iamblichus specifically states that the priest of the Oracle of Apollo
at Colophon was 'inspired when drinking water', and this is

confirmed by Pliny, who tells us: 'In the cave of Apollo of Claros at Colophon there is a pool a draught from which causes marvellous oracular utterances to be produced, though the life of the drinkers is shortened.'[76] Iamblichus says that the prophetess at Branchidae actually was 'overpowered by vapours from the water'.[77]

The priestess at Delphi who prophesied was also said to be intoxicated by fumes rising from a chasm in the earth beneath her. It has been conclusively demonstrated by modern French excavators that the temple at Delphi has no such chasm, and that this story is a fable. Part of the explanation for it lies in the fact that at the original site at Lykoreia, some miles up the mountain, there still is to be found a vast cavern where the Oracle was originally

Figure 20: The Pythia at Delphi seated on a tripod in a state of prophetic frenzy induced by intoxicating fumes rising from incense censers. She is supported by a priest and surrounded by laurel branches, laurel being the symbolic tree of Delphi. Above her towers the statue of Apollo, the legs only being visible. Around the dais crouch enquirers listening to her utterances, which are recorded by a priest in the foreground. These are rendered into hexameter verse by a versifier (extreme left). Engraving from De Oraculis *by Antonius van Dale, 1700*

situated. This was forgotten after about 800 BC, and the 'chasm' came to be thought in popular tradition to have been beneath the priestess. There probably was a source of vapour beneath the priestess, and the story of a chasm beneath her may have been spread by the priests to allay curiosity about the presence of other vapours or fumes which may have been near her.

In figure 20 we see a seventeenth-century engraving of the Pythia, the priestess at Delphi, seated on the traditional sacred tripod and prophesying in a state of wild intoxication. Above her swirl clouds of vapour, and she is surrounded by the sacred laurel, emblem of Delphi. Beside her, a priest prevents her from falling off the tripod in her frenzy. It seems that the tripod stood above a basin filled with a hallucinogenic potion which was warmed gently by lighted charcoal beneath it, so that the vapour issued straight up to the priestess's head, and provided a continual source of intoxication, in which she would utter her oracles. It is known that these utterances were taken down and rendered into hexameter verse by scribes and versifiers retained for that purpose, though not throughout the entire active history of Delphi. The oracular utterances would often be wild and disjointed. Often they may have been disregarded completely, and a sensible answer substituted by a temple official. Also, in later times the whole ritual may have been enacted without any potion or fumes, and without any frenzy on the part of the priestess, who would have had her answer ready in advance (since all the questions asked had to be submitted in writing beforehand!).

I have left the previous two paragraphs as I wrote them, despite the fact that just prior to publication a new discovery about the Delphic chasm has been announced, so that I am inserting a brief account of it here. This new information sheds a new light on the problem altogether. The announcement appeared in the press on 15 August 2001 and my wife, Olivia, spotted it.[78] I was amazed not only at the discovery, but that it had been made by a man who is a professor at the same university as myself (the University of Louisville in America, where I am a 'visiting' or, as they say in America, 'adjunct'

DER HEILIGE BEZIRK VON DELPHI
BLICK VON SÜDOSTEN (ETWA VOM GIPFEL DER HYAMPEIA)

Figure 21: This is what the sacred precincts of the Oracle Centre of Delphi looked like in the classical period. The Temple of Apollo, where the Sibyl prophesied, is the large structure in the centre. The view is from the southeast. This now-forgotten but excellent reconstruction drawing by H. Pomtow was published in 1910 in H. Luckenbach's Kunst und Geschichte (Art and History): Altertum (Antiquity), *Part I, Munich and Berlin, 1910, p.36. (Collection of Robert Temple)*

professor), with whom I have several mutual friends, but whom I had never met. I immediately phoned him and discussed the matter at length, and he sent me his material so that I could summarize it in this book.

The professor is John R. Hale, and he has worked jointly with Professor Jelle de Boer and others on this problem over a period of many years. What they have discovered about Delphi is amazing. They have found that the site of Pytho, which was adopted as the new site for Delphi in the eighth century BC, was chosen because someone discovered that there were strange gas emissions there which did indeed induce prophetic seizures! There is a geological fault line running underneath the Temple of Apollo, and at that precise spot it is crossed by other fault lines. A spring also once welled up beneath the temple, which has now run dry. The French archaeologists who dismissed the chasm theory did not reach bedrock in their excavations, as we had all believed until now, and the story spread by them was clearly misleading. Pytho lies on a cracked bed of bituminous limestone which contains pockets of petroleum products, and careful analyses of the water in nearby springs, and of pieces of ancient stalactites formed on a wall near the temple from springs which have since gone dry, show that in ancient times three hydro-carbon substances were emitted as gas in and around the temple: ethane, methane and ethylene. Where ethane and methane are odourless and would have had no effect, the situation is different with ethylene:

Ethylene is colourless and smells somewhat sweet. This gas was used by surgeons for anaesthesia around the turn of the century [i.e. circa 1900]. When inhaled, induction is rapid, and not disagreeable mental clouding supervenes. Assuming the adyton below the Apollo temple to have been a small, rather confined space, such gases if rising in relatively small volumes, but over extended periods of time, may have been able to accumulate in concentrations sufficiently high to induce mild narcotic effects. . . . Bituminous limestones also contain hydrogen sulphide (H_2S). This gas is colourless, but smells like rotten eggs. During seismic agitation of an area containing gas-enriched limestone, this is probably the gas that is emitted earliest, because it will not form gas hydrates. When Apollo occupied Delphi's oracle, he had to slay a female serpent. Her name Python was bestowed upon this site because he left her corpse to 'rot'. This myth suggests an early phase of H_2S gas emission, which probably followed a seismo-tectonic event along the Delphic fault zone.[79]

Further information about the influence of ethylene was provided by Hale's friend, Henry Spiller, who runs the poison centre at a hospital in Louisville, and who told me that this excellent anaesthetic gas was discontinued in the 1960s, but that it could have had the effects on the Pythia described by the ancient writers, and the simulation of apparently prophetic states. One ancient account, which is probably true, says that a local goatherd noticed that his goats were intoxicated by a gas emitted by a hole, and this led to the site being investigated and adopted for sacred purposes. As Hale and de Boer point out in another article written with J. Chanton for *Geology* Magazine:

> The location of the fault as it passes under the Temple of Apollo is indicated by an ancient spring house built into the massive foundations, below and just to the south of the oracular chamber. . . . Ethylene causes an excitation of the central nervous system. The effect of low concentrations of ethylene is a sensation of floating or disembodied euphoria, with a reduced inhibition. In some cases a more violent reaction may occur, including delirium and frantic thrashing of the limbs. Eventually, the anaesthetic properties of ethylene can cause complete unconsciousness or even death. Plutarch described an event in which the Pythia died as a possible consequence of such an overdose. The effects of low-level intoxication wear off quickly once the subject has been removed from contact with the gas.[80]

People who have visited Delphi may know that there is a large and prominent spring named Kastalia beneath a cliff and alongside the road below the temple complex, which was used in ancient times as a bathing spring before consulting the Oracle. The spring has not dried up, and water pours from it from the wall that runs along the road. A friend of mine who is a native of Delphi fills his bottles with this water to take back to his home in Athens every time he visits his elderly father, so that he can drink the spring water for days afterwards. Anyone can drink from this plentiful spring, and many do. But Hale and de Boer have discovered that there is no ethylene in this spring, and that it is entirely separate from the springs in the temple complex itself. That is how intensely localized these phenomena are.

In all probability, therefore, the use of ethylene gas for intoxication of the Pythia at the site of Pytho was adopted in the eighth century BC and continued throughout most of classical times until Plutarch's time when it had 'dried up'. What I have written about drug plants probably also appertains in a 'supporting role' and a leading role at some other oracle centres, but I am happy in the case of Delphi to stress the precedence of ethylene, as these new discoveries are so convincing. And we must certainly disregard the previous standard view on this subject, as given by H. W. Parke and D. E. W. Wormell in their otherwise definitive two-volume work, *The Delphic Oracle*: 'As to the existence of a chasm at Delphi . . . The French excavators have shown, however, that there can never have been any deep subterranean cleft in the rock beneath that sanctuary.'[81]

It is of course the French excavators who are corrected by these new findings. Let this be a lesson in the fallibility of authority! But as to the site of Pytho, let us remember that it was a late site, and that the original site of the Oracle of Delphi was much higher up the mountain. Now at last a reason other than mere convenience of access has been found as to why the site was shifted. The discovery of the prophetic gas must have been seen as divine dispensation, and moving the Oracle to a point directly over it must have seemed a natural – or should I say supernatural – thing to do.

There seems little doubt that attempts were frequently made in the history of the Delphic Oracle, and at many other oracles, to have utterances produced by a prophetess or priestess in a state of trance. Probably self-hypnosis was attempted, and from time to time gifted 'mediums' would no doubt have held office. But suitable persons could not always be found, and these methods would become impossible. Then the only means of maintaining continuity of the practice would be by the constant use of hallucinogenic drugs, and this would have become part of the ritual on most or all occasions. An ingenious study of prophecy under auto-hypnosis forms part of the scholarly and impressive book *Possession,* written more than half a century ago by Professor T. K. Oesterreich.[82] Oesterreich points out that when oracular pronouncements by priestesses were uttered in the first person as the words of the god speaking through her, then this may reasonably be taken as evidence that she was on the occasion of that utterance actually *possessed*. He says:

> Let us now consider the nature of the psychic state of the priestess during inspiration. Is such inspiration founded on fact or not? While it would be difficult to demonstrate in particular cases, it seems indubitable that inspired states did exist in a general way, as without them the important role played by Delphi would be quite inexplicable.
>
> The reality of a state of possession in the priestess is principally indicated by the fact that the word 'I' in her utterances always designated Apollo.

Figure 22: An ancient Greek painting of Themis seated on the tripod at Delphi, as prototype of the Pythia, and prophesying for Aigeus. She stares down into the phiale bowl in which is contained a liquid which probably had two purposes: first, it may have given forth intoxicating odours and fumes from drugs contained within it, and second, it would have acted as a reflecting surface into which the gaze could be directed in order to induce an auto-hypnotic trance. Such methods of gazing into reflecting surfaces were widespread in ancient times in many cultures. But this is a rare piece of evidence associating that practice with the advanced and sophisticated Delphic Oracle

The Pythoness [the name for the priestess at Delphi] speaks in the name of the god himself . . . in the reply given to Croesus we read:

See, I count the sand, I know the distances of the sea,
I hear even the dumb and understand those who are silent.

. . .This first person supposes that the Pythoness was . . in a

Figure 23: Painting from a red-figured hydra of c. 480 BC preserved at the Vatican. Apollo, with his bow, quiver, and lyre, is here seated on his prophetic tripod. But here the tripod is a great winged tripod soaring into the celestial regions over the sea. The reference may be connected to the intoxication of the Pythia or prophesying priestess. In her hallucinatory visions, she may have experienced the sensation of flying through the air which was experienced by the medieval witches, who went to bed smeared with special drug ointments and had visions of flying to the Witches' Sabbath. This painting is rare evidence that the intoxication experienced by the Pythia was associated with the idea of soaring through the heavens, and strengthens the assumption that drugs were used like those of the later witches

state of inspiration. . . . As proof that the priestesses underwent states of the most acute excitement we may adduce Plutarch's statement that these affected them so greatly that they died young . . . From all that has hitherto been said we are driven to conclude that the states under discussion are auto-suggestive.[83]

Figure 24: From a red-figured vase of the fifth century BC, *Apollo himself is seated on his tripod at Delphi, his bow in his left hand, and upraised in his right hand the* phiale *containing liquid, into which he would gaze, and which might give forth vaporous fumes. Before Apollo is the young prophesying maiden serving his Pythia, and behind Apollo is Pythia's attendant, who significantly holds in her left hand a small jug from which she would either fill or replenish the liquid in the* phiale, *a detail of Delphic procedure possibly otherwise unknown. This vase is in the second Hamilton Collection*

Iamblichus, in his account of the priestess at Branchidae quoted

above, stresses that Apollo 'becomes present as though coming
from outside'. Oesterreich says of this pre-modern concept of
possession: 'The strange soul is conceived as a material breath,

*Figure 25: A drawing of a bas relief in Pentelic marble now at Athens,
and dating from the fifth century* BC. *It shows Apollo seated on the
Delphic tripod, in the presence of his sister Artemis and their mother
Leto. In his right hand, uplifted (but here broken off), he would have
held the* phiale *for divination purposes. The association with Artemis and
Leto may be intended as a reference to the oracle centre of the island of
Delos, which had become defunct by this time. It is interesting to
speculate, in the light of this piece of iconography, that the Delos Oracle
may have had the tripod and prophetic techniques of Delphi before it fell
into disuse*

psyche, and at its entry into the body it enters also into the mind, as yet incapable of distinguishing itself clearly therefrom.'[84]

Clearly, every conceivable means of 'making contact with the future' was attempted in ancient times. In order to keep themselves in business, a vast amount of trickery and pious fraud was perpetrated. But the priests were in earnest much of the time, and even while administering drugs to visitors in such places as the Oracle of Trophonios, they may well have thought they were *offering a genuine means to achieve visions.* We, in our mechanistic era, look upon drugging people as pure manipulation. But who can say that the ancients, even while manipulating, did not truly believe that they were opening doors in the psyche as well?

It would be possible to give many more details about the tricks of the trade. Clues to them are scattered throughout ancient literature. Many of the early Christian writings contain interesting titbits. The early Christians were gleeful when they exposed priestly frauds by the pagans, and wrote naive and boastful accounts of things they found when they destroyed the heathen temples and hurled the idols to the ground. Take, for instance, this intriguing example from Bishop Theodoret's *Ecclesiastical History* (fifth century AD):

Theophilus was a man of great prudence and intrepidity. He delivered the city of Alexandria from the errors of idolatry. He not only overthrew the idolatrous temples from their very foundations, but also disclosed the frauds of the priests to those whom they had deceived. These imposters had provided hollow statues, made of bronze and wood, with the back fitted against the wall; hence they secured an entrance into them. Having secreted themselves within the statues, they issued whatever commands they pleased, and the hearers, deceived by the fraud, obeyed them. By breaking these statues, this wisest of bishops showed to the deceived people the imposture which had been practised upon them . . . In this way were the temples of the demons destroyed throughout the world.[85]

Artefacts of this nature have also been discovered by archaeologists. One of the better guidebooks tell us of Corinth:

> Nearby a sanctuary used by oracles has been excavated from the ruins of shops of the Roman era. It must have been constructed in the fifth century BC around a small, still older altar near to which libations were made before consulting the oracle, and worshippers waited to hear the pronouncement of the gods. A priest used to crawl through a passage only wide enough for him to pass. By this means he arrived at a mobile metope [part of a frieze] which differed in no way from those next to it, and it was through this channel that he voiced the prophecies of the oracle.[86]

Other means of consulting the future attempted at the oracle centres included the use of lots, dice, and a sort of grand roulette-wheel, of which a detailed description survives. There is also evidence of hydromancy, a form of scrying, or telling the future by gazing down into a bowl of liquid, or into a pool. This seems to have assisted in the achievement of a state of self-hypnosis. All these subjects are too broad and complex to be considered in this book. No competent account of them seems ever to have been written, and they cannot be surveyed superficially without making a travesty of the subject matter.

It is difficult for us today to comprehend the power of the oracular establishments in nearly every aspect of ancient life. The importance of the Vatican in modern Italian politics may offer some slight comparison. It is the oracles of ancient Greece itself, of course, which provide the most detailed evidence we have from the ancient world. The documentary and historical evidence from them is enormous, as we might suspect from the foregoing accounts of a few aspects of them. We are not here considering any non-Greek oracles, though there were many. Let us proceed, then, with Greek examples, and turn our attention to some from the *History* of Herodotus, for oracular intervention in public affairs. He recounts a particularly good example of how the Oracle of Delphi managed power-politics in the Hellenic world. The Spartans, before they rose to prominence, were 'the worst-governed' of all the Greeks and had little contact with the outside world. One of their leading citizens, Lycurgus, went to Delphi and as soon as he entered the temple hall, the priestess is said to have announced to him that he was 'dear to Zeus and all the gods of Olympus', and then added for good measure, 'Are you a man or a god? A god, I think.' After that, how could Lycurgus fail? He went back to Sparta and took over the government and completely transformed the state. He reorganized the army and life in general in the way which has led to the common use today of the expression 'a Spartan existence'. It could be said that he instituted a totalitarian state. But this was just the beginning of Delphic influence over Spartan affairs. When Sparta began to cast its eyes about for other nations to conquer, it took a fancy to the region of Arcadia. But before rushing ahead the Spartans sent to the Delphic Oracle to learn the wishes of Apollo. The priests issued this reply of the god to their request for his comments:

> You ask Arcadia of me? 'Tis too much, I cannot grant it.
> Many are the acorn-eaters there who will hinder you.
> But I do not grudge you all: you may have Tegea;
> There may your feet strike a dance
> And measure the fertile plain with the line.

'Acorn-eaters' was synonymous with 'hardy', as the Arcadians were a relatively primitive and rough people who were presumed to be so wild that they ate acorns. According to Pliny, 'when there is a scarcity of corn they [acorns] are dried and ground into flour which is kneaded to make bread.'[87] Pliny specifically adds that 'the acorn-bearing trees . . . first produced food for mortal man and were the foster-mothers of his helpless and savage lot.'[88] Sweet acorns (from the burr oak), either boiled or roasted, were traditionally eaten until recent times by the American Indians, and well-soaked acorn meal, which has had its bitter taste extracted from it, was also eaten by them in the form of cakes.[89]

(A decoction of acorns was widely used also in classical Greece to counteract the effects of too much alcohol.)

No more persuasion was needed: single-handedly the Delphic Oracle prevented an invasion of Arcadia by the Spartans. Instead it directed their warlike intentions towards a single nation of Arcadia, Tegea, towards which the Delphic officials may well have had some grievance. But the outcome is even more remarkable. For instead of conquering the Tegeans, the Spartans were defeated, and many of their soldiers captured and enslaved. And the prediction of the Delphic Oracle was then interpreted as having been true in an unexpected way, for the captives were employed in tilling the ground and *measuring the fertile plain with a line* as slaves rather than as masters. So that it was claimed that the prediction had come true in a literal sense, though in a way no one could have anticipated.

Simultaneously impressed by the fulfilment of the prophecy and in low spirits because they had been defeated, the Spartans went again to the Delphic Oracle to ask 'What do we do now? How can we conquer the Tegeans?' And this time the Oracle answered in a truly bizarre riddle:

Bring home the bones of Orestes, son of Agamemnon.

Agamemnon was one of the heroes of Homer's *Iliad* who was murdered by his wife upon returning home from Troy. His son Orestes later avenged his death by killing his mother. These events, even if they had ever occurred, would have taken place centuries before, but, no doubt, the Delphic officials had some arcane message hidden beneath the riddle. The Spartans, however, were a literal-minded people. They went away and tried to find the bones of Orestes and then, predictably, came back for further advice. This time the Oracle told them:

Go to Tegea in Arcadia's level plain,
Where two winds are ever blowing by hard force,
Where shock answers to shock, where anguish lies on anguish.
There life-engendering earth contains Agamemnon's son,

Bring him away, and thus shall you be the lords of the Tegeans.

All this time, a truce reigned between Sparta and Tegea, and travel between the two was possible. A prominent emissary of the Spartans, Lichas, was one of the men authorized to scout around for the bones of Orestes, whose place of burial was of course unknown, and whose very existence was possibly only mythical. Lichas went to Tegea and wandered about trying to find some sign of a promising tomb, with no success, when fate brought him into a blacksmith's shop. As he sat watching the smith working at his anvil, the words of the riddle turning over and over in his mind, he suddenly realized with a great shock that he appeared to be witnessing what the Oracle had described: the iron being forged on the anvil was 'shock answering to shock', and considering the anguish brought to men by use of iron in warfare, and the suffering endured by the anvil and the iron in the forging process, he thought he saw in this also 'anguish lying on anguish'.

The story goes that Lichas managed to persuade the smith to hire his smithy and home to him, after which he dug in the nearby sepulchre and uncovered some enormous bones in a 'coffin seven cubits long', which he assumed to be the remains of Orestes. He took these back to Sparta and everybody was happy. The Spartans after that were victorious in their encounters with the Tegeans. The entire tale is recounted at length in Book I of Herodotus.[90] A strange sidelight on this subject is preserved by that magpie of miscellaneous information, Pliny. In his *Natural History* he has a section on exceptional human stature and tells us: 'The records attest that the body of Orestes dug up at the command of an oracle measured 10 feet 6 inches.'[91]

The Delphic Oracle continued to order statesmen and public assemblies to find the bones of mythical persons, which were to be interred at the city in question with great ceremony, and to form the basis of a cathartic state religious cult. This is rather similar to the Roman Catholic attitude towards the relics of saints, which are officially encouraged, and believed by the devout to be authentic. To cite one more ancient example, we have from Plutarch this extraordinary tale:

> After the Persian war, in the archonship of Phaedo, the Athenians were told by the Delphian Oracle to take home the bones of Theseus and keep them with the greatest care and honour. There was great difficulty in obtaining them and in discovering his tomb on account of the wild and savage habits of the natives of the island [where they were reputed by legend to lie]. However, Cimon took the island, as is written in my history of his Life, and making it a point of honour to discover his tomb, he chanced to behold an eagle pecking with its beak and scratching with its talons at a small rising ground. Here he dug, imagining that the spot had been pointed out by a miracle. There was found the coffin of a man of great stature, and lying beside it a brazen lance-head and a sword. These relics were brought to Athens by Cimon, on board of his trireme, and the delighted Athenians received them with splendid processions and sacrifices, just as if the hero himself were come to the city. He is buried in the midst of the city, near where the Gymnasium now stands, and his tomb is a place of sanctuary for slaves, and for all that are poor and oppressed, because Theseus, during his life, was the champion and avenger of the poor, and always kindly hearkened to their prayers.[92]

It is immediately obvious that one important purpose of the shrine of the bones of Theseus was to inspire and make official a certain degree of social compassion. Most altars and temples were in any case places of refuge which were sacred and not to be violated. A long treatise could be written about the purely social functions of the religious and oracular establishments, and many such discussions have appeared from a variety of scholars, as one might expect. Extensive and comprehensive surveys have also been made of the political and military aspects of the oracular institutions, the most thoroughly surveyed being

Delphi, for which we have the most evidence. Scholars such as H. W. Parke, D. E. W. Wormell and Joseph Fontenrose, to mention only some who write in English, have accomplished mammoth feats of historical compilation and synthesis in the study of these subjects.[93] It is to be hoped that readers will turn to them for further study of the oracles. But there remains much to be done. At the time of writing I have discovered new evidence which indicates that the original site of the Oracle of Dodona, like that of Delphi, was some distance away from the later site, which has the ruins that are known today. Some investigation of this question is already taking place.

The final aspect of the ancient oracular establishments which we shall consider here concerns the peculiar riddles which they circulated. There was a continuous stream of riddles issuing from Delphi during most of its active history. They have been well documented and collected amongst all the other utterances of the Oracle. They have received attention in their own right by Dr Joseph Fontenrose, but only for a brief five pages in his *The Delphic Oracle*.[94] The extraordinary nature of these riddles was not lost on the more critical of the ancients. Cicero says: 'Chrysippus [a prominent philosopher] has filled an entire volume with [Apollo's] oracles, many of which, as I said before, I consider utterly false, and many others only true by accident, as often happens in any common conversation. Others, again, are so obscure and involved, that their very interpreters have need of other interpreters.'[95]

It has been remarked by many people, not least the ancients themselves, that ambiguity was useful for the priests and prophets, not to mention the fortune-tellers or 'oracle-mongers' who haunted the streets and market-places, because an oracular pronouncement which was sufficiently vague could be said to come true in a wide variety of situations. As Aristotle said, when describing the five principles of correct use of language which are essential to a good writing or speaking style:

The third is to avoid ambiguities; unless, indeed, you definitely desire to be ambiguous, as those do who have nothing to say but are pretending to mean something. Such people are apt to put that sort of thing into verse. Empedocles, for instance, by his long circumlocutions imposes on his hearers; these are affected in the same way as most people are when they listen to diviners, whose ambiguous utterances are received with nods of acquiescence –

Croesus by crossing the Halys will ruin a mighty realm.
[A famous oracular pronouncement which encouraged King Croesus to cross the Halys River and make war, but the realm which he ruined was his own!]

Diviners use these vague generalities about the matter in hand because their predictions are thus, as a rule, less likely to be falsified. We are more likely to be right, in the game of 'odd and even', if we simply guess 'even' or 'odd' than if we guess at the actual number; and the oracle-monger is more likely to be right if he simply says that a thing will happen than if he says *when* it will happen, and therefore he refuses to add a definite date. All these ambiguities have the same sort of effect, and are to be avoided unless we have some such object as that mentioned.[96]

The more arcane and obscure the prophecy, the easier it is to 'interpret'. Emotive words like 'home', 'mother', 'father' were frequently included in oracular messages and whilst seeming to refer to specific people or places would convince the recipient of the message that something important had been said: one's mother could be one's actual mother, one's motherland, or a goddess; 'home' might be one's house, one's city, or even death itself, conceived of as the soul's 'return home' from the bondage of matter. But whatever the advantages to the priests of the ambiguous prophecies, the riddling aspect of oracular utterances was a serious and profound element with quite a different purpose and of quite another kind.

The riddles of the oracular establishments were highly

sophisticated and, I believe, deliberately used to raise the level of culture. Even hostile Christian writers were impressed by this. Take, for instance, the remarks to be found in the *Ecclesiastical History* of Hermias Sozomen (early fifth century AD): 'It is true, indeed, that the sibyl and certain oracles foretold what was about to happen to Christ; yet all the Greeks must not on that account be accused of unbelief: these prophecies were, for the most part, written in verse, and were intelligible only to the few who by their erudition were able to understand more important truths than those commonly taught to the people.'[97]

One oracular scholar, Fontenrose, has taken riddling as a criterion for many reputed oracular utterances of Delphi to be considered spurious. He believes any riddle invariably existed simply as a folk tradition and then sometimes was 'made into an oracle'. What he does not even consider is that this could have been done purposely by the oracular officials themselves. To Fontenrose all riddles are primitive. But there is no reason why oracular officials should not also have invented fresh riddles – indeed, I believe they did. Therefore, many of the Delphic riddles which H. W. Parke accepted as genuine on historical or literary grounds I would reinstate despite their having been deposed by Fontenrose. If one reads through the entire collection of all known Delphic oracles, and considers these in their historical contexts where appropriate, the riddling aspect of the responses comes across very strikingly indeed. Parke's brilliant *History of the Delphic Oracle* provides just such a review.[98]

There are two important German books about riddles in the ancient world, by Wolfgang Schultz and Konrad Ohlert.[99] I must confess I have not read them. But I have read most of the material on riddles in English, and can state with a fair degree of certainty that in this language the question has not been fully considered or explored. Herculean efforts at collection and translation have been made by Archer Taylor and Vernam Hull from Irish, Welsh, and English folklore.[100] A Ph.D. thesis including a full translation of the ancient Greek riddle collection of Symphosius was written in 1928 by Raymond Ohl and published privately in Philadelphia.[101] But a truly satisfactory consideration of riddles yet remains to be written in English. When it is, questions such as the following raised by Plutarch will have to be discussed: Jupiter is enraged with Numa, the founder of the religious rites of early Rome, and according to the story orders him to make a magic charm: '[Jupiter] in a rage ordered Numa to make the charm of "Heads"; and when Numa added, "Of onions", he said "Of men's" – "Hair", said Numa, again taking away the terrible part of the imprecation. When the Jupiter said "With living" – "Sprats", said Numa, answering as Egeria had taught him. The god went away appeased.'[102] (Egeria was Numa's wife – she was a supernatural being, or nymph, and when he died she melted away into a spring of water through grief.)

This riddling to take away the terrible aspects of imprecations, in the form of a ritual matching of wits between a culture-hero and a wrathful god, preserves, I believe, an important clue as to the nature of sacred puns and riddles in general. Plutarch gives this story as part of a long account of Numa's supernatural experiences, and as a means of explaining a very bizarre 'charm against thunderbolts' given to Numa by mystical beings, which consisted of onions, hair and sprats. But as he clearly points out, onions, hair, and sprats are code-words disguising some other deeper truth of an arcane nature. Puns and riddles were the means of saying one thing and meaning another, which was fundamental to the ancient religions, and of course helped to preserve their secrets from the profane.

Let us see some of the best ancient Greek riddles, so that we have a better idea of them. Here are a few:

Speak not and thou shalt speak my name.
But must thou speak? Thus again, a great marvel, in speaking thou shalt speak my name.

Answer: Silence.[103]

I look at you whenever you look at me;
You see but I see not; no sight have I;
I speak but have no voice; your voice is heard;

My lips can only open uselessly.

Answer: A reflection in a mirror.[104]

I am a black child sprung from a bright sire,
A wingless bird, fleeting to heaven from earth.
Each eye that meets me weeps, but not from grief,
And in thin air I vanish at my birth.

Answer: Smoke.[105]

My mother I bring forth, she brings forth me:
I'm sometimes greater, sometimes less than she.

or another version:

There are two sisters; one brings forth the other,
And then is born from her own child as mother.

Answer: Night and day.[106]

No one sees me when he sees, but he sees me when he sees not;
He who speaks not speaks, and he who runs not runs,
And I am untruthful though I tell all truth.

Answer: Sleep (with reference also to dreams in sleep).[107]

If you had taken me in my youth,
Haply you would have drunk the blood shed from me;
But now that time has finished making me old,
Eat me, wrinkled as I am, with no moisture in me,
Crushing my bones together with my flesh.

Answer: A raisin.[108]

I am a member of a man; wherefore iron cuts me.
If you take away one letter the sun sets.

Answer: Onyx, 'nail'. Take away the first letter and you
have *nyx,* 'night'.[109]

The last example is one of many where words were altered to give other words; sometimes the numerical values of letters of words were toyed with (the ancient Greek letters doubled as numerals, as they did not have the Arabic numerals which we use today). It is plain that some of these riddles were highly sophisticated. It would be possible to give a large number of examples of oracles of the same sort, but it would take too much space and is not necessary. In the ancient compilation of poetry, the *Palatine* or *Greek Anthology,* riddles are preserved side by side with oracular utterances and numerical problems. Fontenrose says of this: 'It was not chance or mere convenience that prompted the compiler of the *Palatine Anthology* to place riddles alongside oracles in the fourteenth book: he saw two species of one genus.'[110] It is a pity that Fontenrose did not understand that at least part of the reason for there being two species of one genus was that the oracular pronouncements were purposely made so!

Archer Taylor puts the matter in some historical perspective when he says that in Greece 'riddling has flourished from the beginning of literary history. The riddle of the sphinx is an ancient puzzle; and tradition relates that Homer himself died from vexation at failing to guess a riddle for lice. Although scholars studied riddles in classical times, their works are now lost and we are limited to what Athenaeus tells us.'[111] He pins down the nature of these riddles as follows:

> [It] draws attention to the similarity between two wholly unrelated objects by a very simple rhetorical device. The speaker relates the adventure of a certain Humpty Dumpty who sits on a wall and falls from it. He then suddenly tells us that an egg is intended. He has confused us by the simple device of speaking first in general terms which can be taken in two ways, and then in specific terms which can be taken in only one way. A vague general description contrasts sharply with a specific description that follows it.[112]

In another book, Taylor attempts a definition of a riddle as 'descriptions of objects in terms intended to suggest something entirely different.'[113] In a well-considered article on ancient Greek riddles, the classical scholar E. S. Forster remarked that 'oracles are closely allied to riddles and can often be converted into them by being put into an interrogative form' and points out that 'It is the sign of the antiquity of riddles that among the Greeks they were usually expressed in poetry, showing that they go back to a time before writing was in common use and a verse form was a useful aid to memory.'[114]

Among the most thoughtful remarks about riddles ever written were the following by Aristotle:

> The very nature indeed of a riddle is this, to describe a fact in an impossible combination of words (which cannot be done with the real names for things, but can be with their metaphorical substitutes). . . . Metaphor consists in giving the thing a name that belongs to something else. . . .[115]

> Further, in using metaphors to give names to nameless things, we must draw them not from remote but from kindred and similar things, so that the kinship is clearly perceived as soon as the words are said [as in] celebrated riddle[s]. . . . Good riddles do, in general, provide us with satisfactory metaphors: for metaphors imply riddles, and therefore a good riddle can furnish a good metaphor. . . . Metaphors must be drawn, as has been said already, from things that are related to the original thing, and yet not obviously so related – just as in philosophy also an acute mind will perceive resemblances even in things far apart. Thus Archytas [a Pythagorean philosopher of great repute] said that an arbitrator and an altar were the same, for the injured fly to both for refuge. Or you might say that an anchor and an overhead hook were the same, since both are in a way the same, only the one secures things from below and the other from above. . . . Liveliness is specially conveyed by metaphor, and by the further power of surprising the hearer; because the hearer expected something different,

his acquisition of the new idea impressed him all the more. His mind seems to say, 'Yes, to be sure; I never thought of that.' The liveliness of epigrammatic remarks is due to the meaning not being just what the words say. . . .

Well-constructed riddles are attractive for the same reason; a new idea is conveyed, and there is metaphorical expression. . . . The thought is startling, and . . . does not fit in with the ideas you already have. . . . The effect produced . . . is a surprise.[116]

What, then, may we conclude about these riddles in association with the ancient oracular establishments? That they were associated in the public mind is beyond question. That they were often formulated and issued by the oracular officials is probable. And many such riddles may well have been based on traditional folk riddles. But whatever the degree of conscious involvement and intent on the part of the oracular officials, the establishments were as a result, whether by design or by accident, centres of 'new thinking'. Those who consulted them and were in thrall to their replies were thus stimulated to a great deal of deep speculation and thought. 'The thoughts were startling,' as Aristotle says, and they *did not fit in with the ideas already held*.

They were akin to philosophical enquiry, as Aristotle points out, where 'an acute mind will perceive resemblances in things far apart'. In fact, they served to make minds acute. They fed into the mainstream of Greek culture a virile stream of new ideas and unconventional notions, while at the same time taking a conservative line with regard to those cult practices which acted as the cement binding society together. This was, therefore, a recipe for ferment and change within a stable system.

It may be that one of the secrets to the greatness of Greek civilization was the constant encouragement given to every man in Greece to face problems or ideas which would eventually make him say, with Aristotle, 'Yes, to be sure; I never thought of that.' And when we think of the Greeks, it is largely with awe at just this characteristic of their culture. Let us therefore never underestimate the power and influence of the oracular establishments to stimulate intellectual vitality through posing a continual challenge to settled patterns of thought by setting problems for solution, with the authority of a sacred source and the sanction of the gods.

One final aspect of this view of the oracles is that they were stimulating fresh mental associations by a means which was essentially non-logical; they were – and I believe this was their deepest function – stirring up the creative and non-rational faculty of man. The purely rational and logical thought processes do not lead to brilliant 'connections'. The non-rational or irrational capacities of the psyche can and should be harnessed for creative growth and insight. Since cause and effect are logical and rational, the only way to get a glimpse of the future is by circumventing that route. In another book I have suggested a theoretical framework by means of which to explain the connections between events which transcend cause and effect. [117]

As I have described at length elsewhere, the deepest and most basic level of the human mind does lie beneath the level of rational thought. It is called the *'hidden observer'* and it appears to stand outside time as we know it in our daily existence.[118] I believe this level of the mind can be tapped, and that this was done by the posing of riddles by the ancient oracular establishments. They were trying to speak to the core of the human being by circumventing the logical mind; but they did so in a sensible way which, while non-rational, was nevertheless reasonable. I believe that the 'hidden observer' inside us has a kind of hyper-rationality which seems to incorporate non-rational thought as well, or at least sees the two in joint perspective. Let us call this process *reason*, and state that rationality and irrationality are equal components of it.

The oracular conditioning of ancient Greek culture, therefore, may very well have led to a growth in prophetic experience by this unobvious and apparently circuitous route. And it may have been done entirely by instinct, without a grand plan. Perhaps this was the magnificent irony of the oracles – they may not have been genuine, despite many efforts – but, sometimes, *they worked.*

FOUR

SIGNS

What concerns us here is an alternative form of perception which is rarely discussed by modern psychologists, and is generally left to folklorists, who are hardly the right people to be dealing with all its implications. We need to consider this seriously. I am referring to mankind's age-old awareness of 'signs'. We should take seriously this knowledge of our distant ancestors, of the so-called 'primitives' from whom we are all descended.

These supposed 'savages' had a true knowledge of nature, of the weather, of herbs, of wild foods, of springs, of the movements and flight of birds, of the behaviours of beasts, of the 'ways of the wild'. So much of this knowledge is lost to us today except as fragmentary survivals, bits of flotsam and jetsam on the seas of modernity. The dark satanic mills of commerce and science have ground away the threads which connected us with the true realities of the wild. Nature is for us something of a corpse, whose waxen profile may be seen on display in natural history museums. But it was once alive; it was once, indeed, a matter of life or death.

The ancient Greeks and Romans seem very far away to us, almost as long ago as the cavemen seem to some people, for classical education barely exists today, so that we no longer feel Aristotle at our elbow. Ordinary schools no longer teach the classics, so it is inevitable that the classical writers have receded into dim corners of the cave. But it is fascinating to see that the classical writers – who may seem incredibly ancient now – themselves speculated on our early nomadic or pastoral ancestors: 'The life of men in early times was rude and illiterate,' says Pliny the Elder (AD 23–79), who then praises the early men for being such keen observers. For they were so close to nature that they saw into its secret signs. Their knowledge from observation, Pliny says, was 'no less ingenious for them than our knowledge from theory is today'.[1] As Pliny was to his own mind a 'modern', a dweller in the luxury of cities, he was just as intrigued with mankind's primitive origins as a modern anthropologist is. Within him resonated that haunting chord, full of awe at the secret ways of nature and the lost communion with them, which early man had once enjoyed.

The impulses that stir a modern environmentalist were at work, too, in Pliny, prisoner as he was of the opulent civilization of Rome. A historian of science has said: 'Pliny's *Natural History*, which appeared about AD 77, and is dedicated to the Emperor Titus, is perhaps the most important single source extant for the history of ancient civilization.'[2]

Few works of literature ever written are as evocative of life close to nature as the lengthy poem *Works and Days* by Hesiod, who is believed to have lived in the eighth century BC. It tells us of the daily toil of an ancient Greek small-holder, or 'dirt-farmer', who tries to scratch a subsistence from the rocky soil. This long poem has the authenticity that could only come from one who grew up in such a stark, rural existence. Hesiod is full of practical advice:

> The holm-oak makes the strongest plough-beam. . . . Elm or laurel make the soundest poles. . . . Get two nine-year-old bull oxen. In their prime, they have full strength, and work the best, nor will they quarrel in the furrows, break the plough, and leave the work unfinished.[3]

He describes how you should cut your timber in the autumn: 'The tree you cut at this time, when it sheds its leaves and stops sprouting, will be most free of wormholes.'[4]

All these ancient writers who tell of the pastoral life are alert to the signs of nature. Inextricably combined with Hesiod's descriptions of practical life of the primitive farmer is his advice on how to take one's cues from nature, without which one will perish:

> The crane, returning every year, cries out from the clouds above, and when you hear her voice, know that she means the time has come to plough, the time of chilly rains. She gnaws the heart of men who have no oxen.[5]

And also: 'Men sail in springtime, also; when a man can first see leaves upon the very tops of fig-trees, tiny as the prints the crow makes with her foot, the sea is passable.'[6]

A man should plough in time, but if you're unavoidably late, there is a sign to tell you whether you can survive this delay:

> And though you've ploughed too late, this cure may come: When first the cuckoo calls among the oaks and pleases men over the boundless earth, if, from the third day, Zeus sends constant rain until the water rises to a point no higher than an ox's hoof but not much lower, then the farmer who ploughed late may rival him who did the job on time.[7]

Cruel, relentless fate awaits those who shirk:

> ... do not be caught helpless and poor in cruel wintertime, rubbing your swollen feet with scrawny hands. . . . The horned and hornless creatures of the wood in pain, with chattering teeth, flee through the brush, one care in all their minds, to find a cave or thickly covered shelter. Like the man, three-legged with his staff, with shattered spine, whose head looks to the ground, like him they go wandering, looking for shelter from the snow.[8]

These descriptions from Hesiod are so vivid that one can hardly believe that they were written over two thousand six hundred years ago – and what a miracle that for all of that time they have actually survived!

Pliny firmly believed that nature had a code of signs which could be interpreted, followed and, with great difficulty, comprehended. The much earlier Hesiod's observation of the first call of the cuckoo has always undoubtedly been a folk tradition. Indeed, for anyone who lives in the countryside in Europe today, you can hardly miss the call of the cuckoo unless you have the radio turned up too loud. Says Pliny, when it first comes – that first call of the cuckoo after the ravages of winter – it pierces the heart with the hope of spring. The first call of the cuckoo is like a first love: *indelible*. But in Roman times, the Italian peasants used this unmistakable call as the basis for ridiculing their neighbours. Anyone lazy enough to be still pruning his vines when the bird arrived was called 'cuckoo', as Pliny records:

> . . . this is the origin of the rude habit of jeering at people pruning their vines by imitating the note of the visiting bird called the cuckoo, as it is considered disgraceful and deserving of reproach for that bird to find the pruning-hook still being used on the vines; and consequently wanton jokes . . . are thought to be objectionable as bringing bad luck. To such an extent in the country do they think of every trifle as being really a hint or sign given to us by Nature.[9]

But there is good reason to think in this way if you view nature as being in any way alive. A 'primitive' is called an animist if he or she thinks that spirits are to be found in every tree, every stream, every imposing rock. Were stones thought to be inhabited by spirits? Is such a conception partially responsible for the megaliths and stone circles in various parts of the world? The ancient Egyptians seem to have believed that if the name of a god or goddess were suitably intoned or chanted in front of its image carved in stone, then the power of that deity would be invoked, and would resonate within and virtually animate the stone by an epiphany of the deity's presence.

Greek peasants and countryfolk of today retain a surprising amount of the lore of ancient Greek times relating to animist forces and 'spirits' of the woods and springs. A great deal has been recorded about this in the extraordinary book, *The Dangerous Hour: The Lore and Culture of Crisis and Mystery in Rural Greece*, by Richard Blum, an anthropologist, and Eva Blum, a clinical psychologist with a training in the classics. They reveal that many inhabitants of the modern Greek countryside firmly believe in the existence of spirits whom they call 'the nereids' and also occasionally 'the lamias'. Here are some quotations from remarks made by these people in interviews:

A neighbour of ours told us that his brother and his brother's wife were walking one night. Suddenly the nereids got hold of him, seizing him by the arms, and dragged him along with them. His wife lost him as the nereids carried him away. Some days later he was found dead by a fountain . . .[10]

In Doxario there was a girl who could see the nereids and the lamias (they are the same). These creatures are very beautiful and they dance well. The girl wanted to go out with them and dance with them whenever she saw and heard them. Her brothers had a hard time keeping her inside the house, for she kept saying, 'Oh listen to them singing. Look at their dance. I want to go with them.' . . . All these creatures are cooperators-with-the-devil . . . Only faith will save you from these creatures.[11]

While I was waiting to see the doctor in the public clinic in Athens a woman there told me she had been sleeping under a half-closed window and, after midnight, she heard musical instruments playing and saw the nereids dancing. The following day, while she was sitting by the window and doing some sewing, the nereids suddenly rushed through the window, took her in their arms, and threw her out of the window. She broke her arm when she fell and that was the reason she was waiting there in the hospital when I met her.[12]

We can see from this that Greeks of today are surprisingly like the Greeks of ancient times. The modern nereids are even often described as being associated with springs or trees, although in ancient times a tree spirit was really a dryad and a spring spirit was a naiad, whereas the nereids were originally sea nymphs. The modern Greeks have simplified the many nymphs by calling them all nereids. But these countrified or superstitious modern Greeks are light years away from 'us', that is those of us who live in 'modern societies' where we are 'free from superstitions' such as believing in nereids. Of course we have other superstitions which we often don't admit, but by and large we do not hold what could be called 'superstitions about nature'. The reason for this is doubtless because we are so far removed from any experience of nature that we don't know enough about it to hold any superstitions concerning it.

But let us consider what it really means at the psychological level and in a wider context of meaning for people to believe that 'spirits' inhabit the rocks and trees around them. In the ancient classical world there were various classes of nymphs, water nymphs who lived in streams, forest nymphs who lived in the trees, nymphs of the air, nymphs of the sea; there were earth spirits, emanations of regions of soil; there were spirits of sacred springs, spirits of caves, spirits of wells. Any natural source of either vitality or its opposite (sources of life or serious hazards to life) could be spoken of as being alive somehow, possessing an animating spirit. In one sense this is certainly correct – if the animating spirit is symbolic of the dynamism of the source. When one does not have a language for dynamic forces separate from one's language for spirits, the two inevitably become one. We have not abandoned this habit today. For example, ships and automobiles are usually called 'she', and we say 'she's giving me trouble' when an engine performs badly. By that we project a personality on to the engine, but we do not often confuse this poetic habit with a notion that the engine is truly alive. So in this sense, perhaps we are all animists, because the world is full of dynamic processes which we persist in viewing emotionally. And since emotions are our inner dynamics, viewing exterior dynamics by reference to them is natural behaviour for us. When this becomes literal, it lapses into the extreme of superstition. But on the whole I believe it is wrong to hold ancient or 'primitive' peoples up to ridicule because they viewed natural forces as being 'alive'. 'Alive' was their concept for 'dynamic'.

If we are to live in the world, we have to recognize the dynamics of events. 'Things' seem to be 'alive' because *things happen*. If you do not have a scheme of science or philosophy to explain things for you, you turn either to religion or to superstition (which in many cases amounts to the same thing). The inescapable fact is that one cannot do without explanations, so if one does not have them, one invents them. Sometimes anything will do, even the most errant nonsense. What is handiest of all is if someone else does your thinking for you, what the modern philosopher Ayn Rand called 'secondhand thinking'. This happens in organized religions, where dogma and authority can give you all the answers you need and you don't have to worry your little head about a thing. But if you aren't embedded in such a structure, you have to fall back on your wits, and in ancient times that generally meant the assumption that animistic forces inhabited natural phenomena and were responsible for events. This was *the dynamics of fate*. It was all improvised, of course, but the natural forces could at least be explained by the often whimsical dynamics of capricious spirits. They were the ghosts in the machine of life. It was by this means that ancient or primitive men provided themselves with a ready-to-hand philosophy, something they could take out of a sack as needed upon occasion. They didn't have Newton's Laws of Motion, so they made up their own laws on the spot: the nereids, or whoever it was, were at work. That explained everything. It was an instant system of dynamics to explain the great engine of events. This provided enough comfort that ancient men did not feel completely helpless, for they could try and appease the spirits by sacrifices and offerings, and thereby hope for some amelioration of their condition. And what is more, one could do so while retaining one's dignity, for there was always piety to justify appeasement by calling it respect.

Throughout ancient literature one can find many evocative descriptions of wild nature and of man's animistic relations to its forces. Some of my favourite such descriptions come from *The Voyage of the Argo (Argonautica)* by the ancient poet Apollonius of Rhodes (third to second century BC). Here is the description of how the stranded Argonauts, who are attempting to reach the distant golden fleece, are informed by their seer Mopsus by bird-augury that they may set sail:

For twelve days after this there was foul weather day and night, and the Argonauts were unable to put out. But towards the end of the night . . . a halcyon [a mythical bird] hovered over the golden head of Mopsus and in its piping voice announced the end of the gales. Mopsus heard it and understood the happy omen. So when the sea-bird, still directed by a god, flew off and perched on the mascot of the ship, he went to Jason, who lay comfortably wrapped in fleeces, woke him quickly with a touch and said:

'My lord, you must climb this holy peak to propitiate Rhea, Mother of all the happy gods, whose lovely throne is above – and then the gales will cease. I learnt this from a halcyon just now: the sea-bird flew above you as you slept and told me all. Rhea's dominion covers the winds, the sea, the whole earth and the gods' home on snow-capped Olympus.' . . . This was welcome news to Jason, who leapt up from his bed rejoicing. He hastily woke the rest and told how Mopsus had interpreted the signs. They set to work at once. The younger men took some oxen from the stalls and began to drive them up the steep path to the top. . . . Standing in the woods, there was an ancient vine with a massive trunk withered to the roots. They cut this down to make a sacred image of the mountain goddess; and when Argus had skilfully shaped it, they set it up on a rocky eminence under the shelter of some tall oak trees, the highest trees that grow, and made an altar of stones near by. Then, crowned with oak-leaves, they began the sacrificial rites, invoking the Mountain Mother. . . . Jason, pouring libations on the blazing sacrifice, earnestly besought the goddess to send the stormy winds elsewhere . . . the young men in full armour moved round in a high-stepping dance, beating their shields with their swords. . . . The goddess must have observed the flawless sacrifice with pleasure, for her own appropriate signs appeared . . . beasts left their lairs and thickets and came to them with wagging tails . . . [and] with no digging on their part, a stream gushed forth from the thirsty peak [which had previously had no spring]. And it did not cease to flow; the natives of the place still drink from it. They call it Jason's Spring.[13]

Later in the saga, the Argonauts put ashore to fetch dry wood, fresh leaves from the fields for bedding, and drinking water from a spring. Hercules, whose oar had broken, wanted to find a new one: 'Wandering about he found a pine that was not burdened with many branches nor had reached its full stature, but was like a slender young poplar in height and girth.' He took off his lion skin and pulled the tree up with his bare hands: 'Deep-rooted though it was, it came up clods and all like a ship's mast torn from its stays . . .'

While this was going on, Hercules's beloved, for whom he had a mad passion, a young lad named Hylas, 'had gone off by himself with a bronze ewer in search of some hallowed spring where he could draw water for the evening meal . . .' But awful Fate was brooding over the scene, planning a tragedy:

Hylas soon found a spring, which the people of the neighbourhood call Pegae. He reached it when the nymphs were about to hold their dances – it was the custom of all those who haunt that beautiful headland to sing the praise of Artemis by night. The nymphs of the mountain peaks and caverns were all posted some way off to patrol the woods; but one, the naiad nymph of the spring, was just emerging from the limpid water as Hylas drew near. And there, with the full moon shining on him from a clear sky, she saw him in all his radiant beauty and alluring grace. Her heart was flooded with desire; she had a struggle to regain her scattered wits. But Hylas now leant over to one side to dip his ewer in; and as soon as the water was gurgling loudly round the ringing bronze she threw her left arm round his neck in her eagerness to kiss his gentle lips. Then with her right hand she drew his elbow down and plunged him in midstream. . . . Hercules was the only member of the company to hear the boy's cry. Led by the sound he rushed off towards Pegae, like a wild animal who hears the bleating of a distant flock and in his hunger dashed after them, only to find that the shepherds have forestalled him, the sheep are in the pen, and he is left to roar in protest till he tires.[14]

In the *Argonautica* the mortals and the nymphs mix without there being a clear borderline between real people and imaginary spirits. In other words, the term 'imaginary' did not apply. This is a true expression of the animistic state of mind. Hylas goes along to the spring, and there is the naiad nymph just coming up to the surface, as naturally as you please. The Argonauts do not appear to be in the least ill at ease about doing sacred dances on the spur of the moment to the Mountain Mother; a sacrifice, a carving of a tree, the honouring of the appropriate divine force in the correct way at the right time and place – all of this is as natural to them as breathing. They are not self-conscious about it, their piety is not expressed grudgingly; they are not looking over their shoulders to see if their friends are laughing.

Being this close to the natural forces means that they are more integrated with their surroundings, more in tune with nature, better adjusted, and inevitably happier and more contented than we are. If tragedy strikes, if someone dies, if a house burns down, it is easier for them to accept. They are immersed in the ways of things, what the Chinese call the *Tao*. Psychic pain is more acute in us because of our alienation from nature, our isolation from the comforting stream of natural events.

It is worth stressing all of this if only to show by contrast the way of the ancients and the primitives in its good side. They did not have modern dental care or our medicine; their lives were in

many respects 'nasty, brutal and short'. But they seem to have
been more in balance with the world and with themselves. I do
not mean to promote the myth of the Noble Savage. I mean
instead to stress the closeness to natural forces.

They were searching for signs, always trying to find the cues of
nature, to see which way the flow was going, the wind of change.
They were masters of weather signs, and countless of these are
recorded in the ancient writers such as Pliny, Aratus, Eudoxus,
Hesiod, and Vergil. I will not take the trouble to record where
each sign comes from, but will mention many of them as we go
along as coming from a common tradition. For instance, the
ancients knew that it is a sign of rain or a storm when birds that
are not aquatic take a bath, or when swallows hit the water of
the lakes with their bellies as they swoop. When a sea crow
(chough) puts back its head on a rock which is washed by waves,
or when it often dives or hovers over the water, rain is coming.
Cranes flying high and silent indicate fine weather. You may see
the signs with the livestock too: when oxen sniff the sky, they lick
themselves against the way of their hair, when sheep go skipping
and gambolling in an unusual manner – all this portends a
change in the weather for the worse. Bees, normally so
industrious, will not go so much abroad, earthworms will come
up, ants are more active – this means rain. All the creatures sense
it. And even the plants know: 'It is also a well-ascertained fact
that the trefoil bristles and raises its leaves against an
approaching storm,' says Pliny.[15]

As for the raven, who makes so many different sounds in the
wild, if he should be heard to repeat one of them twice in quick
succession, if he then shakes his wings and makes a whirring
sound, you can take it that he senses the rain coming. If he or
the jackdaw flies high, screaming like a hawk, then it means rain.
So, too, the hawk is affected by the coming rain. He will un-
characteristically alight in a tree, or go under the leaves, and
begin searching for lice in the bark. The hens and cockerels will
also turn to search for lice, rather than pecking the ground in
their usual manner. They have even been known to make a noise
like that of falling rain.

The heron will give signs. If, flying towards the sea, he utters his cry, it means rain. But otherwise a loud cry from him merely means he senses a wind coming. Study, too, the flocks of birds: if a large colony lives together on an island, and they pack together in the summer, it means rain. If their numbers are much larger than in other years it may be a sign of a severe drought coming. They say that crows, if observed closely, can tell much. If they shake themselves and croak with a sort of gurgle, with a continuous sound, it means a storm is coming; but it means gusty rain if the sound is not continuous but is instead swallowed down in gulps. The silly rooks, who make so much noise, give signs of rain too; they are so alarmed that when they look at a pond or other water they will begin to make more noise than usual, and will go to the water and sprinkle themselves. The swallow, if not striking her belly against the pond, will touch it with her wing and keep coming close to it. For the ponds seem to attract the birds when storms threaten, even as they flee from the sea – flocks of gulls are well known to come inland to escape storms.

I am not enough of a naturalist to have personally checked out all of these signs from the behaviour of birds. Cranes, after all, can no longer be seen so easily, and ravens vanished from areas like Wiltshire in the nineteenth century, as W. H. Hudson discovered. But I am struck by the extraordinary persistence of the belief that various birds before the coming of rain will bathe or splash about in the water. According to Sir James Frazer in *The Golden Bough*, and also other authors, it is a 'well-known principle of magic that any desired effect can be produced by imitating it.'[16] Could this belief about magic be rooted in animal behaviour? What, indeed, could be the motivation for these creatures in imitating getting wet?

Dolphins give signs too. If the sea is billowy and they are seen splashing about in it, then it means that calm weather will come. But if the sea is already calm and they are seen diving in and out, then it is a sign that wind will come from the quarter in which they are seen. The dolphin indicates rain is coming when he is seen diving near the land with great frequency. Cicero refers to this also: 'When pilots see the cuttlefish leaping, and the dolphins betaking themselves to the harbours, they recognize these indications as sure signs of storms approaching. Such signs may easily be explained by the laws of nature . . .'[17]

Pliny says:

> A cuttle-fish fluttering out of the water, shellfish adhering to objects, and sea-urchins making themselves fast or ballasting themselves with sand are signs of a storm; so also frogs croaking more than usual, and coots making a chattering in the morning, and likewise divers and ducks cleaning their feathers with their beaks are a sign of wind, and the other water-birds flocking together, cranes hastening inland, and divers and seagulls forsaking the sea or the marshes.[18]

The Latin scholar L. A. S. Jermyn published a series of articles back in 1951 in the classical journal *Greece & Rome* entitled 'Weather-Signs in Virgil', in which he admirably grasped the importance of these signs not only in the sense of natural phenomena, but in their literary and cultural sense as well.[19] His main purpose is to praise the poetry of Vergil, and he says of Vergil's use of weather signs drawn from Greek and Roman scientific writers in his verse: 'Surely there is nothing odd or culpable in Vergil's using the language of his scientific predecessors when treating of (these) subjects! The miracle is that it becomes poetry at his touch.' Jermyn records several instances of his having checked Vergil's weather signs by personal experience and found them to be accurate, as in this quaint confirmation that Vergil was correct to say that frogs sing in chorus in the rain:

> In Singapore I had plenty of opportunity of listening to the chorus of the frogs, which are of the same species as those of Virgil and Aristophanes. The chorus began practising *as heavy rains began to fall*: it was soon at full blast, and continued after the rain had stopped. Of course the creatures were singing in their bath! But in the distance the

sound was certainly mournful, so that Virgil is right in calling it *querelam*.

Jermyn's enthusiasm for the turns of phrase used by Vergil to describe weather signs is most endearing, and anyone interested in Latin poetry would do well to read his lengthy analyses of how Vergil turned his weather signs to good use as a poet. In the process of doing this, Jermyn gives much valuable information about how the weather signs were passed from source to source, entering Latin from a translation of Aratus done by Cicero, which he shows was read by Vergil. He explains that the long poem of Aratus in turn was a mediocre versification of an otherwise lost prose work by the Greek scientist Eudoxus of Cnidus, a contemporary and friend of Plato.

The weather itself was used in ancient times to try to predict the forthcoming weather. Thunder in the winter is said to indicate wind rather than rain; thunder in the morning at any time of year indicates the same. But thunder in summer at midday or in the evening is a sign of rain. When the west wind is accompanied by lightning which comes from the north, it means that rain or a storm is coming. But in the summer, when you have lightning in the evening it may be a harbinger of delayed rain, which will come within three days, if not sooner. In late summer when you see lightning from the north, it means rain. If the south wind blows at early dawn and lightning comes from the same direction, rain will come soon. (Obviously, all these weather signs are meant to refer to Greece and Italy, as they are all drawn from classical sources.)

In ancient Athens they observed the local hills very closely for signs:

If the lesser Mount Hymettus, which is called the Dry Hill, has a cloud in its hollows, it is a sign of rain: so also is it, if the greater Hymettus has clouds in summer on the top and on the side, or if the Dry Hymettus has white clouds on the top and on the sides . . .

These local weather signs must have been personally observed by the man who recorded them, the ancient philosopher Theophrastus (fourth century BC), who was Aristotle's disciple and successor as head of his school, the Lyceum. He adds: 'When at night a long stretch of white cloud encompasses Hymettus below the peaks, there will generally be rain in a few days.'[20]

Over the years, Theophrastus must have made frequent tests of these observations. Otherwise he would not have written them down in what was meant to be a scientific treatise. Theophrastus is known as 'the Father of Botany', just as his colleague and predecessor Aristotle is known as 'the Father of Zoology'. Both were highly acute scientific observers, among the best known from antiquity.

Animals of all kinds can give signs of many different things. If the sheep or oxen dig holes in the autumn and lie with their heads close together – a rare sign indeed, as I have never seen it and know of no one who has in Britain – then a most severe winter can be expected. (Perhaps the mildness of British winters means this would never occur there.) It is well known that when the cattle lie down in the fields they are doing so to keep a spot dry for an oncoming storm. But Theophrastus says that the sign may be further known by the fact that the cattle, before doing this, will eat more than usual and they will almost always, before rain, choose to lie on their right sides and not on their left. He says also that if the sheep fight together for food more than usual they are concerned with getting their meal before a storm, and the ass at that time shakes his ears a lot and the mice will squeak and dance about.

It would be interesting if all the ancient and traditional weather signs could be gathered together, classified and scientifically examined by observation, to see whether there is anything to them or not.

An interesting Chinese example of the scrutiny of weather signs elucidated from accumulated meteorological observations comes from the personal writings of a Chinese emperor himself. The second Ch'ing [Qing] Dynasty Emperor was K'ang-Hsi [Kangxi], who reigned from 1661 to 1722. During his reign the

Jesuit missionaries were prominent advisers and scientists at his court. One of them in particular, the Rev. Ferdinand Verbiest, who later died of a fall from a bolting horse, was an official in the Calendrical Bureau of the Chinese Government, and is mentioned in this extract from the Emperor's autobiographical writings:

There are certain recurrences that I have drawn from the annual *Records of Sunshine and Rain*, and these can be used to forecast the weather, even though each area is not exactly the same. It is likely to rain on the eighth, eighteenth, twentieth, twenty-second, and twenty-fourth days of every lunar month. Between the ninth and fifteenth days there will not be rain if you can see the moon; but if deep clouds obscure the moon, you can expect a storm of rain that will last for several days. I have also observed the wind's directions: southwest winds are rare in all seasons; the northwesters – what the people call 'guest winds' – will only blow three or four days before they change; northeasterly and southeasterly winds are popularly called 'rain winds'. Observing the clouds will only help you for about half a day ahead, and of course when it's completely overcast it's hard to tell when the skies will clear, just as in prolonged drought it's hard to know when it will rain. The day's lengths will also vary in different areas: thus in Heilungkiang [Heilongjiang], which is in the far northeast, near the place where the sun rises and sets, the nights are short and the days long, and even at night it does not get completely dark.

I always have a little flag set up, so that I can tell the wind's exact direction, and compare my own observations with the weather reports that come in from other provinces. Once I took a gnomon and, having marked with my brush the exact point at which the sun's shadow would fall at noon, had the courtiers sit and watch till they could see that my calculations were correct. I have sat out on a clear night and told the time from the star charts that Verbiest had prepared for me. Many of the officials could not even recognize the basic twenty-eight constellations [*My note:* technically these should be translated not as 'constellations' but as 'lunar mansions', but Spence is trying to be clear to general readers], and I showed them such things as the way the constellations *Ts'an* [*Can*] and *Tsui* [*Zui*] paired together in Orion and how the principles of astronomy and geography meshed. So we could see how China's mountain ranges sprang out from the K'un-lun [Kunlun] ranges and also how general principles regulated the rivers, those south of the forty-fifth degree of latitude flowing to the south and east while those north of this line flowed to the north.[21]

When our daily or home lives are invaded by signs or portents, we call them ominous. But perhaps they are reminders, whispers. Some of the simplest, though they may seem especially ominous if you aren't familiar with them in advance, are really only weather signs. There are some fascinating examples from the ancient writers:

If a lamp burns quietly during a storm, it indicates fair weather. So also if . . . a bright line surrounds the lamp nozzle. . . . Again, when in winter the lamp rejects the flame (i.e. refuses to light properly) but catches, as it were, here and there in spurts, it is a sign of rain: so also is it, if the rays of light leap up on the lamp, or if there are sparks. . . . If a lamp burns steadily in fine weather, it is a sign of storm: so it is if in wintertime dark snuff forms: if it is, as it were, full of numerous millet-seeds, there will be stormy weather; and if these in fine weather appear in a circle round the flame, it is a sign of snow. . . . Some say that, if in the embers [of the fire] there is an appearance as of shining hail-stones, it generally prognosticates hail; while, if the appearance is like a number of small shining millet-seeds, it portends fair weather, if there is a wind at the time, but, if there is no wind, rain or wind.[22]

These are recorded by Theophrastus. One can imagine such

signs being looked for as long as man has known the use of fire. The presence or absence of wind does indeed regulate the rate of burning of a fire, and exercises influence over the size of the embers.

A more homely weather sign is that of Pliny: '. . . when we are at table during our meals vessels into which food is put foretell dreadful storms by leaving a smudge on the sideboard.'[23] This can hardly be called an omen! But somehow the invasion of one's home by these signs adds an ominous element to them. It is not the same as going out and observing the birds: in these cases the spirits seem to be stepping over the threshold, reaching into the innermost recesses of our private retreats. Intrusive phenomena can cease to be signs, and often become omens.[24]

But many of the premonitions that animals appear to have of future events, and which therefore seem occult, are really explained by sensitivities unavailable or unknown to us as humans, or by explanations that we might have not thought of or have not been able to formulate because the factors involved are beyond the reach of our human senses. Homing pigeons provide examples of this. They have been investigated a great deal in recent years and scientific research has demonstrated some surprising facts about them, which by inference must apply to other species as well.

In the atmosphere are very low frequency acoustic waves known as *infrasounds*. These are generated by storms, ocean waves, earthquakes, winds, weather fronts, the aurora borealis ('northern lights'), magnetic phenomena in the atmosphere, and thunder. Some artificial infrasounds are also now generated by man's machines. It was proved as long ago as the late 1970s by a group of scientists at Cornell University, that homing pigeons can perceive such infrasounds far below the range of human hearing, and may act on the information which they derive from them.

This information was published in *Nature* Magazine.[25] It marked a new development at that time in the search for answers to the perception of what to us would be faint cues from nature by animals and birds. By observing these animals and birds we may therefore be observing more sensitive beings reacting to information that our own senses cannot perceive. This may therefore be the true answer to *signs*: observation of our more sensitive fellow creatures in order to detect what they are sensing. The guard dog's reaction is the most obvious daily example of a *sign*. We also employ alarm clocks to wake us up; the clock 'senses' the time for us when we wish to awaken. Presumably early men had to wake themselves, as Tarzan does in the novel *Tarzan of the Apes* (one of the things which most struck me in my early reading as a child), and as 'savages' are said to do. Also 'savages' do not need guard dogs as much as we do because they can smell enemies themselves and do not have the need of a borrowed dog's nose to warn of approaching danger. A VCR 'senses' when to tape the film which we will see later because we aren't at home to watch television. We farm out so many of our sensory requirements to devices or to surrogates such as dogs either because we are not there at the time or because our senses have atrophied so that we cannot wake ourselves at a set time any more or cannot smell our enemies approaching. The sense of smell is the one that has perhaps suffered the most from 'civilized living' conditions. As someone who has an unnaturally acute sense of smell, I suffer agonies from being able to smell too much, like a dog.

The scientists studying the homing pigeons said of the infrasounds:

> Many of these atmospheric oscillations are of high amplitudes . . . but because they are outside the normal limits of human hearing they usually go unnoticed (although humans can detect extremely loud artificial infrasounds generated in test chambers, these sounds are louder than most natural infrasounds and verge on the threshold for pain). . . . Unlike sounds easily audible to humans, atmospheric infrasounds can travel huge distances – often thousands of miles – without much attenuation (which is proportional to the square of the frequency). Hence such sounds could potentially provide birds with much useful

information. For example, the ability of birds to sense approaching weather fronts might be aided by detection of infrasounds funnelled to earth by those fronts or by detection of the infrasound components of thunder associated with storms that are still hundreds of miles away. Localization of several remote infrasound sources could serve as a distant landmark system for triangulation of the home site and of the location of a release site. Properly utilized, infrasound information could thus assist in almost every aspect of avian navigation, in both homing and migration.[26]

During the 1980s and 1990s, much work was done on the detection of the earth's magnetic fields by birds and also of the recognition by birds of star patterns. But the combination of these capabilities with the sensing of infrasound should not be forgotten, since it is undoubtedly an orchestrating of all of these that explains the extraordinary navigational feats of our feathered friends. Living as I do in England, I am continually seeing on the television weather forecasts great swirling masses of low pressure coming in from the Atlantic which will bring rain and gales. These pictures are often broadcast when the sky is clear and the weather appears fine. Such prognoses of impending doom seem very unconvincing in such circumstances. But by the use of infrasound, the birds are not fooled by appearances. They can directly hear the storms far out in mid-Atlantic which we with our satellites can only envisage in TV images which appear to be the fantasies of mad meteorologists.

Infrasounds are just one example of cues from nature which we cannot perceive ourselves, but which the animals and birds can, and do, perceive directly. Early man, 'primitive' man, and 'savages' all noticed these things from the signs of the behaviour given by the animals and birds, and they still notice them to the extent that such people are allowed to survive.

Of course if you are covered in clothes you cannot sense the subtle changes of temperature in the air which the animals notice. When I go for walks in the countryside, though quite well clothed myself, I still pay close attention to these air currents as

I feel them on my face or arms. Sometimes a cold stream of air will be felt running along a fold in the ground: this may indicate the site of a spring. Dry air can unexpectedly become moist for a short distance. The sheep paths may go in a curious manner along a hillside – along this path there may be a congenial air current, warmer than the rest. Imagine the external, soft skin of an animal's nose. This is the foremost part of the animal. It is its leading-edge. Not only is it busy smelling and sniffing, but it is feeling the air currents and slight temperature and humidity variations. A naked 'savage' does this with his exposed body, and it is essential to him.

European civilizations have always insisted upon clothing the 'savages', and the missionaries took not only Bibles but clothes with them wherever they travelled. These suits of clothes were as confining as handcuffs. Immediately the 'savage' was drastically cut off from the ambient air and enclosed within the bounds of Western manacles. Then he would begin to develop neuroses about nudity, which in turns leads to sexual obsessiveness and other unhealthy traits.

A perfect example of closeness to nature leading to an understanding of signs is seen in the scientific validation of the sensitivities of the homing pigeons. Primitive man has always 'known' that he could study *signs* from the birds. But only now with our modern science are we beginning to validate primitive man's opinions by providing verifiable scientific explanations and proof. This process will continue. More and more will we come to appreciate the innate wisdom of the 'primitives', and be able to discriminate between what is nonsense in their lives and what is sense. This sense we must preserve, study, and per-petuate. It is our heritage and our birthright.

The 'science of *signs*' is one of the oldest and most distinguished of mankind's accomplishments. From it came the extrapolations of *portents*, attempts to use signs to know more than just the com-ing weather. These were genuine attempts to interpret not merely the future conditions of natural phenomena such as clouds and rain, but situations of human life itself. This further and higher-level endeavour is what we shall consider next.

FIVE

PORTENTS

Portents are a step up from *signs*. Signs indicate what might happen in nature, but portents are supposed to indicate what will occur with reference to *ourselves*, whether we will be fortunate or unfortunate. Portents are also called presages. This comes from the Latin *prae* 'in advance' plus *sagire* meaning 'to observe keenly'. So one is thus still looking for signs, but with greater urgency and, perhaps, less justification. For it all involves the assumption that nature gives a damn about us, or the gods do, or God does, or however one wants to put it. Alternatively, it could involve the assumption that natural processes have some deep connection with human life in a structural sense, so that they can offer hints as to how things are going for us if we know how to read them.

Basically, the former idea was the Western notion and the latter was the notion held in China. Later in this book we shall be seeing just how interesting the Chinese concepts of portents really were, and considering whether there might really be a deep structure of some kind which could conceivably offer us clues as to human events. But for the moment we are considering portents from the viewpoint of ancient Western civilizations. These usually did not have much validity, although the science of anatomy did arise from the curious preoccupation with inspecting the entrails of animals for signs of what was to come. There were two big exceptions to the general futility of portents in the Western tradition: as we shall be seeing later in this chapter, there was something to some of the ancient superstitions about meteors and comets, and we shall now consider those relating to earthquake prediction.

A presage is, as indicated a moment ago, something 'seen keenly in advance'. This is obviously what we would all like to do: see it coming. An example of a genuine portent would not only be something more drastic than a sign, but also a sign of something more drastic than, say, a mere change in the weather. The Chinese were the first people in the world to construct earthquake detectors, or proto-seismographs. They did this as long ago as the second century AD. The Chinese scientist Chang Heng (Zhang Heng in Pinyin) built such a machine in AD 132. I have given an account of this and reproduced photos of a modern reconstruction of his machine in my book *The Genius of China*. I have also published there a diagram of my own calculations as to how the original machine probably functioned, which improves on the previous attempt by a Japanese scholar in 1939 who considered the same problem.[1] The Chinese seismologists of the present day still have a reputation for being the best predictors of earthquakes in the world. Some of their ideas are strange, but their techniques appear to have excellent results.

What ancient people would have called *portents* of earthquakes are now called *precursory phenomena* of earthquakes. These precursory phenomena were discussed by Chinese seismologist Chen Yun-tai (Zhen Yun-tai) at a meeting of the International Union of Geodesy and Geophysics in 1977, just as China was emerging from the Cultural Revolution. He discussed them in relation to the earthquake at Haicheng in 1975 and the famous one at Tangshan in 1976, which was reported in all the newspapers of the world at the time. He said that the Chinese had observed prior to these earthquakes some significant changes in the measurements of gravity in those same areas. He suspected that enormous changes and movement of underground water could have accounted for this. There was one case in Yunnan Province in the southwest of China where the quality of the underground water had definitely altered in terms of its radon concentration and its electrical resistivity.[2]

It is interesting to compare these tentative scientific approaches to a theory of earthquake prediction by observation of underground water with some of the traditional ancient portents said to herald earthquakes. Pliny wrote in the first century AD:

> ... a remarkable and immortal inspiration is attributed (if we can believe it) to the natural philosopher Anaximander of Miletus, who is said to have warned the Spartans to be careful of their city and buildings, because an earthquake was impending; and subsequently the whole of their city collapsed, and also a large part of Mount Taygetus projecting in the shape of a ship's stern broke off and crashing down on it added to the catastrophe. Also another conjecture is attributed to Pherecydes the 6th century BC supposed teacher of Pythagoras, this also inspired: he is said to have foretold to his fellow-citizens an earthquake, of which he had obtained a premonition in drawing water from a well.[3]

Not much is known about Pherecydes of Syros. The leading expert on him at the moment is H. S. Schibli, who has written the only book about him.[4] Schibli clearly has never had occasion to add seismology to his list of interests, and so he pays little attention to this titbit of information about Pherekydes, saying that it belongs 'Wholly to the realms of the fantastic . . .'[5] But let us learn a little more about this incident of the well water. Apollonios Paradoxographos says: 'Such are the things told about Pherekydes. Once on the island of Syros he was thirsty and asked a little water from one of his acquaintances; after drinking he predicted that there would be an earthquake on the island after the third day.'[6] We get more details – and these are the crucial ones – from Cicero:

> Physicians, pilots, and husbandmen have likewise many presentiments of many events; but I do not choose to call this divination; as neither do I call that warning which was given by the natural philosopher Anaximander to the

Lacedaemonians [Spartans], when he forewarned them to quit their city and their homes, and to spend the whole night in arms on the plain, because he foresaw the approach of a great earthquake, which took place that very night, and demolished the whole town. . . . In the same way, it is not so much as a diviner, as a natural philosopher that we should esteem Pherecydes, the master of Pythagoras, who, when he beheld the water exhausted in a running spring, predicted that an earthquake was nigh at hand.[7]

Here we learn that Pherecydes had made a careful observation of the failing of water from a spring which normally never failed. From this he inferred massive changes in the movements of underground water, and thus predicted that an earthquake was imminent. (It is doubtful that he really said 'in three days' time', though the earthquake may really have occurred three days later; it is more likely that he merely said 'soon', which was later said to have matched the true time.) But as we can see, this is very similar to what the Chinese seismologists were successfully doing in the AD 1970s, 2500 years later – detecting massive movements of underground water prior to an earthquake – although in their case they were detecting this from changes in gravitational measurements. The Chinese do, however, also inspect wells and springs in the manner of Pherecydes.

Pliny elaborates further on the signs to be derived from underground water in predicting earthquakes. He says the water in the wells will be muddier and will have 'a somewhat foul smell'.[8] This makes perfect sense if there are vast movements of this underground water. He also says that earthquakes are known for 'sending out rivers . . . or hot springs'.[9]

There are various other interesting precursory phenomena noted by Pliny, relating to elements other than underground water. He says that 'in Lycia an earthquake is always followed by forty days' fine weather'.[10] Could this be a genuine observation? Has anyone ever bothered to make a note of such an apparently unrelated circumstance? Pliny makes other qualifications which presumably fit his own earthquake reports:

Earthquakes are more frequent in autumn and spring [this is interesting because it is also true of flood tides]. . . . Similarly they are more frequent by night than in the daytime. The severest earthquakes occur in the morning and the evening, but they are frequent near dawn and in the daytime about noon. They also occur at an eclipse of the sun or moon, since then storms are lulled, but particularly when heat follows rain or rain [follows] heat.[11]

Another curious observation of Pliny's is that if earthquakes do not stop, but continue for some time, then 'if they go on, they do not stop before forty days, and usually even longer, some in fact having gone on for one or two years' time'.[12]

Perhaps all these strange hints should be seriously considered. They do, after all, represent generalizations from accumulated ancient observations. It may not be as far-fetched as it would seem, that one or more of these signs might genuinely portend an earthquake for reasons we cannot yet fully understand.

There is, I am happy to say, a specific example to prove this very point. The Chinese have come up with a sharp observation that Western scientists condescendingly find 'amusing'. The Chinese say that they have observed an 'earthquake light' which illuminated the night sky during an earthquake.[13] It is suggested as a possible explanation that 'an electrical discharge represented by an earthquake light may build up before the quake'.

Now let us turn back to Pliny, where we see that he also knew of a sky-sign for earthquakes. He maintained that in fine weather, when an earthquake is imminent, either during the day or a little after sunset, a thin streak of cloud will appear stretching over a wide space.[14] One's instinctive reaction to this might be to say that it must be ridiculous – what has the sky to do with earthquakes?

But we now know that a long thin cloud such as Pliny mentions would be what we call a cirrus cloud, which exists at extremely high altitudes, and that such clouds sometimes align themselves with the lines of force of the earth's magnetic field. The Chinese suggestion that earthquakes might be related to electricity in the sky can be extended to suggest that earthquakes might also be related to the earth's magnetic field, as displayed by the cirrus clouds in the sky. Notice that Pliny says it must be in fine weather. This is because only when there are no clouds at a lower level (which come with bad weather) can these high clouds be seen. What we now know is that cirrus clouds contain tiny particles of micro-meteorite iron dust suspended in them, which enable them to take up their alignments through magnetism. Several scientists have found general evidence of a relation between earthquakes and atmospheric phenomena.[15] One speaks of 'zonal wind changes which affect the rotation of the Earth . . . [which triggers] the release of [a] large amount of elastic energy . . . setting off global seismic activity'.[16]

As for the underground water signs traditionally known for so many millennia, scientists concluded in 1975: '. . . the water level of wells is able to monitor . . . coseismic strain changes . . . wells less than 60 metres deep could reflect tectonic strain . . .'[17]

So Pherecydes, the teacher of Pythagoras, may even be the father of seismology – vindicated 2500 years later! And as one seismologist has stated in *Nature*: 'It now seems . . . the best prospects [are with] seismicity patterns, with the new concept of precursory swarms for the establishment of long-term predictions, and a fuller understanding of methods used by the Chinese . . .'[18] What he is saying is that portents should be adopted as the chief method of predicting earthquakes, for we have already seen that 'precursory swarms' are merely a more modern and scientific version of the ancient portents collected by Pliny and utilized by Pherecydes and Anaximander.

In ancient times signs and portents blended imperceptibly into one another at the edges. The entire matter is deeply embedded in our everyday language. How many of us realize that when we are describing events which are important to us, we nearly always use a cluster of words derived from our ancestors' attempts to divine the future? We say something is significant: this comes from *sign*. We say something is portentous (from *portent*) and fateful (from *fate*). If it is prodigious, then this comes from *prodigy*, which is a kind of portent. It is only in latter days that the word prodigy has become most common in describing that prodigy of nature, a child whose precocity amounts to genius.

In Latin the word *portentum* means 'a prodigy, a portent'. But because a portent is more extreme than a mere sign, as I have said, we find that this word in Latin also comes to mean 'something monstrous'. In drawing the line between signs and portents it is this aspect of extent and size of the event which seems to make the difference. If the weather changes, something indicating it is simply a sign. But if something monstrous is about to occur, it is preceded instead by a portent. The difference is, of course, that something that momentous will effect *us*, not just the wind and sky. This is further indicated in that the word *monstrum* in Latin, which is the origin of 'monster' and 'monstrous', means 'a supernatural event, a prodigy, a portent'.

The ancient Romans, Tuscans, and Etruscans had a quaint tradition. They believed that there were 'family meteors'. The first meteor seen after a man set up house was called his 'family meteor' and according to certain principles its significance was determined, which then foretold his entire life to follow.

There could also be 'individual meteors', or 'private meteors'. The more important ones were those such as the meteor seen at a man's first marriage, or less important, the meteor seen on his birthday. Other private meteors were thought only to prophesy for ten years to come, rather than a lifetime.

Towns too could have meteors (an example of extraterrestrial twinning, perhaps!). These 'public meteors' were not thought to prophesy for more than thirty years ahead, however, unless the extraordinary occurrence of a meteor came at the colonization or founding of the town in question. Such a wonderful portent would be the 'public foundation meteor' and would be almost as important as, and presumably might help to define, the astrological sign under whose auspices this town might be said to lie.[19]

Every country and town had its own astrological sign after the time of Alexander the Great (fourth century BC), when the Babylonian/Assyrian influence spread to the classical world.

Claudius Ptolemy lists these at great length in his book on astrology called the *Tetrabiblos*.[20] See Figure 26 for a table of the astrological affiliations of different regions of the ancient world according to Ptolemy. He makes quaint remarks such as these:

> ... the inhabitants of the Cyclades Isles, and of the shores of Asia Minor and of Cyprus, are more particularly under the influence of Taurus and Venus, and are therefore voluptuous, fond of elegance, and over-studious in their attention to the body.[21]

Comets were considered by the ancients to be much more grandiose than meteors and therefore less applicable to individual mortals, except for kings of course. The Emperor Augustus had a personal obsession or fixation on a particular comet, although he disguised this feeling in public. Pliny gives us an amusing account of this, which is interesting from several points of view, not least the disguising of this personal fixation as something entirely different for purposes of state:

> The only place in the whole world where a comet is the object of worship is a temple at Rome. His late Majesty Augustus had deemed this comet very propitious to himself; as it had appeared at the beginning of his rule, at some game which, not long after the decease of his father [meaning his adoptive father, since Julius Caesar was really his great-uncle] Caesar, as a member of the college founded by him he was celebrating in honour of Mother Venus. In fact he made public the joy that it gave him in these words: 'On the very days of my Games a comet was visible for seven days in the northern part of the sky. It was rising about an hour before sunset, and was a bright star, visible from all lands. The common people believed that this star signified the soul of Caesar received among the spirits of the immortal gods, and on this account the emblem of a star was added to the bust of Caesar that we shortly afterwards dedicated in the forum.' This was his public utterance, but privately he

TABLE SHOWING ALL THE COUNTRIES BELONGING TO EACH SIGN RESPECTIVELY

Signs.	Aries.	Taurus.	Gemini.	Cancer.	Leo.	Virgo.
Triplicity.	North West.	South East.	North East.	South West.	North West.	South East.
Quadrant of the Countries.	North West.	South East.	North East.	South West.	North West.	South East.
Countries remote from the middle of the earth.	Britain Galatia Germany Barsania	Parthia Media Persia	Hyrcania Armenia Mantiana	Numidia Carthage Africa	Italy Apulia Sicily Gaul	Mesopotamia Babylonia Assyria
Quadrant of the Countries.	South East.	North West.	South West	North East.	South East.	North West.
Countries near the middle of the earth.	Cælesyria Idumæa Judæa	Cyclades Cyprus Asia Minor	Cyrenaica Marmarica Lower Ægypt	Bithynia Phrygia Colchis	Phoenicia Chaldæa Orchynia	Hellas Achaia Crete

Signs.	Libra.	Scorpio.	Sagittarius.	Capricorn.	Aquarius.	Pisces.
Triplicity.	North East.	South West.	North West.	South East.	North East.	South West.
Quadrant of the Countries.	North East.	South West.	North West.	South East.	North East.	South West.
Countries remote from the middle of the earth.	Bactriana Casperia Serica	Metagonitis Mauritania Getulia	Tuscany Celtica Spain	India Arriana Gedrosia	Sauromatica Oxiana Sogdiana	Phazania Nasamonitis Garamantica
Quadrant of the Countries.	South West.	North East.	South East.	North West.	South West.	North East.
Countries near the middle of the earth.	Thebais Oasis Troglodytica	Syria Commagene Cappadocia	Arabia Felix	Thrace Macedonia Illyria	Arabia Azania Middle Æthiopia	Lydia Cilicia Pamphylia

Figure 26: A table prepared by J. M. Ashmand showing the regions of the world assigned to various astrological signs by Claudius Ptolemy in the second century AD. Britain is under Aries and was governed by Jupiter and Mars. Because of their familiarity with Mars, the British 'inhabitants are accordingly wilder, bolder, and more ferocious' than other peoples, although they share these traits with the Germans. (From J. M. Ashmand, Ptolemy's Tetrabiblos, London, no date, p. 51)

rejoiced because he interpreted the comet as having been born for his own sake and as containing his own birth within it; and, to confess the truth, it did have a healthgiving influence over the world.[22]

Great occasions of state were assumed to have related but mysterious manifestations occurring all round – as portents. The dangerous conspiracy of Catiline, whereby Rome came near to falling under a dictatorship of a young psychopath before the time of the Caesars, was only prevented by the prompt and forceful action of Cicero, who happened to be consul in that year, and who arrested and executed Catiline so quickly that the conspiracy then collapsed. Ever since, Cicero's action has been a model to some and a source of controversy to others, though there can be no doubt that Cicero saved the tottering Republic at that time, which some years later was to succumb forever to the imperial reign of the Caesars. But the manifestations of portents must have been thought to be pretty widespread, for Pliny records one occurring as far away from Rome as Pompeii, and seems to think no justification for this is required: 'Among the portents in connection with Catiline, a town-councillor of Pompeii named Marcus Herennius was struck by lightning on a fine day.'[23]

You might think that a town-councillor in a provincial town couldn't have less to do with a political upheaval in Rome, but to the ancient Roman mind, this was a portent of the Conspiracy of Catiline!

Cicero himself records a portent which he witnessed personally:

When Sulla was in the territory of Nola, and was sacrificing in front of his tent, a serpent suddenly glided out from beneath the altar; and when, upon this, the soothsayer Posthumius exhorted him to give orders for the immediate march of the army, Sulla obeyed the injunction, and entirely defeated the Samnites, who lay before Nola, and took possession of their richly-provided camp.[24]

Portents were in full swing during the Renaissance. The famous Renaissance physician, mathematician, and philosopher, Jerome Cardan (Girolamo Cardano/Hieronymus Cardanus, who lived 1501–76), mentions them in his autobiography *De Vita Propria Liber* (*The Book of My Life*). This extraordinary book is well worth a read and is noted for its scandalous, sensational, and candid revelations. Cardan liked to describe the portents that occurred throughout his own life. Here is an example:

> An incident ... occurred in 1531 when a dog of the neighbourhood, ordinarily a well-behaved beast, howled for hours without stopping – an extraordinary performance; ravens sat on the ridgepole, croaking with unwonted persistence; when the house-boy broke the kindling faggots, fiery sparks flew forth, and before I rightly knew what I was about, I found myself married![25]

Here we have many of the familiar elements: croaking ravens, howling animals, sparks from the fire. These are similar to the signs and portents noticed by man for thousands of years until our modern age. Cardan did not invent these nor was he slavishly copying ancient observations – despite the fact that this group of portents could just as well have been quoted from some work written 1500 years earlier. But what the animals and the birds and the fire do are simply the obvious things to notice, and when something extraordinary occurs with regard to them, it is taken as an indication of an extraordinary course of events, signified by them just as a 'precursory swarm' comes before an earthquake.

An interesting comment upon the state of mind of those who insist that everything is a portent was made by Pliny:

> Everywhere in the whole world at every hour by all men's voices Fortune alone is invoked or named, alone accused, alone impeached, alone pondered, alone applauded, alone rebuked, and visited with reproaches; deemed volatile and favouring the unworthy. To her is debited all that is spent and credited all that is received, she alone fills both pages in

DE DIVINATIONE ET ORACVLIS.

Figure 27: A fanciful engraving from 1675 showing divinatory themes. An augur stands on the right, observing the flights of birds for augury. In the background on the left a prophet lies in the entrance to an oracular cavern prophesying. At the augur's feet, extreme foreground on the right, are seen chickens pecking grain from the ground, a reference to the ancient Roman technique of divination practised by that method, whereby if a chicken pecked its food or not the outcome of an event would be favourable or unfavourable. In the foreground on the left is an object which is evidently meant to refer to the oracular tripod at Delphi, though this one has four rather than three feet. The oracular temple in the centre is a seventeenth-century fantasy

the whole of mortals' accounts; and we are so much at the mercy of chance that Chance herself, by whom God is proved uncertain, takes the place of God. Another set of people banishes fortune also, and attributes events to its star and to the laws of birth [deterministic astrology], holding that for all men that ever are to be God's decree has been enacted once for all, while for the rest of time leisure has been vouchsafed to Him. [In other words, God has made a predetermined universe in which everything is inevitable and he can sit back and relax, enjoying the show.] This belief begins to take root, and the learned and the unlearned mob alike go marching towards it at the double: witness the warnings drawn from lightning, the forecasts made by oracles, the prophecies of augurs, and even inconceivable trifles – a sneeze, a stumble – counted as omens. His late Majesty [Augustus] put abroad a story that on the day on which he was almost overthrown by a mutiny in the army he had put his left boot on the wrong foot.[26]

This stinging critcism may sound contradictory from someone who took astrology very seriously and spent so much of his time recording omens, signs and portents. One scholar who has made a study of Pliny remarks:

In Pliny we also detect signs of the conflict between science and religion. In a single chapter on God he says pretty much all that the church fathers later repeated at much greater length against paganism and polytheism. . . . He believed that the soul had no separate existence from the body. . . . The hope of personal immortality he scorned as 'puerile ravings' produced by the fear of death. . . . In short, natural law, mechanical force, and facts capable of scientific investigation would seem to be all that he will admit and to suffice to satisfy his strong intellect. Yet . . . [he has] the greatest difficulty in distinguishing between science and magic, and [he gives] credence to many details in science which seem to us quite as superstitious as the pagan beliefs concerning the gods which he rejected. But if any reader is inclined to belittle Pliny for this, let him first stop and think how Pliny would ridicule some modern scientists for their religious beliefs, or for their spiritualism or psychic research.[27]

Or he might be inclined to point out that modern cosmologists who speak confidently of such things as 'superstrings' have little but their theoretical preferences to justify such talk, since 'superstrings' may or may not exist, and they would probably seem far less tangible to Pliny than many a sign or portent. We must not think that just because we are modern (or 'post-modern', as some now prefer to say) we are necessarily the clever ones who can justify our claims, while ancients like Pliny could only deal in nonsense. There is plenty of nonsense still around today. Some would say there is too much of it.

Possibly the most dramatic example of modern science seriously vindicating ancient man's superstitions regarding portents has been with regard to comets. I well recall buying the 17 November 1977 issue of *The New Scientist* at a newsstand and being astonished to see a very strange article in it by the astronomer Sir Fred Hoyle and a man I had not heard of before, but whose name I recognized as being Sri Lankan, Chandra Wickramasinghe. (I had numerous friends from Ceylon, now called Sri Lanka, and instantly recognized a typical Sinhalese tongue-twister surname.) The article bore the title 'Does Epidemic Disease Come from Space?' The article was accompanied by a strange special editorial in which the editor felt called upon to justify himself for daring to publish Hoyle and Wickramasinghe's article! The editor, Bernard Dixon, said:

> On p. 402 this week, we publish an article by Sir Fred Hoyle and Chandra Wickramasinghe ... *New Scientist* may well be criticized in some quarters for helping to publicize a notion so far at variance with established theories ... [but] because, as Hoyle and Wickramasinghe point out, their theory has important practical implications, we have decided to publish it, in the hope that it is fully appraised and criticized by the scientific community.[28]

A few years before, the article would probably never have been published at all. So this horribly condescending – some might say insulting – editorial by Dixon actually marked a slight thawing in the climate of intolerance in the scientific community. Today it is laughable, but then it was deadly serious. After all, Hoyle and Wickramasinghe were, in Dixon's own words, '*at variance with established theories*', and the implication is clear that this was then considered to be a most dreadful thing. One imagines Bruno at the stake only the day before for some similar crime.

Long may as many people as possible be *at variance with established theories*! After all, since no established theory can ever be wholly correct due to the imperfection of human knowledge, it is only if we are perpetually at variance with them that any progress can ever be made at all.

I read on, past the notorious breast-beating and *mea culpa* of the editor who seemingly believed himself to be ever so courageous and brave, and came to the article itself. Its subtitle announced: 'An impact of a comet-type body on the Earth about four billion years ago could have led to the start of terrestrial life. Even today continuing influxes of cometary debris may bring to the planet viruses and bacteria responsible for diseases of plants and animals.'[29]

Throughout history comets had been thought to be portents of pestilence. Now a scientific theory had been evolved which suggested that that was literally true! This was not lost on me from the first moment, though few readers of the article can have been as concerned about the obscure subject of ancient portents as I was. In the text of the article the authors stated:

> Comets have been regarded with awe and trepidation by many ancient cultures in widely separated parts of the globe. Almost invariably they have been regarded as bad omens – bringers of pestilence and death. In this article we argue that … the periodic influx of cometary debris in the form of micrometeorites may be responsible for waves of disease which sweep the planet. … Further major epidemics of disease could be caused when the Earth crosses the debris of long-period comets. Relatively minor variants of the 'same' disease – e.g. the common cold – could be due to more frequent, regular passages of the Earth through debris of shorter-period comets.

The authors call on historical information to justify their theory:

The abrupt appearance in the literature of references to particular diseases is also significant in that they probably indicate times of specific invasions. Thus, the first clear description of a disease resembling influenza was in the 17th century AD, while the earliest reference to the common cold was in about the 15th century AD. Also it is significant that earlier plagues, such as that in Athens [described by the historian Thucydides as occurring in 429 BC], do not have easily recognizable modern counterparts ... if bacteria or viruses are dispersed in a diffuse cloud of small particles, the incidence of disease may well be global. ... A continual microbiological vigil of the stratosphere may well be necessary to eliminate the havoc which will ensue from extraterrestrial invasions [of cometary germs] in the future.

I was most impressed by these clever suggestions. Within days there was an atmosphere of the lynch mob in some quarters in reaction to this article which dared to be *at variance with established theories*. The shrill and hysterical outrage at which British academics surpass all others in the world was not in short supply. Of all the neurotic, self-indulgent, spoilt and vain academics in the world, there are none worse than some which occur in Britain. Even the haughtiest and most preening French academic can come nowhere near them for arrogance. The mass outpouring of vituperation was like a thunderstorm, drenching all onlookers. But Fred Hoyle, who likes walking in the rain, was an expert at surviving inclement weather, and his stout walking shoes, which he used daily on his walks in the fells, helped him wade through this ordure.

The following year, I became joint editor of a magazine dealing with the frontiers of knowledge entitled *Second Look*. I had kept up with the cometary debates and was aware that Hoyle and Wickramasinghe were bringing out a book on the subject entitled *Lifecloud*, which duly appeared in 1978.[30] I arranged to serialize *Lifecloud* in three lengthy instalments in three successive monthly issues of *Second Look,* appearing in February, March, and April of 1979.[31]

I edited the instalments from the book personally, and they were also sold separately as a collection of extracts. I was thus one of the most active campaigners on behalf of Hoyle and Wickramasinghe's theories at the time. One of my proud possessions is a copy of *Lifecloud* signed by both of them.

The next year, Hoyle and Wickramasinghe published a sequel volume expounding their theories at greater length, entitled *Diseases from Space.*[32] Other books or pamphlets by one or both of them on the same subject include *Space Travellers: The Bringers of Life* (1981), *Is Life an Astronomical Phenomenon?* (1982), *Proofs That Life Is Cosmic* (1982), *Living Comets* (1985), *Viruses from Space* (with John Watkins, 1986), *Astronomical Origins of Life: Steps Towards Panspermia* (2000), and *Cosmic Dragons: Life and Death on Our Planet* (2001).[33] The books and the material in them are too vast for me to summarize adequately, but suffice it to say that Hoyle and Wickramasinghe comprehensively support their theories with extensive research and argument.

As time went on, slowly and painfully, the tide began to turn. The first thing that happened was that lots of hostile scientists and academics proceeded to die off – always a useful way for progress to happen! (And sometimes the only way!) Over the course of the 1980s, evidence continued to accumulate that Hoyle and Wickramasinghe were right about the chemicals necessary for life existing in space. Then in the 1990s, interest in comets took a new turn. It began to be accepted that the dinosaurs had been killed off by a cometary impact with earth. This theory too had originally been met with howls of neurotic outrage by all the usual suspects. But the power of the pack was weakening: new developments such as the Internet, and an entire new generation of disrespectful young scientists in anoraks, who spent their lives staring at computer screens and cared nothing for High Table at Oxford and Cambridge, were beginning to replace the old-style cocks-of-the-walk. Screams of protest

trailing off into rambling monologues were decreasingly effective, and began to sound as petulant and pouting as they truly
were. The unthinkable began to seem possible: it was beginning
to be possible to envisage the tolerance by the so-called 'scientific
community' of that mortal sin, that offence against the gods
known as *variance with established theories.* It actually became
possible to believe that perhaps the dinosaurs really had been
rendered extinct by a cometary impact without shrill accusations
of madness, congenital lunacy, bad character, evil intentions, or
a psychopathic disposition. In fact, fewer and fewer people in the
world at large seemed to care any more that that heinous offence
of *variance with established theories* was taking place.

And so now the once-outrageous theories of Hoyle and
Wickramasinghe do not seem so very outrageous after all. And
thus it is that if you live long enough, you can survive your most
hysterical opponents. And at the end of 1999 and beginning of
2000, when everybody came down with a rather nasty flu, there
were not a few people who wondered if the close encounter in
December 1999 with the Leonid meteors (a cloud of cometary
debris) may have brought us that latest mutated variety of a
virus, which might live in the dirty snowballs of that debris,
breeding and altering themselves over the years, the better to
infect us when they get sprayed down on our atmosphere from
time to time. My wife and I were near the closest point of
approach of the Leonids, actually observing the meteor shower
in Egypt, and we noticed at the time that everybody came down
with the flu in Egypt first, and in Britain two or three weeks later.
We brought it back with us – a souvenir we would rather have
done without.

Amazing physical confirmation of the Hoyle and Wrickramasinghe hypothesis occurred in the summer of 2001, as was
reported in the *Times* of London on 31 July 2001. Large quantities of bacteria, apparently of extraterrestrial origin, were
captured by balloons at the extraordinary altitude of 41 kilo-
metres above the surface of the Earth, on the very edge of the
atmosphere and its dissipation into space. The high-altitude
balloons that captured this material were launched from India

and they used sophisticated sampling devices that kept the air sterile to avoid any contamination. The quantitles of bacteria captured are described as 'between one and ten clumps . . . per litre of ambient air'. Chandra Wrickramasinghe rightly says: 'That's a huge amount.' For such enormous quantities of bacteria to be floating at the very edge of the Earth's atmosphere like that looks like proof of the theory that life was seeded from outer space, that it was originally transported by comets, and continues to be brought here by them on a regular basis. It seems that huge quantities of bacteria sink down through the atmosphere to the Earth's surface daily. This means that we all 'come from outer space', and that every living thing on this planet is extraterrestrial in origin.

So we see that the classical portent of the comet as a bringer of disease may well be all too true. And the ancients may have observed the coincidence of these two things so many times that they drew the obvious conclusions. And it was not until Hoyle and Wickramasinghe that modern scientists figured out that comets might well harbour viruses which showered down upon us, so that the ancient portents were literal descriptions of what was actually happening.

The most famous ancient portent in the world is doubtless the so-called Star of Bethlehem. What was it? Did it even exist? If it existed, was it Venus? A supernova? A conjunction of Saturn and Jupiter? Every astronomer who dabbles in the subject tends to have his own pet theory. It is a great game to play.

According to the New Testament of the Bible, the three wise men – or as the revised translation of the Gospel of Matthew has it, 'astrologers from the east' – saw the Star of Bethlehem and 'followed' it, and it led them to the infant Jesus. As the Gospel of Matthew (revised translation) says: '. . . the star which they had seen at its rising went ahead of them until it stopped above the place where the child lay. At the sight of the star they were overjoyed.'

The astrologers are described as coming from the east, having observed the star rising in the east. It then 'went ahead of them', travelling westwards, and they, too, travelled westwards. It was clearly therefore not a circumpolar star because it is specifically described as having risen, and circumpolar stars do not rise or set. It seems likely that the 'star' was near the Ecliptic or Zodiacal Band in the sky. Perhaps the most interesting theory about the Star of Bethlehem is that it may have been an exploding supernova which suddenly appeared in the sky. When thinking of this possibility, it is very important to remember that our chronology of AD and BC is computed wrongly. The monk who counted backwards to arrive at it made a mistake and neglected to take note of four years of the reign of the Emperor Augustus, so that by using his inaccurate system, we must realize that the birth of Christ cannot have taken place in 0 BC at all, but would have to have occurred in either 4 BC or 5 BC, according to the mistaken system that we now use. This is further confirmed by the evidence from the Gospels of Matthew and Luke, where it is clearly emphasized that the birth of Christ took place at the end of the reign of King Herod. But we know for certain that Herod died in March, April, or May of 4 BC!

Having lived through the gigantic hype of the Millennium and the year 2000, it is perhaps safe now that it is all over and no commercial interests will be threatened to point out that 1 January of the year 2000 was really 1 January 1996. All the raving loonies who wanted to commit mass suicide in Jerusalem and such places 'at the Millennium' were four years late. And they didn't commit mass suicide after all, which was a bit of a letdown.

The world is always 'coming to an end', a Messiah is always coming, and there are always raving loonies who are convinced of it. But if only they would get their calendars right! Why didn't they all kill themselves on 1 January 1996? Then they would have got it right. But alas, as we all know, 2 January 1996 was quite an ordinary day like any other, and no Messiah came. Perhaps he forgot. And as for the Millennium, all those wonderful fireworks and the exploding Eiffel Tower – they were all four years late.

Having pointed out the calendrical correction we should make, we can now consider the conclusion of a brilliant article

written by three astronomers at about the same time that Hoyle
and Wickramasinghe were launching their comet theory. They
concluded: 'The *Star of Bethlehem* was most likely to have been
a bright nova recorded by the Chinese as appearing in the spring
of 5 BC . . . the birth [of Christ] probably took place within a year
or so of the spring of 5 BC.'[34]

Here we have another example of the application of modern
scientific investigation to the question of ancient portents. In
their article the astronomers give revised astronomical
calculations to show that the conjunction of Saturn and Jupiter,
which had previously been thought to be the Star of Bethlehem,
was not sufficiently striking at the time, as the planets were too
far apart: 'Thus it is clear that the conjunctions were
unspectacular, the planets never coming closer than approximately two apparent lunar diameters and so there is no
possibility that the two planets could be close enough to appear
to merge together to form a single, bright object.'

Let us hope that such serious and methodical examinations of
historical portents continue, whether for the propounding of
new theories or the exploding of old ones. But let us always
realize that ancient man's observations must be treated with
respect, and our ancestors do not deserve ridicule.

So we see, looking especially at the question of the comets and
disease, that affinities thought to have been entirely mystical
(comets and pestilences appearing to have no causal connection)
may after all be related in ways that are quite simple. It was just
difficult to figure it out. It merely *seemed* impossible. Long
experience had appeared to teach early men that there was some
connection. They 'knew' it. But how to *explain* it? In the years
ahead, there will certainly be more examples of modern scientific
theories being put forward to explain 'mystical' phenomena. Our
minds are lagging behind the phenomena. Progress is slow, but it
is happening.

Ancient man was conscious of affinities of many kinds, as we
have seen. He knew that many phenomena were similar or
seemed to share qualities, or were related by signs or appearances. Attempts were made to systematize such relationships.

The Greek philosopher Proclus (AD 410–85) in his treatise 'Upon Sacrifice and Magic' – which is preserved only in the Latin translation of Marsilio Ficino done in Florence during the Renaissance from a now-lost Greek manuscript – describes the way in which 'the ancient priests' (evidently he means centuries or millennia before his time) set about this problem:

> In the same manner as lovers gradually advance from that beauty which is apparent in sensible forms, to that which is divine; so the ancient priests, when they considered that there was a certain alliance and sympathy in natural things to each other, and of things manifest to occult powers, and by this means discovered that all things subsist in all, they fabricated a sacred science from this mutual sympathy and similarity.[35]

Theories of affinities spreading themselves throughout nature came to prominence especially during and after the Renaissance. The leading exponent of such theories in the sixteenth century was the physician Paracelsus. He was succeeded by the religious mystic Jacob Boehme (1575–1624). Boehme wrote a book entitled *The Signature of All Things* (*Signatura Rerum*), which was published in 1621, not long before his death, in which Boehme's creed is summed up in this saying: 'The whole outward visible world with all its being is a signature, or figure of the inward spiritual world . . .'[36]

This Doctrine of Signatures, as it is called, has antecedents in the Platonic philosophers. Proclus (fifth century AD, mentioned earlier) says:

> Thus the sun-stone, by its golden rays, imitates those of the sun; but the stone called the eye of heaven, or of the sun, has a figure similar to the pupil of an eye, and a ray shines from the middle of the pupil. Thus too the lunar stone, which has a figure similar to the moon when horned . . . So that all things are full of divine natures . . . some things turn round (and follow) the revolutions of the sun, and others . . .

imitate the solar rays, as the palm and date: some of the fiery nature of the sun, as the laurel ... Hence the authors of the ancient priesthood ... saw that some simple substances possessed a divine property . . . of which they were participants.[37]

Proclus gives an example to illustrate how things participate in the divine nature:

Thus if a piece of paper is heated, and afterwards placed near a lamp, though it does not touch the fire, the paper will suddenly be inflamed ... the procession of fire in the paper aptly represents the presence of divine light, to that nature which is capable of its reception ... the inflammation of the paper may be compared to ... the illumination of material natures, which are afterwards carried upwards like the fire of the paper.[38]

He speaks of the lotus flower, sacred to the ancient Egyptians:

... the lotus before the rising of the sun, folds its leaves into itself, but gradually expands them on its rising: unfolding them in proportion to the sun's ascent to the zenith; but as gradually contracting them as that luminary descends to the west. Hence this plant by the expansion and contraction of its leaves appears no less to honour the sun than men by the gesture of their eye-lids, and the motion of their lips. But this imitation and certain participation of supernal light is not visible only in plants, which possess but a vestige of life, but likewise in particular stones.[39]

I have never seen any account of the Doctrine of Signatures which traced its origins back this far. There are many accounts of the Doctrine as it existed in much later times, and most of them concern the extraordinary individual whose full name is in itself so incredible: Philippus Aureolus Theophrastus Bombastus Paracelsus von Hohenheim, better known simply as Paracelsus;

born 1493, died 1541 (aged only 48). This preposterous personality is well described by one of his names: Bombastus. Maybe that would suit him better than Paracelsus. But I do not intend by any means to deride his amazing intellectual attainments, his courage, or what he managed to accomplish in medicine and philosophy. In evaluating him the historian of science, George Sarton, found that he could not ignore his life and its extreme vicissitudes:

> He then resumed his vagrant life, never staying as long as a year in a single place. At the age of 35 he found himself a kind of outcast, and his rejection by society caused him to become more truculent and abusive than ever, thus aggravating his social disgrace. In spite of poverty and insecurity he wrote a great many books, but he was unable to obtain publication for most of them; even when the public censors permitted it, academic and medical intrigues were strong enough to stop the printing. [After all, he was *at variance with established theories*.] The worst period of poverty seems to have been the years 1531 to 1534. At the end of it he reached Innsbruck in rags and was soon driven out. His reaction to such contumely was increased contempt for the medical education and practice of his day.[40]

Paracelsus was incapable of tact. He seemed to love fighting orthodox opinion more than anything else, including getting on with his work. He had allowed himself to become obsessed with the stupidity and viciousness of those who opposed him – the injustices he suffered, compounded by poverty and even near-starvation, distorted his perspective. He held theories of medicine which differed drastically from the orthodoxy of his day, so much so that the entire medical establishment was quite genuinely threatened, for ideas are more powerful than armies. But Paracelsus combined these theories with a violent hatred of the vested interests of the orthodox. He taunted them continually: he threw Avicenna's *Canon of Medicine* into a St John's Day bonfire just to irritate them. He insisted on lecturing

to his university students at Basle in German rather than in Latin.
Sarton comments:

> It is possible that having been brought up in a mining
> environment instead of an academic one he could not do
> otherwise, but this was a final provocation to his colleagues.
> It was much as if a medical professor of today should lecture
> in thieves' argot. Moreover, it was a betrayal of professional
> secrecy. Latin was the esoteric language used to prevent the
> dissemination of learning to people who were deemed
> unworthy of it . . .[41]

Paracelsus used the Greek word *chaos* to describe different
kinds of air. His disciple van Helmont changed this word into the
form *gas*, and that is the origin of that word in the meaning it has
come to have for us today. There are many instances one could
cite of the formative influence of Paracelsus in the history of
science. But we are not considering most of his accomplishments.
Here we must restrict ourselves to his theory of the Doctrine of
Signatures, and related matters.

A Greek philosopher much earlier than Proclus, who was the
friend and teacher of the Emperor Julian, in a work entitled *On
the Mysteries of the Egyptians, Chaldaeans, and Assyrians*,
describes the manner in which divine sympathies are meant to
operate:

> A divine nature, therefore, whether it is allotted certain parts
> of the universe, such as heaven or earth, or sacred cities and
> regions, or certain groves, or sacred statues, externally
> illuminates all these, in the same manner as the sun
> externally irradiates all things with his rays . . . the solar
> light is present with the air in an unmingled manner . . .
> [which] is manifest from no light being left in the air [after
> the sun has set] . . . though heat is still present [when the sun
> has gone] . . . thus also the light of the Gods illuminates . . .
> [and] proceeds through all beings. . . . But this light is
> everywhere one and the same whole . . . [although] through

an all perfect power it fills all things. ... Hence the world
causes all things to be in each other, and to tend to each
other, makes the end of one thing to coalesce with the
beginning of another ... [42]

Iamblichus continues to describe his elaborate system, and
then comes to the question of futurity: How is it possible to have
a knowledge of future events? The physical world of change and
decay he refers to as the realm of 'becoming to be'. Prophecy, he
says:

> ... is not, however, one of the things which have their
> existence in becoming to be ... nor is it invented and
> devised as something useful for the purposes of life, nor in
> short, is it a human work, but is divine and supernatural,
> and is supernally sent to us from the heavens. It is also
> unbegotten and eternal ... the principle of divination ...
> neither originates from bodies, nor from the passions [of]
> bodies ... nor from any human apparatus. ... But neither
> does it originate from a certain art, externally acquired ...
> it pertains to the Gods, and is imparted by them; it is also
> affected by works, or signs . . . divine spectacles and
> scientific theorems ... the prophetic power of the Gods ...
> is wholly everywhere present with the natures which are
> capable of receiving it. It likewise externally illuminates
> and fills all things, pervades through all the elements,
> comprehends earth and air, fire and water, and leaves
> nothing destitute of itself, neither animals nor any of the
> productions of nature, but imparts from itself a certain
> portion of foreknowledge, to some things in a greater, and
> to others in a less, degree. Moreover, existing itself prior to
> all things, by its own separate nature, it becomes sufficient
> to fill all things, so far as each is able to partake of it. [43]

He says later:

As, therefore, the Gods generate all things through forms, in a similar manner they signify all things through signs, impressed as it were by a seal . . . from divine portents . . . the Gods, therefore, produce the signs . . . through nature. . . . But these signs symbolically premanifest the decrees of divinity and of futurity, as Heraclitus says: 'neither speaking nor concealing, but signifying' . . .[44]

The tradition of the mystery religions of the Middle East, and this Greek Platonic tradition that drew upon them, envisaged a divine efflux which permeated all things, resulting in a true unity of all. This, they imagined, was the cause of prophecy. God's light (which was 'supreme' light, not physical light) extended through physical bodies as if they were not there, illuminating them 'externally' both within and without. The emphasis on the 'external' was so as to make clear that the divine light was not mixing with matter but merely illuminating it. It was considered essential to make the distinction, lest the divine light be thought of as capable of admixture with matter, which it was not. This theory, in fact, has much in common with the now-discredited nineteenth-century theory of a universal aether.

Discussions of the Doctrine of Signatures today are to be found occasionally in books on herbs. One such author tells us:

In accordance with Hermetic tradition Paracelsus was convinced that human life was mysteriously bound up with that of the universe. . . . It is an inescapable fact that many of the herbal remedies still prescribed were first discovered because someone took the trouble to read the botanical signature believed to have been left by a providential nature. Our friend the lesser celandine does, after all, cure haemorrhoids, although whether this is because of or despite the pile-like nodules on its root is anybody's guess. And the wild pansy [generally known as heartsease], blessed with tiny heart-shaped leaves, really does cure valvular disorders of the heart. There are many more examples to be found, but those readers who are interested can find them for themselves. While doing so, they may take care to note that even [Giambattista] della Porta's extension of the Doctrine to the actual site favoured by wild plants can be justified by a host of examples. Take the willow tree, for instance, which because it grows in damp places was assumed to provide a cure for rheumatism, a condition aggravated, if not caused, by a damp atmosphere. In accordance with the Doctrine, willow bark was duly prescribed for the easing of rheumatic pain, and, curiously, it worked. But still more curious is that when modern science deigned to take an interest in the willow, it discovered a substance to which it gave the name of salicin [Latin *salix* means 'willow'], once an important stand-by in the treatment of rheumatic fever. The same substance plays its part too in the history of aspirin [acetylsalicylic acid], undoubtedly one of the safest and most efficient painkillers yet discovered.

By now the Doctrine of Signatures is an historical curiosity, but we all have reason to feel glad it had its day.[45]

The Doctrine of Signatures was particularly important to the alchemists, and Paracelsus was prominent as an alchemist himself. In one of the best historical surveys of alchemy we read: 'The alchemists attached great importance to the doctrine of signatures, a quaint conception which received universal credence throughout the alchemical era.'[46]

Elias Ashmole, the seventeenth-century intellectual after whom the Ashmolean Museum in Oxford is named, wrote: 'Nor are these remarkable *Signatures* made and described by Chaunce, for there is a certaine Providence which leades on all things to their end, and which makes nothing but to some purpose ...'[47] This might just as well have been written by Iamblichus, so similar are the sentiments.

Here is how Paracelsus describes in his own words the principles involved in the Doctrine of Signatures:

I have reflected a great deal upon the magical powers of the soul of man, and I have discovered a great many secrets in

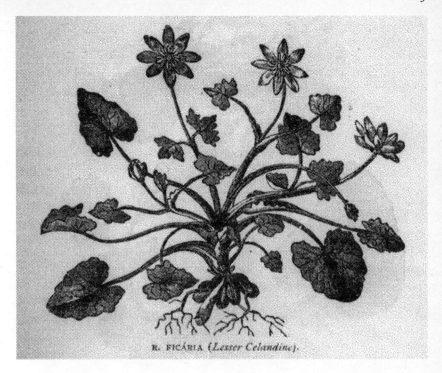

R. FICÁRIA (*Lesser Celandine*).

Figure 28: Lesser Celandine, the tiny herb which was said to cure haemorrhoids. According to the Doctrine of Signatures this was because it had pile-like nodules on its root, and there was thus an affinity between the plant and the ailment. From the Rev. C. A. Johns's Flowers of the Field, *1911*

Nature, and I will tell you that he only can be a true physician who has acquired this power ... The soul does not perceive the external or internal construction of herbs and roots, but it intuitively perceives their powers and virtues, and recognizes at once their *signatum* [sign or signature].

This signatum (or signature) is a certain organic vital activity, giving to each natural object (in contradistinction to artificially made objects) a certain similarity with a certain condition produced by disease, and through which health may be restored in specific diseases in the diseased part. This signatum is often expressed even in the exterior

form of things, and by observing that form we may learn
something in regard to their interior qualities. . . . We see
that the internal character of a man is often expressed in his
exterior appearance, even in the manner of his walking and
in the sound of his voice. Likewise a hidden character of
things is to a certain extent expressed in their outward
forms. As long as man remained in a natural state, he
recognized the signatures of things and knew their true
character; but the more he diverged from the path of
Nature, and the more his mind became captivated by illusive
external appearance, the more this power became lost.[48]

An even more critical account of man's alienation from nature
occurs in another passage written by Paracelsus:

All natural forms bear their signatures, which indicate their
true nature. Minerals, vegetables, and animals remain true
to their nature, and their forms indicate their character.
Man, who has become unnatural, is the only being whose
character belies his form, because, while his character may
have changed into that of an animal, his form has retained
the human shape. If such men could re-enter the *Limbus* [the
spiritual matrix] of Nature and be born again in forms
which correspond to their true nature; and if this should
take place, many of our Pharisees, strutting about in scarlet
coats and pretending to be benefactors of mankind, while
they in reality care for nothing but for the gratification of
their ambition and lusts, would be born in the shape of
monkeys, camels, and buffaloes.[49]

Personally, I think that is rather hard on the monkeys, camels,
and buffaloes.

In leaving our subject of portents, we should just take a last
look at the subject from the point of view of politics and power.
Obviously, the observation and interpretation of portents on
countless occasions concerned political and military affairs in
antiquity, and it takes little imagination to think of it. But one

scholar has come up with a most astounding aspect of the 'politics of portents' which is so unusual and amusing that I thought I ought to mention it, as few people will have encountered the rather obscure book which contains this information. As a matter of fact, the information comes from the Ph.D. thesis of a Swedish scholar named Hans Bielenstein published in 1953 in Göteborg, Sweden, apparently privately.[50] The four people to whom it is dedicated include Allyn Rickett, under whom I once studied Chinese literature at university.

The thesis is entitled *The Restoration of the Han Dynasty*, and it concerns the history of China two thousand years ago. The Early Han Dynasty existed between 207 BC and AD 9. Later, the Han Dynasty was restored in AD 25 and it lasted then until AD 220 and was known as the Later Han Dynasty. The period in between was when the ruling Liu family lost power, and the usurper Wang Mang took over the country and styled himself Emperor. Eventually he was overthrown and the Liu family regained the Empire. I am very keen on the Han period of Chinese history and I have a considerable collection of original rubbings of the tomb carvings of this period. They are extraordinarily beautiful and I only wish I had enough spare wall space to hang them all and gaze at them in the awe which they fully deserve. But I do unroll them and shiver with delight when I can.

In his thesis, Bielenstein considers the question of portents from a unique point of view. He is trying to discover how popular or unpopular Wang Mang may have been during his rule, since many of the records of it were lost after the Han Restoration. Here is the fascinating passage from Bielenstein:

Wang Mang ascended the throne in AD 9. He was killed in AD 23. From AD 10 to 19 not a single attempt was undertaken to overthrow him. This indicates that whatever the ruling class might have thought about Wang Mang's reforms, it was still to its advantage to remain obedient, and even the Liu clan for one decade abstained from revolts. Hence, if the gentry harboured resentment against the emperor, these feelings were not strong enough to call forth insurrection. ... It would be welcome if this picture of Wang Mang's reign could be corroborated. One way of doing this is furnished by the portents recorded in Wang Mang's rule ... the high officials had a means of criticizing the emperor and his government indirectly by memorializing [sending in official reports of] the occurrence of unnatural phenomena. These phenomena were regarded as portents, warning from Heaven of bad rule, and hence the officials in question could not be punished for drawing attention to them. As a rule, the officials memorialized real events. Only when no unnatural phenomenon was at hand did the temptation arise of inventing a portent, if the reasons for criticism seemed strong enough. In this way, during the rule of the Empress, née Lü, (187–180 BC) an eclipse was memorialized which actually had never occurred. However,

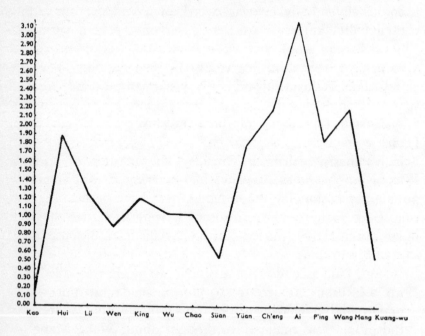

Figure 29: The number of portents reported each year during the reign of Wang Mang in China. From Hans Bielenstein's Restoration of the Han Dynasty

it was a dangerous thing to do, because if such a fraud was detected, the culprit could be fairly sure of his execution. In case unnatural phenomena were lacking, it was therefore more sensible to manufacture a 'portent' rather than only

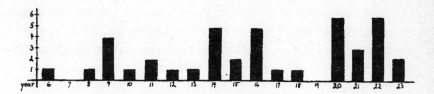

Figure 30: The total number of recorded portents (except eclipses) per year for each reign during the Han Dynasty in China. From Hans Bielenstein's Restoration of the Han Dynasty

pretend that it had occurred. To this category probably belong the frequent 'visitations of fire' in different parts of the imperial palaces.

From the average number of portents per year for each successive reign it is possible to see the strength of the indirect criticism directed against the various emperors. . . .[51]

Bielenstein has actually produced graphs to show this! In Figure 29 is a graph showing the number of portents reported during the reign of Wang Mang, to show the years in which Wang Mang was popular and when he was not. And in Figure 30 is a graph showing the numbers of portents (excluding real eclipses) reported for a series of emperors, to compare which ones were liked with those which were disliked. As Bielenstein says of this graph:

. . . the curve reveals the strength of the indirect criticism expressed by the high dignitaries during each reign. . . . Indeed, the curve reveals the stability of government under the successive emperors. The more criticism there was expressed, the more the machinery of state creaked in its operation.[52]

So this is an aspect of portents that many people may never have thought of! What would they think at the White House or Number Ten Downing Street, I wonder, if, instead of mail complaining about political decisions, a lot of letters started coming in from the public reporting the births of two-headed calves and fictitious eclipses? Or even more to the point, what would the president or the prime minister think if the memos from members of their cabinets took the form of warnings about the economy because a new comet had appeared in the sky?

There are times, surely, when we would all be tempted to invent an eclipse if that is what it might take to change a government policy!

SIX

DIVINATION BY ENTRAILS

> '. . . the whole Etruscan nation has gone stark
> mad on the subject of entrails.'
>
> *Cicero*, On Divination, *1, 18, 35*

Anyone who has closely studied the cultures of ancient Greece, Rome, the Etruscans or, especially, Babylonia and Assyria, will inevitably have come across the curious subject of divination by entrails. This form of divination is perhaps the least understood of all today, and yet it was the leading form of divination in all of those cultures for thousands of years, its importance far exceeding that of astrology. In the history of humanity, it can truly be said that divination by entrails has had a foremost place. Not only was it central to these ancient Mediterranean cultures, but the millennia of its continuance, with the constancy of its principles over all that time, make it a genuine phenomenon of the ages. It is still practised in a rudimentary way by primitive people today. While religious beliefs changed, while rites and worship drastically altered, over countless centuries, divination by entrails persisted.

Divination by entrails is known as *extispicy,* from the Latin *exta,* 'entrails', and *specere,* 'to view'. (It takes some practice to be able to pronounce it without getting your tongue twisted. The accent is on the second syllable.) One of the greatest scholars of extispicy was the late Dr Morris Jastrow Jr. He puts it in some perspective when he writes: 'We thus [have] an uninterrupted chain of Babylonian influence, embracing Etruscans, Greeks, and

Romans, as well as Hittites.'[1] And before the spread of this Babylonian influence:

> . . . it was because of the perfection of [the priests'] elaborate system that the rite managed to survive throughout the phases of culture through which the Babylonians and Assyrians in the course of many centuries passed. From the earliest period down to the days of the last king of Babylonia, [it] continued in force as the official method of divining the future; and while other methods were also resorted to, none equalled in importance and scope the system of divination through the liver.[2]

Another noted scholar, Dr C. J. Gadd, makes the point that extispicy took precedence over astrology:

> If it is impossible to decide which was the older of these two 'sciences', it is at least certain that inquiry by the entrails was in higher esteem at an early, even prehistoric period. . . . The first alleged astrological omen relates to Sargon. . . . Despite the evidence that, in the late Assyrian kingdom, the heavens were as anxiously scanned as the entrails, all the indications are that until then astrology had been quite a subordinate factor in the conclusions which kings drew from natural data as to the will of the gods.[3]

What was at the bottom of this strange practice? At a casual glance it seems total madness. Were the ancients out of their minds? Who would want to plunge his hands into the steaming innards of a freshly killed animal, pull out some of its organs, and study them with intense scrutiny? And more important, what possible connection could this disgusting activity be supposed to have with predicting the future? Was fate to be read in such a bloody place?

There is probably no better way to appreciate the chasm separating the ancient from the modern mind than by exploring this subject. For there are perfectly sensible answers to be found.

The point is that the ancients sought them in a different way from the way we think reasonable. But their way was strangely rational, and eerily proto-scientific. It was, after all, not for nothing that Morris Jastrow wrote an article about this subject for the *Transactions of the College of Physicians of Philadelphia* entitled 'The Liver in Antiquity and the Beginnings of Anatomy'.[4] Science of a kind was there, but it was turned to ends we may find incredible. No popular account of extispicy seems ever to have been written in English, though there is a semi-popular survey in a French anthology.[5] This, therefore, is an attempt to set down the system and its major implications for the general subject of this book.

I have published two other accounts of this subject in journals. A technical one, which appeared in the *Journal of Cuneiform Studies* in 1982, is reproduced as Appendix 3 to this book. A general survey for medical readers was published in 1995 in the Glaxo-Wellcome medical journal, *Odyssey*.[6]

The main subject of entrail inspection in ancient times was the liver, though other portions of the entrails were also examined. Thus it is the examination of the liver of a sacrificial victim which is portrayed by the Greek historian Plutarch, probably from contemporary evidence, as portending the death of Alexander the Great. Alexander died of fever at Babylon, having been clearly warned not to go there by 'the Chaldaeans' (the Babylonian diviners).

As Plutarch relates:

Just as Alexander was on the point of starting for Babylon, Nearchus who had returned with his fleet up the Euphrates, met him, and informed him that some Chaldaeans had warned Alexander to avoid Babylon. He took no heed of this warning, but went his way. When he drew near the walls he saw many crows flying about and pecking at one another, some of whom fell to the ground close beside him. After this, he heard that Apollodorus, the governor of Babylon, had sacrificed to the gods to know what would happen to Alexander. He sent for Pythagoras [not the philosopher of that name, who lived centuries earlier], the soothsayer, who had conducted the sacrifice, to know if this were true. The soothsayer admitted that it was, on which Alexander inquired what signs he had observed in the sacrifice. Pythagoras answered that the victim's liver lacked one lobe. 'Really!' exclaimed Alexander, 'that is a terrible omen!' He did Pythagoras no harm, but regretted that he had not listened to the warning of Nearchus, and spent most of his time in his camp outside the walls of Babylon, or in boats on the river Euphrates. Many unfavourable omens now depressed his spirit. A tame ass attacked and kicked to death the finest and largest lion that he kept; and one day, as he stripped to play at sport, the young man with whom he played, when it was time to dress again, saw a man sitting on the king's throne, wearing his diadem and royal robe. For a long time this man refused to speak, but at length said that he was a citizen of Messene, named Dionysius, who had been brought to Babylon and imprisoned on some charge or other, and that now the god Serapis had appeared to him, loosed his chains, and had brought him thither, where he had bidden him to put on the king's diadem and robe, seat himself on his throne, and remain silent.

When Alexander heard this, he caused the man to be put to death, according to the advice of his soothsayers; but he himself was much cast down, and feared that the gods had forsaken him: he also grew suspicious of his friends. Above all, he feared Antipater and his sons, one of whom, Iolas, was his chief cup-bearer, while the other, Cassander, had but recently arrived from Greece, and as he had been trained in the Greek fashion, and had never seen any Oriental customs before, he burst into a loud, insolent laugh, when he saw some of the natives doing homage to Alexander. Alexander was very angry, and seizing him by the hair with both hands, beat his head against the wall.[7]

This splendid evocation of the decline of Alexander's character, and of the seedy, omen-riddled last days of his life before the fatal fever, is confirmed by the account given by the historian Arrian, who also stresses the importance of the liver's lack of a lobe, and the demoralizing effect of this fact on Alexander.[8] The liver inspection offered the opportunity to send Alexander into the self-induced decline which his own guilty conscience required. Alexander became enraged when, for example, Cassander refused to worship him and in a rage smashed Cassander's head against a wall. Alexander wanted to be treated as a god, and pretended to himself that he was a god. But in his heart of hearts he knew that Cassander's laughter was justified. He knew also that his old teacher Aristotle was ridiculing his present pretensions to divinity, and he could not endure the feelings of guilt which these sensible people back in Greece were arousing in him. Above all, he knew that he had succumbed to vanity, that he had betrayed what was best in his own character. Hence his increasing resort to meaningless acts of violence, his drunken fits of rage, and, finally, his sinking into a superstitious torpor and a terror of omens. He succumbed to the portents in a spell of self-destructive gloom. He had lost all his bearings, and is a terrible witness to the maxim that those whom the gods would destroy they first make mad. And the defective liver in a sacrificial animal was truly an omen.

An interesting account is preserved of a disaster which befell the two Roman consuls who were trying to defeat the invading Carthaginian general Hannibal. Rome was at that time ruled by two elected consuls whose term of office lasted for a year. The two at this time were Marcellus and Crispinus. Liver divination is again central to the story:

> The Romans were surprised at Hannibal, that, having had the first choice of so excellent a position as this, he had not occupied it, but left it to the enemy. ... Now Marcellus determined to ride forward with a few horsemen and reconnoitre it, so he sent for a soothsayer and offered sacrifice. When the first victim was slain, the soothsayer showed him that the liver had no head [the term used by the Romans for the protruding lobe known anatomically as the

processus pyramidalis). On sacrificing for the second time
the head appeared of unusual size, while all the other organs
were excellent, and this seemed to set at rest the fear which
had been caused by the former. Yet the soothsayers said that
they were even more disturbed and alarmed at this; for when
after very bad and menacing victims unusually excellent
ones appear, the sudden change is itself suspicious. But 'Not
fire, not walls of iron can hinder fate', as Pindar says.
Marcellus rode forth with his colleague Crispinus and his
son, who was military tribune, in all two hundred and
twenty horsemen. . . . On the overhanging crest of the woody
hill, a man, unseen by the Romans, was watching their
army. He signalled to the men in ambush what was going
on, so that they permitted Marcellus to ride close to them,
and then suddenly burst out upon him, and surrounding his
little force on all sides . . . Marcellus was pierced through the
side with a lance. . . . Crispinus, after a few days, died of his
wounds. Such a misfortune as this, losing both consuls in
one battle, never before befell the Romans.

Hannibal heard of the fate of all the rest with indifference,
but when he was told that Marcellus had fallen he himself
hastened to the place and stood for a long time beside the
corpse, admiring its strength and beauty. He made no
boastful speech, and showed no joy in his countenance, as a
man who had slain a troublesome and dangerous enemy,
but, wondering at the strangeness of his ending, he drew the
ring from the dead man's finger, and had the corpse decently
attired and burned.[9]

Yet another tragedy is recorded as having been foretold by the
missing lobe of a liver in a sacrificial victim. This time the
incident concerns Pyrrhus, the fierce king of the Molossians, of
whom Plutarch says: 'The appearance of Pyrrhus was more
calculated to strike terror into the beholder than to impress him
with an idea of the dignity which becomes a king. He had not a
number of separate teeth, but one continuous bone in his upper
jaw, with only slight lines showing the divisions between the

teeth.'[10] From his successes in battle Pyrrhus came to be known as 'The Eagle'. Here is how the liver omens forewarned him of a disaster:

These reinforcements piqued Pyrrhus into making several more attempts to take the city, in which however he was repulsed and wounded. He now retired, and began to plunder the country, professing his intention to winter there. But no man can resist his destiny. ... Areus occupied the most difficult of the passes on the road with an ambuscade, and attacked the Gauls and Molossians who formed the rearguard. Pyrrhus had been warned by his soothsayers that the livers of the victims lacked one lobe, which portended the loss of his relatives, but at this crisis the disorder and confusion into which his army was thrown by the ambush made him forget the omen, and order his son Ptolemy to take his guards and go to the help of the rearguard, while he himself hurried his main body on through the defile. When Ptolemy came up a fierce battle took place. The flower of the Spartan army, led by Eualkus, engaged with the troops immediately around Ptolemy, and while they fought, a Cretan named Oryssus, a native of Aptera, running forward on the flank, struck the young man, who was fighting bravely, with a javelin, and killed him. His fall caused his troops to retreat. ... Pyrrhus himself, who had just heard of the death of his son, in an agony of grief now ordered the Molossian cavalry to charge them. He was the first to ride among the Spartans, and terribly avenged his son by cutting them down. Pyrrhus in battle was always a terrific figure, whom none dared to resist, but on this occasion he surpassed himself in courage and fury. ... [He] fell from his horse, and, fighting henceforth on foot, slew all the chosen band commanded by Eualkus. This was a severe loss to Sparta, incurred as it was unnecessarily, after the war was really over, from the desire of the generals to distinguish themselves.[11]

These stories have been given at some length in order to show that liver divination was taken very seriously, and many more such examples could be cited, from a variety of sources. But lest the reader think that these might perhaps be exceptional, isolated incidents, we shall briefly skim over a single, extended history. The reader should note how successive incidents of entrail divination form a continuous background to the events of the story.

One of the best-known stories from antiquity is the extraordinary *Anabasis* of Xenophon. This amazing tale, written by an eyewitness, is more like a Hollywood epic than a classical history. Xenophon himself was one of the most interesting personalities in ancient Greece. Cicero, three hundred years later, exclaims of him: 'What a man he was!'[12] He was an aristocratic Athenian, who as a young man had been a disciple of Socrates. But Xenophon, though quite close to Socrates and dependent upon him for advice, was not himself a philosopher. He was a restless young man who thirsted for adventure. And adventure he was to find aplenty!

A friend of Xenophon, named Proxenus, then aged about thirty, had been appointed a general for a mercenary Greek force under Cyrus, the younger brother of the Persian king. Proxenus did not know the true purpose of the force, but he enthusiastically wrote to Xenophon in Athens and in effect said, 'Come on over! I can probably get you a commission as an officer and it will be great fun.' Xenophon was very excited and went to Socrates to ask whether he should go. Socrates was not in favour, and insisted that Xenophon go and enquire of the Oracle of Delphi about the matter. But Xenophon phrased his enquiry in such a way that the Oracle could hardly advise him not to go, and so off he went to Persia to seek adventure. When he got there it turned out that the real purpose of the force was to enable Cyrus to march on the main Persian army and seize power from his brother in a military coup. Largely because they did not wish to lose face and appear afraid, the Greeks reluctantly followed Cyrus on this madcap mission. Xenophon went along, still in the status of mere onlooker and friend to Proxenus. Over the next year and three months, Xenophon was to be involved in some of the most dramatic and hair-raising episodes ever recorded in history, and was to march an astonishing 3360 miles. We cannot go into the details of his fantastic adventures here, but we shall briefly survey the incidents where extispicy obtrudes into his narrative in a major way, in sequential order, and marked by the numbers which can identify the location in the text for those who wish to consult the work directly[13] (Xenophon wrote the book under a pseudonym, which is why he refers to himself in the third person):

I, 8, 14–15: Cyrus, riding by at a moderate distance from his army, surveyed from thence both the lines, looking as well towards the enemy as to his own men. Xenophon, an Athenian, perceiving him from the Grecian line, rode up to meet him, and inquired whether he had any commands; when Cyrus stopped his horse, and told him, and desired him to tell everybody, that the entrails and the appearances of the sacrificial victims were favourable.

II, 2, 3–4: But afterwards, when the sun was setting, having assembled the generals and captains, [Clearchus the commander] spoke as follows: 'My friends, when I offered a sacrifice with reference to marching against the King, the signs of the victims were not favourable, and indeed it was with good cause that they were not so; for as I now learn, there is between us and the King the River Tigris, a navigable river, which we could not cross without vessels; and vessels we have none. Yet it is not possible for us to remain here; for we have no means of procuring provisions. But for going to the friends of Cyrus [who had been killed, and whose rebellion had collapsed, leaving the Greeks stranded in the middle of Asia surrounded by millions of unfriendly people and by hostile armies], the sacrifices were extremely favourable. We must accordingly proceed thus . . .

The Greek generals attempted to parley with the Persian king for permission to march unmolested back to Greece, though even the coast was some hundreds of miles away. But the Persian king seized the Greek generals who were his guests at the conference, tortured them savagely, and put them all to death. This left several thousand Greek mercenary soldiers leaderless. One Greek captain staggered back from the Persian camp, his stomach slit open, holding his intestines in his hands, and managed to warn his fellows of what had happened. Xenophon's friend, the young general Proxenus, was among the dead. The entire Greek force fell into despair. They did not even bother to light their fires, but spent the night lying wherever they were, in fear of what the morrow might bring, when they would probably all be massacred. Xenophon too lay down in a torpor, in the state of shock common to them all. Eventually, he drifted off briefly to sleep and had an alarming dream which woke him and caused him to think clearly. He realized that he must organize a new leadership, and rally the forces to defend themselves. He sought out whatever officers were left and called a conference. He persuaded them to appoint replacements for the slain officers, to prepare their defences and plan their escape. He himself was appointed general in place of Proxenus. For the rest of the tale, Xenophon is the leading figure in the saga, as he successfully manages to get back home to Greece from this seemingly impossible situation. His account is riddled with constant consultations of the entrails of animals, which are consulted to guide almost his every action:

> V, 2, 9: . . . it seemed impossible to bring off the first part without the loss of many lives, and the captains were of opinion that they might take the place. Xenophon accordingly yielded to their judgement, placing some reliance, at the same time, on the sacrifices; for the augurs had signified that there would be an action, and that the result of the excursion would be favourable.

> V, 4, 22: Thus they rested for that day. On the next, when

they had sacrificed, and found favourable omens, and had taken their breakfast, they formed themselves in columns . . . and marched forward. . . .

V, 6, 27–9: Xenophon was in consequence obliged to rise and speak as follows: 'I sacrifice, as you see, soldiers, to the best of my ability, both for you and for myself, in order that I may say, and think, and do such things as may be most honourable and advantageous for both yourselves and me; and I was just now sacrificing about this very consideration, whether it would be better to speak and treat with you on this subject, or not to touch on the point at all. Silanus the augur informed me, what was the most important particular, that the victims were favourable, but added (for he knew that I was not unskilled in such matters, from being constantly present at the sacrifices), that some fraud and treachery was indicated against me by the sacrifices, as being conscious, in fact, that he himself was treacherously proposing to slander me to you; for he it was that spread the report that I intended to carry this scheme into execution without gaining your consent.'

VI, 1, 22–32: While he was perplexed as to his decision, it appeared to him [Xenophon] that the best thing he could do was to lay the matter before the gods; and having placed by the altar two victims, he sacrificed to Jupiter the King, who had been pointed out to him as the god that he should consult, by the oracle of Delphi; and he thought that he had received from the god the dream which he saw, when he was first appointed to take charge of the army. . . . While he was sacrificing on the present occasion, the god clearly directed him [by the signs in the entrails] not to seek any additional command, and not to accept it if they should elect him. . . . The army came together, and all suggested that one commander should be chosen; and, as it was resolved to do so, they proposed Xenophon. As it seemed evident too that they would elect him, if anyone should put it to the vote, he rose up and spoke as follows [gracefully declining the proposal]. . . . After he had thus spoken, far more persons than before rose up, and said that he ought to take upon him the command . . . the assembly showed by a murmur their opinion that [they agreed]. . . . Xenophon, seeing that there was need of something additional on his part, came forward and said, 'But, my fellow-soldiers, that you may be fully informed on this subject, I swear to you by all the gods and goddesses, that after I learned your inclination, I sought to ascertain by sacrifice whether it would be better for you to confer this command on me, and for me to undertake it, or not; and they gave me such manifest signs, by the [entrails of the] victims, that even an untaught person would have understood that I ought to decline the command.' They in consequence chose Cheirisophus. . . .

VI, 2, 15: Xenophon was also inclined to detach himself from the army altogether, and to sail away; but as he was sacrificing to Hercules the Conductor, and consulting him whether it would be better and more advisable to march in company with such of the soldiers as remained, or to take leave of them, the god signified by the victims that he should march with them.

VI, 4, 9–25: . . . they longed to return in safety to Greece. When the day after their meeting together began to dawn, Xenophon offered sacrifice with regard to an expedition, for it was necessary to lead out the troops to get provisions; and he was also thinking of burying the dead . . . Cheirisophus was now dead. . . . Xenophon stood up and said: 'It seems evident, fellow-soldiers, that we must pursue our journey by land, for we have no ships; and it is necessary for us to set out at once, for there are no provisions for us if we remain. We will therefore,' he continued, 'offer sacrifice; and you must prepare yourselves, if ever you did so, to fight; for the enemy have recovered their spirit.' The generals then offered sacrifice; and Arexion the Arcadian assisted as augur; for

Silanus of Ambracia had already fled, having hired a vessel from Heraclea. They sacrificed with a view to their departure, but the victims were not favourable. This day, therefore, they rested. Some had the boldness to say that Xenophon, from a desire to settle a colony in the place, had prevailed on the augur to say that the victims were unfavourable to their departure. Xenophon in consequence, having made a proclamation that whoever wished might be present at a sacrifice on the morrow, and having given notice also, that if there was any augur among the soldiers, he should attend to inspect the victims with them, made another sacrifice, and a great number of persons were present at it; but though they sacrificed again three times with reference to their departure, the victims were still unfavourable to it. The soldiers were on this account extremely uneasy, for the provisions which they had brought with them were exhausted, and there was no place near for them to purchase any. They therefore held another meeting, and Xenophon said, 'The victims, as you see, fellow-soldiers, are not yet favourable for our departure; and I see that you are in want of provisions. It seems to me necessary, therefore, to offer sacrifice with regard to this matter.' Here someone rose up and said, 'It is with good reason, indeed, that the victims are unfavourable; for, as I heard from a person belonging to a vessel that came in yesterday by accident, Cleander, the governor of Byzantium, is on the point of coming hither with transport vessels and galleys.' In consequence they all resolved to stay. But it was necessary to go out for provisions; and to this end sacrifice was again offered three times, but the victims were still unfavourable.

The soldiers now came to Xenophon's tent, and told him that they had no provisions. He however replied, that he would not lead them out while the victims were adverse. The next day sacrifice was offered again, and, as all were concerned, almost the whole army crowded around the sacrifice; and the victims fell short. Still the generals did not lead out the troops, but called them, however, together; and

Xenophon said, 'Perhaps the enemy may be assembled in a body, and it may be necessary for us to fight: if, therefore, leaving our baggage in the strong part of the ground, we march out prepared for battle, the victims may possibly prove more favourable to us.' But the soldiers, on hearing this observation, cried out that it was of no use to lead them to the part that he mentioned, but that they ought to sacrifice without delay. Sheep were no longer to be had, but they bought an ox that was yoked to a wagon, and sacrificed it; and Xenophon begged Cleanor the Arcadian to be on the alert if anything in the sacrifice should appear propitious. [Xenophon appears to have absented himself, to dispel suspicions.] But not even on this occasion were the signs favourable.

Neon was now general in the place of Cheirisophus, and when he saw how the men were suffering from want of food, was desirous to get them relief, and having found a man of Heraclea, who said that he knew of some villages in the neighbourhood, from which it might be possible to procure provisions, he made proclamation that whoever was willing might go out to get a supply as there would be a guide to conduct them. A party accordingly proceeded from the camp, to the number of two thousand, equipped with spears, leather bags, sacks, and other things for holding what they might find. But when they had reached the villages, and had dispersed themselves to plunder, the cavalry of Pharnabazus fell upon them ... cutting off not less than five hundred of the Greeks; the rest fled to the mountain.

One of those who escaped immediately carried the news of the occurrence to the camp; and Xenophon, as the victims had not been propitious that day, took an ox from a wagon (for there were no other cattle) and, after sacrificing it, went forth to give aid, with all the other soldiers not above thirty years of age. They brought off the rest of the party, and returned to camp.

The reader may by now be astounded at the reliance placed upon divination by entrails. Here we find an army of several thousand men literally starving to death and, because the entrails indicate that it is unwise to stray from the camp in search of food, they sit still! Furthermore, they use up their few remaining beasts of burden in order to have a further supply of entrails to examine. (The meat would be eaten, and only small portions burnt on an altar to the gods. This being the standard practice, at least the animals provided some food for a few men and were not simply wasted.) The story continues with more examination of entrails the next day:

> VI, 5, 1–3: A vessel meanwhile had arrived from Heraclea, bringing barley-meal, cattle and wine. Xenophon, rising early, had sacrificed with reference to an excursion, and in the first victim the omens were favourable. Just as the sacrifice came to a conclusion, Arexion of Parrhasis, the augur, saw a lucky eagle, and encouraged Xenophon to lead forth. The men, therefore, crossing the trench, ranged themselves under arms; and the heralds made proclamation that the soldiers, after taking their dinner, should march out equipped for battle. . . .

Later the same day:

> VI, 5, 8: As soon as the enemy perceived the Greeks, they halted at the distance of about fifteen stadia. Upon this Arexion, the augur of the Greeks, immediately offered sacrifice, and in the very first victim the omens were favourable.

The Greeks were hemmed in and had no choice but to fight their way out. As he marshalled the forces, Xenophon gave the soldiers this encouragement:

> VI, 5, 21–32: 'It is better therefore for us to fight now, when we have dined, than tomorrow, when we may be without a dinner. The sacrifices, soldiers, are favourable, the omens

encouraging, the victims most auspicious. Let us march against the foe.' ... Singing the paean, therefore, they immediately advanced upon them; and the enemy withdrew ... the enemy's horse fled down the hill. ...

The Greeks, having put the Persians to ignominious flight by their charge, were safe for a time. Much later in the story, Xenophon is still sacrificing as energetically as ever:

VII, 6, 44: Many other persons, too, sent notice to Xenophon that he had been made an object of calumny, and ought to be upon his guard. Xenophon, on receiving these communications, took two victims and sacrificed to Jupiter, consulting him whether it would be better for him to stay with Seuthes on the conditions that he proposed, or to go away with the army. Jupiter signified to him that he had better depart.

VII, 8, 1–5: From hence they sailed across to Lampsacus, when Euclides the augur [an old friend] ... came to meet Xenophon. He congratulated Xenophon on having returned safe, and asked him how much gold he had. [Expecting him to be loaded down with booty.] Xenophon assured him, with an oath, that he should not have enough for his expenses in travelling home, unless he sold his horse, and what he had about him. Euclides did not believe him. But after the people of Lampsacus had sent presents to Xenophon, and Xenophon was proceeding to sacrifice to Apollo, he made Euclides stand beside him at the time, who, on inspecting the victims, said that he was now convinced he had no money. [This is from seeing signs in the entrails.] 'But I observe,' he added, 'that even if money should ever be likely to come to you, there will be some obstacle, and, if no other, that you will be an obstacle to yourself' [through Xenophon's generosity and the fact that he was always giving everything away]. Xenophon assented to the justice of the observation.

VII, 8, 8–23: . . . they reached Pergamus in Mysia. Here Xenophon was hospitably received by [a woman named] Hellas . . . She told him that Asidates, a Persian, resided in the plain, and said that if he would attack him in the night with three hundred men, he might take him, with his wife and children, and his wealth, which was considerable. To guide him in the enterprise, she sent her own cousin . . . and Xenophon . . . offered sacrifice. Basias, an augur from Elis, who was present, said that the omens were extremely favourable, and that the man might easily be captured. After supper, accordingly, he set out, taking with him such of the captains as were most attached to him, and had constantly been his friends, in order that he might do them a service. [They were to share the plunder, as they were all completely penniless.] . . . Asidates, hearing that Xenophon had again sacrificed with a view to an attack upon him, and that he would return with all his strength, went out to encamp in some villages lying close under the little town of Parthenium. Here Xenophon with his troop came round upon him, and captured himself, his wife and children, his horses, and all his property; and thus the omens of the first sacrifice were verified. They then marched back to Pergamus; and here Xenophon had no cause to complain of the god; for the Spartans, the captains, the rest of the generals, and the soldiers, all agreed that he should receive select portions of the spoil [just taken from Asidates], consisting of horses, oxen, and other things; so that he was now even able to help out a friend if need should be.

Thus ended Xenophon's adventures in Asia, and he returned to Athens to write histories and works of literature most of which have survived. The vivid and colourful character of Xenophon, though he died about 354 BC as an old man in his eighties, is still very much with us. But many of those who read him today, finding his endless sacrificing and divination incomprehensible, are tempted to gloss over that side of his life. But it is our duty to note the key remark he makes at the end of his tale: 'thus the omens of the sacrifice were verified'.

Figure 31: A drawing from an ancient Greek vase showing a warrior inspecting a sacrificial liver presented to him by a boy. Hanging down in front of the liver is its processus pyramidalis, *its most important part. The reason why the warrior is dressed in full armour with his spear, is that the entrails were consulted before going into battle*

At every step of his perilous way, Xenophon thought himself to be in communication with divine beings or higher powers. He was never 'alone'. And the surprising thing is that when the omens told him to sit still and starve, and finally another general disregarded them, a disaster occurred to the other general. At nearly every turn, Xenophon's omens were proved right. This must have reinforced his almost fanatical belief in them. And lest we dismiss Xenophon as a foolish, idiotic and superstitious man who was not typical of his age, let us remember that not one of the soldiers is recorded as having objected to sitting and starving because divination by entrails was ridiculous superstition. They did not say, 'This is nonsense, I'm going out to get something to eat.' The quarrel was not over the fact that omens were sought, and should be obeyed, but over whether the omens were being interpreted correctly and honestly. They didn't say 'let's disregard the omens', they said 'try another animal'! They were willing to indulge in a little pious cheating, but it seems never to have occurred to them to question the process itself. And the fact that Xenophon makes meticulous note of his divination results indicates quite clearly that he must have expected his readers to be sympathetic to him, that they would believe him to have acted wisely and with proper reverence to the divine will, the very embodiment of religious piety and a sage circumspection.

To put this matter in its final perspective, let us return for a moment to Socrates. Xenophon wrote a long and vivid description of Socrates, entitled *Memorabilia*. It is generally thought to be more reliable and accurate as a portrait of the actual historical Socrates than the often misleading writings of Plato, Socrates's most famous pupil. We now appreciate what must also have been evident in antiquity, that Plato distorted most of his accounts of Socrates for reasons to do with the philosophical discourses in which they appear. This is only really inconvenient if one wishes to know more about Socrates the individual. For Plato's purposes, Socrates was idealized and turned into a convenient mouthpiece for Plato himself. But people feel that they know what Socrates *should be like,* and they therefore disregard much of the information about him which is to be found in Xenophon. There is a very large scholarly 'vested interest' in holding up Socrates as a model of the thoroughly rational and 'enlightened' thinker, a kind of freak 'modern' man who just happened to live in ancient Athens. Many of us wish Socrates to have been a forerunner of ourselves, holding views similar to our own, and we will not willingly be deprived of this illusion. This inevitably involves casting aspersions on Xenophon's account, and purging Socrates of all 'primitive' and 'demeaning' beliefs which no Man of the Enlightenment could possibly hold. One brief example will suffice. Here is the deathbed scene of Socrates, as recorded by Plato:

> By this time [the hemlock poison] had reached somewhere about the pit of the stomach, when he removed the covering which he had put over his face, and uttered his final words: 'Crito, we owe a cock to Asclepius; pray do not forget to pay the debt.' 'It shall be done,' said Crito. 'Is there anything else you can think of?' There was no reply to this question; a moment afterwards he shuddered; the attendant uncovered his face again, and his gaze had become rigid; seeing which Crito closed his mouth and eyes.
>
> And that, Echecrates, was the end of our friend, the finest man – so we should say – of all whom we came to know in his generation; the wisest too, and the most righteous.[14]

I well remember Glenn Morrow, my professor at university, who was a distinguished translator of Plato and later of Proclus, saying to us in a lecture that why Socrates should ask his friend to remember to offer a cock to Asclepius was a complete mystery. My professor said: 'This may have been some private reference or have some special significance to Plato. It makes no sense, and no one understands it.' The translator Hackforth actually said in a footnote: '. . . it is of course idle to speculate about the occasion for the vow.'[15] For years I unquestioningly accepted their views. But when I began to acquire an understanding of the ancient Greek medical and religious traditions, of the kind never taught in universities because it does not 'fit' the carefully structured curriculum, it became immediately obvious to me that Socrates's remark made complete sense *in the context of a man of his time,* and for that reason no doubt had to be classified as a 'mystery' in today's blinkered classicism. The answer is so simple as to be absurd: it was the custom to sacrifice a cock to Asclepius, the god of medicine, in return for a cure of an illness. Socrates was merely making a wry remark about the efficacy of the hemlock, and how it was 'curing' him by setting him free of his body altogether. But what disturbs the 'rationalistic' picture of Socrates was that he could be so inconveniently atavistic as to refer to such a practice even in a joke. Or perhaps the professor under whom I studied Plato (though otherwise I have a very high opinion of him) really did not know about the custom of sacrificing to Asclepius, so studiously had he avoided any contamination of his studies with primitive superstition and so certain was he that Socrates would disdain such things as well. Even the scholar Wilamowitz dismissed the idea just suggested (which I am by no means the first to suggest) with the contemptuous remark: 'Life is not an illness.'[16] In other words, the question is settled in his mind by his own opinion, and whatever Socrates may have thought is irrelevant.

My old professor maintained that Socrates was condemned to death by a hysterical assembly of Athenians for not believing in their superstitions and for daring to be an enlightened modern man in barbarous times. It is true that Socrates was condemned for impiety because he thought for himself and was a challenge to complacency and orthodox thinking. But the notion that he died because he refused to believe the religious and divinatory superstitions of his time is contradicted by countless facts, and will not stand up to serious scrutiny. Before taking our leave of Xenophon, let us read some telling remarks he makes about Socrates at the very beginning of his *Memorabilia*:

I have often wondered by what arguments the accusers of Socrates persuaded the Athenians that he deserved death from the state; for the indictment against him was to this effect: 'Socrates offends against the laws in not paying respect to those gods whom the city respects, and introducing other new deities; he also offends against the laws in corrupting the youth.'

In the first place, that he did not respect the gods whom the city respects, what proof did they bring? For he was seen frequently sacrificing at home, and frequently on the public altars of the city; nor was it unknown that he used divination; as it was a common subject of talk that 'Socrates used to say that the divinity instructed him'; and it was from this circumstance, indeed, that they seem chiefly to have derived the charge of introducing new deities. He however introduced nothing newer than those who, practising divination, consult auguries, voices, omens, and sacrifices; for they do not imagine that birds ... know what is advantageous for those seeking presages, but that the gods, by their means, signify what will be so; and such was the opinion that Socrates entertained. Most people say that they are diverted from an object, or prompted to it, by birds ... but Socrates spoke as he thought, for he said that it was the divinity that was his monitor. He also told many of his friends to do certain things, and not to do others, intimating that the divinity had forewarned him; and advantage attended those who obeyed his suggestions, but repentance, those who disregarded them.[17]

Therefore, we see that Socrates was as convinced of divinatory procedures and their efficacy as Xenophon himself. And that Socrates recognized the process of divination by entrails which Xenophon so frequently describes in his own adventures. For Xenophon explicitly says that Socrates not only frequently offered sacrifice, but followed as well the customary inspection and practised divination from, among other things, 'omens and sacrifices' (though Socrates's most frequent divine promptings occurred from hunches which he said were the whisperings of a guardian spirit which he called his 'daemon'). Socrates must therefore have had at least a routine familiarity with liver divination; and it is to be suspected that if Socrates had in any way disapproved of extispicy, Xenophon would not have relied on it with such fervour.

This suffices for our examination of liver divination and extispicy among the Greeks, for we are not making a thorough survey, but merely examining a sample of the evidence. The reader now has an idea of how divination by entrails fitted into the life of a typical person in classical times, thanks to the superb documentation of the Greek and Roman historians. We have far less such material in the records surviving from Babylonian and Assyrian times, and no native accounts at all of Etruscan history as such. But those three cultures were the ones where liver divination had the greatest importance, and in fact the diviners by entrails amongst the Romans were invariably Etruscans brought down from the north – the region now known as Tuscany – for this purpose.

But let us now turn to the ancient Assyrian culture. The diviner by entrails was known as a *baru*. What were his ritual and his incantations as he prepared to examine the liver of a sheep or lamb for the king? Fortunately, we have a precise written record. An Assyrian king named Esarhaddon (he became king in 680 BC) was hard pressed by a rebellion in the northeast led by a man named Kashtariti. These rebels included the Medes, the Manneans and the Gimirrites. The king was extremely worried and asked his official *baru* to examine the entrails of a sacrificial victim in order to determine what the future would hold. But the questions asked of the gods had to be framed very carefully in order to cover all possibilities and close any 'loopholes' for fate. Also, it was just as well to restrict the questions to some reasonably limited period of time, for this would result in a more precise answer. Thus, it was decided to ask the gods in this case only what would happen in the crucial next hundred days. The *baru* begins by addressing the sun-god Shamash:

> O Shamash! Great Lord! As I ask thee, do thou in true mercy answer me.
> From this day, the third of this month of Iyar to the

Figure 32: The augurs and diviners by entrails amongst the Romans were mostly Etruscans, from the region now known as Tuscany. Although there is little textual material surviving about the Etruscan religion and culture, a vast number of Etruscan metal mirrors survive, the backs of which bear ornate, elaborate, and brilliant artistic depictions of Etruscan ideas. One such metal mirror, preserved in the Etruscan Museum at the Vatican in Rome, shows the traditional Greek diviner Chalchas (his name inscribed in Etruscan characters beside his figure) as a winged figure bending over a table of entrails of a sacrificial animal, and closely examining a liver, which he holds in his left hand, as with his right hand he traces the fissures and signs on its surface. Behind him, on the ground, is a pitcher with which he would perform sacred ablutions after the inspection. His left foot rests on a rounded stone, which may be meant to represent an oracular omphalos. (This drawing is reproduced from Plate 223 of Edouard Gerhard's large and magnificent collection of Etruscan mirror designs, Etruskische Spiegel, 1884–97)

eleventh day of the month of Ab of this year, a period of one hundred days and one hundred nights. . . . Will within this period Kashtariti, together with his soldiers, will the army of the Gimirrites, the army of the Medes, will the army of the Manneans, or will any enemy whatsoever succeed in carrying out their plan, whether by strategy or by main force, whether by the force of weapons of war and fight or by the axe, whether by a breach made with machines of war and battering rams, or by hunger, whether by the power residing in the name of a god or goddess, whether in a friendly way or by friendly grace, or by any strategic device, will these aforementioned, as many as are required to take a city, actually capture the city Kishassu, penetrate into the interior of that same city Kishassu, will their hands lay hold of that same city Kishassu, so that it falls into their power? Thy great divine power knows it.

The capture of that same city, Kishassu, through any enemy whatsoever, within the specified period, is it definitely ordained by thy great and divine will, oh Shamash? Will it actually come to pass?[18]

It will immediately be appreciated by any readers who are in the legal profession that the enquiry is drawn up with all the care of a legal document. The fickleness of the gods was much dreaded, and legion are the examples in antiquity of answers to divination or oracular pronouncements which were seen in retrospect to have been literally true but utterly misleading in almost a perverse sense, as if the gods were sporting with humanity. Thus an attempt is made to cover every contingency and ensure that the gods were left no opening to fool or mislead the enquirers. The *baru* took no chances. It was a case of pitting his ingenuity against the devious perversity of a bored and restless god who was always trying to make life more interesting for himself by stirring up trouble on earth. So the *baru* official required a great deal of legalistic skill. He was in a very real sense a barrister in the divine courts, or at least a lawyer defending his clients' interests in the impossible task of trying to make contracts with the gods. For in the king's mind, there would be some such contract as the following: 'I, Esarhaddon, king of Assyria, do contract to supply the god Shamash with so many hundred pounds of incense, and so many cattle and sheep on his altars amounting to not less than so many dollars' worth per annum not later than the day and month above said and in return the god Shamash or his assigns shall be kind to me.'

Now the *baru* continues his appeal to Shamash with this prayer:

> See to it that after the specified period no catastrophe may come to pass,
> See to it that whatever the enemies may plan may not be carried out,
> See to it that they shall not make a slaughter or take plunder,
> And whether the decision of this day be good or bad, ward off a stormy day with pouring rain.[19]

This last plea was an element of flattery, since if it poured with rain, the god Shamash, the Sun, would be obscured from sight and they would not be able to admire his beauty. One imagines that the kings and emperors of the period themselves required such nauseating toadying so that it came to be applied to the gods as well.

Now the *baru* comes to the sacrificial lamb and intones the following ritual prayer, which must have been standardized over a very long period:

> Prevent anything unclean from defiling the place of inspection,
> Prevent the lamb of thy divinity, which is to be inspected, from being imperfect and unfit,
> Guard him who takes hold of the body of the lamb, who is clothed in the proper sacrificial dress, from having eaten, drunk, or handled anything unclean,
> Make his hand steady, guard the seer, thy servant, from

speaking a word without proper care or in haste.[20]

It is from similar origins to this that the preoccupation with ritual purity in Greece must have been derived. Not many people who admire the supposed 'liberality' and 'the enlightenment' of classical Athens take the trouble to note that a sacrifice offered there to the gods by anyone who was 'impure' (a relative term!) was punishable by death.[21] And of this the philosopher Plato heartily approved. In his own prescription for an ideal state, he said of such a person: 'Let him be punished with death, for his sacrifice is impure.'[22] Acknowledgement of this fact is one of many correctives which might be administered to those romantics who talk about how splendidly and thoroughly rational the 'divine' Plato was, or how free and idyllic his contemporaries must have been. The step from the barbarity of the Assyrian empire to the glories of the Acropolis was not as great as is sometimes made to appear. There is far more continuity in human development than we sometimes like to admit. The sale of Indulgences against which Luther ranted was not so far removed from the legalizing formulations of the *baru* who sought to tie the hands of the gods with clever wording.

The *baru* official now repeats his query in summary form, to make doubly sure that the party of the first part has fully taken in what the party of the second part has written into the contract:

> I ask thee, o Shamash! Great Lord! Whether from the third day of this month of Iyar, up to the eleventh of the month of Ab of this year, Kashtariti with his soldiers, whether the Gimirrites, the Manneans, the Medes, or whether any enemy whatsoever will take the said city of Kishassu, enter that said city, Kishassu, seize said city, Kishassu, with their hands, obtain it in their power.[23]

Now the lamb was slaughtered and laid out on its back on the altar in front of the *baru* (see Figure 33, page 226). Assistants would no doubt be struggling to cut away the fleece and pull it from the stomach to allow access to the *baru's* knife. As this took place, the *baru,* standing with his knife ready, perhaps raised to the sun, would intone:

> By virtue of this sacrificial lamb, arise and grant true mercy, favourable conditions of the parts of the animal, a declaration favourable and beneficial be ordained by this great divinity. Grant that this may come to pass. To thy great divinity, oh Shamash! Great Lord! May my enquiry be pleasing, and may an oracle be sent in answer![24]

We do not know the answer to King Esarhaddon's enquiry, because the *barus* were not historians, and quite commonly omitted the responses and the outcome of events. The records which we have are often detailed accounts of the questions asked, and the anatomical findings upon inspection of the entrails. But any *baru* would know immediately upon seeing a summary of the entrail examination what the oracular verdict was – these would be an 'open book' to him, so standardized was the 'science'.

What then, were these *barus* continually looking for, or hoping not to find? The first thing to be said is that animal entrails vary far more than one might imagine. In itself this must have fascinated early man. And especially it would have struck him that totally unexpected diseases could be seen upon examination of the entrails. An animal may look perfectly healthy but in fact be dying of cancer of the liver. Young lambs are especially deceptive, for they may not have had time to develop exterior symptoms of an illness which would be all too plain upon examination of their entrails. These facts will inevitably have come to seem to have an arcane significance to early man no less than to modern pathologists! After all, when we want to find the cause of death of a person it is customary to perform an autopsy. And what is that, if not an examination of the entrails?

Even in ancient times, acute minds at their most sceptical were not slow to recognize the obvious advantages to examining entrails from the practical point of view. Architects will be familiar with the name Vitruvius, for he wrote a treatise *On Architecture*, early in the reign of the Roman emperor Augustus, towards the end of the first century BC. This work has been aptly described as 'a complete guide to Hellenistic and Roman town planning, architecture and civil engineering.'[25] In Book One there is an entire chapter on the subject 'Of the Choice of Healthy Situations', in which he sternly lectures us on the siting of cities and buildings so as to minimize the adverse effects on our bodies. He then describes how various animals differ from one another in their constitutions, and then says:

Since, then, we are thus constantly reminded by our senses that the bodies of animals are so constituted and we have mentioned that they suffer and die from want or super-abundance of any one element not suitable to their temperament, surely much circumspection should be used in the choice of a temperate and healthy site for a city. The precepts of the ancients, in this respect, should be ever observed. They always, after sacrifice, carefully inspected the livers of those animals that fed on the spot whereon the city was to be built, or whereon an encampment was to be placed. If the livers were diseased and livid, they tried others, in order to ascertain whether accident or disease was the cause of the imperfection; but if the greater part of the experiments proved, by the sound and healthy appearance of the livers, that the water and food on the spot were wholesome, they selected it for the garrison. If the reverse, they inferred, as in the case of cattle, so in that of the human body, the water and food of such a place would become pestiferous; and they therefore abandoned it in search of another, valuing health above all other considerations. That the salubrity of a tract of land is discovered by the pastures of food which it furnishes is sufficiently clear, from certain qualities of the lands in Crete situate in the vicinity of the river Pothereus, which lie between the two states of Knossos and Gortyna. There are pasturages on each side of this river: the cattle, however, pastured on the Knossian side, when opened are found with their spleens perfect; whilst those on the opposite side, nearer to Gortyna, retain no appearance of a spleen. Physicians, in their endeavours to account for this singular circumstance, discovered a species of herb eaten by the cattle, whose property was that of diminishing the spleen. Hence arose the use of the herb which the Cretans call *asplenōs,* as a cure for those affected with enlarged spleen.[26]

Here we see that liver divination may occasionally have led to medical progress, though of an obscure kind. The knowledge of anatomy obtained in liver divination was truly extensive and impressive. But, unlike modern scientific anatomy, its systematizations were designed not to explain how the organism worked, but rather as clues in the microcosm of what was supposed to be happening in the macrocosm. How the microcosm worked was relatively insignificant to the minds of the ancients as compared to their larger concerns with fate. Perhaps that was why modern science in that sphere never developed in ancient times: it was a pursuit which seemed futile to people obsessed with prophecy. It is essential to realize, therefore, that the body was studied not for its own sake but merely for what use it was supposed to have in connection with divination. Extispicy was thus the exact opposite of a 'pure' science. It was an applied science with a vengeance, one which could be said to have been based on an insane premise, and fantastically elaborated with the relentless logic of a paranoiac.

However, before we come down too hard against the ancients, let us pause for a moment to notice an anomalous modern scientific fact which has so far not been discussed in a popular publication. In 1963, Dr H. von Mayersbach of Nijmegen, in Holland, demonstrated by a series of experiments with rats that the circadian ('near-daily') rhythm of glycogen content of the livers of female rats varied considerably in a way which dramatically matched fluctuations in the earth's magnetic field strength.[27] Different points on the earth's surface have different magnetic field strengths, and the healthy or unhealthy qualities of these places vary accordingly. The liver is a sensitive organ, and it registers these changes.

Can it be that the ancients somehow instinctively knew or 'sensed' this, or that there may be actual visible changes in the organ of the liver over a prolonged period due to the earth's magnetic variations, which the ancients actually saw with their own eyes? These are possibilities which cannot be entirely dismissed. No one in modern times has ever looked for such anatomical variations related to magnetic field conditions. One reason why this search has never been made is that only in the past few years has the sensitivity of organisms to the earth's magnetic field been established. Our preconceptions had blinded us to this fact, for we had thought such sensitivity was physically impossible. I wish to draw the reader's attention to a new word which will become increasingly familiar in the years to come: 'magnetoecology'. This word, a contraction of 'magnetic ecology', has been coined to describe the study of differing habitats and environments from the point of view of their magnetic properties. The plain fact is that some regions which are 'magnetically anomalous' are extremely unhealthy places: crops do not thrive on some farms; people are depressed, even to the point of suicide; livestock and humans alike may be continually prone to disease. This is not a mystical notion, but one which has been scientifically demonstrated with complete rigour. The subject has extremely serious economic implications. If the public were properly informed and accepted the magnetoecological evaluation of certain localities, incalculable changes would occur in property values, which would make millionaires out of paupers, and paupers out of millionaires almost overnight, with far-reaching environmental implications. Some day such information will be widely and easily available. When it is, we may see the modern equivalent of ancient extispicy. Experimental (no longer 'sacrificial') animals will be routinely cut open and examined in autopsies (no longer 'divination') and their entrails will indeed decide the fate of a given area, in a method thoroughly analogous to that described by Vitruvius – by offering scientific evidence of the anomalies of the earth's magnetic field in that area, and its effect on organisms. I do not believe that the ancients were as ignorant of magnetic phenomena as we sometimes assume. I have already published evidence of this and will publish more.[28]

But let us return to the entrails themselves, and what it was about them that the ancient priests were scrutinizing so intently. We have seen that they differ widely in their appearance. But so what? It was at this very point of questioning that I was forced to do the only obvious thing: if I wanted to know what divination by entrails was like, I had to do it myself. And I did! I happened to know someone whose family owned a number of butchers' shops in the West Country of England, where I live. They have a small private abattoir where they slaughter their own lambs, sheep and cattle. Fewer and fewer of these private abattoirs exist these days, and so this was a most convenient coincidence.

Furthermore, I was told that I was welcome to come along to watch, and to inspect the entrails if I so desired. I took advantage of this kind offer, but only after I had made a fairly intensive literary search and study of the ancient liver anatomies, made various drawings and diagrams and collected those that were already published in obscure learned journals. Knowing what I was looking for, but not knowing quite what to expect when faced with 'the real thing', I went along for my introduction to the business of killing and butchering of carcasses for food.

The fact that the meat we eat comes from the dead bodies of animals who are murdered for our pleasure at the table is one of the major sources of guilt today. Most of us know vegetarians who enter into an emotional discourse about 'killing poor dumb animals' for food, saying that the sight of blood makes them faint, and that the idea of eating meat is disgusting. Such diatribes discomfit meat-eaters because the slaughtering of animals has been so severely repressed in our consciousness that we prefer not to think about it. It touches our fear of death, our squeamishness about physical facts and about dead bodies in general, our panic at the sight of blood, our terror of needles which go beneath the skin, our horror of pain, and so forth. It is important to refer in passing to these aspects of the question because our emotional reactions to these things severely cloud our understanding whenever the subject of slaughtering animals for food comes up. In my opinion, it is a sign of neurosis that the slaughtering of animals is repressed and banned from ordinary conversation.

I am now about to describe what happens in an abattoir. I advise the faint-hearted or squeamish reader to skip the next few pages.

People who shop only in supermarkets will probably not be familiar with butchers' shops. In supermarkets meat is wrapped in cellophane, and you cannot smell it. Every effort is made to make the meat seem cleaner and more sanitized even than the vegetables. But for those people (and I am thinking primarily of people outside America) who in their daily lives have occasion to enter small butchers' shops and buy fresh meat, and where whole carcasses are to be seen hanging on hooks, or bits of them on boards or dripping blood in the corner, the butcher's shop is entirely misleading as a preparation for the abattoir. Butchers' shops smell of dead carcasses. But, surprisingly, this is not true of abattoirs. Since even in England probably less than 1 per cent of the population has ever set foot in an abattoir, it seems important to describe the atmosphere.

First of all, the animals. I carefully observed the expression in the eyes of a bullock who was standing patiently waiting to be killed. Beside him were the butchered carcasses of other bullocks with whom he had romped in the fields. Pieces of them were hanging on hooks in front of him; before his eyes one of them lay cut open. The reek of fresh, warm blood which covered the floor was very strong, and the bullock could not have been insensitive to it. Surely he must have realized what was going to happen to him? Surely he was alarmed at all these signs of mortality, at the sight of his butchered friends? Not at all. He was as complacent and bored as someone waiting at a bus stop. There was not even a slight flicker of fear, no hint of apprehension, and the fact is that he was just not very bright. But that is just it: cattle and sheep are unbelievably stupid. Eventually, one of the workers went up to the bullock with a gun in his hand, and carefully placed it against his forehead. The bullock had not the faintest notion of what was going on. He continued to look around with a blank stare. Then the gun was fired, and he instantly dropped dead. That was that. So much for the supposed suffering of the animals which I had heard so much about from people who have never witnessed it. The essential difference between the butcher's shop and the abattoir is that the abattoir smells of warmth and life, not of coldness and death. This was the most astonishing of the many surprises I experienced. The atmosphere of a slaughter-house is strangely reminiscent of that of a maternity ward. One is a place of death; the other a place of new life – but both are places of warmth, blood, fluids, soft tissues, and bodily transitions. The bodies of the freshly slaughtered animals are quite hot, steam often rises from them when they are cut open, and lambs are after all children under a year old, so that their flesh is soft and gentle. Cutting open the body of a creature which has just been killed and which is of this size brings a disturbing sense of intimacy and familiarity with flesh which almost seems to be still alive, or from which the mysterious qualities of life are ebbing away and not completely gone. The dead and cold meat of butchers' shops bears almost no resemblance to it. The horror one would expect from blood – and it is all over the concrete floor, running down to the drains – is much muted by the fact that it is warm, and has a friendly, natural feel about it. It is not threatening or ominous, which may perhaps explain why the animals seem no more disturbed by it than ewes are disturbed by the smell of each other's afterbirths at the lambing season. A barn in the middle of the night which is full of the smell and atmosphere of ewes lambing, with lambs being born two a minute as if it were a snowstorm of delicate, fleecy little creatures popping into the world, has an air of manifestation, of epiphany, of 'life-force coming in'. The slaughterhouse has a somewhat similar atmosphere of 'life-force ebbing slowly out', a place of exit. But entrances and exits resemble one another in this – that the raw life-force seems somehow closer than usual, less disguised, in fact revealed. One feels closer to what lies under the surface of appearances. Somehow, one feels that one can almost grasp the intangible, but it slips through one's fingers. But its presence is strong, and the elemental smell of warm blood is enhanced by the heat of organic tissues either newly brought to life or newly brought to the end of life. The mother who loves the smell of the baby in her arms would recognize the dead lamb in the abattoir, the proximity of warm flesh, wet, palpitating, and soft. So fragile are the bodies of beasts before they become stiff meat, which is cold and dead.

My butcher friend was extremely accommodating. Every time I asked him to alter his routine in order to follow more closely the ancient practices, he obliged. Lambs which have been killed and had most of the blood drained from them are generally hung up and butchered as they are suspended, which is more convenient and quicker for purposes of removing the fleece and obtaining the desired cuts of meat. But this will not do for the proper inspection of entrails. In Figure 32 we see a ram being stretched out on its back on an altar preparatory to the inspection of its entrails. I asked the butcher to prepare one of the lambs in this way, and he did so. It proved easier than he had imagined.

The fleece is removed from a lamb only with great difficulty. The operation requires considerable strength. The fleece is cut at the stomach, folded back a little, but this is not easy. As soon as a respectable flap is available, it is pounded repeatedly by fist from inside, while the other hand pulls mightily. The tough membranous tissues are not in any way injured by this hard pounding. Finally, the fleece hangs to either side and the stomach is revealed, soft and downy. The ribs are then cut in the middle, and pulled apart. At this point, unless it is a hot day, steam pours out of the interior of the body. The heat of the carcass is most unexpected. I reached inside and put my hand on the heart of this lamb just after it was cut open, and it was as hot as an electric light bulb which has been switched off less than a minute before.

It was considered extremely inauspicious by the ancients if there was any accidental damaging of the crucial organs, so the greatest care had to be taken at every stage of their removal and

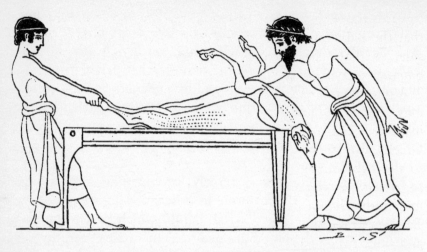

Figure 33: Preparing a sacrificial ram, stripped of its fleece, preparatory to inspection of the entrails by an Etruscan diviner. (From an ancient Roman painting reproduced by Blecher and Bezold, 1905)

handling. It is probable that the first action was to remove the intestines. If this were not done, they would slither around and hinder removal of the set of organs – lungs, heart and liver with gall bladder attached – which lie above them. After the intestines had been set to one side the oesophagus would be cut and the other organs carefully lifted out. The liver had to be most gently handled, especially so that the tissues attaching the gall bladder remained intact. It was considered a terrible omen by the Babylonians if the gall bladder was torn out of the small depression it had made in the liver: 'it portends hostility', says one of the ancient texts, and might even signify the advent of war.

Primary attention was paid to the liver and gall bladder. In order to inspect them properly, they had to be severed from the heart and lungs and laid on a flat surface, the gall bladder lying on top of the liver. The most minute inspection could then be made of the liver, which requires intense scrutiny, since it is so dark. All modern anatomical drawings of the liver lying flat are done with the liver lying so that the gall bladder hangs down towards the observer. But we know from the many ancient texts that the Babylonian priests viewed the liver from the opposite side, so that from their point of view the gall bladder was hanging away from them.

A photograph of a lamb's liver with the gall bladder attached may be seen in Plate 32. This was one of the livers I personally inspected. The most important single feature of the liver to the Greeks, Romans and Etruscans, and one of the most important to the Babylonians, is what is called in modern anatomy the *processus pyramidalis*. The name indicates the shape: it does look rather like a pyramid – a three-sided rather than a four-sided one; thus with its base it forms a tetrahedron. It is not rigid, and flops over unless supported in some way. I took a photograph of one I had propped up (see Plate 33). To the Babylonians this protuberance was known as the *ubānu* ('finger'). I understand that some orthodox Jewish kosher butchers still call it the 'finger' even today, not suspecting that in doing so they preserve a term from their people's Babylonian captivity. The 'finger' is strikingly portrayed in a complete Babylonian terracotta model of a liver dating from *c.* 2000 BC and now in the British Museum, which may be seen in Plate 34. The long, thin organ lying on top of the model is the gall bladder. Both 'finger' and gall bladder are very prominent in Figure 34, which shows an ancient Etruscan liver model, cast in bronze, found in the last century at Piacenza in Italy. We shall return to these models shortly.

The pyramid-shaped protrusion of the liver was known to the Romans as the *caput* or 'head'. As the Roman author Pliny tells us, in describing animal organs: 'The liver is on the right-hand side; it contains what is called the head of the internal organs, which varies a great deal.'[29] This reference to the *processus pyramidalis* as 'the head of the internal organs' implies that it was the chief of them, and this is reinforced by the fact that the 'head' was given the highest divine assignment or sympathy: it was 'dedicated to the hypercosmic gods'.[30] And in divination by the entrails, no omen was more serious than the absence of this 'head', as we have seen in the stories already recounted about

Marcellus and Alexander the Great, and in other such stories to be found in the ancient literature. For instance, this omen portended the assassination of Julius Caesar: 'On the following day there was no head to the liver of the sacrifice. These portents were sent by the immortal gods to Caesar that he might foresee his death . . .'[31]

Figure 34: A drawing of a scene portrayed on the Column of Trajan at Rome, showing the Romans cutting open the belly of a sacrificial ox to examine its entrails. In the centre of the picture, the man with the axe has just slaughtered the ox, and bending down, the diviner is inspecting the entrails. Distinguished senators and perhaps the emperor himself stand nearby awaiting the divinatory results

The reader may very well wonder whether such a major portion of the liver could be missing, or whether an animal lacking it could live. I am assured by veterinarians that a farm animal which is not overstressed by modern intensive rearing techniques (which impose a great strain on the organism) can survive with up to seven-eighths of its liver destroyed by disease. The 'head' may thus easily be missing in a seriously diseased animal, along with most of the rest of the liver. I am told that with very seriously ill animals the liver crumbles and disintegrates within hours of death, whereas a healthy animal's liver will remain intact for many days after death.

The liver takes its position in the body from the support it gets from surrounding organs. It more or less 'floats'. But essentially, the liver is shaped like a very large plano-convex lens. If the lamb were to stand on its hind legs, the convex surface of the liver would be uppermost. The liver when removed from a freshly killed animal is extremely shiny and reflective; but it becomes dull as time elapses. This attribute of the liver was not lost on the ancients: there are many references to it as a 'mirror' in their literature. This led to all sorts of esoteric doctrines, and immeasurably added to the reputation of the liver as an arcane and highly special organ.

Plato gives an extraordinary account of the liver in his discussion of the constitution of the human body in his dialogue *Timaeus*. He says that the gods placed it for its function as a mirror down into the bowels so that it might reflect the thoughts and images of the mind, bringing an improvement to the bestial part of man which is placed in the bottom of his guts. Here is what Plato says:

> The part of the soul which desires meat and drink and the other things of which it has need by reason of the bodily nature, they placed between the midriff and the boundary of the navel, contriving in all this region a sort of manger for the food of the body; and there they bound it down like a wild animal which was chained up with man, and must be nourished if man was to exist. . . . And knowing that this lower principle in man would not comprehend reason, and even if attaining to some degree of perception would never naturally care for rational notions, but that it would be led away by phantoms and visions night and day – to be a remedy for this, God combined it with the liver, and placed it [the liver] in the house of the lower nature, contriving that it should be solid and smooth, and bright and sweet, and should also have a bitter quality, in order that the power of thought, which proceeds from the mind, might be reflected

as in a mirror which receives likenesses of objects and gives back images of them to the sight; and so might strike terror into the desires, when, making use of the bitter part of the liver, to which it is akin, ... [and] when some gentle inspiration of the understanding pictures images of an opposite character, and allays the bile and bitterness ... [and] corrects all things and makes them to be right and smooth and free, and renders the portion of the soul which resides about the liver happy and joyful, enabling it to pass the night in peace, and to practise divination in sleep, inasmuch as it has no share in mind or reason. For the authors of our being placed in the liver the seat of divination. . . . Such is the nature of the liver, which is placed as we have described in order that it may give prophetic intimations. During the life of each individual these intimations are plainer, but after his death the liver becomes blind, and delivers oracles too obscure to be intelligible. The neighbouring organ [the spleen] is situated on the left-hand side, and is constructed with a view of keeping the liver bright and pure – like a napkin, always ready prepared and at hand to clean the mirror.[32]

The statement that the liver 'becomes blind' is probably a reference to the fact that after death the liver quickly becomes dull and ceases to have good mirror-like properties. Plato's remark that the surface of the liver-mirror is wiped by the spleen reminds us that perhaps the ancients did not appreciate that it was the interior tissues of the internal organs which were necessarily the only functioning elements; they evidently believed that the *surface* of the liver had more of a function that anyone today would assume.

To Plato, if the liver acted as a mirror when removed from the animal, then it must be a mirror inside the animal, and reflect images there as well! We must also remember that the entire subject of mirrors was one which in ancient times was, awe-inspiring. I have written at length about optical phenomena in antiquity in my last book, *The Crystal Sun* (Century, London,

2000), where I have also referred to livers as reflecting surfaces and many related matters.

In a culture which was totally separate from most of those which we are considering in this book, the liver may also have been regarded as a mirror. In ancient Mexico, the Toltec civilization (which was adopted by the conquering Aztecs not long before the arrival of Cortes) had a major god and Lord of the Night whose name means 'Smoking Mirror' (the name in Nahuatl is Tezcatlipoca). Since the Toltec and Aztec cultures practised human sacrifice, and would rip the still-beating hearts out of victims cut open by sharp obsidian knives on the tops of temple platforms, they would presumably be quite familiar with livers as well as hearts. Thus the mirror-like properties of the fresh liver would not be unknown to them, nor the fact that the liver ripped from a man just cut open would smoke with steam: it would be, literally, a 'smoking mirror'. Tezcatlipoca's fetish was an obsidian knife – just the knife which was used in the act of human sacrifice. Furthermore, Tezcatlipoca was a 'dark god', and the liver is also dark. Moreover this god's mirror was also specifically described as being a 'black' mirror and sometimes referred to as an 'obsidian' mirror. Obsidian, a shiny, black volcanic glass which occurs in Meso-America, was considered very precious by the Indians of that part of the world. They actually used it to make mirrors; but obsidian mirrors do not smoke. Nor is it easy to think what kind of mirror could possibly smoke, except the liver. And being dark, the liver does resemble an obsidian mirror. Since the liver reflects illnesses more acutely than many other parts of the body, it may not be an accident that 'Maladies, famine and death were the manifestations of Tezcatlipoca's justice'.[33]

A further Toltec tradition may possibly be explained by a liver cult. I am referring to the strange reclining figures carved in stone which are to be found in the city of Tula, and for which no satisfactory explanation has ever been offered. They are called 'the Chacmools'. These enigmatic statues feature a man with a dish of offering held directly over his liver. It is generally assumed that these dishes are meant to be awaiting the offering of human hearts. But they are from the point of view of their size and location more appropriate as receptacles for livers. And a liver placed there would enable a smoking mirror to lie upon the surface of the Chacmool's belly, reflecting the sky. I must emphasize that these are merely hypotheses, and I offer them strictly in that vein. But if they were to be true, they would show that the characteristics of the liver which are so obvious to anyone inspecting entrails were appreciated on another continent, and came similarly to be included in the religious rituals of another culture which was obsessed with entrails, though in a more sinister fashion!

The ancient concept of the liver as a mirror is connected with the belief that it was the seat of the soul. It is not widely appreciated that in ancient cultures not the heart or brain, but the liver, was considered to be the organ in which the soul resided inside the body. Morris Jastrow collected the evidence for this belief in his long essay 'The Liver as the Seat of the Soul'.[34] He has established his point absolutely beyond question, for the evidence is overwhelming. I shall not attempt to summarize his excellent study, to which I refer the curious reader. But in another essay he comments in connection with the mirror-like properties of the liver as follows:

> The life or soul, as the seat of life, in the sacrificial animal, is, therefore, the divine element in the animal, and the god in accepting the animal, which is involved in the act of bringing it as an offering to the god, identifies himself with the animal – becomes, as it were, one with it. The life in the animal is a reflection of his own life, and since the fate of men rests with the gods, if one can succeed in entering into the mind of a god, and thus ascertain what he purposes to do, the key for the solution of the problem as to what the future has in store will have been found. The liver being the center of vitality – the seat of the mind, therefore, as well as of the emotions – it becomes in the case of the sacrificial animal, either directly identical with the mind of the god who accepts the animal, or, at all events, a mirror in which

the god's mind is reflected; or, to use another figure, a watch regulated to be in sympathetic and perfect accord with a second watch. If, therefore, one can read the liver of the sacrificial animal, one enters, as it were, into the workshop of the divine will.[35]

I have found an important and remarkable ancient account of the liver as a mirror by a writer ignored by all previous scholars of liver divination. He is the Jewish writer Philo Judaeus, and the account appears in his obscure treatise 'On Animals Fit for Sacrifice', which he wrote in Greek in the first century AD. Philo lived in Alexandria, is thought to have been a Roman citizen, and his life's work was to try to harmonize the traditions of the Greeks and the Jews. He therefore continually tried to interpret Jewish laws and customs for the Greeks and the Romans, trying to make them compatible with Platonism, and attempting to reconcile the two communities of people. He says:

> . . . the nature of the liver being of a lofty character and very smooth, by reason of its smoothness is looked upon as a very transparent mirror, so that when the mind, retreating from the cares of the day (while the body is lying relaxed in sleep, and while no one of the outward senses is any hindrance or impediment), begins to roll itself about, and to consider the objects of its thought by itself without any interruption, looking into the liver as into a mirror [for Philo no longer accepted that the liver was the actual seat of the soul], it then sees, very clearly and without any alloy, every one of the proper objects of the intellect, and looking round upon all vain idols, and seeing that no disgrace can accrue to it, but taking care to avoid that and to choose the contrary, and being contented and pleased with all that it sees, it by dreams obtains a prophetic sight of the future.[36]

Here we have, clearly expressed, the idea that the liver affords prophetic vision by reflection of the divine. We are now in a position to begin to appreciate what may have seemed extraordinary if we had been told it without explanation: that there is a direct link between divination by entrails and scrying – that is, crystal gazing, or prophesying by staring at pools of ink or into bowls of water. And this in turn connects with the induction of trance in the gazer and trance is compared to dreaming, the liver being the mirror or pool or crystal into which the dreaming soul gazes – a reflecting surface suitably and perfectly placed within the man himself. But since we cannot conveniently cut men open to inspect their livers, animals were used instead, for divination outside of sleep.

Philo, quoted above, refers to the 'head' of the liver and makes some interesting remarks about it. But he calls it the 'lobe' *(ho lobos)*, which was the Greek term for it. He says: 'And the lobe of the liver is the first fruit of the most important of the entrails . . .', which tallies with what we have seen elsewhere about this pyramid-shaped protrusion. It was the one portion of the liver which was laid on the altar by the Jews.[37] This habit obviously came from their familiarity with the traditions of Babylon. However, the Jews were not keen on liver divination, which they certainly knew about. In Ezekiel 21:21 we read: 'For the King of Babylon stood at the parting of the way, at the head of the two ways, to use divination: he made his arrows bright, he consulted with images, he looked in the liver.' Though the Jews disapproved of what the Babylonians did, liver lore left its mark nonetheless in other ways: there can be little doubt that leaving the 'head' or 'finger' of the liver on the altar in Jewish custom has its origins in the great reverence accorded to this part of the organ in Babylonian tradition.

It is an extraordinary fact that the Dogon tribe of Mali in West Africa apparently also place the 'head' of the liver on their altars. The Dogon call the liver *kinne na*, 'the seat of the heart' – in other words 'the organ of the soul'. This is in accord with the wider traditions of the Mediterranean in pre-classical times as elucidated by Jastrow.[38] The Dogon say of the liver specifically that 'it is also the privileged seat of the being's vital force'. A particular small piece of the liver is thrown onto the altar by the Dogon, and it would seem that this must be the *processus pyramidalis;* unfortunately the anthropologists reporting this were not precise about the anatomical details of the liver. However, it is difficult to imagine what else they could be referring to, as the gall bladder is discussed separately and has its own name. It is also interesting that, just as Plato preserved a tradition that the liver was continually wiped clean and purified by the spleen, so the Dogon envisage the function of the spleen in a similar fashion: 'This organ's role is to regulate the "words" cast out by the liver; it is said: "the spleen purifies evil words".'[39] It is even more remarkable that the spleen is now known to have a purifying action. One of its functions is blood filtration, by which bacteria and worn-out red cells are taken out of the blood. This is strangely close to what the Dogon claim for the spleen, since to the Dogon 'words' circulated in the blood! What the Dogon are in effect saying is that the spleen is a blood filter – which indeed it is. But how does a primitive tribe in Africa without modern science know this? Finally the Dogon also describe the liver as 'the mirror of heaven', indicating that they too are aware of its reflecting properties, which they connect with the reflection of the divine quite in the Mediterranean tradition.

Plutarch in the first century AD described some fairly elaborate concepts concerning 'divine illumination' in the esoteric Greek religious tradition, which may be seen in relation to the idea of the liver as reflecting divine images. Connected with these ideas is the concept at that time of 'daemons', which are nothing like 'demons' as they are conceived today. Daemons were 'higher' sorts of souls which were disembodied, and in fact had no need of bodies. They were conceived of as helping the better sort of men, described as 'daemonic' men:

> ... the understanding may be guided by a higher under-
> standing and a divine soul, that lays hold of it from without
> by a touch, which is the way in which it is the nature of
> thought to impinge on thought, just as light produces a
> reflection ... the thoughts of daemons are luminous and
> shed their light on the daemonic man. Their thoughts have

no need of verbs or nouns, which men use as symbols in their communication, and thereby behold mere counterfeits and likenesses of what is present in thought, but are unaware of the originals except for those persons who are illuminated, as I have said, by some special and daemonic radiance . . . just as the sound of sappers' blows (attempting to undermine a fortress) is detected by bronze shields, which re-echo it as it rises from the depths of the earth and strikes them, whereas through everything else it slips unnoticed; so the messages of daemons pass through all other men, but find an echo in those only whose character is untroubled and soul unruffled, the very men in fact we call holy and daemonic. In popular belief, on the other hand, it is only in sleep that men receive inspiration from on high. . . .[40]

Plutarch takes this line of thought even further, and specifically relates it to the liver and entrails in divination, in his essay 'The Oracles at Delphi'.[41] He was High Priest at Delphi and was thoroughly steeped in the esoteric lore of the place, as we have already seen. In this essay he speaks of the first Sibyl who in legend was supposed to have prophesied at Delphi. He paraphrases verses which she is said to have written of herself, and which had presumably been preserved at Delphi (though whether they are actually genuine is another matter):

. . . that even after death she shall not cease from prophesy-ing, but that she shall go round and round in the moon, becoming what is called the face that appears in the moon; while her spirit, mingled with the air, shall be for ever borne onward in voices of presage and portent; and since from her body, transformed within the earth, grass and herbage shall spring, on this shall pasture the creatures reared for the holy sacrifice, and they shall acquire all manner of colours and forms and qualities upon their inward parts, from which shall come for men prognostications of the future.[42]

In another essay, 'On the Apparent Face in the Moon's Orb',[43]

Plutarch carries all this still further. He speaks there of what were known to the ancient Greeks as *eidōla* – prophetic visions or spectres – and says of them: 'Of these *eidōla* the moon is the element: for they are resolved into her substance, like as bodies into earth, of the dead. . . . The daemons do not always pass their time upon the moon, but they come down hither and take charge of oracles; they are present at and assist in the most advanced of the initiation rites. . . .'[44]

In my last book, *The Crystal Sun*, I wrote an entire chapter on the subject of these *eidōla*, which was chapter 6, 'Phantom Visions'[45] In it, I surveyed the use of the concept in the whole of Homer's *Odyssey*, considered the possible Egyptian origins of the concept, and dealt with its treatment by the Greek philosopher Democritus and his successors, the Epicurean School. I also described its implications for ancient theories of optics.

By bringing together these disparate remarks we can begin to discern a remarkable body of tradition of which no coherent single account has survived. The liver is a mirror and reflects the divine; the divine daemons illuminate the liver with their radiance and inspire the daemonic man; the body of the first Sibyl of Delphi was buried in the earth and came up again in the plants, which were eaten by the sacrificial animals (evidently grazing in the area of her tomb, or reputed tomb), which affected the livers and entrails of those animals; visions of the future may be seen in these livers, reflected from divine images in the moon where the daemons live when they are not supervising the operations of oracles and divination.

The connection of entrails with celestial concepts goes much further than this. In Figure 35 we see a drawing of the bronze Etruscan liver model known as the Bronze Liver of Piacenza. This model is extremely important. We know from several textual sources that the Etruscans divided the sky into sixteen regions. These regions are inscribed round the edge of the bronze liver, each being marked with the name of a god. The ancient writer Martianus Capella in his *Marriage of Philology and Mercury* preserves the Etruscan sky-lore, describing the sixteen regions and the gods in them in considerable detail. Martianus's account and the bronze liver have sufficient points in common for the connection between them to have been the subject of an entire book by Dr Carl Thulin, entitled *Die Götter des Martianus Capella und der Bronzeleber von Piacenza* (The Gods of Martianus Capella and the Bronze Liver of Piacenza).[46]

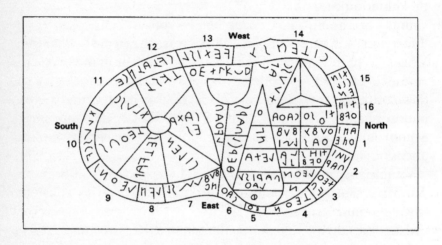

Figure 35: Drawing of the bronze liver of the Etruscans discovered at Piacenza. The view is from above; top right is the three-sided pyramid of the processus pyramidalis; *the long conical shape near the centre represents the gall bladder. The points of the compass associated with the liver are shown N, E, W and S, and the sixteen regions of the sky are numbered in sequence, as they are inscribed around the edge of the liver model*

We see here that the idea of the liver as the mirror of heaven has been carried to extraordinary extremes. On the bronze liver we actually see the heavens depicted! So pronounced are the heavenly aspects of this model that, when it was found and first studied, scholars did not even recognize it as a liver model. The German scholar W. Deecke even had to publish a rather embarrassing public correction of himself in 1882 saying that he had just found out that the object was a liver, and taking back everything he had so far said on the subject.[47]

In 1987, L. B. van der Meer published an entire book about the bronze liver entitled *The Bronze Liver of Piacenza*.[48] He translates all of the Etruscan inscriptions, correcting many misreadings by previous scholars, and discusses the names and natures of the gods. He concludes that the bronze liver was made about 100 BC and was probably an instruction model for Etruscan diviners.

The cosmic symbolism of the spiral colon of the sacrificial animal seems to have been described at some length by Martianus Capella. In Figure 36 we see an anatomical drawing of the colon of a pig, which resembles that of a lamb or sheep, and we can see that it descends in centripetal coils, then retrogrades and rises again in centrifugal coils. The planetary motions, and particularly the motions of the planet Mercury, as seen from the earth, involve forward motion, then turning back, then moving forward again. If charted against a star map, they resemble spiralling patterns. The historians of science De Santillana and Von Dechend have commented on this at length, with diagrams.[49]

I first discussed this subject and published illustrations in a book of mine published in 1976, and reissued in expanded form in 1998.[50] Subsequently, I discussed the matter further at length in notes and commentary to my translation of the *Epic of Gilgamesh*, in my book, *He Who Saw Everything: A Verse Translation of the Epic of Gilgamesh*, in 1991.[51] The planet mercury and the intestines are inextricably linked in the ancient tradition, and these ideas permeate the whole of the *Epic of Gilgamesh*, as I have explained in considerable detail for every relevant passage.

The face of the demon god Humbaba (Huwawa) of the Sumerians and Babylonians, well known from the *Epic of Gilgamesh*, was formed of the convolutions of intestines. This is represented in a famous object in the British Museum (Plate 35). There is another fragmentary Humbaba mask in the British Museum, a photograph of which would be disappointing – but Dr Sidney Smith in 1926 made a reconstruction of its entirety in a drawing.[52]

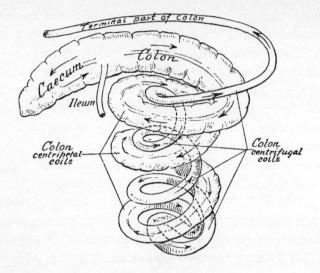

Figure 36: The spiral colon of a pig, from Septimus Sisson's Anatomy of
the Domestic Animals, *showing the spiralling configuration which the
ancients seem to have associated with the planetary motions, particularly
that of the planet Mercury*

Veterinarians have told me that if the spiral colon is cut open,
the contents of each successive spiral winding are dramatically
different both in consistency of material and colour. Martianus
Capella appears to refer to this when the god Mercury ('the
Cyllenian') takes the goddess Virtue on a tour of some cosmic
'rivers' bearing relation to the planetary spheres of heaven,
described as follows:

The Cyllenian also showed to Virtue some rivers flowing
down from heaven which, he said, they had to cross to reach
the god whom they were trying to find. The streams swept
along in multicoloured billows. [The translator here adds in
a footnote: 'The seven rivers represent the seven planets, and
their different colours and other properties derive from this
identification.'] The first stream, a wide and far-spread body
of leaden colour, eddied with a cloudy swirl and its currents
were extremely cold and sluggish. Within it, another one,

like milk ... steady in movement. ... The third one was sulphurous, and with breathless swiftness was twisting. ... The next one was golden. ... Within shone a river purer than amber. ... There were besides two narrower streams hurrying along with a tighter curve inside the others; each of these added a little of its own character to a mixture from other sources as it was blended with the other streams close by. For one, hastening along at an excessive speed, frequently halted and reversed its course. ... .'[53]

There are several reasons for thinking this to be a description of the intestines of a sacrificial animal. First, the fact that there are seven streams each inside the other indicates that these are concentric, as indeed we should expect for orbital paths of planets. But Martianus Capella cannot be speaking directly of the planetary orbits themselves, for he quite specifically held to the heliocentric theory and stated that Mercury and Venus revolved around the sun, not the earth.[54] Therefore, to suggest that these 'streams' are concentric goes against Martianus's own astronomical ideas. Then, the streams are said to blend their characters, implying that they are connected. But, most important of all, Martianus describes the inner 'stream' as hurrying along with a tighter curve inside the others but halting and reversing its course. This is precisely what happens with the innermost coil of lamb or pig intestines.

Furthermore, seven is the standard number of coils in Babylonian extispicy, which has been suggested to be the origin of Etruscan extispicy. In Plate 36 we see a photograph of an object in the Yale Babylonian Collection, dated to c. 600 BC, which portrays perfectly the spiral pattern of a lamb colon laid flat, with seven concentric coils, the innermost turning and spiralling out again, and an 'omen count' of 14. The entire subject of the intestines in ancient extispicy is dealt with at greater length in an article by me (Appendix 3), where I have managed to confirm a translation of a technical term in Babylonian/Assyrian extispicy from examination of lambs in the abattoir, and more importantly, I was able to reconstruct the technique of making the intestinal 'omen count' in a way which fits all the surviving textual evidence.

Plate 37 is a photograph of a lamb's spiral colon (centre of picture) laid out by me in the manner of the ancient extispicy examinations. I believe this pattern of the spiral colon to be the origin of the sacred spirals and spiral mazes in many cultures. For instance, an ancient Stone ball from Glas Towie in Scotland, dated to the third millennium BC, contains several perfect representations of the spiral colons of lambs or pigs. (It is AS 10(7) in the National Museum of Antiquities of Scotland in Edinburgh.) One could collect a vast number of such illustrations from a variety of cultures with little difficulty.

The indentation in the outline of the liver between the two main lobes was known to the Babylonians and Assyrians as the 'Palace Gate'. In Greek it was simply the 'Gate' – and it may be no coincidence that the Greek god Hermes, who is the Roman god Mercury and identified with the planet Mercury, had an epithet in Homeric times of *pylē-dokos,* 'Watcher at the Gate'. For the intestines watch at the gate of the liver, and Hermes/Mercury, and the planet Mercury, were identified with the intestines because of the tight winding of Mercury's orbit in the sky, and especially because he turns and runs again with such sudden twistings, like the central spiral of the colon.[55]

In the notes to my translation of the *Epic of Gilgamesh*, I explain in detail how the references to 'gates', 'doors' and even 'blows', in connection with Hermes/Mercury are astronomical and anatomical references, not merely vague or abstract mythological ones.[56]

But a full elucidation of the cosmic associations between entrails and the planets is not yet possible. Despite the vast labours of Thulin[57] and Deecke,[58] details of Greek, Roman and Etruscan extispicy are still vague. Weinstock has listed in passing the Greek terms for parts of the liver.[59] They bear such colourful names as: God, Dioskuri, Charioteer, Head, Tongues, Nail, Sword, Doors, Table, Hearth, Mirror, Basket, Knot, River and Tomb. But some of these may be inaccurate translations, or at least inapt ones. The Greek word *machaira,* meaning 'sword', for instance, also means 'knife'. An alternative word for the same feature of the liver, according to Suidas, is *spathē*, which can

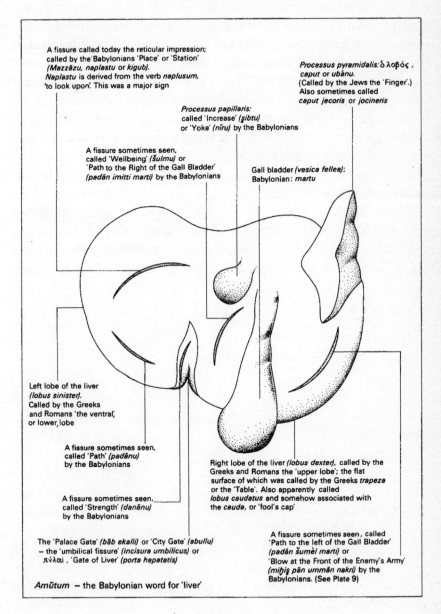

A fissure called today the reticular impression; called by the Babylonians 'Place' or 'Station' *(Mazzāzu, naplastu* or *kigub)*. *Naplastu* is derived from the verb *naplusum,* 'to look upon'. This was a major sign

Processus pyramidalis: ὁ λοβός , *caput* or *ubānu.* (Called by the Jews the 'Finger'.) Also sometimes called *caput jecoris* or *jocineris*

Processus papillaris: called 'Increase' *(ṣibtu)* or 'Yoke' *(nīru)* by the Babylonians

A fissure sometimes seen, called 'Wellbeing' *(šulmu)* or 'Path to the Right of the Gall Bladder' *(padān imitti marti)* by the Babylonians

Gall bladder *(vesica fellea)*; Babylonian: *martu*

Left lobe of the liver *(lobus sinister)*. Called by the Greeks and Romans 'the ventral', or lower, lobe

A fissure sometimes seen, called 'Path' *(padānu)* by the Babylonians

A fissure sometimes seen, called 'Strength' *(danānu)* by the Babylonians

Right lobe of the liver *(lobus dexter)*, called by the Greeks and Romans the 'upper lobe'; the flat surface of which was called by the Greeks *trapeza* or the 'Table'. Also apparently called *lobus caudatus* and somehow associated with the *cauda*, or 'fool's cap'

The 'Palace Gate' *(bāb ekalli)* or 'City Gate' *(abullu)* – the 'umbilical fissure' *(incisura umbilicus)* or πύλαι , 'Gate of Liver' *(porta hepatatis)*

Amūtum – the Babylonian word for 'liver'

A fissure sometimes seen, called 'Path to the left of the Gall Bladder' *(padān šumèl marti)* or 'Blow at the Front of the Enemy's Army' *(miḫiṣ pān ummān nakri)* by the Babylonians. (See Plate 9)

Figure 37

mean 'oar-blade', 'spatula' or 'stem of a palm frond'. How are we to choose?

The Babylonian terminology is every bit as colourful. Babylonian terms for parts of the liver are: Path, Increase, Finger, Strength, Palace Gate, Wellbeing, Station, and Blow-at-the-Front-of-the Enemy's-Army! Far greater progress has been made by Assyriologists in identifying these than has been made by classical scholars at their end. But there is still much confusion. If you want your head to spin, try sorting out the terms and techniques of ancient extispicy! A small army of scholars has been working at this for over a century now. Some valuable high ground has been taken, but the final action has not yet occurred. I have pored over a mountain of material in different languages on this tantalizing subject. Although in Figure 37 I give a partial mapping of liver features in different languages and traditions, which is the result of dozens of hours of study, I hasten to emphasize that it is strictly tentative and preliminary because so much remains to be done in sorting out the areas and parts of the liver.

PART TWO

The Chinese Tradition

SEVEN

THE BOOK OF CHANGE

Many people in the West have become familiar in recent decades with a Chinese oracle book called the *Book of Change* (or *Book of Changes)*, the Chinese name of which is *I Ching*. It is not a craze for an Eastern religion which is responsible for this. The *Book of Change* attempts to reduce a means of consulting fate to a system, and it is a genuine response both to its claims and to its apparent success in fulfilling them that has brought the *I Ching* such popularity in an entirely alien culture.

Behind the system of the *Book of Change* lies a profound tradition of the nature of time, space and the universe – the Chinese tradition of these things which has been properly comprehended in the West by only a handful of scholars educated in the history of Chinese philosophy. Some of the most passionate devotees of the *I Ching* show a lamentable ignorance of the book and its history, not to mention its deeper implications.

The first helpful thing to know about the *I Ching* is how to pronounce the name. Do not say 'I, Ching . . .', as if your name were Ching and you were about to begin a monologue. It should be pronounced instead 'ee jing'. The title of the book can mean either *Book of Change* or *Book of Changes* because in Chinese there is no singular or plural in our sense. The context of a statement usually conveys the number of subjects or objects referred to. When the context is unclear, there is no certain way of knowing. Hence it is that *I Ching* can refer to either *change* or to *changes*.

There is an alternative spelling for the name *I Ching*: it can also be spelled *Yi Jing*. The reason for this is that there are two different systems for writing Chinese words in English letters, known as transliteration systems. The system where one writes *I Ching* is called the Wade-Giles System, and has been the traditional system used by Western scholars. However, the rival system, known as the Pinyin system, has been officially adopted by the Chinese Government and is now universally used in all the newspapers of the world. This can make for confusion, as everything can now be spelled 'correctly' in two different ways! In scholarly books there is a concern for continuity and often scholars hesitate to change the spellings of names they have been discussing for decades. In my own book about the history of Chinese science and technology, *The Genius of China*,[1] I have used the Wade-Giles System for this reason. However, in both the French editions of my book, the two successive French publishers wished to use the Pinyin System, and I agreed. Here, I will only use the spelling *I Ching*, but in the case of other Chinese names I will put the Pinyin spelling in parentheses so that both systems are covered. This is becoming increasingly necessary, since many people familiar with the system now used in China have no knowledge of the old scholarly system, and have understandably become confused. It is even beginning to happen to me. I spend so much time in China, where I use the Pinyin System all day, every day, that I now have to struggle to mentally convert things. The moral of the story is: life is such a trial!

The *I Ching* has not always been known as the *I Ching*. The word *Ching* [*Jing*], meaning 'classic book', is a later addition. There are several Chinese *chings* – there are the *Shih Ching* [*Shi Jing*], the *Book of Songs*, and the *Shu Ching* [*Shu Jing*], the *Book of History*. These are works which came to be considered classics and thus were called *Ching*. A book which is made *Ching* is like a distinguished person who is given a knighthood – instead of being Sam Smith, he becomes Sir Samuel Smith. That is what happened with the *I Ching*.

Originally there were three great oracle books – 'the three *I*' – under the guard of the Grand Augur (*Ta Pu* [*Da Bu*]) of the

Chinese Imperial Court, during the Chou [*Zhou*] Dynasty of 1122–249 BC. (The name of this dynasty is pronounced 'Joe'.) The first of these books was *Manifestation of Change in the Mountains (Lien Shan [Lian Shan])*, which is known to have had a text of 80,000 words.[2] The second was *Flow and Return to Womb and Tomb (Kuei Tsang [Gui Zang])*. These two books are lost, but fragments survive, which have never been translated into English.

The third oracle book was the *Chou I [Zhou Yi] (Book of Changes of the Chou Dynasty)*. In other words, it was the book of *I* which was more closely identified with the Chou period, and may have been brought originally from the West, as the Chou rulers were provincial western Chinese who conquered the unenthusiastic defending armies of the preceding dynasty. This conquest was said to be facilitated by the unpopularity of the last king of the old dynasty, who had built a 'pleasure dome' called the Stag Tower for his barbarian concubine, and he and she together ran a reign of terror, mutilating and executing people upon mere whim. One minister offended them and so they had his body chopped up and salted like pork. The king had another wise man killed and cut open 'so that he could examine the structure of a sage's heart'. He ripped open the bellies of pregnant women, roasted people alive, and had the legs chopped off people he had seen wading in the winter 'so that he could examine the marrow of the bones of those who could so well withstand the cold'. When it came to the battlefield, this tyrant king's armies mutinied. According to an account written by conquering Chou historians, '. . . they offered no opposition to our army. Those in the front inverted their spears and attacked those behind till they fled; the blood flowed till it floated the pestles of the mortars.'[3] The last image is, I think you will agree, amazingly vivid.

It was during the Chou Dynasty that the philosopher Confucius lived. His followers formed themselves into coherent schools of philosophy known as the Confucian Schools, each led by a different disciple and claiming to be truer to Confucius's oral teachings than the others. This is exactly what had happened with the Socratic Schools in Greece, as students of the classics will know very well. Later, Confucianism was more unified and was adopted by one of the Chinese emperors as the official imperial creed. In this way Confucianism came to resemble a state religion, except that its emphasis was on society and ethics rather than on metaphysical speculation or on so merely personal a thing as salvation of the soul.

Confucians were notoriously loath to speculate on the after-life. It is quite clear from the *Analects* – his sayings recorded by his disciples – that Confucius himself believed in an after-life and in an active 'Heaven'. He revered the spirits of his ancestors in the traditional Chinese way. But he discouraged philosophical speculation on such matters as being a distraction from the true concerns of living, which are to be a 'gentleman' and to follow 'the Way'. The basic tenet of Confucianism is the same as that of Christianity, namely, to treat others as one would like to be treated oneself. One of Confucius's disciples was always asking him questions about spirits and ghosts, and Confucius is recorded as having snapped at him: 'How can you hope to understand the dead when you do not yet understand the living?'

When the Confucians were seeking to form a canon, or collection of essential texts, for themselves, they took the *Chou I* as their classic concerning the *I,* just as they had a classic concerning music, a classic concerning rites or proper behaviour, and a 'history classic'. They wanted to select these texts for their students as a curriculum and also to single out for special honour the texts most congenial to their own opinions. Thus the *Chou I* was adopted and became the *I Ching* or 'change classic'. They took the basic, and earliest, text, and then added to it. The commentaries which form a part of the *I Ching* of today are thus the work of these later scholars, though they are not necessarily any less interesting for that.

Confucius himself was said to be such an admirer of the *I Ching* and its profundity that he is recorded as saying: 'If many years were added to my life, I would give fifty to the study of the *Book of Change,* and might thereby manage to avoid great mistakes.' However, it has been suggested that he did not actually say this himself and that it is a later interpolation by a zealous Confucian scribe who wanted to give an extra boost to the reputation of the *I Ching*. We simply do not know whether Confucius himself actually wrote some of the commentaries which are now part of the *I Ching*. There are arguments for both sides. It can safely be concluded that he did not write them all, but whether the earlier layers of commentary are by the Master himself we may never know. But does it matter one way or the other? Whoever wrote them must have been an interesting man (or men) whether called Confucius or John Doe. Let us disregard the intellectual snobs who say: 'Oh, we can't be sure that is by Confucius, it could be by his grandson or some insignificant disciple . . .', implying that anything lacking the imprimatur of someone famous should of course be ignored.

It is not only the Confucians who have traditionally been keen on the *I Ching*. The rival Taoists, the other great native Chinese philosophical and religious school, are just as avid in their liking for the 'change classic'. While the Confucians were primarily an ethical school, the Taoists were decidely mystical. Later, when Buddhism became entrenched in China as an import from India, the mystical Taoists seemed to blend their ideas and doctrine with the Buddhists, and for a while the combined forces of the mystics nearly eclipsed the Confucians.

The Taoists took delight in being obscure and tantalizing. Perhaps that is why they instinctively liked the *I Ching* so much. A Taoist monk of the fifth century AD made this provocative statement about it: 'The fundamental idea of the *I Ching* can be expressed in one single word, Resonance *[Kan]*.' But a gentleman named Mr Yin was not satisfied with this, and said to the monk: 'We are told that when the Copper Mountain collapsed in the West, the bell Ling Chung responded, by resonance, in the East. Would this be according to the principles of the *I Ching?*' But the monk – in a typically irritating fashion – 'laughed and gave no answer to this question'.[4]

The philosopher Tung Chung-Shu [*Dong Zhong-Shu*] (c. 179–c. 104 BC), who was instrumental in making Confucianism the state doctrine in 136 BC, wrote more lucidly on this same subject:

Suppose the seven-stringed and the twenty-five-stringed lutes are tuned and played. When the note F in the one is struck, the note F on the other will respond to it, and when the note G in the one is struck, the note G in the other will respond to it. Among the five notes each one that matches will sound of itself. There is nothing supernatural in this. It is their natural course that they do so. A beautiful thing calls forth things that are beautiful in kind and an ugly thing calls forth things that are ugly in kind, for things of the same kind arise in response to each other. For example, when a horse neighs, it is horses that will respond, and when an ox lows, it is oxen that will respond. Similarly, when an emperor or a king is about to rise, auspicious omens will first appear, and when he is about to perish, unlucky omens will first appear. Therefore things of the same kind call forth each other. . . . When the night comes, the sick person's sickness becomes worse. When the day is about to dawn, cocks all crow and press on each other, their force becoming more and more refined.[5]

A famous Confucian statesman and poet of the late third century AD is credited with solving a mystery from his profound knowledge of harmonics in the following story:

Attached to the Chin [*Jin*] court was a man who had in his charge a bronze washing tub. Morning and night it gave forth a sound, as though someone were beating on it. He asked Chang Hua [*Zhang Hua*] about it, and Hua said: 'This tub is sounding in sympathy with the gong in the Loyang palace. In the palace, they strike the gong morning and night, and this tub responds to that. If you could make this tub lighter by using a grindstone on it, the harmony between them would be destroyed, and the sounding would cease of itself.' It was done as he suggested, and after that, the noise was heard no more.[6]

Thus did a Confucian sage, through his comprehension of

principles said to be at the basis of the *I Ching,* solve a thorny problem and amaze his colleagues.

The *I Ching* itself is notoriously difficult to understand and is indeed a book of many mysteries. But the Taoist author Wang Pi [*Wang Bi*] said of it: 'The dark sentences in the *I Ching* contain purest truth. After an intense study the hidden meaning will manifest itself.'[7] What does he mean by 'dark sentences'? Why is it that an understanding of the *I Ching* is so difficult to attain?

In all of Chinese history there has never been a single book held in so much awe and reverence as the *I Ching.* If it were simple to understand, perhaps it would not have been held in such awe. One of the most famous Confucians, Chu Hsi [*Zhu Xi*] (AD 1130–1200), expressed a typical opinion when he said:

> As a book it is comprehensive, great, and perfect. It is intended to bring about accord with . . . destiny, to penetrate the causes of the hidden and the manifest, to reveal completely the nature of things and affairs, and to show the way to . . . accomplish great undertakings . . . Although we are far from antiquity, the Classic that was left to us is still extant. But former scholars have lost sight of its ideas and have only transmitted its words, and later students have recited its words and have forgotten its meaning. Since the Ch'in [*Chin*] dynasty [221–206 BC], its ideas have been no longer transmitted. Now, living a thousand years later, I mourn the obscurity and possible disappearance of our cultural tradition.[8]

It is strange to read these remarks of Chu Hsi written nearly eight hundred years ago, and to hear him speak of himself as 'living a thousand years later' – and remarkable to think that nearly the same amount of time has elapsed again, and still we have the *I Ching,* and still the cultural tradition which Chu Hsi thought might die out survives in some form or other.

It should be noted that Chu Hsi in his lament about 'the future of our cultural tradition' implies that the *I Ching* is at the centre of it. That is just the case. We in the West may scratch our heads and wonder why, but the fact is that this strange oracle book is, and has been for two and a half thousand years, at the very heart of Chinese culture. And before that there were other, related, texts and techniques of divination which were held just as sacred.

Chu Hsi complains elsewhere: 'In reading the *Book of Change* one must know how to apply its remarks in accordance with the circumstances. . . . People today read the *Book of Change* but do not know what it is.'[9] But he also says that he cannot explain it all himself. He cites a previous philosopher who had written a *Commentary on the Book of Change;* when the Confucian in question showed his commentary to his pupils, he said to them: 'It tells only seventy per cent. People who read it must later realize the rest themselves.'[10]

The Chinese are always conscious of mental attitude, especially in studying or reading. Chu Hsi chides us:

In reading a book, one should recite it silently. Often excellent thoughts will come to him at midnight or while he is sitting in meditation. If one does not remember what he reads, his thoughts will not arise. After one has thoroughly understood the great foundation of a book, however, it will be easy to remember.

The reason for reading is to resolve one's doubts and to clarify what one does not understand. If with each reading one learns something new, his learning will advance. When one doubts where nothing doubtful seems to exist, one really advances.

The Six Classics must be gone through one after another, in repeated cycles. The student will find that their moral principles are unlimited. With every step that he advances, he sees something different.

In reading books like the *Doctrine of the Mean,* one simply must understand all the sentences so that they can develop and clarify each other's meaning.

In ancient times there was no *Spring and Autumn Annals* [the one supposedly certain writing of Confucius which we possess]. Confucius himself wrote it. And Mencius alone understood it. Unless one thoroughly understands moral principles, one is not qualified to study it. Former scholars studied it without this qualification and their theories are therefore mostly forced.[11]

It is worth knowing what a Confucian sage says about reading these texts because it helps us understand how different these Chinese classics are from what we are normally accustomed to reading. When we in the West pick up a book, we usually expect to be able to sail through it while riding in a train or a plane, or before we turn out the light at night. We think that a book is like a newspaper, something to go through, without trouble, and then to discard without further thought. The best way to score nought for comprehension of a Chinese classic is to treat it as an ordinary Western book. Different habits of reading are required.

Chu Hsi's statement that 'one must simply understand all the sentences so that they can develop and clarify each other's meaning' is quite literally true. In my own reading of such books as he describes I can recall the gradual process of sentence upon sentence piling up an increasing luminosity until a mass of incandescence is reached, where whole paragraphs then glow like burning charcoal and a tremendous heat and light are generated from what had at first been dead and cold words. In generating laser beams scientists keep the photons trapped, furiously going back and forth in a small mirrored chamber, until suddenly a coherent beam bursts through. The focusing of ideas from the Confucian classics is like that. You have to be prepared to mull everything over, to concentrate and meditate on what you are reading; each sentence becomes a precious pearl, prized for itself but also within a context. The statements are not errant meteors but are constellations, each with a place. Confucius said to one of his disciples: 'I believe you look upon me as one whose aim is simply to learn and retain in mind as many things as possible.' The disciple replied, 'That is what I thought.' But Confucius said, 'No; I have one thread upon which I string them all.'[12]

With the *I Ching* we are dealing with something far more

profound even than the normal Chinese classic. It is because the Chinese have appreciated this fact that the *I Ching* has held such a special place in their culture for so long – longer than the English language has even existed.

The *I Ching* consists of many levels. Perhaps the earliest is what we could call the 'folk level'. Throughout the book are embedded nuggets of quaint 'folk wisdom' and traditional sayings, which are so ancient that they go back to a time before history was recorded. This level of the *Book of Change* was brought to light by the great Arthur Waley, a self-taught scholar of Chinese literature who brought vitality and originality to everything he touched. Scholars are notoriously stuffy and savagely jealous of their fields of study. But Arthur Waley, who was not trained to be an orientalist, nevertheless achieved universal respect and affection, and is acknowledged as one of the ultimate authorities in the field which he chose belatedly to enter. Waley seems to have had one of those guns that fire drugged darts into lions, for he stunned and paralysed the jealousies and opposition of the professional sinologues in order to rise to the top of their field, in their very midst.

In 1933, Waley published a fascinating essay on the *I Ching*,[13] which concentrated on the 'folk level' of the book. Waley was uniquely qualified to discuss this, for his was the most noted translation of the *Book of Songs (Shih Ching)*, which contains poems as ancient as the *I Ching*. The simplicity and genius of some of the poetry of the *Book of Songs* has never been equalled, a fact realized by the poet Ezra Pound, who attempted a translation of them which with all its fine points often falls short of Waley's.[14]

The early folk level of the *I Ching* contains such statements as these: 'If in the field there are birds, it is favourable for initiating a parley.'[15] 'When the *ming-i* [bird] in its flight droops its wings, that means that my lord on his journey for three days will have no food.' 'When [one sees] a *ming-i* [bird] while hunting in the south, [that means] one will capture a big head of game.' 'When the wild-goose skims the bank . . .' 'When the wild-goose skims the rock-ledge, you may eat and drink in peace.' 'When the wild-goose skims the tree . . .'

These statements are age-old traditions of signs given by the behaviour of birds such as those which we have seen, are extremely common in ancient Western cultures. Waley points out the similarity to wild-goose omens noted in the ancient poetry of the *Book of Songs:* 'When the wild-goose in its flight follows the land, [it means that] my Lord will not return.'[16] Here we have an undeniable base rock of folk culture. Traditional signs and portents leave their trace in stray formulae throughout the *I Ching:*

A willow-omen: 'When the rotten willow bears sprouts, the old husband will get a lady-wife. . . .' A sign from the poplar: 'A withered poplar puts forth flowers. An older woman takes a husband.' An omen from the behaviour of a fox: 'If a little fox when almost over the stream wets its tail, your undertaking will completely fail.' An omen from the behaviour of a ram: 'If a ram butts a hedge, and cannot go back or go in [but gets stuck in the hedge], your undertaking will completely fail.' And omens indicated by feelings in the body: 'If you fidget and can't keep still, it means that a friend is following your thoughts.' 'A feeling in the big toe, in the calf, in the thigh . . .' There are references to 'feelings' in the back, the corners of the mouth, the cheeks, and the tongue; and to omens seen in animal tracks: 'The footprints run criss-cross. . . . Seriousness when footprints run criss-cross. . . .'

Stumbling was an omen to the Chinese as it was to the Romans. When Julius Caesar stumbled and fell onto the beach as he stepped ashore in North Africa, he turned this terrible omen to good account by cleverly saying in a jocular manner to his troops: 'Africa, I have tight hold of you.' This relieved them all and dispelled their forebodings. But in the *I Ching* stumbling is a favourable sign: 'He who goes stumbling shall come praised. . . . A great stumble means a friend shall come.'

An ancient maxim in the *I Ching* derives from primitive marriage rites, in which the bride rode on a horse to her husband's house: 'If the horse she rides on is brindled, tears and blood will flow profusely.' Perhaps an even older relic is the passage referring to the lucky or unlucky aspects of finding something in your food, as indeed (until the coins were abolished) it is considered lucky to find a sixpence in your Christmas pudding in England: 'If in biting the gristle of dried meat you come on a metal arrow-head . . . If in biting the soft flesh of dried meat you come on a bit of gold . . .' Imagine a time when arrow-heads could still be found in one's meat!

Extremely ancient rites of sacrifice to the moon made in a pit in the ground (like the sacrifice to Hecate made in a pit at night by Jason at Colchis) are referred to in a passage embedded in the *I Ching*: 'Enter into the arcana of the pit. . . . Goblet wine bowl, fill from earthenware crock. . . . Before the pit is filled, the bottom already levelled.'

The ancient superstition of parasitic plants has also left its trace in the *I Ching*. Just as the Druids were in awe of the mistletoe, so the Chinese in very ancient times were in awe of the dodder, a golden, leafless parasitic plant with a thread-like stem. An ancient Chinese riddle says: 'The thing of which the stem is invisible. What is it? – The dodder.' And so we read in the *I Ching*: 'I saw the golden husband; but he had no body,' referring also to the dodder. Just as the ancient Chinese seem to have imagined the dodder as male, so they also called the mistletoe 'twisty boy'.[17]

Those who study the *I Ching* have long puzzled over the curious image given under the heading of *The Marrying Maiden*, where the text says: 'The woman holds the basket, but there are no fruits in it. The man stabs the sheep, but no blood flows.'[18] This refers to the stabbing of the sacrificial sheep by the bridegroom; it is a terrible omen if the sheep does not bleed when he does this. As for the basket, the bride was presented with one in the ancient marriage ceremony; if it contained no fruits, this was also a bad omen.

A modern scholar has suggested that the *I Ching* is 'perhaps an accumulated record of a rather loosely worded and long-existent oral tradition.'[19] In a sense that is true, as we have just seen. The examples given above are relics from an archaic era of China's history. Variations in the basic early text of the *I Ching* have been proved, so that we know there was a certain fluidity of content to the book.[20] But to view the *I Ching* as a hodge-podge thrown together without organization would be totally wrong. The *I Ching* is both a miscellaneous grab-bag and a brilliantly unified entity which is entirely coherent and ultimately (though with difficulty) comprehensible.

What gives the *I Ching* this unity is the bizarre skeleton of mathematical symbols on which the flesh, pieced together, it would seem, from bits of dragon, phoenix and tortoise carcasses which have been found lying about, hangs with baffling splendour. The whole thing is every bit as complex as a totem pole, with just as many strange faces grimacing from it. But it stands up straight, it seems to know what it is doing, and it was carved with a single-mindedness which cannot be disguised by its plethora of exotic imagery.

This skeletal structure of the *I Ching* is the famous system of the sixty-four hexagrams, with which anyone who has ever seen the *I Ching* will be familiar. I shall avoid describing them too pedantically. I hope that readers not familiar will bear with me for not pursuing a full description, which can easily be found in one of the translations of the *I Ching* by consulting its introduction.

I should perhaps take a moment to say which are the ones which in my opinion are good and reliable. A superior translation in English or German is the one by Richard Wilhelm.[21] A simpler one, but also sound, is by John Blofeld.[22] Blofeld was a friend of Hellmut Wilhelm, whose father's translation I have just recommended. The younger Wilhelm says of this translation that 'Blofeld aims at a version . . . in the simplest possible language'.[23] Another which I like to consult and which has much interesting material in its introduction and notes, is the early one by James Legge.[24] The fourth version commonly available is by Alfred Douglas,[25] whom I have met, and who has told me that he does not know Chinese. His work is therefore not actually a translation, but rather largely a simplification of Legge's translation which also takes into account later translations of specific passages. There are other translations, such as that by Z. D. Sung.[26] Various corrected readings to Richard Wilhelm's translation have been made by his son Hellmut Wilhelm, and are scattered throughout the latter's many and various writings. A more recent translation of the *I Ching* by Alfred Huang, a mainland Chinese scholar who is now settled in America, was published in 1998 and has been highly praised for conveying Chinese psychological attitudes that were thought to be lacking to some extent in previous translations by Westerners, though Huang does not have the international scholarly reputation of the Wilhelms.[27] The Huang translation is an extremely useful supplementary text to anyone using the Wilhelm translation. I recommend it very highly indeed. Throughout his book, Huang often gives his own translations of key terms first, and then gives those of Wilhelm and Blofeld for comparison. This is a remarkably open and non-egotistical approach which says a lot for Huang's character and also makes his book that much more useful and effective. He devotes a great deal of space to the supplementary *I Ching* material, and tries to be both clear and faithful to Chinese attitudes. He succeeds admirably. He is continually trying to make obscure aspects of Chinese tradition clear to Western readers, and he manages to be both conscientious and inspiring. He must be an extraordinary man, and he has certainly produced an extraordinary book. I don't think anyone seriously interested in the *I Ching* should be without it.

An even more ambitious modern translation of the *I Ching* is the one by Rudolf Ritsema and Stephen Karcher, entitled variously *The Eranos Yi Jing* and also *I Ching: The Classic Chinese Oracle of Change*, which was intended to reach levels of meaning and significance that the translators believed to be lacking in other versions (it should be mentioned that Huang's translation had not yet appeared at this time).[28] I met both Ritsema and Karcher a few years ago on a visit to the Eranos Centre (Casa Eranos) on the shore of Lake Maggiore near Ascona in Switzerland. The Eranos Conferences, which were held annually at this place from the 1930s, were famous to historians of religion, and Carl Jung generally attended them during his lifetime, as did Mircea Eliade, Karl Kerenyi, and many other noted scholars. The organiser was Frau Olga Fröbe-Kapteyn, and when she died the place was left to the custody of Adolf Portmann, and after his death to Rudolf Ritsema. Ritsema changed the policy of Eranos to focus it on the *I Ching*, and for this and other reasons a split took place amongst the survivors, with many old Eranos loyalists no longer visiting Casa Eranos, but setting up rival gatherings in Ascona, which dealt with a wider variety of subjects in the more traditional way. The two camps were not on speaking terms with each other when I visited. Nowadays, Stephen Karcher lives in Wales and left Casa Eranos long ago, while conferences at Casa Eranos continue, though they now also cover subjects other than the *I Ching*. I am very kindly invited to these but have never yet had the time to attend one. It is a pity that Ascona and its surrounding area have become so expensive in modern times, thereby excluding a great deal of the scholarly and even Bohemian lifestyle which once flourished there and has been described in such a compelling and astonishing manner in the book *Mountain of Truth: The Counterculture Begins; Ascona 1900–1920* by Martin Green.[29] As for the Casa Eranos, whereas originally Carl Jung and his friends could amble up into the hills from the lakeside along a pastoral lane, the construction many years ago of a highway along the north shore of Lake Maggiore has savagely cut off the precincts, and it is now so dangerous to get out of a car and attempt to go in the gate because of speeding traffic, that one feels a great peril to life and limb just attempting to visit the place unless one approaches it by boat. But this remarkable island of tranquillity and contemplation is very much the traditional spiritual home of the *I Ching* in the West. And whether one accepts Carl Jung's psychological theories or not, he was certainly responsible for bringing Western respectability to the concept of synchronicity and to a serious attitude towards the *I Ching*. Lake Maggiore and the other lake near Zurich where Jung lived are thus like two great reflecting mirrors which gaze at the great hexagrams in the sky, in the confidence that every Chinese sage has something to say to us.

As for the Ritsema and Karcher translation itself, it is a magnificent accomplishment, with decades of work behind it. It is such a triumph of scholarship that the Chinese themselves might find it advisable to learn English in order to consult it. Furthermore, it has at the back a massive concordance, which is a unique feature of great value. There are also extensive examples presented of the psychological benefits obtained by people who used the system, vast amounts of explanatory material of many kinds, and attempts to understand what the *I Ching* really is. Many hints of this occur in various discussions in the book. For instance:

> Using the *I* in this way is like working with dreams. The images do not offer standard predictions of an unalterable future. They describe the way energy is moving to create possible futures. This presents you with an opportunity to interact with the energy clusters or complexes of the psyche. Changing your relation to these forces can change what will happen to you ... [you] make conscious the imaginative background and the goal of the situation in which you find yourself, giving you the information necessary to make choices.
>
> In a traditional culture, where myth is alive, people take a step back into the imagination before they start on any significant action. They encounter an image there and move into the action through the image that they have found. This oracular image carries them, keeping them connected with the imaginative ground.[30]

I agree with all of this.
Elsewhere they say:

> Much of traditional Chinese science began in the *I Ching*. The system behind it, first codified in the Han Dynasty, grew out of imagistic, correlative or magical thinking. ... This system describes the way psychic energy moves in the world and in the individual in a precise yet imaginative way. ...

This system is organic and complicated . . . [it] describes the quality and direction of moving energy . . . a fluid, changing world whose ground is imaginative energy.[31]

As we shall see as we proceed, such ideas are close to my own. But I differ from Karcher and Ritsema in being convinced that the scientific insights of the *I Ching* precede the Han Dynasty and were 'organized' long before it began, though perhaps they are correct to say that during the Han they were 'codified' in the sense that the texts were collected and the commentaries written. I would not really consider the origins of the *I Ching* as 'magical thinking'. I prefer to describe them as *proto-scientific*. Although Karcher and Ritsema are correct to stress the 'imaginative energy', or 'psychic energy', which is portrayed in the images of the *I Ching*, I look upon this all as being ultimately much more scientific and less psychological than Karcher and Ritsema do.

The version of the *I Ching* presented by Karcher and Ritsema is nothing short of a masterpiece. It cannot be recommended highly enough. But please, please, don't wallow in it. They themselves would be the first to advise against the over-use of the *I Ching*, and they specifically caution that it is for people in distress. It is not for daily use, any more than caviar is for daily consumption. Just take it easy!

The Legge translation is the earliest of those still in print today. James Legge was a pioneer in Chinese studies, an indefatigable worker who devoted his life to the elucidation of the wisdom of China. He says in his introduction:

I wrote out a translation of the Yi King [his old-fashioned spelling of *I Ching*], the Text and the Appendices, in 1854 and 1855 . . . [but even afterwards] I knew very little about the scope and method of the book. I laid . . . the result of my labour aside, and hoped . . . that I would one day get hold of a clue that would guide me to a knowledge of the mysterious classic.

Before that day came, the translation was soaked, in 1870, for more than a month in water of the Red Sea. By dint of careful manipulation it was recovered so as to be still legible; but it was not till 1874 that I began to be able to give to the book the prolonged attention necessary to make it reveal its secrets. Then for the first time I got hold, as I believe, of the clue, and found that my toil of twenty years before was of no service at all.[32]

If anyone thinks the *I Ching* gives away its secrets easily, let this be a lesson.

A modern scholar has been quite blunt about the problems:

Even to call the *I Ching* a 'classic' – and, hence, a book – presents a problem: for it is a book only in the sense that it contains written material. But this material is merely peripheral to the true core, or nucleus of the book, which is a double set of diagrams: the eight trigrams ... and the sixty-four hexagrams. ... The actual text is a series of explanations and commentaries and appendices which interpret these diagrams in terms of a very complicated and abstruse system of divination.[33]

Now, no matter how difficult and abstruse it appears, the fact is that the entire system makes almost unbelievable sense. It is now possible to explain so much that is amazing about the brilliance of the *I Ching* system that, if once the full facts have been absorbed, it is no longer possible to dismiss the *I Ching* as the embodiment of mere superstition. Rather one must regard it with awe, and wonder how such a work could ever have been created.

First we should look at a few basic building blocks of the system. Many people have heard of the Chinese idea of *yin* and *yang*. The well-known *Yin-Yang* diagram is shown in Figure 38. The idea is that the *yang* (male, strong, active) force and the *yin* (female, weak, passive) force are two opposing forces in the universe; but, far from being entirely separate, the seed of each is to be found at the centre of the other. This is represented in the diagram as the small dot of dark in the light area and the small dot of light in the dark area. The way the two forces swirl round each other represents their mutual caressing, interlocking and constant interaction. From this activity all things are said to be created.

The Chinese were great correlators. Everything, to them, seemed to relate to something else. Taking natural objects and classifying them as *yin* or as *yang* was a game to which the Chinese took with delight. A cliff is strong and masculine – very *yang*. A field is flat, receptive and yields to the plough – *yin*. One can go on and on with this sort of thing. The Chinese never seemed to tire of it. A symbolic representation of *yang* and *yin* was at the basis of the *I Ching*. The diagrams are all based on these two simple things: a solid line and a broken line. The solid line is strong, masculine, firm – *yang*. The broken line is weak, broken, feminine – *yin*. From these simple elements the entire system is developed.

Figure 39 shows the two different kinds of lines, and the four combinations which can be made of them taking them two at a time. It has been suggested that originally the *yang* line represented a 'yes' answer to a question asked in divination and the *yin* line represented a 'no' answer. There may be some truth in this, but it is not the whole story, and is not how the lines are used in the *I Ching*. The way the *I Ching* system is worked out shows a striking correspondence with the mathematical system

Figure 38: The yin-yang *symbol*

of binary arithmetic, which has become the basis for the operation of modern computers.

The human nervous system operates in the same way: nerve cells either fire or they do not – either 'yes' or 'no'. It is the simplest system imaginable, and yet it remained unknown in Europe until its discovery by the philosopher Leibniz (1646–1716), who was also the co-discoverer of calculus. One of the greatest ironies and coincidences in the history of ideas is that after Leibniz discovered binary arithmetic he found that a Confucian, Shao Yung [*Shao Yong*], had several centuries earlier arranged the *yin*- and *yang*-based *I Ching* hexagrams in a sequence which precisely matched his own new discovery (see below). With this fine tool (and though it is simple, it *is* a fine tool), it is not surprising that extraordinary results can follow with the *I Ching*.

The system of the *I Ching,* however, concentrates on using the lines six at a time, to form what are known as hexagrams. By a certain divination technique (described in all the translations) you get either a *yin* or a *yang* line. This is the base line. You then repeat the divination technique five times, drawing above the base line all the succeeding lines as they occur. The hexagram is thus formed from the ground up, like building a house. (There is a highly elaborate theory of the places of the lines in the hexagrams which specialists can consider.) Figure 40 shows the complete set of sixty-four hexagrams which can be obtained by this method. (This particular array, the King Wen Sequence, is not the sequence matching binary arithmetic.)

Mathematically, 64 is the result of 2^6 ($2 \times 2 \times 2 \times 2 \times 2 \times 2$). There are known to be associations between the *I Ching* and early forms of the game of chess, which is played on a sixty-four-square board and had its origins not in India, as many have supposed, but in China (although some supposedly authoritative books on the history of chess are ignorant of this fact). Chess was invented in China no later than the sixth century AD, and spread from there to India, from where it eventually reached Europe. Few historians of chess are aware of its Chinese origin, but it was established beyond all doubt by my old friend Joseph Needham.

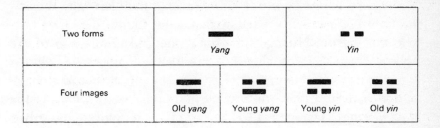

Two forms	Yang		Yin	
Four images	Old yang	Young yang	Young yin	Old yin

Figure 39: Yin *and* yang *lines (solid and broken) and their simplest combinations in the* I Ching

In fact, the game seems to have been invented by Emperor Wu of the Northern Chou [Zhou] Dynasty (561–78 AD), unless he took credit for the invention of one of his courtiers. I have written an account of the history of the invention and spread of chess in my book *The Genius of China*.[34] Joseph Needham believed that the opposing kings of chess originally represented the sun and moon, or *yang* and *yin*. Ancient Chinese chessmen survive which are actually marked with symbols from the *I Ching*. I have a small collection of old Chinese chessmen, including a set from the seventeenth century made of ebony and ivory. But to bear *I Ching* symbols, one would have to have pieces nearly a thousand years older than that, and they would belong only in a museum.

Originally chess was concerned with such subjects as astrology, divination, the compass, and early uses of magnetism. Apparently the elephant used in some sets of chessmen to portray the rook or castle was adopted in India either through a mistranslation of the Chinese word *hsiang* [*xiang*] which means both 'image' (of a celestial body) and 'elephant', or: 'It may even have been a substituted homophone ["sound-alike"] for another word meaning "diviner".'[35] It is assumed that the 'militarization' of chess took place in India because the game, though basically astrological, 'yet had a sufficient combat element to enable it to be vulgarized into a purely military symbolism.'[36]

Divination could actually be practised using chessmen and board. An ancient Chinese book with the tantalizing title of

Garden of Strange Things (I Yuan) records that 'Divination using the twelve chessmen started with Chang Liang (died 187 BC), who got it from Huang Shih Kung (the Old Gentleman of the Yellow Stone) ... of Shensi [Shanxi].'[37] Of course, if Chang Liang 'got it from' someone else, then it cannot be said to have started with him, but presumably he popularized it. During the Sung [Song] Dynasty (AD 960–1279), a writer described divination by chessmen as follows: 'Our present-day [Sung] method is to divide the twelve "chess" or divination pieces into three classes, upper, middle, and lower; these are then thrown [onto the board] and by the result obtained the decision is given as to good or evil fortune.'[38]

There was another form, *tan ch'i,* or 'crossbow-bullet chess', and yet another, *liu-po,* or 'the Six Learned Scholars'. In this version the pieces were moved according to the results of throwing six sticks, which is reminiscent of the throwing of the dried stalks used in the traditional means of consulting the *I Ching.*[39] But the most bizarre form of chess ever played must surely be the ancient Chinese game using magnetized chessmen! Here is an old recipe for the manufacture of magnetic chessmen: 'Take the blood of a cock and mix it with iron [filings] from the grinding of needles, pounding it with a lodestone powder. In the daytime, put the paste on to the heads of the chessmen and let it dry in the sun. Then put them on the board and they will constantly bounce against and repel one another.'[40] Anyone could follow this recipe today and cause a sensation at an International Chess Congress. Or you could magnetize the bottoms of the chessmen, setting them on a thin board, and lead them around the board with a magnet held underneath. Something of this kind must have been done in the case of the ancient Chinese chessmen which could not be picked up from the board: 'They moved to and fro and pushed each other about, yet if you tried to pick them up you could not do so. This was called "spirit chess" (*hsien i* [*xian yi*]).'[41]

These magnetized chessmen could be used not just for fun but for divination. An ancient writer named Ko Hung [Gou Hong] refers to 'playing with the three [sets of] chessmen, in order to foretell the success or failure of military enterprises'.[42] Joseph Needham, from whom I have taken all this information on early chess, summarizes the matter as follows:

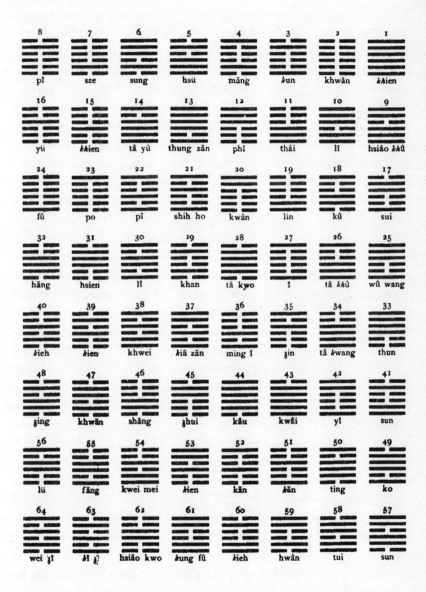

Figure 40: The hexagrams of the I Ching (the King Wen sequence)

Our immediate object must be to explain how a cosmic-astrological technique used for divination could have turned into a war-game used for recreation. The answer is not far to seek; the image-chess of the emperor Wu was nothing but a mimicry of the eternal contest between the two great forces in the universe, Yang and Yin. It was desired to determine the general balance between Yin and Yang in the existing cosmic situation, and if the model pieces were well chosen, their moves properly adjusted, and the board oriented and arranged according to the concrete circumstances, the players, being themselves part of that situation, could not fail to proceed to a valid and informative decision. ... the image-chess ... must have seemed at the time a brilliant device, evoking respect somewhat analogous to that accorded to the elaborate computing-machines of today.[43]

Although Needham disparages the *I Ching* itself as superstitious and pseudo-scientific, which is certainly true in that it does not adhere to strictly logical or analytic procedures, my own conclusions differ from Joseph's. The operations of the *I Ching* impress many people who are not considered unduly credulous. Where is the line drawn between credulity and open-mindedness? From the way some academics react, it would seem that the very act of considering a possibility is treachery to reason, for the siren is certain to bewitch you. Rigid orthodoxy is simply fear; for fixed boundaries are erected by those who have no confidence and who feel threatened. The ancient Greek city of Sparta was so confident of its invincible land armies that it had no walls around it: it knew no enemy would ever get that far. Modern science and true scholarship of all ages should feel enough conviction in their own sound principles to be able to throw down the long walls which guard the corridors of academe. They were built not to keep the barbarian hordes out, but to confine those within. Tear down the barriers, remove the barbed wire, fill in the foxholes. Science and learning must not be bound and gagged by stuffy opinions, but must be open to free and unlimited enquiry. Hence it is that a serious consideration of something which is not understood, of something 'superstitious', is to be encouraged. It would be insufferable arrogance to insist that we have nothing to learn from the strange system of the Chinese *Book of Change*.

So let us now commence a deeper study of its principles and their implications. Surely some surprises lie in store for us.

We may perhaps be led to notions of time, futurity, and natural process which will relate to our own advanced scientific concepts. We may have as much of a shock as Leibniz had when he saw the hexagrams arranged by Shao Yung in a sequence matching his own binary arithmetic. Shao Yung's sequence is shown in Figure 41, with the binary digit equivalents shown below each corresponding hexagram in the way that Leibniz matched them together. As Hellmut Wilhelm has said (in his book *Change)* of this amazing coincidence:

Shao Yung's schema has led to one of the most extra-ordinary episodes in the history of the human mind, and to this day it has never been satisfactorily cleared up. More than six hundred years after its origin, Shao's diagram fell into the hands of Leibniz through the agency of Jesuit missionaries, and he recognized in it a system that had previously sprung from his own mathematical genius. To facilitate the solution of certain mathematical problems, Leibniz had thought out the so-called binary, or dyadic, numeral system, which makes use of two numbers only, instead of ten, but otherwise follows the same principle as the decimal system. The two figures are 0 and 1. The numerical sequence of the binary system would look as follows:

1, 10, 11, 100, 110, 111, 1000, etc.

In the Sequence of the Earlier Heaven Leibniz now rediscovered his own dyadic system, though he had to begin with zero for the correspondence to emerge. He took the

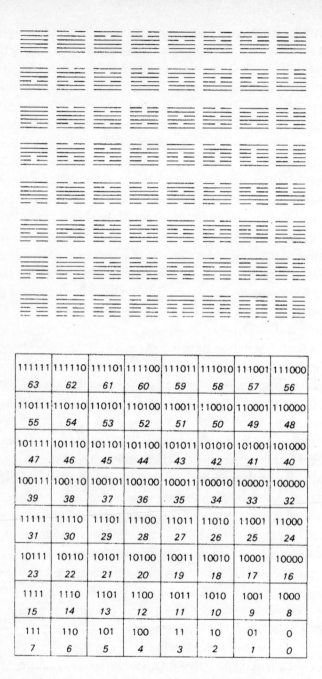

Figure 41: *Shao Yung's sequence of hexagrams and Leibniz's matching binary sequence of zeros and ones*

broken line for a zero, and the unbroken for a 1. Thus the hexagram Po [Bo] was 1, if zeros preceding 1 are disregarded, and stood in the first place in his system; the next, Pi [Bi], was 10, that is, our 2; and so on. Leibniz placed the zero (=K'un [Kun]) at the beginning of the sequence, and so Shao Yung's system corresponded point for point with the binary system, right up to the last hexagram, Ch'ien [Chien], which for Leibniz was 111111, or 63. The only difference is that this correspondence is not a direct but an inverted one, that is, in order to obtain it, one must begin at the end of the series, which serves to emphasize once more the fact that parallel cultural phenomena in East and West are as mirror images to each other! Nonetheless, the correspondence arrived at by these two great minds independently, each having started from a completely different basis, is truly an astonishing phenomenon.[44]

Shao Yung [Shao Yong], who lived in the eleventh century (AD 1011–77), was a truly extraordinary philosopher and thinker, whose name will be forever associated with the *I Ching*, his central inspiration. In English, his main work is called *The Supreme Principles for Ordering the World*, although it has unfortunately never been translated in its entirety. Shao Yung advocated lifelong continuing education, and in that sense is extraordinarily modern. He wrote: 'Learning lies in not stopping [i.e. never stopping learning]. Therefore Wang T'ung [Wang Tong, AD 584–618] said, "Just give your life to it." . . . If learning does not arrive at delight, you cannot call it learning.'[45]

In the words of a modern scholar, Shao Yung believed that 'learning means to arrive at or perfect one's nature and destiny. Its progress should be endless and all-consuming.'[46] It is ironic that now, in the twenty-first century, in the post-industrial world where people are forced to re-train continuously through their working lives in order to remain employed, we are finally arriving at a society that in some ways matches the expectations of a medieval Confucian! But Shao Yung was modern in an even more extraordinary way. For he believed in a kind of 'distributed

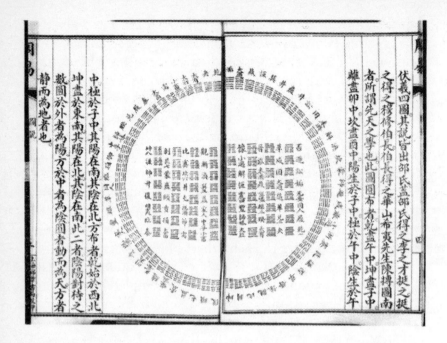

Figure 42: The circular form of the Fu Hsi (Fu Xi) or 'Preceding Heaven'
sequence of hexagrams. The circular array represents heaven, moves, is
active, and is yang and the inscribed square array represents earth, is still,
and is yin. Western sources generally portray these in modern re-
drawings, but I thought it would be more authentic if I reproduced a
traditional diagram from a late Ch'ing (Qing) Dynasty edition of the I
Ching *which I acquired in China. This comes from the* Illustrated
Version of the 'Imperially Authorized' I Ching *(Pinyin title:* Huitu
Jianben Yi Jing*) published in the second half of the nineteenth century at*
Shanghai (no date) by the Jinzhang Tushuju Publishing House. In that
book, the text explains that this is Fu Hsi's Fourth Illustration, that the
Shao Clan received it and Li Ji-Tsai (Li Zhicai) 'corrected' it. I explain
more about this figure in the main text. The crease in the middle is due to
the fact that this illustration is spread over two facing pages in the
original. (Collection of Robert Temple)

intelligence' of the kind which is only coming to be suggested
seriously now in the West by philosophers of what we call
'cyberculture', such as the deeply profound French thinker Pierre
Lévy. Cyber-thinkers are thus one thousand years behind Shao

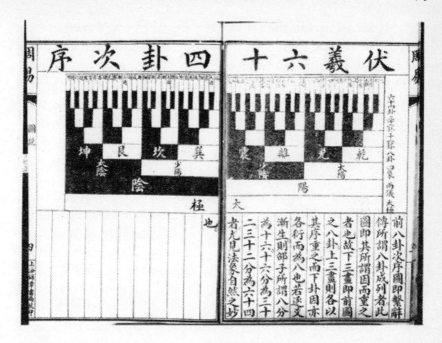

Figure 43: Another I Ching *illustration from the* Illustrated Version of
the 'Imperially Authorized' I Ching *from which the previous Figure was
taken. This is also a view of the Fu Hsi (Fu Xi) diagram called 'Preceding
Heaven'. The title given above the illustration says: 'The Order of Fu
Hsi's 64 Diagrams'. At the bottom of the diagram everything merges into
a unity called 'The Great Absolute' or 'The Supreme Ultimate'. Just
above it the line which is half black and half white represents* yin *and*
yang, *also known as 'the two modes'. Then in ascending order the two
('the two modes') split into four ('the four images', Greater and Lesser*
Yang *and Greater and Lesser* Yin), *the four into eight ('the eight
trigrams'), the eight into sixteen, the sixteen into 32, and the 32 finally
become the 64 hexagrams. The text explains the process of splitting 16
into 32, etc. This diagram also was spread across facing pages of the
original book, and the difference in quality between the two sides is due
to the two pages having been printed at separate times from separate
blocks. (Collection of Robert Temple)*

Yung. First let us see what he wrote about this, and then let us
compare it to what a contemporary cyber-thinker has to say.
Shao Yung said a millennium ago:

. . . one can use all the eyes of the world as one's own eyes; there is nothing these eyes do not contemplate. One can use all the ears of the world as one's own ears; there is nothing these ears do not hear. . . . One can use all the minds of the world as one's own mind; there is nothing these minds do not think about. . . . [this is done by] not contemplating things from the perspective of the self.[47]

. . . [the sage] is a person able by means of his own single mind to observe a myriad of other minds. . . . What I mean by the observation of things does not mean observing them with the eye. No, it is not observation with the eye, but observation with the mind . . . one is thus able to observe things in terms of those things. . . . In this way one acquires the ability to use the eyes of the entire world as one's own eyes, with which eyes there is nothing that is not observed.[48]

A near contemporary of Shao Yung's, a fellow philosopher of the Neo-Confucian school named Ch'eng Hao [Cheng Hao; AD 1032–85], expressed a similar idea in a slightly more enigmatic form and specifically mentions the *I Ching* as embodying the essence of a world-mind: 'The constant pattern of heaven-and-earth is that its mind pervades all things, yet it has no mind. . . . The *I* is without thought and without activity. Silent and unmoving, when stimulated it then penetrates all situations . . .'[49]

Shao Yung explains how it is that an individual who has stepped outside of self can commune with the world-mind: 'Now, what is meant by contemplating things is not using the eye to contemplate them. It is not contemplating them with the eye but contemplating them with the mind.'[50]

Now let us see what the French cyber-philosopher Pierre Lévy has to say in his book *Collective Intelligence*:

What is collective intelligence? It is a form of *universally distributed intelligence* . . . My initial premise is based on the notion of a universally distributed intelligence. No one knows everything, everyone knows something, all knowledge resides in humanity. There is no transcendent store of knowledge and knowledge is simply the sum of what we know. .... There is little doubt that intelligence is universally distributed. .... New communications systems should provide members of a community with the means to coordinate their interactions within the same virtual universe of knowledge. This is not simply a matter of modelling the conventional physical environment, but of enabling members of delocalized communities to interact within a mobile landscape of signification. Events, decisions, actions, and individuals would be situated along dynamic maps of shared context and continuously transform the virtual universe in which they assume meaning. In this sense cyberspace would become the shifting space of interaction among knowledge and knowers in deterritorialized intelligent communities. .... This project implies a new humanism that incorporates and enlarges the scope of self knowledge into a form of group knowledge and collective thought. .... Far from merging individual intelligence into some indistinguishable magma, collective intelligence is a process of growth, differentiation, and the mutual revival of singularities.[51]

Shao Yung and his friends would have felt very comfortable with this, and indeed if one could go back in time to the eleventh century and hand Shao Yung a laptop computer, he would probably become a geek within a week. After all, he did invent binary arithmetic, which underlies the operations of all computers!

All of this is not just of casual interest, but is fundamental to what we have to consider now of Shao Yung's interpretation and use of the *I Ching*. This is yet another astonishing tale to tell. Shao Yung believed that phenomena could be mathematically plotted by complex arrangements and arrays of numbers, which represented a variety of what we might call today 'phase spaces'. And these phenomena being in a sense mental, the selfless mind of the sage could roam over them like a helicopter searching for a sailor lost in the sea. Basically there was a clockwise roaming across the number arrays, which followed the natural order of events, and a counter-clockwise roaming across the number arrays which went against the natural order and therefore 'went against time'; this direction contrary to the flow of time enabled prediction to take place. Such processes were best modelled on a circular pattern such as that seen in Figure 42, which is a form of the traditional *I Ching* diagram known by the name of 'Preceding Heaven'. Shao Yung called it this because he believed it existed before heaven even came into existence, so fundamental was it to the universe.

In the circular diagram of Figure 42, the top symbol or hexagram is the one consisting entirely of solid lines (just to the left of the page fold). At the bottom of the circle is a symbol or hexagram consisting entirely of broken lines (just to the right of the page fold). The top one is entirely *yang* (wholly solid) and the bottom one is entirely *yin* (wholly broken). According to Shao Yung's scheme, physical processes begin at the top and slide down to the bottom, and then rise up again, in a clockwise cycle. But if we move back in a contra-flow, like someone driving in the wrong direction up a one-way street, we can 'cheat' and find out what will happen in the future. As Shao Yung says:

> Knowing what is to come is contrary motion . . . all the trigrams [and hexagrams] have not yet been produced. Therefore it says, 'knowing what is to come.' . . . Knowing what is to come is contrary motion [*ni*, which has the double meaning in Chinese of 'going against' and 'in advance']. Therefore the *I* 'goes against' (*ni*) its numbers [in the Preceding Heaven Diagram].[52]

This gives us an inkling of how Shao Yung was plotting processes in both space and time according to number series. But for many centuries, the full complexity of his number schemes was not properly understood. It is only in modern times that Western scholars have been slowly unravelling it. And the most inspired treatment of the subject that I have encountered is in a pamphlet which is so extraordinarily rare that there is no copy of it in the British Library. As with so many of the books that are not in the British Library and which I have required in my research, this one magically came into my hands. I suppose I must have about a hundred important books or pamphlets of which mine are probably the only copies in Britain (some of them Chinese books and manuscripts, of course). In this case, it is only a little pamphlet of 16 pages published privately in Jerusalem in 1948. It is by a Jewish scholar named Immanuel Olsvanger. He normally wrote in German or in Yiddish, and his speciality was Jewish folklore studies. I have reproduced a small portion of this pamphlet as Appendix 4. The pamphlet is entitled *Fu-Hsi: The Sage of Ancient China*. Fu-Hsi [Fu Xi] was a legendary founder of Chinese culture, credited with some of the ideas for the *I Ching*, including the diagrams called Preceding Heaven.

Olsvanger analysed the *I Ching* diagrams, as well as other related mysterious diagrams called Ho and Lo, in a new way. In the square 'chessboard' King Wen sequence (Figure 40), he replaced the hexagrams with their corresponding numerical values and came up with the diagram reproduced as Figure 44. He then broke this pattern down into a series of regions having special mathematical properties, namely several adjoining 'magic squares'. Magic squares are squares filled with numbers which, if added up in any direction, across, up and down, or whatever, always give the same total.

I was first introduced to magic squares in my teens. When I was sixteen, both Shao Yung and magic squares were explained to me by my scientific and philosophical mentor, Arthur Young. But by the time I was eighteen, I had befriended the world's leading expert on Chinese magic squares, Schuyler Cammann, who gave me his offprints on the subject and discussed them with me. Cammann was a very shy and rather lonely man who was an Associate Professor in the Oriental Studies Department (as it was then called) at the University of Pennsylvania, where I was a Sanskrit student (the only Sanskrit student, as it happens). He was descended from one of the original Dutch families who settled America, when the city we call New York was known by its original name of New Amsterdam. He was also independently wealthy. Cammann was on very bad personal terms with Professor Derk Bodde, under whom I was studying Chinese philosophy and whom I never found to be a warm personality (to put it tactfully), and he was alienated (though not for personal reasons) from the very amiable Allyn Rickett under whom I was studying Chinese literature. I was one of the few people who was prepared to befriend and talk to Cammann, who was ostracized by various people who shall be nameless because of his political views (he was opposed to Mao). It is actually difficult to be frank about these matters even after all these years, since some parties are still alive. To say that there was a lot of intrigue around would be an understatement! It is almost impossible to take an interest in Chinese studies without encountering political passions. But I ignored all the politics and concentrated on scholarly matters, despite a lot of pressure to the contrary. I was the only person on campus poor Cammann had to talk to about his magic squares! I felt really sorry for him, and used to go and chat about magic squares not only because I found them interesting but to try and cheer him up. I did get bored when he showed me items from his huge collection of old Chinese snuff bottles, however, as I have never found those interesting.

Schuyler Cammann had published a pamphlet entitled 'The Magic Square of Three in Old Chinese Philosophy and Religion' in 1961.[53] The famous Confucian 'Lo Diagram', sometimes associated with the I Ching, is really a magic square of three. But magic squares have never been a familiar phenomenon in Western culture. According to the German mathematician Hermann Schubert, the first known occurrence of a magic square in the West is its portrayal in a famous drawing by Albrecht Dürer, entitled 'Melancholy', where it may be seen inscribed on a tablet and hanging on the wall behind a depressed and brooding angel.[54] This magic square contains the numbers from 1 to 16 and always adds up to 34 in any direction. As we shall see later, Albrecht Dürer was remarkable for his geometrical researches, and here we see that he dabbled in odd mathematical puzzles as well, the source of which was China, though by which route we do not know.

In the bizarre group of adjoining magic squares that we see in Figure 44, we see the true nature of one of the famous *I Ching* diagrams. The boxes shown in black add up in every direction to 104, the ones in the rectangle at top left add up in every direction to 132, there are two partially overlapping rectangles in the top right that add up in every direction to 240, all the remaining numbers add up to 532, and so on. (The Figure gives the text direct from Olsvanger.) Olsvanger appears to have worked all of this out by tinkering – he must have had a lot of time on his hands!

Olsvanger continued his analysis and discovered that the King Wen Sequence also shows that 'Column I . . . has been construed in a beautiful process of symmetrical additions of the numbers in the original tablet containing the powers of 2'. Olsvanger's analyses are too long and complex to reproduce here. He even found a meandering line in the King Wen Sequence that separated two groups of numbers, each of which added up to 1008 on either side of the meander. With these and other findings, Olsvanger was more than justified in insisting that the King Wen Sequence 'was not at all arbitrary'. He stressed that he had only discovered some of the deep mathematical aspects of these diagrams, and he was convinced that there were more.

With the circular form of the Preceding Heaven Diagram (Figure 41), Shao Yung envisaged the birth of *yang* at the bottom, which rose to the top, and the birth of *yin* at the top, which then fell to the bottom, all of this taking place clockwise. He says: '. . . there is nothing that does not come from this!'[55] He also said: 'The Supreme Ultimate having divided, the two modes were established. *Yang* rose and interacted with *yin*. *Yin* descended and interacted with *yang*. . . . Things must come into being by going with . . . time can be known by going against . . . The Supreme Ultimate is one (unitary). Unmoving, it gives birth to two (duality, i.e. *yin* and *yang*). Duality, then spirit. Spirit gives birth to number. Number gives birth to images. Images give birth to objects.'[56]

We see here that there was an immensely complex mathematics and cosmology elaborated around the basic *yang* and *yin*

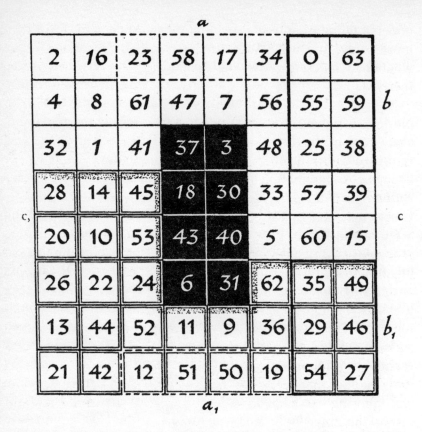

*Figure 44: The King Wen Sequence as analysed by Immanuel Olsvanger:
A particularly complex and intricate Chinese magic square, of a multiple
nature. In this one, the sum of the numbers plainly written equals the
sum of those inserted in thin frames (904). The sums in the two parts of
the black middle column are equal (104); the sum in the upper rectangle
a is equal to that in the lower rectangle a (132); the sums of the numbers
in the two right corner rectangles b and b are equal (240); cutting out the
four rectangles just mentioned, the sums of the remaining groups in
either group will remain equal (532), these two groups now forming a
symmetry by reflection, partly vertical (c and c), and partly horizontal*

concepts in China, patterns which later in this book I explain as
'flow' and 'stasis' in modern physical terms. As Olsvanger
discovered, we do not yet by any means have a full

understanding of all the ideas embedded in this lore. It calls for more study, and will doubtless prove to be as inexhaustible as what the Chinese call 'the ten thousand things' (i.e. everything there is).

No less intriging, however, are some new discoveries which we shall now proceed to consider, and for this purpose we shall return to the traditional Chinese preoccupation with universal change. A fascinating early Chinese novella entitled *The Emperor and the Two Sisters,* written shortly before the birth of Christ, gives an indication of the popular attitudes. In the story, a remote barbarian tribe in the southwest corner of the Empire sent some gifts of tribute to the Emperor, Fan I. The leader of this mission from the barbarians was 'an extraordinary man who with a single meal of vegetables absorbed so much strength that for days and nights he did not need to sleep. The Colonial Office reported this fact and added that this man's figure was surrounded by a remarkable radiance.' The Empress was a moody, self-indulgent woman who was entirely preoccupied with the fact that the Emperor had eyes only for her sister, and was ignoring her. This drove her to desperate measures to try to attract the Emperor's love once more:

> . . . she had the stranger asked what sort of magic he used. 'My magic consists in this,' he answered, 'that Heaven and Earth are balanced in me, that life and death are one and the same. Growing and passing away, being and not being, in their transmutations mark the ten thousand different shapes – but I remain eternally unchanged.'
> The Empress sent him a thousand gold pieces through a younger brother of Fan I's in order to win him to her, but the stranger sent the message: 'He who wishes to learn my art must first abandon concupiscence and lies.' To this the Empress gave him no answer.[57]

Here we find in popular fiction a perfect example of what the Chinese traditionally viewed as the 'be-all and end-all'. The 'ten

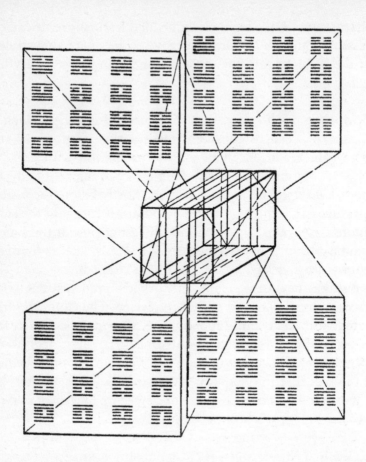

*Figure 45: Z. D. Sung's extraordinary diagram entitled 'the cube of three
quadrinomial dimensions' appearing on page 48 of his book* The
Symbols of Yi King, or The Symbols of the Chinese Logic of Changes,
*Paragon Book Reprint Corporation, New York, 1969 (original edition,
Shanghai, 1934). This and other similar diagrams are part of Sung's
attempt to explain the mathematics of the* I Ching *by rather complicated
and sometimes baffling means. A full comprehension of his theories
about the* I Ching *can only be attained by long and close study of his
book, and it cannot possibly be summarized. But I wanted to give one of
his diagrams just to give an idea of his techniques*

thousand shapes' is a phrase referring to the infinite number of
changes. (To the Chinese 'ten thousand' has always been a form
of saying 'infinite': it is like our Western habit of saying 'I had

hundreds of things to eat at the banquet', meaning, simply, lots.) Despite all the flux of change, the universe does not change. It says in the *I Ching*: 'Change – that is, the unchangeable.' This seems to be a paradox, but refers to the fact that amidst all the things which cannot be relied upon, the one which is constant is change: transformations will inevitably occur. This the Chinese view as a comfort. But this change is inherent, is from within. As Hellmut Wilhelm says:

> The concept of change is not an external . . . principle that imprints itself upon phenomena; it is an inner tendency according to which development takes place naturally and spontaneously. . . . To recognize that man moves and acts, that he grows and develops, this is not deep insight, but to know that this movement and development take place in typical forms and that these are governed by the law of change, from which there is no escape, this is the knowledge that has fostered in early Chinese philosophy its gratifying integrity and lucidity.[58]

It is worthwhile trying to discover how far back these attitudes go. To do so, we can look at the oldest surviving Chinese texts, which are even older than the *I Ching* itself. They come from the *Shu Ching (History Classic)*, which records the most ancient Chinese history. The most recent episode recounted in the *Shu Ching* was 2500 years ago, but most of the history recorded there is far earlier, and some of the documents seem to be genuinely 3500 years old or more. It is remarkable that any of these writings survive.

Near the beginning of the *Shu Ching* we find an admonition addressed to the Emperor: 'Let him be wary and fearful, remembering that in one day or two days there may occur ten thousand springs of things.'[59] Here we find a sensitivity to the ineffable and manifold origins of events which are springing up all around one at every moment, noticed shortly afterwards in this further counsel: 'Find your repose in your proper resting point. Attend to the springs of things, study stability.'[60] The

Chinese realized that the 'springs of things' are the most important phenomena to watch for. In Chinese cuisine, for example, there is considerable emphasis on beansprouts, bamboo shoots, baby corncobs, and other young, budding, or sprouting foods.

The *Shu* also emphasizes the minute scrutiny which must be applied: 'We must deal cautiously with the favouring appointment of Heaven, at every moment and in the smallest particular.'[61] And the Emperor is told by a minister: 'It is yours to lead on and originate things.'[62] Thus the Emperor, who holds Heaven's mandate, tries to emulate Heaven – and he does so by originating and noting the springs of all.

The ends of processes were also viewed with circumspection. It was just as important to note the time of decay as the time of growth. As the *Shu* suggests in advice to another Emperor: 'When you thus accelerate the end of what is of itself ready to perish, and strengthen what is itself strong to live, how the states flourish!'[63] There is also the pungent maxim: 'Be careful for the end at the beginning.'[64]

In following the changes one must realize that they form sensible patterns. And our own behaviour must emulate the sense and purpose of universal process: 'Your course must be as in ascending high: you begin from where it is low; and when in travelling far: you begin where it is near.'[65] All of this is combined with sage advice: 'He who likes to put questions becomes enlarged; he who uses only his own views becomes smaller than he was.'[66] And we are given this vivid description of an early Emperor who reigned beneficently and brought peace to his land: 'The former king, before it was light, sought to have large and clear views and then sat waiting for the morning.'[67]

Responsibility for one's own fate is emphasized: 'Calamities sent by Heaven may be avoided, but from calamities brought on by one's self there is no escape.'[68] And: 'It is not Heaven that cuts short men's lives; they bring them to an end themselves. Some men who have not complied with virtue will not acknowledge their offences. When Heaven has by evident tokens charged them to correct their conduct, they still say: "What are these things to us?"'[69] Here we see the philosophy of signs and portents. 'Heaven' or 'fate' or 'the universe' or 'God' or 'the spirits' or whatever we want to imagine – or possibly just the flow of processes below and beneath us, in grander forms and patterns than we consciously know, at levels of reality which the logical or even the conscious mind cannot touch, warns us by 'evident tokens' of the direction that things are taking.

According to the ancient *Shu*, only a fool refuses to see the signs and make adjustments accordingly with all due speed.

The *Shu* shares with the *I Ching* that fine sense of balance, the delicate touch, the awareness of the knife-edge of events, of how success can tumble at any moment into disaster as into a pit, and how from the bottom one can suddenly be catapulted up to the top. As the *I Ching* says: 'The explanations in the book express a feeling of anxious apprehension, and teach how peril may be turned into security, and easy carelessness is sure to meet with overthrow.' This statement from the *I Ching* is nearly identical with one from the *Shu Ching*: 'In the enjoyment of favour think of peril and never be without a cautious apprehension; he who is without such apprehension finds himself amidst what is really to be feared.'[70] And we are the ones who are responsible for being aware of these small springs of things, for turning them to our advantage and guiding bad developments gently away as we see the stream beginning to flow towards us. If we fail to be vigilant, then, as the *Shu* says: 'It is not Heaven that does not deal impartially with men; men ruin themselves.'[71] The responsibility is awesome. An Emperor in the *Shu* says: 'The trembling anxiety of my mind makes me feel as if I were treading on a tiger's tail, or walking upon spring ice.'[72] This reminds us of a passage in the *I Ching* where Hexagram 10 has the Judgement: 'Lu. Treading upon the tail of the tiger.'[73]

The *Shu* and the *I Ching* share images and notions which seem to go back to distant antiquity. Throughout the oldest layers of the *I Ching* text there are recurring examples of the phrase 'It will be advantageous [or disadvantageous] to cross the Great Water'. The emphasis in the *I Ching* is on the right moment to act thus. Likewise, in the *Shu*, we find the same recurrent image: 'The case is like that of sailing in a boat; if you do not cross the stream at the proper time, you will destroy all the cargo.'[74] 'Suppose me crossing a great stream; I will use you for a boat with its oars,' says an Emperor to his new prime minister, who is supposed to navigate all the hazards of state. One can 'cross the Great Water' at the wrong time and find disaster. The collapse of the Shang Dynasty (1776–1122 BC) was described this way in the *Shu*, as it was about to occur: 'Its condition is like one crossing a large stream who finds neither ford nor bank.'[75] An Emperor seeks guidance and phrases it this way: 'Yes, I am but ... in the position of one who has to go through a deep water; I must go and seek where I can cross over.'[76] The Emperor says to his minister: 'Now with me ... it is as if I were floating on a great stream. With you, O Shih, let me from this time endeavour to cross it.'[77]

The *I Ching* itself mentions some of the historical figures in the *Shu Ching*, showing some of the links between these earliest Chinese books. Hexagram 63, Commentary on the Third Line, mentions the Emperor Wu Ting [Wu Ding], who reigned from 1324 to 1266 BC.[78] The *Shu Ching* in turn mentions the techniques of divination by yarrow stalks used for the *I Ching*. Every major act of state had to be coordinated with the universal currents and patterns. Before the attack which brought the downfall of the Shang Dynasty and its replacement by the Chou, the king says: 'My dreams coincide with my divinations; the auspicious omen is double. My attack on Shang must succeed.'[79] So we see that the extremely early texts of these two separate books, as well as some of the contemporary poems, interweave in common phrases and concepts and are very much a part of the same culture. We have already seen that the *I Ching* had somewhat similar relations to the poems of the third most ancient book, the *Book of Songs (Shih Ching)*, which means that these three most ancient *Ching* are like three sisters dressed alike, all with the same smile. There is nothing to be gained from maintaining, as most superficial books on the *I Ching* do, that the *I Ching* stands alone, is the earliest Chinese book, and has nothing in common with any other.

One of the postulates of the *I Ching* is that change, when it takes place, endures in extended periods rather than being a flash at an instant. As the change consists of more than just a central dot in space, being rather a configuration or larger pattern surrounding the event, so also in time the change is extended. This is central to the Chinese attitude towards understanding and harnessing change. It is because change is extended once it has commenced that we can sometimes tiptoe round it and get out of the way, or even tease it in our own direction if it appears favourable. This is like standing in a large field in which springs – the 'ten thousand springs of things' – suddenly burst forth out of the ground, and, as the water runs forth in endless streams, and the rivulets rapidly criss-cross, we have the task of avoiding the unpleasant ones and seeking out the ones we like.

At Grayson Springs, near the Kentucky–Tennessee border, there are seven springs in a row over a space of about a hundred yards. As you walk along with your cup to try the water, each spring tastes more strongly of sulphur than the last, the last one of all being very potent. Imagine these springs overflowing drastically and forming seven deep streams. If you wanted to swim in one of them you would try to choose the sweetest water, and to avoid the most sulphurous in case you swallowed some of it or it stung your eyes. This is what it is like dealing with change. You try to find the sweetest stream, and you swim in that one instead of leaping into a bitter one full of sorrows and vicissitudes. Some streams are swift and help you on your journey, while others are sluggish and murky, retarding all progress and leaving you struggling in the mud.

The idea of swimming through life, of sampling the different pools, but of choosing the best streams, expresses very well the way the Chinese see change working. As Hellmut Wilhelm comments: 'Development is not a fate dictated from without to which one must silently submit, but rather a sign showing the direction that decisions take. Again, development is not a moral law that one is constrained to obey; it is rather the guideline from which one can read off events. To stand in the stream of this development is a datum of nature; to recognize it and follow it is responsibility and free choice.'[80]

Or, as both the *I Ching* and the *Shu Ching* tell us: 'Cross the Great Water' – but do so at the right time and in the right company.

EIGHT

THE ORACLE BONES

In order to understand what lies at the basis of the ancient Chinese system of thought as represented in the *I Ching*, we must investigate those extremely ancient and important objects, the oracle bones. Most are shoulderbones of oxen made into tablets, or shells of tortoises, which also made covenient 'tablets'. They were first discovered in ancient Chinese sites by peasants, who sold them as dragon bones for aphrodisiac purposes.

They came to the attention of archaeologists, and since then many tens of thousands have been excavated. Many of the bones and shells are inscribed with archaic Chinese writing, and they are thus a prime source of our knowledge of ancient China. The first comprehensive book written in English about the culture from which the oracle bones come appeared in 1980, and is entitled *Shang Civilization*.[1] The book is important and deserves to be more widely known.

To my knowledge, no one has ever suggested how the oracle bones might relate to the *I Ching*. However, since they were used for divination in a manner which I shall shortly describe, and they date from a period when we know the yarrow stalks of the *I Ching* system were used for the same purpose, it seems reasonable to suppose some connection must have existed between them.

In working out such a connection I managed to gain some insight by trying to imagine how one of the Chinese diviners might have seen things. Those ancient thinkers were close to nature in a most intimate way which we can hardly understand

Figure 46: The carapace of the tortoise which was used in Shang Dynasty oracle consultations represented Heaven, and here it is seen depicting the constellations of the night sky. Along the rim of the carapace and also scattered in the sky are the trigrams of the I Ching system, and thus the two divination systems are fused in this one design, probably

*commissioned for a Taoist temple. This picture in my collection is
unique, and its survival in this authentic form is apparently unknown to
historians of Chinese art. It is entitled 'The True Abode of the Tortoise
and the Snake', i.e. 'Dark Warrior', meaning the northern sky. It is a
very old rubbing of a carving in stone by the famous Tang Dynasty artist
Wu Tao Tzu (Wu Dao Zi), who was active* AD 710–60. *The original
carving is believed to have been destroyed long ago, and it apparently
survives only in this rubbing, although paintings copied from it without
attribution – or copied from copies – survive in museums, without
anyone seeming to realize that they are based on a lost original by Wu. I
also own one of these later scroll paintings, done in white paint on a red
background, but it is very inferior to the rubbing in quality of drawing
and calligraphy and makes some errors such as giving the tortoise the
wrong number of toe-claws. No actual original painting by Wu has
survived, but one of his other stone carvings, 'Flying Demon', is still
preserved at a temple in Quyang, Hebei Province. Apart from that
carving, this rubbing is thus the only surviving genuine work of Wu, who
is such a famous figure in the history of Chinese art that he was actually
deified after his death as the Patron God of Painters. Most of his work is
said to have consisted of temple murals commissioned for Buddhist and
Taoist temples, as was obviously the case with this one, though in this
instance it was certainly Taoist rather than Buddhist. Wu was the
founder of the 'loose' style of painting, whereby the artist attempted to
convey as much as possible with as few strokes of the brush as possible;
later this became the ideal of the whole of Chinese art and calligraphy.
Wu gave street performances of this technique, which dazzled the public.
In one famous incident, he painted a halo in a single freehand stroke, and
we are told: 'He raised his brush and swept it around with the force of a
whirlwind, so that everyone said a god was aiding him.' Wu's paintings
of heavenly dragons were said to be 'so lifelike that mist swirled around
them whenever it was about to rain'. In this picture, the edges of the
celestial tortoise's carapace are subtly drawn not as lines but as clouds,
according to Wu's famous technique of 'flowing water and scudding
clouds', and yet are done so simply that one can almost not notice. The
square seal in the centre, rubbed in red, merely says* lei
*('Thunder/Thunder/Thunder' . . .) ten times. Wu's signature is to the
right of the seal, and the bottom character is* bei, *which means the
equivalent of* fecit *('made this') in Latin. This rubbing of the title and of
Wu's signature is presumably the only surviving example of his personal
calligraphy. I can honestly say that this is the only thing I have which
was 'made by a god', other than natural objects which were made by a
higher one. (Collection of Robert Temple)*

today, and which yielded, I am convinced, an extraordinary profundity of both observation and thought. By 'close to nature' I do not mean sitting beside a brook and drifting off into a reverie, or being inspired by the sight of a waterfall, or feeling the light breeze 'that breathes upon a bank of violets'. These are merely momentary respites from a technological world. Rather, I mean having experience of growing things, of woods, and glades, and springs, and streams, knowing how the birds fly and where they nest, and where the rare orchids bloom, following the vixen to her lair and watching her lick and nudge her bumbling cubs – this brings us closer.

What I am referring to is a very deep communion with nature which is essentially mystical in its intensity, and basically scientific in its structure. This latter quality rules out the pure mystics, because they tend to speak in mere generalities. The essence of knowing nature would seem to be to combine the generalities of 'the way things happen' with the most rigorous and intense observations of particulars. Somebody who sits in a trance all day will neither have the time nor consider it worth his while to observe the particulars of nature.

I believe the ancient Chinese achieved the true form of natural science. It was intensely particular, and yet was at the same time general to a sublime degree. The ancient Chinese seem to have achieved this profundity through listening to nature's voice and allowing wholeness to grow naturally within them, from the root of nature which exists inside the heart of every man. I also believe that man's most profound way of being is to allow the way of nature to become his way, inside himself, and while being truly and fully himself, to become at the same time truly and fully nature. The two give strength to and support one another in their growth.

Perhaps as we proceed with some of the uncovered secrets of the *I Ching,* what I mean will become clearer if you attempt to imagine the kind of mentality that could have constructed the *I Ching* system and observed the rather selective and peculiar aspects of nature which it uses. The things that these ancient thinkers noticed and incorporated into their system are all meaningful within a certain framework. Let us try as we examine these things to simulate the mental stance – so alien on the surface, and yet so familiar deep within our suppressed natural selves – of these men, to whom thinking and observing in this way was the most natural and unquestioned method of trying to penetrate the secrets of the universe. I really do believe that if we ourselves could think like this once in a while, and apply the fruits of it to our own world, we might achieve a higher intellectual synthesis. Can we not salvage these lost ways of thinking, combine them with our contemporary modes, and make breakthroughs which are otherwise unobtainable?

Let us turn our attention to the tortoise. The pattern of hexagons on a tortoise's shell would have been considered a certain sign of his sacred character for divination by the Chinese, who would have equated these with their concepts of hexagrams. In modern Chinese tradition, the land tortoise *(Ocadia sinensis)* is known as the Black Warrior. He is a powerful guardian of graves, and also a symbol of long life. He is one of the Four Sacred Animals who preside over the four points of the compass and the four seasons. The tortoise himself represents north and the winter. The Chinese have a curious folk belief that tortoises are all female, and that if they are to reproduce, they must mate with serpents! Because of this belief, to call a man a 'tortoise egg' *(wang pa)* is the worst insult which you can offer him. It implies that he is a bastard, and does not know his own father, and indeed that his father was of a different kind altogether.

In the ancient times of the Shang Dynasty, 1776–1122 BC, tortoises were sacred and were specially bred for a particular purpose. The tortoises in use then are now extinct; they have been given the name *Pseudocadia anyangensis* retrospectively, after the name Anyang, site of important archaeological discoveries.

Underneath the carapace of the tortoise is a softer underlayer, the plastron, which was used for divination. (Less often the carapace itself was used, usually broken in half.) In Figures 47 and 48 we can see a rare whole tortoise plastron which has

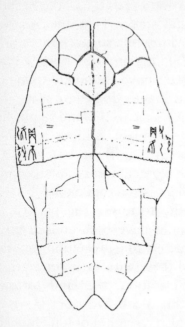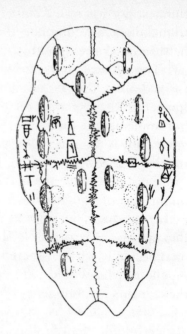

*Figure 47 (left): Drawing of the top surface of the same tortoise plastron.
To the left and right are a few archaic Chinese characters concerning the
divination*

*Figure 48 (right): Drawing of the bottom surface of a complete tortoise
plastron. Sixteen lentoid (bean-shaped) cavities have been cut into it. The
roundish, lightly shaded areas to the side of them are scorch-marks from
the application of the red-hot divination instrument*

survived unbroken, and is now in the Royal Ontario Museum in
Toronto, among an extensive and valuable collection of such
items.

To prepare these plastrons for divination purposes, cavities
were cut into them. When the question was put – usually by, or
on behalf of, the king – a red-hot implement, probably in the
form of a metal rod,[2] would be applied to the cavities, working
from the bottom up, although often some of the cut cavities were
purposely left unscorched, indicating that there was a definite
system of selection, which we do not fully understand.

The scorching of the cavity caused sufficient heat in the

thinnest portion of the plastron, at the very bottom of the cavity, to make cracks along the surface underneath. These cracks may be seen on the reverse (top) of the plastron, as shown in Figure 47. The normal pattern for a crack is a straight vertical line formed along the line of the centre of the cavity bottom, and a further crack at an angle to the first one, which was caused by the hot implement resting to the side of the cavity bottom, at a right angle. It was these side cracks which gave the oracular response, for they varied in their nature.

It can be seen in the plastron that there has been no cheating on the part of the diviner. The hot implement was obviously held reasonably straight each time, causing uniform scorch marks. But the resulting side cracks vary nevertheless and it is in such unexpected variation that the divination technique of the tortoise oracle lies. The normal side crack would be at right angles, like the implement. In the figures you can see that most of the side

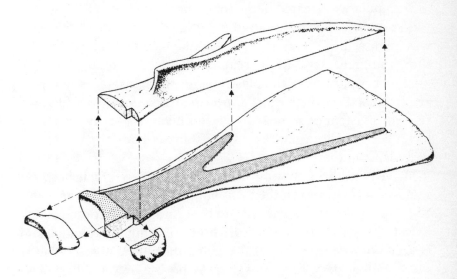

Figure 49: The shoulderblade of the ox was prepared for divination by making it flat and tablet-like. These tablet-bones could then be stored in rows to form archives. Many rows of carefully filed bones have been found in excavations. (Redrawn from Hung-hsiang Chou, Scientific American, *April 1979)*

cracks are indeed like this. Only one side crack on the entire shell is different: the one on the bottom left. This one shoots up at an angle of roughly 60° to the vertical and 30° to the perpendicular.

The Chinese character *pu* [*bu*], 'to divine', is ⋏. It is recognized by scholars that this character derives from the variation pattern of a side crack which branches out at 60°/30° rather than at the right angles of the hot implement. This ancient character is still used to day, but goes back unchanged to the Shang period, 3500 years ago, when these tortoise plastrons were in constant use.

Sometimes, instead of tortoise plastrons, the shoulderblades (scapulae) of animals were used; divination by these is called 'scapulimancy'. Cavities were cut into these bones and scorched, as with the tortoise plastrons. The procedure has been deduced to have been from the bottom, fan-shaped, end of the bone, working upwards. Right shoulderbones were scorched from the right side of the cavities, and left ones from the left side of the cavities.

A scapula was treated in the following way. Half of the socket was sawn off, and the longitudinal ridge on one side of the bone was removed. This made the scapula flat and tablet-like (as shown in Figure 49). Many scapulae have been found buried in piles or rows, as have the plastrons. In some instances numbers are scratched on their ends, appearing to conform to a filing or reference system of some sort. The archives of the diviners must have been well organized. The Chinese had a passion for precedents in these matters.

I have been through some hundreds of Chinese oracle bones in London, where most of the items happen to be scapulae and very few are plastrons. There are two separate collections in the British Museum, the better of the two being catalogued and treated not as objects but as texts, and they bring them to you at your reading desk in trays. There is no list or survey of these objects, though they are numbered. They are merely dumped together. You order them as if they were books. They are kept in drawers, which come from a wooden cabinet, which is very shallow – if the drawers are pulled out too hastily, they flip over in your hand and the bones fall on the floor and shatter. Once in the old library building I went along into the stacks to help find the bones (which apparently had not been consulted by any 'reader' in years) and when we found the cabinet eventually and the attendant pulled out the drawer, it overturned and the contents were spilled all over the place, and one of the bones broke into pieces. Such are the vicissitudes of 3500-year-old objects which survive excavation only to be broken in libraries!

One of the most interesting shoulderbones in the British Library is to be seen in Plate 38 (front and back views of the same bone). This bone is split part of the way down the middle of its length, which gives a dramatic demonstration of the heat that must have been applied in the scorching. This is a right shoulderbone, so the black scorch-marks may be seen very clearly to the right of the equally clear cavities, behind four of which the bone has split clean in half. Both the cracks and the writing on this bone preserve the dark colouring matter which was rubbed into them to make them more easily visible (presumably before being deposited in the archives).

The scorching on this bone would have started at the bottom. The first sideways crack is at a perfect right angle. The number 2 is written by it (two scratches). The second sideways crack is also at right angles; the number 3 is written by it (three scratches). The third is not right-angled, and the number 2 is by it. The fourth is a right angle and has the number 1. The fifth crack is double: two sidelines go shooting out, each at 30° to the vertical, making a 120° angle between themselves. This is numbered 1 also. The sixth crack is at 60° to the vertical and 30° to the perpendicular. It appears to have no number. The seventh crack is at right angles and is numbered 1. The eighth and final crack at the top sends out a side crack which then shoots into two, which make a 120° angle between themselves, as happened with the fifth crack. At the top, to the left of the seventh crack, and again at the very top on the right of the eighth crack is (upside down) the Chinese character pu, 'to divine'. It may be clearly seen on this bone that this written character resembles the sideways crack which occurred with the sixth and the top parts of the fifth and eighth cracks.

The numbers which are inscribed on the bone obviously do not simply ascribe a 'value' to the crack, otherwise similar cracks would not have different numbers, nor do they designate the order of the cracks. They do not even designate a straightforward sequence of scorching, for if that were the case there would not be different cracks with the same number. These inscribed numbers must therefore refer to something else, possibly concerning the divination system and its rules, which we no longer possess. I believe that it may be possible to unravel the system by a systematic study of all the known bones and plastrons; but these are all over the world in China, Canada, Britain, and elsewhere. Furthermore, there are some forgeries which must be excluded (though experts can usually spot these quite easily). Some forgeries are done on original old bones, but the forgers never get the Shang script right, and I have held in my hand other forged pieces which were much too light in weight. I even own one, which was forged about 100 years ago. Original inscriptions on tortoise plastrons were cut while the plastrons were green and fairly soft so that the cuts are clean; forged inscriptions on old plastrons are rougher because the material had become hard before the inscription was cut.

One may well ask what all these weird cracks were meant to represent. The theory appears to have been that the 'force field' or 'way things are going' or 'tendency' is represented – or almost depicted – by the crack. Probably there was a basic distinction between right-angled and not-right-angled, as there is between *yin* and *yang*. The further complications which can arise in the sideways cracks may be considered as addenda, further elaborations of the answer (rather like what are called the 'moving lines' in the *I Ching* system – see below). Obviously the diviners never settled for just a single cracking. They did a series. A series is necessary also in the *I Ching* system with the yarrow stalks (of which I shall give an account shortly); there is never just one parting of the stalks, there must always be many, so that out of the multiplicity of the changes the answer may result. This series of attempts within the framework of a system is meant to ensure, I assume, that chance alone had a diminishing place in it.

For, although a diviner might think that a single such act of consultation could have a chance result, an accumulation of consultations would be viewed as being purged of chance and truly indicating 'the way things were going'. For such a purpose, the yarrow stalks were a considerable improvement over the tortoise shell, or at least that is what I surmise. But in Shang China, the tortoise shell was, at least publicly, honoured above the yarrow stalks, and both methods were practised simultaneously. Professor Shih-Chuan Chen has found evidence that the system of the yarrow stalks was a state secret of the court until 685 BC![3]

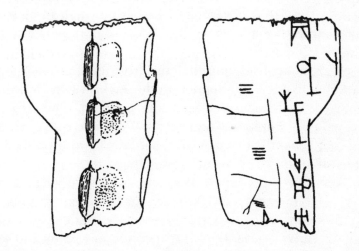

Figure 50: Left: Underside of a scapula, with cavities and scorch-marks Right: The resulting topside cracks from the two scorchings. Both of these were rare multiple crackings

I reproduce in Figure 50 a scapula with a crack in it which started out at a right angle and then sent an offshoot up at 30° to itself. This multiple cracking is unusual. The crack below it also appears normal until it splits, the bottom part then having a tiny 30° offshoot at the end. Some rare cracks are even more complicated than these. But 95 per cent or more of all the cracks seem to fall easily and comfortably into commonplace patterns which could readily be systematized. Their significance would be impossible to mistake. As for their interpretation, I assume that there must have been either a written text coexisting with this system, or else one which evolved from its practitioners. It is possible that one or both of the two lost oracle books which I mentioned at the beginning of Chapter 7 may have been a text specifically associated with the interpretation of the tortoise oracle. This would be an interesting possibility to follow up. It might explain the significance of the numbers written beside each crack – the numbers may refer to passages in a lost text which were similarly numbered. Some such cross-reference appears to have been used. We know that both the lost books also contained a system of sixty-four hexagrams.[4] Perhaps a way can be found of interpreting the cracking oracles according to a hexagram system.

But we are not considering all of this from antiquarian interest. I would now like to call attention to the angle at which the non-right-angled side cracks seem usually to form. This angle of 60°/30° is, in my opinion, significant. When there are two side cracks, they generally form an angle between themselves of 120°. We know that the 30° side crack branching off the vertical crack is the basis for the Chinese character for 'to divine'. I now propose a connection (and scholars have generally found it difficult to imagine any hitherto) between the tortoise oracle and the yarrow stalks oracle. Look at the common yarrow and see if you notice anything familiar. What I am suggesting is a product of the search for natural correspondences which is part of the 'coordinative thinker's' view of nature.

Yarrow is a useful herb: it makes you sweat profusely if you are trying to combat a cold or fever, and has other medicinal uses. Imagine that your house is full of herbs hanging upside down in bunches, drying. These you will store for future use to make infusions and decoctions. In the old days everyone did this, without a second thought. They just went out and got the herbs, brought them back and had recourse to them as naturally as a dog eats grass. So there you are, a diviner of the tortoise oracle cult, sitting quietly at home, drinking your rice wine and perhaps composing a poem. You have had a rough day; the king was in a rage because he had not killed a stag that afternoon in the hunt, and also there came news of trouble from barbarians on the border. Everyone was ill-tempered, and you just want to sit there, drink your rice wine and relax. Slowly, you unwind. You begin to cast your eyes around the room; the rice wine is warming you very well and you begin to think everything is marvellous. You are in a mood to welcome people, but there are no guests. Your mind is receptive to a new idea.

Your eye drifts to your bunches of herbs. There, hanging in the window so that it will dry in the sun, is the *shi*, the yarrow. It is hanging upside down, boldly silhouetted against the red sky as the sun sets. Then, you are startled. That very day you have been writing on one of the tortoise shells and have written the character 'to divine', *pu*. And there it is again – several *pu* characters just there in front of you. The side branches go off the main stem of this plant at the same angle as the 30° side cracks which you see every day on your plastrons. It is quite astonishing. This is an omen, a correspondence: there must be a significance to it. You brood on it for some days, and then you decide that the *shi* plant is indeed especially favoured by nature with virtues and efficacy far surpassing its mere medicinal use to which you had so foolishly thought it restricted. What a lesson this is to the arrogance of man, who overlooks the subtle secrets of nature. This cannot be coincidence. You, after all, are a diviner. You must look for these phenomena. You will set to work thinking about what can be done with this revelation. A way must be found by which this plant can be treated with the respect which it obviously deserves. It shall be brought into the sphere of the diviner. Nothing less will do!

Our common yarrow, *Achillea millefolium,* known as 'milfoil' in the West, takes its Latin name from Achilles, for this herb staunched the flow of blood from his wound in the *Iliad. Millefolium* refers to its being 'thousand-leaved'. But what no one who has written about the *I Ching* has ever taken the trouble to do is to find a likeness of the true Chinese yarrow, the one used in divination with the *I Ching.* I have discovered a nineteenth-century Japanese woodcut of this plant, with the help of the librarian of the Linnaean Society in London, and it is represented in Figure 51. This plant evidently has many fewer leaves than our European yarrow, and the *pu* character and angle of 30° may be clearly seen. The branching angles are even more striking in Plate 39, a photograph taken especially for this book of a live plant at Kew Gardens in London, where the only yarrow plants of this type outside the Orient are to be found. Apparently it has never been photographed before.

This Chinese yarrow is botanically known as *Achillea sibirica,* but it has also been referred to as *Achillea mongolica* and as *Ptarmica sibirica.* There are four different kinds of yarrow in China, including our own common yarrow. But it is only this plant, *Achillea sibirica* (Figure 51), which is meant to be used in divination. It grows several feet high – generally five or six feet, and some exceed this. In England, the stalks which I originally picked and dried for my own use were of common yarrow, and only a foot and a half long. This is better than the pathetic stalks which I have seen for sale in some occult bookshops, which are a few inches long and are not of yarrow at all! But for real style, I think nothing can beat the ancient Chinese, for we read that the lengths of the stalks were prescribed by tradition as follows: the emperors used stalks nine feet long (which must have been extremely difficult to find!), feudal princes were allowed to use stalks seven feet long, high officers of the realm could use stalks five feet long, and graduates of academic standing could use stalks three feet long.[5] Imagine being the Emperor and wielding fifty stalks nine feet long! (Fifty stalks are necessary for divination.) Today, I use stalks five feet long myself, like a 'high officer of the realm'. You can see me with these in Plate 41.

In order to make quite sure that the angles I am talking about are what I suspect them to be, I have traced them out and measured them. The Chinese character *pu,* the tortoise plastron cracks, and the stem and branch of the Chinese yarrow are all either 30° or 60° from the vertical (60° from the vertical is 30° from the perpendicular, of course). You may think that all this is quite interesting, and that it may explain why the yarrow was

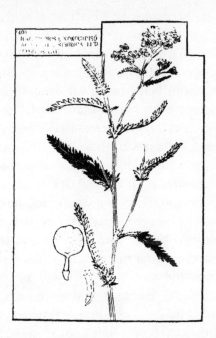

*Figure 51: A rare nineteenth-century Japanese woodcut of the true
Chinese yarrow,* Achillea sibirica, *traditionally used for the* I Ching.
'*The ch'i plant [yarrow] will yield, when a hundred years old, a hundred
stalks from one root and it is also a spiritual and intelligent being,*'
*according to the ancient Chinese sage Chu Hsi. 'Divination by the
yarrow is a questioning of a spiritual being because of its mysterious
intelligence . . . it indicates its intimations . . . by our manipulating in a
prescribed way forty-nine stalks of the plant eighteen different times until
the diagrams appear*'

brought into divination procedures; but you may wonder why I
am so concerned about the actual angles. There is a very good
reason. But before I explain it, I should describe how the
divination procedure of the *I Ching* is actually carried out with
the yarrow stalks.

Real yarrow stalks have a marvellous feel to them: it carries a
great deal of conviction that something special is being done
when they are handled. Perhaps it is because so many similarly
sized stalks bunched together look as if they must have a

purpose. (A bundle of anything is striking because it must have a purpose even though what it is may be a mystery.) The impression they give is that they may very well be able to help bring about some arcane intent. Their consistency is such that they are firm without being hard, yet delicate without being soft. This in itself is something. How many stalks have such qualities? When I handle elder stalks I am often impressed by them, but they are lighter for their size than yarrow. Yarrow is nobler: it has presence. If you like plants and do not think what I have said is silly, some good dried yarrow stalks will surely make an impression upon you. Yarrow stalks do, however, have their disadvantages. As you manipulate them, you discover that they have tiny sharp bits where you have rubbed the leaves off, and these prick you. And then there is the yarrow dust, undoubtedly combined with some mould, which will get up your nose and make you sneeze. The hazards of divining are as numberless as all the grains of sand in all the hour-glasses of the world.

Having decided that you will endure these discomforts, you proceed. Light a candle, which establishes a certain atmosphere. Place your bundle of dried sticks in front of you, remove one and set it aside. It is not clear why fifty sticks are required when only forty-nine are actually used; but it is the tradition.

Your left hand is the refuse collector. The right hand does the sorting. Part the stalks at random into two smaller bundles. Take a stalk from the right-hand pile and place it between the two smallest fingers of your left hand. Then take the left-hand pile and hold it while you repeatedly count off four stalks at a time and put them down. Having cast the majority of the stalks away by fours, you will be left with a residue. Take these leftovers and put them between the next two fingers of your left hand. Then take the right-hand pile and cast away by fours until you have the residue from this pile. Take the two residues plus the single stalk between the two smallest fingers, and count them. There will be either nine or five, five being far more common. Then set these stalks aside and combine the two piles back into a single bundle, which you again divide into two. As before, take one from the right, cast away by fours from both piles, and count the residues.

Set these aside as previously, then combine and divide the remaining stalks a third time and repeat the process. Take the three numbers you got by way of the residues from the three divisions, and add them up. The resulting number will then, according to a standard procedure, tell you which kind of bottom line of your hexagram you will have.

Go through this process six times altogether, to get the six lines of your hexagram, which you draw from the bottom up, just as the tortoise diviners scorched from the bottom up. (Both of these facts are strange, as Chinese is written from the top down.) You have then divided the yarrow stalks a total of eighteen times to get your hexagram – three times for each line.

If the lines are what are called 'moving lines' your answer is not the simple hexagram with its associated text, but involves other more complicated qualifications and addenda. Since there are two basic kinds of line, the *yin* and the *yang* (broken or solid), you may well be confused as to what a 'moving line' is. It is simply a *yin* or a *yang* line which *is changing at that moment to its opposite.*

If there were no moving lines, there would be only sixty-four answers. But because there are these moving lines which change into their opposites, a hexagram will, when its moving lines are considered, transform into another hexagram which must also then be considered. The transformations of hexagrams into one another by this means are 4096 in number. And so there are 4096 basic answers to be obtained by consulting the *I Ching*. That gives a very wide range of replies, and makes more sense than the mere sixty-four replies which superficially seem to be available from the sixty-four hexagrams. To consult the *I Ching* and get a hexagram which does not transform into another hexagram is comparatively rare, and by its very rarity, that answer may be taken to be doubly emphatic and precise.

I hope I have not been too confusing in explaining these things. Even so, I have omitted many details. Most modern Westerners who use the *I Ching* consult it by throwing three coins. This derives from the coin oracle which came to prominence in China during the 'Northern and Southern Dynasties' period of AD

420–581, in a book supposed to have been written by a man named Ma I.[6] The use of coins came at the very least a full thousand years later than the *I Ching* and cannot be viewed as authentic at all. That is why I have had to explain the system of the yarrow stalks to a certain extent. Using the yarrow stalks takes, at the very least, twenty minutes. People today say that they have no time; they want quick answers. They might as well know, then, that if they want quick answers from the *I Ching*, they have their priorities wrong. If their problems are serious enough to drive them to consult an oracle, then they are serious enough to merit proper consultation. Frivolous, superficial consultation of the *I Ching* over petty or even serious problems will merely result in less chance of significant help. If you will not go to the trouble of seeking out stalks or even joss sticks, it is better not to use the *I Ching* at all.[7]

But the reader will now have sufficient familiarity with the techniques of consulting an oracle either by means of cracking shell or bone or by the complex and interweaving multiple division of yarrow stalks to be able to take the next step, which is to understand something of what may be revealed by those two divination processes. It is more obvious and more startling in the case of the cracking. And we shall see in Chapters 9 and 10 just how extraordinary an underlying natural phenomenon had been discovered by the ancient Chinese, which must have led them to a greater surety about their techniques. For there really is, beneath it all, something quite astonishing. And that is what I now endeavour to explain, for the first time.

As to the origin of all this, we do not know where the Chinese came from before their civilization sprang up in China. But there is evidence that the yarrow stalk oracle technique existed also in the ancient Middle East – certainly in Persia, and possibly in Babylonia – though this evidence is fragmentary and indecisive. In a book on ancient religious traditions of this area, we find a suggestive passage:

> . . . to complete the picture of Median Magism, and to finish the comparison of points of resemblance with the system we

studied amongst the Accadians [Akkadians], we must mention that the practices of incantation and sorcery were greatly developed in it. ... Dinon also describes the incantations to which the Magi devoted themselves with their divining wand in their hand. They foretold the future by throwing little sticks of tamarisk wood; this custom is said by the classical writers to have been of Scythian or Turanian origin. The *Bareshma,* having become after a certain period an essential part of the insignia of the ministers of the [Persian] worship, was originally nothing else than a bundle of these wands, the use of which was introduced into Persia under the influence of the Magi.[8]

More details of this are given by Rawlinson, who says:

... the Magi claimed to exercise the prophetical office. From a very early date they had made themselves conspicuous as omen-readers and dream-expounders; but, not content with such occasional exhibitions of prophetic power, they ultimately reduced divination to a system, and, by the help of the *barsom* or bundle of divining rods, undertook to return a true answer on all points connected with the future, upon which they might be consulted. ... The Magian priest was commonly seen with the *barsom* in his hand. ...[9]

There can hardly be any doubt that divination with a bundle of tamarisk wands must have borne some relation to the Chinese use of the yarrow stalks. It may be, however, that these Magi got the custom from China rather than the other way round, as the evidence we have concerning Persian divining wands is rather late – earlier material is scarce. Herodotus, writing in the fifth century BC, tells us of divination by the Magi of his day and even quotes them as saying: '. . . some of our predictions terminate in trifling results; and dreams, and things like them, are fulfilled by slight events.'[10] This indicates to me that the Magi had at that time already a highly sophisticated attitude towards divination.

But the account is very slight, and no wands are mentioned. Diogenes Laertius, writing much later, tells us of the Magi: 'Further, they practise divination and forecast the future, declaring that the gods appear to them in visible form. Moreover, they say that the air is full of shapes which stream forth like vapour and enter the eyes of keen-sighted seers.'[11] This would seem to indicate a sensitivity towards natural forms, expressed here rather obscurely.

We do know that the Magi used the wands in connection with at least two specific religious rites. One was the water rite (their second rite after the fire rite, in earlier times): '... in the water sacrifice the Magi are said to have held a bundle of rods, a practice among the Zoroastrians that still survives.'[12] Of the other known use we are told by Strabo, the ancient geographer, that the Magi in Cappadocia 'enter [their temples] by day and chant for almost an hour in front of the fire, holding a bundle of rods, wearing felt head-gear which falls down on both sides so that the cheek-pieces cover the lips'.[13]

The Magi may often have used tamarisk rods, but Strabo, in his description of the ancient water sacrifice, also gives evidence that they used myrtle rods: 'They continue their incantations for a long time, holding in their hands a bundle of slender myrtle rods.'[14]

We may conclude, then, that divination with bundles of sticks or wands was far more widespread in the ancient world than has been acknowledged by those who have to date written about the yarrow stalk divination of the Chinese. There is an entire book, published in 1894, which maintains that Chinese civilization originated from the Middle East, though many of the arguments have since been found to be quite incorrect.[15] The author of this work also wrote a book about the I Ching.[16] He refers to divination wands as having been acquired by the Chinese from Babylonian sources.[17] But such wider contexts, though of great interest, need not detain us, and it is enough that I have suggested them. A thorough examination of the origins of the yarrow stalk technique cannot be undertaken here.

An article appeared a number of years ago in Scientific

American, entitled 'Chinese Oracle Bones', by Hung-hsiang Chou.[18] It is from his article that I have taken the interesting diagram showing the preparation of the shoulderbones in Figure 49. Here is his description of how he tried to prepare a bone:

> Working with the shoulder blades of steers, I have tried to 'flatten' and otherwise prepare the bones to receive an inscription. My instrument was a modern metal saw fitted with a detachable steel blade 17 centimetres long and a quarter of a centimetre wide. The unwanted projections on a shoulder blade are the spine on the reverse side and higher parts around the shoulder socket. (The obverse side of the bone is naturally smooth.) To rid a single bone of these projections cost me four hours of labor and two broken saw blades.
>
> To engrave an inscription on the obverse side of the bone I worked with a modern stainless-steel engraving knife. Although I am not unskilled in writing Chinese, I found it next to impossible to produce the kind of engraving most commonly seen on the oracle bones. I did not even attempt to make the pairs of [cavities] . . . that the Shang diviners scooped out on the reverse side of the bone. If I found my task too difficult, working with steel tools, how much harder must it have been for the Shang, who had only knives or saws of bronze and engraving tools of soft jade?[19]

Since over 115,000 oracle bones and plastrons are known to have been found so far, and vast quantities are presumed to remain in the earth, awaiting future discovery, it may be realized that a considerable industry must have existed for the preparation of these items, and their inscribing!

The *Scientific American* article points out that the questions asked in the cracking oracle were often phrased in pairs: 'Will X happen? Will X not happen?' The author has a certain appreciation of the angular features of the cracking, for he says:

> If the perpendicular crack was more or less at a right angle

to the upright crack, that is, within 20 degrees of an exact 90 degrees, the oracular reply to the diviner's question was considered to be affirmative. If the angle of the crack did not fall within this 40-degree range (from 70 to 110 degrees), the reply was negative.[20]

This further underscores the importance of the angles I mentioned earlier, and which I shall be discussing in Chapters 9 and 10. However, I believe that this author's conclusions may be oversimplified, or even entirely wrong, when he confidently announces that a right-angled side-crack means simply 'Yes', and anything outside roughly right-angled means simply 'No'. Such a simple suggestion does not in any way account for the variation in numbers scratched beside the cracks, as noted earlier. It may well be that the basic idea of what he suggests is valid, namely that a right angle means 'Yes' and a non-right angle means 'No'. But if so, it is still within a complex context, just as the broken and closed lines of the *I Ching* hexagrams are in a vague sense 'Yes' or 'No', though that apparent simplicity is utterly lost within the labyrinthine complexities of the actual hexagram divination system, if not wholly negated and rendered irrelevant by it. And there is the further qualification that if texts were used, or if an unknown pattern sequence were used, this would add further complications.

But the *Scientific American* author, though we can, with considerable caution and many pinches of salt, tentatively accept his simplistic 'Yes' and 'No' schema, errs entirely when he discusses the character *pu*, which I have discussed earlier. He says that this character is 'a vertical line joined at about the midpoint from the right by a more or less perpendicular line'.[21] This is simply wrong. It is true that in modern Chinese the character can be written in such a way that it almost appears to be right-angled. But that is irrelevant. I have studied this character on too many original oracle bones to have any doubts – and I have, as I said earlier, measured with a compass the angle of several such *pu* characters from ancient bones from tracings and reproductions. The possibility that anyone could think this character was right-angled is utterly incomprehensible to me. In the *Scientific American,* there is even a photograph of a right-angled crack in a bone reproduced, and underneath in the caption it says: 'Each set of cracks is in the general shape of the character "*pu*" . . .'[22] I can only conclude that the author who has made such statements has been carried away by oversimplification in an attempt to communicate with his readers to such a point that he has, in trying to keep things simple, accomplished the opposite of what may have been his intent, by purveying a total error! So not only was the article disappointing in some respects, it is marred very seriously by error. I regret having to say this, for its author's obvious enthusiasm is only to be commended, and by writing for the *Scientific American* at all he was doing a splendid service in bringing these matters to the attention of a wide public for the very first time.

Another publication on the oracle bones is a truly splendid major book about them by the scholar David N. Keightley of the University of California, entitled *Sources of Shang History.* This large-format work will for many years be a definitive contribution to the subject. But here again we meet with disappointment. For what interests us is, according to Keightley's preface, to be discussed in a book by him which has not yet been published, and which will be called *Studies of Shang Divination.* It may be years before anyone can read his forthcoming scholarly work. But there are some few passages in the other book which has been published which shed light on what we have so far considered.

The sequence of scorching puzzled me, and I insisted it was complex, and that this had been ignored in the *Scientific American* article. David Keightley says: 'The crack numbers subsequently engraved beside the cracks presumably reveal the order in which the hollows were burned.'[23] But he can only say *presumably,* and is obviously as puzzled by the numbers as I was, and yet Keightley must have studied every important oracle bone in public collections in the world! The plain fact is that we still do not know what the system was. Keightley is well aware of this, and is obviously determined to figure the system out. His forthcoming book should contain his findings, though it has been delayed for many years.

It is in order to try to find some answers that we now turn to what may lie beneath the surface of the ancient Chinese cracking system and, in the process, learn much about the natural phenomena underlying also the very process of physical change.

NINE

THE ORACULAR HEXAGONAL
LATTICE

I once attended a scientific conference at which a lecturer showed a diagram illustrating the decision process. It looked like this:

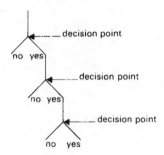

Figure 52: The decision process

If you imagine yourself going along (straight line) you come to a fork, and must decide either 'Yes' or 'No'. All your decisions then extend in a series of such forkings. They may weave back and forth, as you decide differently about things, but you could draw them as a track darting this way and that on a pattern rather like the one above. If you fill in the missing lines above, you will find that the pattern looks exactly like a section of a honeycomb. We have here, in fact, a hexagonal lattice. (Technically a plane lattice is known as a tessellation, but we shall for the moment use the word 'lattice'.)

Regular hexagons fit together perfectly, as honeycombs demonstrate. All the sides of a regular hexagon make angles of 120° between themselves, and if you set a hexagon on its point (vertex), the flat surface upon which you set it will be at 30° angles to the two sides of the hexagon meeting at that point, as in Figure 53.

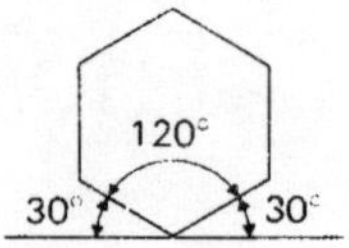

Figure 53: A regular hexagon

If we turn this diagram on its side (Figure 54), we have a picture which we can set beside some of our ancient Chinese crackings:

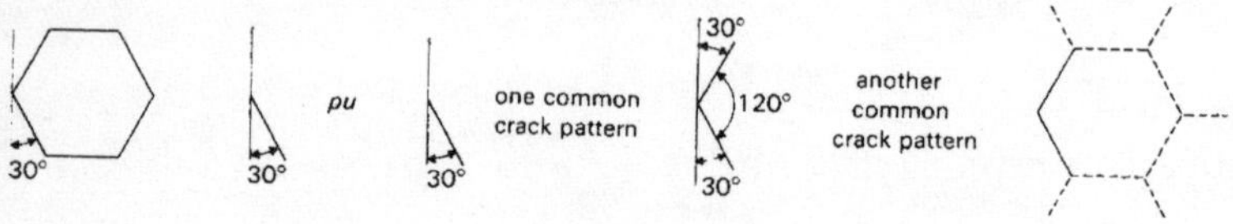

Figure 54

At the bottom of the angles emanating from the line beside the hexagon is the shape of the Chinese character *pu*. Here in this figure we see the most common non-right-angled cracks of the oracle bones and plastrons: either the 30°/60° crack or the double crack which gives the 120° angle of the hexagonal lattice. This, simply, is the way these bones and shells crack.

It may seem ridiculous that anyone should want to study patterns of cracking in anything. We regard cracks as aberrations, insignificant and weak. Or we consider them simply beneath our notice. Believe it or not, however, I have stumbled across a scientific paper giving the results of a study on pavement cracks![1] I found it in a 1935 issue of a Japanese technical journal which I was consulting for quite another purpose. I was unable to resist reading what seemed to be an absurd piece of academic mania, and to my consternation I discovered that this extraordinary article was not as silly as I had imagined. In fact, it was to end up being crucial in my work on a major problem.

In Figure 55 is reproduced one of the diagrams from the

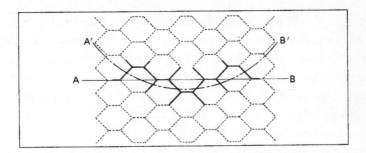

Figure 55: The cracks in the sidewalk pavement shown as portions of a hexagonal lattice pattern by Terada and Watanabe

article: it shows a sidewalk crack plotted against a hexagonal lattice. For, apparently, the seemingly meaningless and meandering cracks in pavements are all partial hexagonal lattices.

The Japanese authors, Terada and Watanabe, say:

[Regarding] a system of cracks found on a concrete pavement. . . . This type of crack is of a very common occurrence. Its origin may be explained in the following manner. When a layer of plastic material such as mud or plaster spread on a rigid substratum is subjected to a uniform contraction, cracks are formed constituting quasi-hexagonal cells as shown by broken lines. If in such a case a field of tension be superposed which is perpendicular to a line A'B' . . . and the magnitude of which is greatest at somewhere about the middle point of A'B', decreasing towards A' and B' as well as with the increase of distance perpendicular to A'B', then the cracks developed will be of the type as shown by the full lines in Fig. [55] . . . [and] we take the form of cracks shown by Fig. [55] as a typical one and adopt it for the standard of reference to all the other forms of crack lines belonging to a similar type.

One of the authors of the above, T. Terada, published in 1934 an article called, in translation, 'Crack and Life', in which he 'pointed out different classes of phenomena, inorganic as well as organic, which may compare with the formation of cracks or creases, from a physicist's point of view'. He adds: 'In the cases of biological phenomena belonging to these classes, the comparison, even if it may ultimately turn out to be merely formal, seems to enable us to review these phenomena in question under an entirely new light which may at least suggest a fresh promising line of investigation in a still unexplored region.'[2] Unfortunately, this article has never been translated from Japanese. Terada became famous in his own country, but foreigners have never heard of him. This is a pity.

Terada and Watanabe were not primarily interested in cracks as they occurred in such solid materials as pavements. Their real interest was in the apparently meaningless meandering ripples and blotches to be seen on the skins of some animals, and they carried out valuable experimental work in this field. It is exciting to follow their lines of thought and see them make some sense out of what one would superficially assume to be totally arbitrary products of chance: the colour patterns in the fur of domestic cats. They developed a theory that seemingly random fur patterns were a result of the original cracking of the surface of the very early embryo, leaving permanent traces: '. . . some kind of crack phenomenon was involved at an early stage of embryonal development of the animal and . . . in the subsequent development the ectoderm cells produced within the domain of the cracks were deprived of the faculty to endow the proper pigment.'[3] They believed that their discovery was 'of some significance and not to be overlooked'.[4]

Let us pursue this line of thought. What Terada and Watanabe did to prove their case was to take the skins of several cats and trace on thin paper the boundary lines of the apparently random markings. From these tracings they cut matching pieces of silk or linen, which were then sewn together as patches to form a closed envelope: 'The front end of the patch belonging to the head of the animal was put in juxtaposition with the hind end of the hind-most patch, omitting the tail.'[5]

They then stuffed these envelopes with cotton wool and studied the geometrical and topological characteristics of the markings on the skins. Then they took these stuffed envelopes (which were like odd truncated bodies) and marked the seam lines with ink. These seam lines were then projected upon a spherical surface or globe.

From these projections what they concluded is that early embryos undergo some kind of rupture as they grow, and the rupture marks show up in the variegated patterns of the animal skins. The rupturing takes place in a way which is just like the process of a pavement cracking. Terada and Watanabe hypothesized that this all happened 'in the earliest stage of embryonal development where "the inner cell group" had just been formed [and] a system of cracking lines of discontinuity was produced on the surface of the cell group'.[6] (They do not believe, however, that this process explains the regular skin markings characteristic of animals who have the same type of markings more or less uniform in species.) They say:

> It must be remarked here that the more or less regular and specific colour patterns of giraffes, zebras, tigers, leopards, etc., are of the class quite different from those irregular and statistical patterns of domestic animals here dealt with. The former are most probably produced at [a] later stage of maturity. . . . Some animals are even known to change their colour pattern in the course of their growth after birth.[7]

They even apologize that their hypothesis is not fully worked out: 'The present paper is in short nothing more than a rather clumsy attempt to get an insight into the physical factors which might have played some role in determining the morphology of animal patterns.'[8]

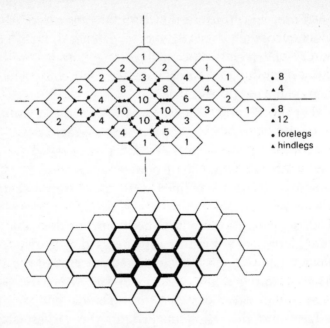

*Figure 56: Terada and Watanabe's hexagonal lattices showing the
statistical plotting of their data regarding the skins*

Terada and Watanabe statistically plot these morphological
phenomena on hexagonal lattices, as in the two diagrams above.
They also make some statements about the nature of cracks in
general: 'A crack or crease is one of the most characteristic
phenomena in the domain of physics by means of which a
macroscopic discontinuity is produced in the field which is
apparently uniform and homogeneous but subjected to
microscopic "Schwankungen" [fluctuations].'[9] The universe
itself is known in modern relativity theory to be subject to
microscopic fluctuations.

The phenomenon of the crack, and its frequent occurrence on
a hexagonal lattice, may therefore be of considerable and
fundamental significance to an extent which has never before
been realized. Terada and Watanabe conclude their article with
the splendid metaphysical observation that: 'In the domain of
physics, cracks and creases are phenomena by means of which a

discontinuity or a localization of energy may spontaneously be produced in an apparently uniform field, with homogeneous distribution of matter and energy; in other words, something is produced out of nothing.'[10] We shall return to this idea later.

It is interesting that these ideas are being put forward by Orientals. Do the Orientals really have a monopoly on seeing certain kinds of phenomena? The ancient Chinese seem to have stumbled upon the special significance of cracks and apparently had at least a partial understanding of the basically hexagonal lattice upon which these cracks could be plotted. In any case the specific angles involved seem quite clearly to have been appreciated by them, and these angles are the ones which make up hexagonal lattices.

The ancient Chinese even seem to have known about the animal skins! Apparent proof of this is easy to find. It is in the introduction by James Legge to his translation of the *I Ching*.[11] A scheme known as the Ho Scheme – the Ho being the Yellow River in China – is often called the Ho Map. (The word 'map' is probably not a suitable one, and 'scheme' is better.) This is drawn in various ways, using dark and light circular symbols. *'The difference in the colour of circles occasioned the distinction of them and of what they signify into Yin and Yang, the dark and the bright . . .'*[12] (italics mine).

This scheme is specifically identified with an animal skin. In the *Book of Rites*, the Confucian classic, the scheme is specifically said to be 'borne by a horse'.[13] Legge points out that 'the thing, whatever it was, is mentioned in the Shu as still preserved at court, among other curiosities, in BC 1079'.[14] He is referring to the *Shu Ching (History Classic)*, which is familiar to us already, and the passage he is thinking of is in Document 22 of the *Shu*.[15] This document describes the death and funeral of King Ch'eng [*Cheng*], who is quoted as saying: 'Oh! my illness has greatly increased and it will soon be over with me. The malady daily comes on with more violence and maintains its hold. I am afraid I may not find another opportunity to declare my wishes about my successor.'[16] Eventually, in the account, the ailing king dies, and there follows a minute description of the

ceremonials and surroundings of his funeral. In the course of this
description we are told many things about the king's palace, and
are informed, for instance, that the screens in it were ornamented
with figures of axes. Then the sacred objects of the State are
described:

> the five pairs of jade and the precious things of display.
> There were the red knife, the great lessons, the large round-
> and-convex symbol of jade, and the rounded and pointed
> maces – all in the side-space on the west; the large piece of
> jade, the pieces contributed by the wild tribes of the east, the
> heavenly musical stone, and the river plan – all in the side-
> space on the east; the dancing habits of Yin, the large
> tortoise shell, and the large drum – all in the western
> apartment; the spear of Tui, the bow of Ho, and the bamboo
> arrows of Ch'ui – all in the eastern apartment.[17]

The 'river plan' mentioned above is, in fact, the Ho Scheme. It
seems that it was an object of some kind, and all scholars seem to
think that it was a skin, on which the Ho plan was clearly to be
seen. Now, in giving an account of the origins of the system of the
I Ching, the ancient Chinese tell us that 'a dragon-horse issued
from the Yellow River, bearing on its back an arrangement of
marks, from which Fu-Hsi [*Fuxi*] got the idea of the trigrams'.[18]
This seems to me fairly specific. Fu-Hsi is a legendary ancient sage
credited with being the first to conceive the system of the *I Ching.*
Notice that we are not told that the system of consulting the
yarrow stalks as such was found on the animal skin, but merely
the system of the eight trigrams which combine to form the sixty-
four hexagrams. All three ancient oracle books are said to have
had these signs, and we have already speculated that the cracks
may well have been interpreted in relation to the hexagrams of
one or all of the three great divination books, of which three the
I Ching is the sole survivor. So although most people have
assumed that what we were being told was that the yarrow oracle
was revealed by the 'dragon-horse', what we are in fact told is that
the *hexagrams* were revealed by the 'dragon-horse'. And I

therefore propose that somehow, in some absolutely astounding stroke of genius or proto-science, the ancient Chinese actually recognized the significance of hexagonal cracking *and its manfestation in animal skin patterns* thousands of years ago, and that this was the true basis of their arcane systems of divination. Even today, with all our highly touted scientific insight, we are still largely blind to the phenomenon of cracking and its universal theoretical implications.

Once you have discovered the hexagonal lattice (which, after all, is obvious in the honeycomb and other natural phenomena), you need only an active brain to begin constructing extra-polations of it in other forms. You can consider the six sides of the completed hexagon not as a closed polygon, but rather as six separate lines taken individually. Perhaps these lines have different qualities – just as the 'dark and the light' *(yin* and *yang)* patches on the skins are separated by their agency. Perhaps some virtue of darkness or lightness attaches to each line itself, and may be divined. Thus you can quickly arrive at a concept of the dark line and the light line, and represent them as broken lines and whole lines. Taking these one at a time, methodically, and building them upwards in the way you crack the plastron, you find yourself with a hexagram.

A hexagram is a perfectly valid alternative picture of a hexagon if you are interested primarily in the *yin* or *yang* qualities of the lines (sides) of the hexagon. In fact, it may make for an easier system of study of the various hexagons, and the sixty-four hexagrams do indeed correspond to the very same sixty-four possible variations of the hexagon. The mathematics are identical; it is merely a different arrangement of the same elements.

Can this, then, be the origin of the system of the *I Ching*? Strictly speaking, the hexagonal lattice is not really a lattice, but a tessellation: 'A plane tessellation (or two-dimensional honeycomb) is an infinite set of polygons fitting together to cover the whole plane just once, so that every side of each polygon belongs also to one other polygon. It is thus a *map* with infinitely many faces.'[19] The modern mathematical use of the word *map* reminds me of the persistence with which modern translators have wished to describe the Ho Scheme as the Ho Map. Tessellations are quite clearly a kind of mapping, and if the Ho Scheme refers to hexagonal tessellations, then perhaps we may really call it the Ho Map after all.

There are only three regular tessellations possible: squares may be fitted together evenly and indefinitely, of course. But they do not really have any character. And furthermore, they seem to be more an abstract possibility than a persistent and recurring feature in nature. The other two tessellations are hexagonal (each hexagon of which can be divided up into six triangles pointing inwards), and a series of diamonds, which are two equilateral triangles base to base.

A tessellation is considered regular if its faces are regular and equal.[20] The first person ever to discuss plane tessellations scientifically was Johannes Kepler (1571–1630) who also discovered the three laws of planetary motion.[21] There seems to be no surviving record of anyone considering them scientifically before Kepler, whom the philosopher Immanuel Kant considered to have been 'the most acute thinker ever born'.[22] But it is essential to give credit also to that brilliant artist and investigator of perspective and geometry, Albrecht Dürer. For I discovered in his book *Treatise on Measurement*,[23] published in 1525, half a century before Kepler was born, considerations of hexagonal tessellations. In Figure 57 I reproduce his drawings of them which he published in that book. If the ancient Chinese were really aware of tessellations in some way or other, there was apparently a gap of approximately three thousand years between the comprehension of the principles of tessellations (in however rough a form the theory may have been conceived) by the early Chinese and the revival of the subject in the sixteenth century. This is reminiscent of the revival of the principles of binary arithmetic by Leibniz, which we discussed in Chapter 7.

The hexagon itself might have been considered by ancient peoples to have had mystical properties, due to the inherent but profound simplicity of its constitution. It is easy to construct a regular hexagon: draw a circle, take its radius, and you can then inscribe a hexagon in the circle, using the radius itself as the

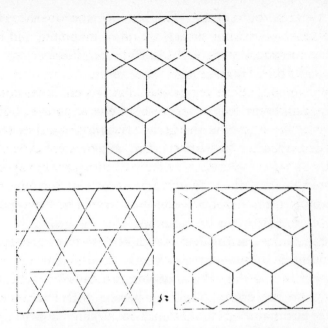

Figure 57: Albrecht Dürer's studies of hexagonal tessellation and other hexagonal patterns, from his book Underweysung der Messung *(1525)*

length of each side. Simply mark off any point of the circle, draw a line equal to the radius from that point until it touches the circle again, and that is a side; do this six times and you can draw your hexagon inside the circle.

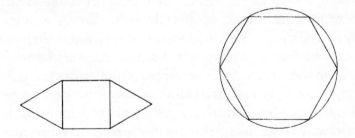

Figure 58 (right): Hexagon inscribed in a circle. The radius of the circle is equal to each side in length, and the hexagon is thus the simplest of all to inscribe
Figure 59 (left): Construction of an irregular but equilateral hexagon

An irregular but equilateral hexagon may be constructed by drawing a square and attaching two equilateral triangles to opposite ends of the square, as in Figure 59.

You may think that hexagons are monotonously similar, but that is not true. Snow crystals are hexagonal, and every snow crystal is different from every other. What more variety could you wish? Here is how the great crystallographer Sir William Bragg described the formation of snowflakes:

We can imagine the way in which snowflakes grow. One or two molecules of water become associated in the upper air; molecule after molecule adds itself to the growing, falling crystal, filling out the details of the pattern until at last the six-pointed snowflake rests gently on the ground. If the weather is cold the flake may continue to grow in the same way, and the crystals develop perfect little facets, which glitter like diamonds in the sunshine. When the snow crystal first forms, it is very often feathery; the six arms grow outwards and other little arms grow out from each of them to right and left, and from these yet smaller arms, and so on; all the arms joining each other at the angle of 60° [this is precisely what happens in the cracking oracle bones and plastrons] so that the whole is like a six-pointed star of fine lace. These feathery forms are peculiar to the early stages of crystallization, and seem to be the consequence of sudden and rapid freezing. The arms stretch out from the centre because they have used up the nearer molecules that are ready to join up into the structure, and they must stretch out into new fields. . . . When the snow crystal has had time to grow, and there is an available supply of molecules, the gaps fill up, and the crystal becomes a hexagonal plate. Sometimes, it is supposed, the plates grow in that form from the beginning. Strange to say, these plates are often connected in pairs by a hexagonal prism. . . .[24]

The crystallization of ice on the earth's surface is also hexagonal, though this may be difficult to see:

Ice when it forms quietly on a water surface exposed to the sky crystallizes in a form analogous to that of the snow crystal, all the six-sided figures being horizontal. That it does so is not generally very obvious, though in books of Arctic exploration pictures are to be found of table ice breaking into six-sided vertical columns, like the basalt columns of the Giant's Causeway. . . . In the accounts given by Antarctic explorers, it is especially mentioned that the ice on fresh-water lakes was found to be divided into six-sided prisms, all standing upright on the surface. The planes of separation were marked by lines of air bubbles.[25]

In advanced modern relativity theory, physicists talk about 'superspace', conceived of as the arena within which the dynamics of space-time operate. Here is an interesting observation from a highly technical text on this subject: 'Fischer has studied the topological structure of superspace. He finds that it is a stratified manifold, in which spaces of high symmetry are contained in the boundary of the spaces of lower symmetry.'[26] This is called by the author in question an 'unattractive feature'.[27] But, in fact, the phenomenon which we witness with air bubbles in lines between the hexagonal prisms, and in lack of pigmentation in the skins of animals along their embryonal rupture marks, may be universal in some sense, and certainly sufficiently so to show up at some remove from normal space and time altogether, and be seen in the 'unattractive' features of boundary regions in 'superspace'. After all, did not Terada and Watanabe generalize their findings to say that 'In the domain of physics, cracks and creases are phenomena by means of which . . . something is produced out of nothing'?[28]

Bragg tells us about studies which can be carried out on the nature of ice:

A slab of clear ice is placed in the rays from an arc lamp and is focused on [a] screen. . . . The heat of the lantern begins to 'undo' the crystals, which come to pieces in the order inverse to that in which they were put together. Little six-rayed cavities appear and grow, looking like flowers of six petals, and other cavities having a fern-like form in which the fronds are inclined to the stem at an angle of 60°. Soon the whole screen is covered with these 'flowers of ice', as they are called. . . .[29]

Here we see in ice a phenomenon reminding us of the angles of growing yarrow, and of cracking shells and bones in China. All of the phenomena in question are inherently planar – phenomena of *surfaces*. We think that many things are three-dimensional solids in their inner structure, whereas the most unlikely things are really inherently planar within their secret interiors, and these surfaces, crystalline as they are, generally have hexagonal properties concealed from casual sight. The perfect example of what I mean is that unlikeliest of all substances, clay. You would – would you not? – think that clay was just a lumpen mass without any inner structure to speak of. Well, you would be wrong. In Plate 40 is reproduced a striking photograph which shows us the truth about clay. Here we see a photograph taken by a scanning electron microscope, magnification *three thousand times,* of the substance kaolinite, which is the principal constituent of china clay. You can see that deep inside this slimy mass there are these slightly distorted six-sided crystals, which are irregular hexagons. You can also see that these crystal lattices are in chains – such is the true nature of clay. When we are told in ancient texts such as the Bible and the *Epic of Gilgamesh* that man is made of clay, are we really meant to believe that we are constructed from the primeval slime? Or may we perhaps conclude that we are really built of secret crystal lattices and structures at the microscopic level – a concealed order in the heart of the apparent random ooze?

Soil can manifest hexagonal structure from within itself, as it were. 'Frost polygons' appear in the soil in areas of extreme cold, such as tundra regions, and they can be seen from aerial photographs. These are shaped as hexagons some tens of feet across. They are caused by the soil's shrinking and drying and cracking. So we see that soil, that most basic of earthly substances next to water, can manifest the hexagon just as water does when it becomes ice. Therefore, all the basic materials of soil, water, ice and clay are seen to have hexagonal manifestations. They all demonstrate those very angles and patterns over which the ancient Chinese brooded.

How can ooze conceal hexagonal crystalline properties? The microstructure of clays reveals that clay is basically composed of planar molecules, that these molecules form two-dimensional sheets of polymers, and that there is very little interaction between the layers. That is why clay is so slimy – the micro-surfaces within it simply slide over each other all the time. Clays are, in short, two-dimensional silicates, or plane silicates. (Asbestos is a chain silicate, whereas beryls are three-dimensional silicates.) The molecules of clays would extend infinitely in planes if not fractured. And, being planar, the inherent hexagons in the clays are based on the atomic structure of the silicates, which are hexagonal structures at the deeper level, at the true interior – at the level of the very atoms themselves. And when we get down that far into the heart of matter, we are dealing no longer with substance but with its underlying mathematics.

The fact is that, if you want a regular tessellation with the maximum number of lines coming together at the meeting points (called vertices), it must be hexagonal. This is therefore nature's greatest possibility of economy for a maximum number of events on a planar surface. The alternative regular tessellations of squares and triangles do not allow for as many connections; they are inferior. So that is why, underlying so many phenomena, the hexagonal tessellation appears time and time again. *It is fundamental geometry.*

In Figure 60 we see chemical diagrams of substances with hexagonal rings in their structure. Benzene is basically a hexagonal ring, and its related chemicals incorporate hexagonal rings. Sir William Bragg tells us:

> The conception of the closed hexagonal ring leads at once to a simple and beautiful explanation of a number of remarkable chemical observations, of which we will

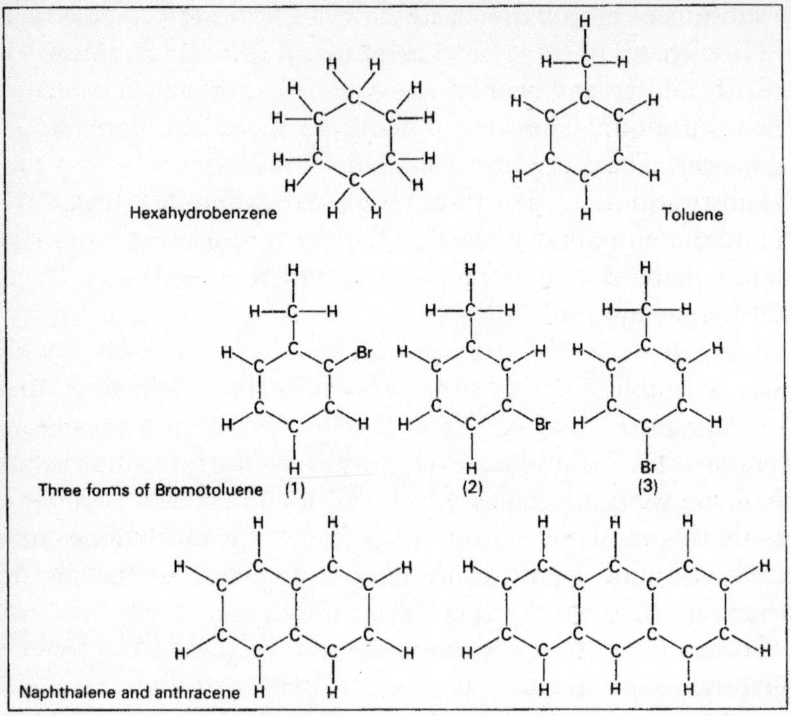

*Figure 60: The transformations of the hexagonal 'benzene ring'. We start
with benzene itself, which transforms into the substance at top left by
adding more hydrogen atoms. Or it may transform instead to toluene
(top right). Or it may transform to the molecules shown in the middle
row. At the bottom we see naphthalene, which is a double benzene ring,
and beside it anthracene, which is a treble benzene ring. All of these
substances with their different properties are in a sense pure geometry, as
their differing properties arise from positional shifts of atoms. And their
geometrical dance takes place around the hexagonal ring*

consider one example. The benzene molecule consists of the
hexagonal ring of carbon atoms, with one hydrogen at each
corner. .... Taking the benzene molecule as it is, chemists
find that they have the power to alter its constitution,
pulling off one or more of the hydrogen atoms, and
substituting other atoms or groups of atoms. ... It is very
remarkable that when this has been done three different

substances are obtained, all having the same composition. How are we to explain the existence of these three, endowed with different properties, yet all having the same constitution? The ring hypothesis gives an immediate answer. There are three ways and no more of making the substitutions. . . . The three molecules have different shapes, and therefore may be expected to have different properties; and there is no doubt that these are actually the three different substances.[30]

Here is a sublime demonstration, once again, of appearing to get *something for nothing,* to hark back to the observations of Terada and Watanabe. You have a substance and, without changing what it is made of, you can get a new substance simply by altering its shape – around a hexagonal ring. Here again, the crack or boundary of the hexagon is where all the changes take place.

Some of the most fascinating studies of hexagonal cracking have taken place since the fly-past of Jupiter by the satellite-probe Voyager 2. Photos of Jupiter's moon Europa (which is a little smaller than our own moon) revealed that Europa has a smooth surface criss-crossed with highly complex fracture patterns and 'many of the lines intersect with an angle of 60–70°.'[31] Europa is very eerie when seen in a huge colour slide, being rather green and looking like a huge cracked ice-ball. And indeed, Europa is believed to be covered in ice, and shows only three craters on its surface. It is thought that 'An early liquid water "ocean" (with thin ice crust) covered the satellite. . . . Continual freezing of the liquid layer resulted in large-scale expansion of the crust, producing fracture patterns, filled with fluids from below, now visible as dark markings.'[32] Considerations of these ice cracks on Europa have led to some profound observations on cracking in general. In order to consider the remarks made by various experts, it is necessary to know one technical word: 'isotropic'. This word simply means 'the same in every direction'. (If things are not the same in every direction, they are *anisotropic*). If someone pulls one of your arms, it is an anisotropic tug, and you fall over. But if you have both arms pulled equally hard, you stay where you are and do not fall either way; that is *isotropic stress!* Events and situations in the universe are either one or the other: either evenly stressed (isotropic) or unevenly stressed (anisotropic).

Dr Pieri, who has considered the cracking patterns on Europa, speaks of hexagonal cracking as follows: 'The common feature of these examples is their formation in isotropic or near isotropic stress conditions, which is not surprising as the ideal hexagonal pattern maximizes the reduction of strain energy per unit surface area by cracking and is therefore the most efficient pattern given an isotropic stress field. . . . In an isotropic stress environment . . . [critical stress] . . . tends to create [non-right-angled] intersecting fractures with intersection angles of about 120°. . . . The more isotropic and uniform the stress, the more likely it will be that six-sided polygons [i.e. hexagons] will form.'[33] He does not mean that one will get hexagon patterns exclusively, for nature is not perfect, and 'the ideal perfectly-formed pure-hexagonal pattern will never form in nature', but 'hexagons would be more numerous in situations where conditions were more uniform'.[34] Pieri points out that when the field of stress is not the same in all directions, but strongly biased in a flow from a particular direction, then 'fracture patterns from strongly oriented stress fields tend towards having [right-angled] intersections'.[35]

Here we have interesting information about the two variations of cracks which we also find on the ancient Chinese oracle bones: hexagonal cracking and right-angled cracking. The first represents a situation where the stress is the same from all directions, and the latter represents a situation where the stress is unequal, and comes more from one direction than another. Looked at another way, if we were to imagine it in the context of what we might consider as 'event-fields', we would have the two alternatives: 1. situation static, little change, no flow in a particular direction; 2. situation fluid, a distinct 'flow' may be detected, change now unavoidable. The first would show a hexagonal crack and the second would show a right-angled crack. If we are in a stagnant situation, would such a stationary and isotropic 'event-field' *influence material objects within it* such that the average crack would tend to be hexagonal? And if we were in an 'event-field' of flow and change, would material objects in such a 'field' be influenced such that the average crack would tend to be right-angled? Can the Chinese possibly have hit upon a genuine physical manifestation of the nature of such 'event-fields'? This should be capable of experimental test, and I hope that such tests might one day be carried out in laboratories.

Let us look again at the *I Ching*. What are the two opposite hexagrams? They are Ch'ien (all solid lines), 'The Creative', and K'un (all broken lines), 'The Receptive'. Let us equate them with the hexagonal cracking and the right-angled cracking as follows. Ch'ien is quite obviously related to fluid-flow, anisotropy, and active change. The text associated with this hexagram is very specific: 'The clouds pass and the rain does its work, and all individual beings flow into their forms.'[36]

The Image associated with Ch'ien is: 'The movement of heaven is full of power.'[37] This could not be more specific. Of Ch'ien we are told: 'Its image is heaven. Its energy is represented as unrestricted by any fixed conditions in space and is therefore conceived of as motion. . . . The course of the Creative alters and shapes beings. . . . It is the same heaven moving with untiring power.'[38]

On the other hand, the Image associated with K'un is this: 'The earth's condition is receptive devotion. . . .'[39] Here we find that the Chinese text even gives the earth, which as we know frequently cracks hexagonally, as the central image for a situation which gives rise to hexagonal cracking. Can this be no accident? Another connection with hexagonal patterns is that the Chinese text of the Judgement for K'un specifically associates it with the mare, which seems to be another reference to the horse whose skin was preserved (with its cracking pattern of hexagons) in the Emperor's palace. The Receptive does not attempt to take a direction; as the Judgement says: 'If the superior man undertakes something and tries to lead, he goes astray.'[40] In other words, there is to be no directionality in such a situation; the situation is isotropic. We are told of K'un that 'The receptive is yielding' and if the person yields in such a situation, it will bring him success, 'Furthering through the perseverance of a mare'.[41] In other words, the mare is taken as a symbol of yielding to the forces around one; cracking hexagonally, in response to isotropic stress and the absence of a directional, creative flow. With K'un also, 'Taking the lead brings confusion because one loses his way' and 'If the Receptive were to push ahead on its own initiative, it would deviate from its natural character and miss the way. By submitting ... it attains its appropriate permanent place.'[42] We even seem to have a reference to the surrounding equipotentiality of forces when we are told by the text of the Image: 'The earth's condition is receptive devotion. Thus the superior man who has breadth of character carries the outer world.'[43] All of the emphasis here is on yielding, breadth of acceptance, and the outer world being without particular direction or flow.

Thus the two primary and opposite hexagrams of the Chinese *I Ching* seem to represent the two opposite and primary conditions which give rise to the two primary and opposite modes of cracking. The underlying attitudes of the oracle bone system and the *I Ching* system are the same. And, in their simplest expression, are the *yin* and the *yang*. Or, in other words, the *yin* being yielding would give the hexagonal cracking, and the *yang*, being active, would yield the right-angled cracking.

This study of the ancient Chinese divinatory concepts is not absolutely conclusive. But I do believe that we must seriously consider the possibility that the ancient Chinese, who were almost unbelievably observant of the minutiae of nature, did hit upon something so fundamental about physical change, that in doing so they achieved one of the greatest advances in protoscientific thought in the history of civilization. And furthermore, they may even have been correct in making their intuitive leap by assuming that *events* have a structure too, and that they undergo processes of change similar to physical matter. If so, we still have much to learn from the oracle bones and the *I Ching*.

TEN

Higher-order Events

I believe we can understand events better if we recognize that *events have structure*. But what does this mean? How can an event have structure? What *is* an event? Surely just something happening, a nothing, some things taking place, but without a structure – since what is an event made of, that its constituents could be structured? How can something that is made of nothing have any structure to it?

Today it is scientifically respectable to speak of space itself having structure. We all presume that space is neutral, just 'there'. But then, cavemen assumed that air was neutral, just 'there', and when we at last realized it had structure and was a fluid which could be exploited, we were able to make aeroplanes fly. So perhaps if we realize that space too has qualities and is not just 'there', we may make the equivalent of aeroplanes fly in it too. But something more surprising than aeroplanes. For I propose that it is not aeroplanes that fly in space, but events. In other words, events have shape because space has structure.

There is a fascinating book called *Patterns in Nature* by Peter Stevens which discusses this problem in such a lively way that I will quote the relevant passages:

Of all the constraints on Nature, the most far-reaching are imposed by space. For space itself has structure that influences the shape of every existing thing.

The idea that space has structure may sound strange, since we usually think of space as a kind of nothingness that is the

335

absence of structure. We think of space as the emptiness within an empty container, as the passive backdrop for the lively play of all material things.

It turns out, however, that the backdrop, the all-pervading nothingness, is not so passive. The nothingness has an architecture that makes real demands on things. Every form, every pattern, every existing thing pays a price for its existence by conforming to the structural dictates of space.

Our ignorance about the effects of space parallels the ignorance of fish about the effects of water. And just as fish would understand their environment better through studies of buoyancy, pressure, and stream-lining in different liquids, so we have come to understand our own environment better through studies of transformation, extension, and curvature in different spaces. . . . More and more in physics, the idea seems to be taking hold that space has real material structure. That thought shocks most of us.[1]

So it is not only material things that can form themselves into lattices and patterns, for empty spaces can do the same! This is a bit like the 'flowers of ice' we encountered in the previous chapter, whereby regular hexagonal patterns of emptiness form in melting snow, as the ice 'undoes' itself. Since the 1970s, a strange concept has emerged in a branch of physics known as Materials Science. Researchers in metals now routinely use the term 'void lattice'. This refers to the fact that holes or *voids* appear in metals, which arrange themselves in elaborate patterns just as if they were *things*. As one scientist expressed it at the time when this new concept was just emerging:

In some metals, voids have been found to arrange themselves in an orderly three-dimensional array – a 'void lattice'. . . . A very extensive and effective research effort has developed during the past decade [he was writing in 1979] into the genesis and growth of individual voids in the alloys used to contain nuclear fuels and also into the inhibition of void formation; but the origin of the void 'lattice', which is of purely fundamental interest, has only intermittently attracted attention.[2]

Another peculiar aspect of the voids is that they do not form a lattice structure in a medium that is the same in all directions, but only in one that is somehow uneven, with an elasticity different in one direction from another.[3] I look upon this as being analogous to whether the metal has a 'flow' or not. If the metal 'flows' it seems to generate void lattices rather in the way a fluid with sufficient flow generates eddies, which also have their patterns.[4]

A very bold and advanced interpretation of void lattices was advanced by an Indian scientist named Krishnan in 1980. I cannot give a full account of his ideas because they are far too technical to repeat at any length. But Krishnan pointed out that the initial discovery that voids could form lattices was made in 1971, and that attempts to explain them had all been unsatisfactory. As a result, he was driven to develop a radical new theory of his own about them. His interpretation bordered on the mystical, perhaps appropriate for a scientist with a name so redolent of Hindu philosophy as Krishnan. He spoke of void lattices as having 'an inherent capability of self-organisation'.[5] His work was based upon the ideas of Nobel Laureate Ilya Prigogine, which are now known as 'complexity theory'. I have visited Prigogine in Brussels, where he is based, and I discussed his work as long ago as 1982 in a book of mine which was published only in German.[6]

Prigogine was an interesting fellow. His office in Brussels was full of African, tribal, and archaeological artefacts, and he behaved with the grandeur of a Gallic chieftain. It could be said that his ego was not altogether diminutive. His extremely brilliant team of colleagues treated him with the deference one might have expected of the staff of Charles de Gaulle rather than of a scientist. He dressed impeccably and behaved with the formality of a diplomat. But there was no mistaking the fact that one was in the presence of a genius, an attribute he was at no pains to conceal. To turn, however, from Presences back to voids:

If one wanted to become picayune about it, one could point out that material things are composed of atoms, and atoms are 99 per cent empty space, so that 99 per cent of the volumes of atoms are empty of matter. Therefore even the things we call 'solid' are only one per cent solid at most. It would be better for us to view matter as a kind of illusion, which it most certainly is in my opinion, than to take it so seriously that we are blinded to the more pervasive realities. The physicist John Wheeler has compared matter to clouds in the sky – substantial in appearance, but in fact as insubstantial as wraiths, as anyone may discover by flying through them.

Let us consider for a moment just how important voids are in the universe as a whole. Since the 1980s, it has been known that 90 per cent of the known universe consists of giant voids. If that be so, then voids are pretty important, aren't they? Because the comments that people make when they first discover things are often so revealing, I quote here from a lengthy report published in December 1982 about the voids in the universe:

> This picture, particularly the presence of giant voids, differs completely from earlier expectations and raises several questions. First, is a revision needed of the fundamental cosmology ... of the Universe? ... Recent observations indicate that most galaxies are concentrated in superclusters. . . . Giant volumes exist between superclusters which are almost empty of visible objects. . . . [The Universe now has] a cellular structure of high density sheets, strings in sheets and knots connected by strings. At this stage dense regions fill less than 10% of the total volume of the Universe, while isolated low density regions [cell interiors] fill the remaining major part of the volume of the Universe.[7]

I was delighted when this picture of the universe came out at that time. I had decided already that the universe *must* be full of voids before I ever read that it *was* full of voids. A void-filled universe may be thought of according to the criteria of Terada and Watanabe in the previous chapter: the strings and threads and sheets of matter may be seen as cracks or creases in the universe, where bubbles and efflorescence of matter well out – the creation of something out of nothing. As soon as the voids were reported I knew that they must manifest geometrical properties, and in particular, hexagonal lattices on a grand scale, in keeping with a cellular structure to space. Hexagonal lattices are the three-dimensional equivalent of hexagonal tessellations, although another mysterious 'shape' appears in connection with them, as will be clear shortly.

It is worthwhile looking briefly at the structure of empty spaces, or voids, so that we can appreciate whether on the microscopic scale in metals, or on the largest scale known to us – that of the entire visible universe – structure and pattern does not need to be shown only by things or matter, but can be shown also by voids and holes. As far as I am aware, no one has ever made this particular point in quite this way before. There are various ways of phrasing it. We could say it like this:

The presence of matter is not necessary for the manifestation of form.

By excluding matter, I also exclude radiation and fields. This brings up the interesting philosophical question as to whether *substance* can exist anterior to matter, or indeed what substance might actually be.

Hexagonal lattices have been discovered to be the important mediator in many crucial physical processes which once were naively imagined not to have any such underlying geometry. We shall be considering more of them. But first let us cast a glance at a long-standing mystery of geology. For a long time, the pheno-menon known as 'honeycomb weathering' defied explanation. It appears in rocks all over the world, and has even been seen on rocks on Mars, as shown by a photo taken from Viking 2 at its landing site in Utopia Planitia.[8] In the NASA photo some of the pits in the Martian rock are distinctly hexagonal in shape. The phenomenon is highly peculiar, and has no definite and known cause. As a scientist who wrote on the subject at the time stated:

'Honeycomb weathering is the evocative name given to the small (up to 10 cm) cavities found on the surface of various rock types around the world. The phenomenon is easier to name than to explain, however ... honeycomb-type patterns also occur on rocks beyond the Earth.'[9]

The phenomenon is so widespread, in every kind of rock and on every continent, that we read of it:

> With so many independent observations of so many examples in so many different places, it is perhaps not surprising that it has come to have a variety of names. The French tend to call it alveolar weathering, although others have used the terms fretting, stone lattice and stone lace ... it has even been called miniature tafoni, which means to say miniature caverns. But the most common, and certainly the most evocative, name is honeycomb weathering. ... The phenomenon itself does require explanation, however; and that is where the controversy starts. ... many, if not most, examples of honeycomb weathering are to be found in rocks that were apparently homogeneous to begin with ... few have speculated on its cause and even fewer (if any at all) have tried to investigate its origin ... The existence of honeycomb weathering depends not only on the formation of cavities but also on the failure of the weathering to proceed to the point at which the walls between the cavities are also eroded away, leaving no honeycomb pattern at all. ... For the time being ... questions about honeycomb weathering ... must (largely) go unanswered.'[10]

What we seem to have in this mystery is an example of void-formation in rough (i.e. imprecise) lattice patterns. The purely weathering explanation falls down because if the rocks were simply going to weather, there would, as the above writer notes, be no walls left between the cavities, and hence no honeycomb at all. There is clearly a factor at work in honeycomb-weathering which has eluded all conventional modes of attack on the problem. The mystery is probably intimately connected with the void-lattices mentioned earlier, and may be another example of holes emerging in matter with patterns of their own. But all holes require walls, to maintain their cell-like nature; the walls of the cavities in the rock are analogous to the cracks which appear in homogeneous substances. Note that honeycomb-weathering seems to occur always, or mostly, in *rocks that have been homogeneous.* Let us look at it this way: weathering causes the rocks to begin changing from something into nothing, or from matter into absence of matter. But as we have seen, absence of matter does not necessarily mean absence of form. So, in becoming non-material, the rocks develop form-patterns which belong not to the rock, but to the lattice of non-materiality into which the rock is being driven by its own material disintegration. Patterns emerge from the rock's decay which are a kind of super-lattice or hyper-lattice which has stood 'behind' the rock, and transcended its material constitution.

How like what I envisage for events! For if one grants the premise that events have structure, then the change of event-structures would involve the transformations of event-cells and would result in 'walls' and 'shapes' emerging as event succeeds event. Cracks and creases in space and time would succeed one another, yielding successions of patterns, lattices, and 'weathering'. These hyper-patterns might well influence material objects within the fields of the events, and directly influence cracking of physical materials.

We may feel slightly more comfortable with the idea that *events have structure.* After all, if form can exist without matter, then why shouldn't there be form to things which happen, i.e. events? For we will be well aware that events are non-material. We have long been used to structure being a property of material things, but we have now shown that material things are not necessary. Hence we can allow events to have structure.

But in speaking of 'structure' we should at once differentiate two different kinds of structure. The late Lord Todd, Nobel Laureate in 1957 for Chemistry, made the point to me in conversation quite succinctly (and I have this on tape):

When a chemist talks about structure, he usually means the internal structure of the molecule. But the physical shape of the molecule also has to be determined, and this is not what I as a chemist would call *structure*: it's *conformation*. Conformation is more physical than chemical. If you put individual molecules together so you make a thing like a snake, it can coil up in all sorts of ways. And that is the sort of thing you can see using X-ray methods of analysis. By X-rays you thus determine the physical conformation of the molecule, not the structure of the molecule itself.

Lord Todd and his colleagues worked out the chemical structure of DNA, but it was Watson, Crick, and Wilkins who worked out the *conformation or shape* of DNA. As Lord Todd put it to me: 'They took the chemical work that my colleagues and I had done and used it to interpret their X-ray pictures. In science everybody stands on everybody else's shoulders.'

Actually, when I quoted this remark about DNA to an equally distinguished scientist, he became very agitated, which I suppose goes to show that shoulders are not always smooth, but can be lumpy.

My acquaintance with Lord Todd was amusing. I never visited his home. Although at the time I met him he was retired as Master of Christ's College, Cambridge, he still kept a very fine set of rooms there, which was where he liked to meet people. The rooms were immaculate, impersonal, and devoid of any sign of individual personality except for a single startling item which was prominently displayed on his desk for everyone to see. This object was so unusual that it would have been impossible for any visitor not to comment upon it. Indeed, this was Lord Todd's little game – for in this he was like a determined old dog who will insist upon fetching his stick for the fortieth time – and he lay in wait for when the inevitable enquiry would come so that he could hold forth about his desktop curiosity. I naturally trod the path of all the others when I said: 'Excuse me, Lord Todd, but what is this strange creature? It looks like a duck-billed platypus.'

'It *is* a duck-billed platypus,' he said eagerly and on cue.

'Well, is it stuffed?'

'No, it is freeze-dried,' he said proudly. 'I was given it in Australia where they freeze-dry them.'

Let no one say that Cambridge scientists are not eccentric.

The point made by Lord Todd in distinguishing between internal and external structure is highly sophisticated. I believe the first person to have an insight of this nature was the brilliant German mathematician Karl Friedrich Gauss (1777–1855). One of his great achievements was to distinguish clearly for the first time between the *intrinsic* and the *extrinsic* curvatures of surfaces. I originally learned of this from E. T. Bell's utterly delightful book, *Men of Mathematics*.[11]

Extrinsic curvature is determined when you look at, for example, a glass in your hand, and say: 'This curves, I can detect it with my fingers.' But intrinsic curvature is more subtle; if you live on the curved surface of a planet like the Earth, and you draw an immense triangle on the ground, and then measure the angles and add them together, you will discover that they add up to a little more than 180°. And if you are clever, you will realize it is because the triangle is buckled outwards with the spherical distortion of the planet's surface. This is *intrinsic* curvature. But I am being too simplistic in order to get the idea across. The important mathematical point about intrinsic curvature is that it need not be referred to exterior coordinates or objects. It inheres in the very surface itself and may be determined from within, on self-referential terms. Indeed, the occurrence of a mysterious tiny 'correction factor' relating to matter, such as the Comma of Pythagoras which I discussed at such length in my book *The Crystal Sun*,[12] is probably an indicator of an intrinsic curvature which we have otherwise not noticed.

When I say that events have structure, I wish to emphasize that they have structure of more than one qualitative kind, or category.

Another thing which we must keep in the forefront of our minds is that structures *change*. Such transitions are the essence of what preoccupied the ancient Chinese. In modern science, the words which have come to be used to refer to drastic changes in the nature and type of structure are those magic words *'phase transition'*. An example of a phase transition is the melting of ice. Another is the boiling of water, where the liquid boils away as a gas. The matter undergoes a transition in its state, like that of solid to liquid, or liquid to gas. Another example of a phase transition is when you magnetize a piece of iron – iron with no magnetic field undergoes a phase transition when it is given a magnetic field. And if you heat the iron enough, the magnetism will suddenly disappear when it reaches a certain temperature. These are all 'phase transitions', and there are of course many more.

The concern with phase transitions in recent years has led to an increasingly sophisticated attitude towards the ones which we thought we understood quite well. For instance, it has become obvious that we don't really understand *melting*. Some scientists never thought we did, but others had been rather complacent. But now the issue has become well recognized. What *is* melting? Does it occur all at once, in stages, or what? A sensible scientist today would say that it is a problem which is currently under investigation.

Strange appearances of hexagonal patterns have crept into this apparently simple business of *melting*. 'Liquid crystals' when they were discovered were found to be neither liquids in the conventional sense nor crystals in the conventional sense. Although they are not crystals in their volume aspects, they are evidently semi-liquids consisting of an immense number of crystalline hexagonal sheets stacked on top of one another. They are rather like a more fluid version of clay, which we have already seen consists of slippery layers of hexagonal sheets sliding over one another.

And there are certain solids which when they melt do not become liquids straight away, but pass through an intermediate 'hexatic' phase first, which are related to what has just been mentioned, but are another exotic variation. These solids are ones which are so thin and flat that they are essentially two-dimensional. As the scientists working on them have said: 'Although it is not obvious, nature abounds with two-dimensional formations. . . . Such systems have received a great deal of experimental attention recently . . .'[13]

When these solids have the chemical bonds between their atoms break down, as happens in melting, they do not have to plunge directly into the liquid state. Instead, they can undergo a hexagonal lattice shift of 60° by rotating their crystalline structures. After doing this, they can later become liquids. This strange new state of matter after its discovery was named 'hexatic'.[14] Its full implications are still being investigated.

We should recognize that it is at least conceivable that the ancient Chinese oracle bones, and their cracking patterns, might have indicated something about 'the way things are tending'. Our knowledge of cracking is still so primitive that, as one expert wrote: '. . . despite many laboratory studies, we have only a rudimentary idea of the actual modifications that cracks undergo in stressed rocks.'[15]

Something of the way events may 'crack' into being and manifest themselves, with the source or originator of every event being a kind of stress-centre, may be imagined from reading these comments dealing with basalt rocks:

> In natural conditions, in an essentially unbounded basalt flow, one would expect the crack pattern to begin forming in a random manner; conditions can never be ideal enough for the entire pattern to develop in one cracking operation. Thus it can be expected to grow from randomly distributed stress centres.[16]

If we view human beings and other agents of change as essentially randomly-distributed then 'event-space' would evolve its cracks and patterns at first in the random manner of basalt; but these random crackings would very quickly take up regular shapes. It has been pointed out that beginning with random processes, basalt cracks into blocks which 'always have a mean polygon side number of six'.[17] In other words, although each block will not necessarily be hexagonal, *the average block will be hexagonal.*

Hexagonal arrays appear spontaneously out of nothing in the strange form of what are called 'Bénard cells' in liquids. These curious liquid 'cells' have become well known in popular books about chaos theory, although at one time they were known only to a handful of specialists. One of the best such popular books is *Turbulent Mirror*, and here is the authors' description of these strange cells:

If a pan of liquid is heated so that the lower surface becomes hotter than the upper surface, heat at first travels from lower to upper by conduction. The flow in the liquid is regular and smooth . . . as the heating continues, the difference in temperature between the two layers grows . . . and gravity begins to pull more strongly on the upper layer, which is cooler and therefore more dense. Whorls and eddies appear throughout the liquid, becoming increasingly turbulent until the system verges on complete disorder. The critical bifurcation [branching] point is reached when the heat can't disperse fast enough without the aid of large-scale convection currents. At this point the system shifts out of its chaotic state, and the previously disordered whorls transform into a lattice of hexagonal currents, the Bénard cells.[18]

The authors also say:

Scientists think the spherical shell of the atmosphere, possibly the whole atmosphere, might be a sea of seething Bénard cells. . . . An aerial photograph of the Sahara Desert shows prints left by this atmospheric Bénard sea. These prints of the atmosphere's vortices also show up in snow-fields and icebergs.[19]

We thus see that the entire atmosphere of the Earth may be structured in an array of hexagonal cells!

Before we move on to consider cells, whether atmospheric or others, I want to mention the seminal work by Victor Goldschmidt which preceded all of what I have just discussed

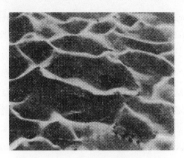

Figure 61: The Sahara Desert seen from the air sometimes shows hexagonal pockmarks which appear to be caused by hexagonal cells in the atmosphere called Bénard Cells. The hexagonal imprints also show up in snowfields and icebergs, apparently. This photo (no source given) is reproduced from one of the best books on chaos theory, Turbulent Mirror *by John Briggs and F. David Peat, who are two of the finest popularizers of modern science at the present time*

about voids. Victor Goldschmidt was one of the greatest geniuses of modern science since Newton, though since his voluminous writings are all in German and only a few pages have ever appeared in English, he is known in the English-speaking world only by specialists. Even in Germany much of his work has been forgotten, since his laboratory was destroyed by Hitler and many of his publications were apparently burnt. He took refuge from Hitler in Norway, where his second laboratory was then lost when the Germans invaded. He only escaped being sent to a death camp in Poland by jumping off a train and hiding in a forest, and apparently making his way by foot to neutral Sweden. His health was ruined by these unnatural exertions, and he died prematurely in the 1940s.

A moving tribute to Goldschmidt was published by the famous British scientist J. D. Bernal, who knew him.[20] It is the text of a lecture given in 1948 to the Chemical Society in London and it commences: 'I feel very sad at giving this lecture. It was from this very table nineteen years ago at a meeting of the Faraday Society that V. M. Goldschmidt gave his first account in English of the new crystal chemistry that he had done so much to found . . . he became the founder of modern Geochemistry and of Crystal Chemistry, sciences that will always be associated with his name.'

Bernal emphasizes, however, that the importance of Goldschmidt's work extended far beyond this. He ranks him equally with Sir Lawrence Bragg and Linus Pauling:

The works of Goldschmidt, Bragg, and Pauling are therefore inextricably combined in this foundation of modern inorganic chemistry.

Before leaving this field, however, Goldschmidt entered the last remaining large area of chemical ignorance, that of the metals and alloys. . . . He was able to draw up the first table of metallic radii . . . the work of Goldschmidt marks him here also as one of the founders of modern alloy chemistry. . . . Goldschmidt must rank after Vernadsky as the founder of modern geochemistry. Not only did he establish an enormous amount of factual data in geochemistry, but he also gave all geochemical problems that he touched a rational interpretation in terms of crystal chemistry and ultimately of physics. . . . Goldschmidt was, indeed, one of the really great men of science, one with that rare combination of comprehensive grasp of a complex subject and deep penetration which revealed its underlying structure. We know already that his work will last, that it has taken its place in the permanent structure of science. His work in geochemistry and crystal chemistry would each by themselves suffice to give him an outstanding place in the history of science, to say nothing of his contribution to petrology. . . . It is to Goldschmidt more than to anyone else that we owe the picture of atoms and ions of definite measurable sizes, and of their combination at least in organic and metal chemistry as a function of their size. In a few years' time, Goldschmidt's crystal chemistry will take a place beside, if it does not replace, the work of Lavoisier in the merit of not merely being true, but also extremely simple and beautiful.[21]

PLATE 20: The strange trapezoidal corridor of the Sibyl's grotto at Cuma, with its many side openings along the hillside, as described in the *Aeneid*. When the Sibyl uttered her prophecies, 'a hundred doors' flew open in these various openings so her message could be heard by a crowd gathered outside. The Sibyl sat in a side chamber to the rear of this photo (see plate 24), flanked by savage hounds, whose tetherings carved into the solid rock may still be seen. It was this Sibyl who led serious enquirers prepared to incur vast expense to the nearby Oracle of the Dead at Baia, after their consultation with her at Cuma. She was the guide of Aeneas in the *Aeneid*. (*Robert Temple*)

PLATE 21: The Chamber of the Sibyl at Cuma, as seen from the opening opposite it in the hillside. The stone benches either side are for enquirers to await the moment of admission to the Sibyl's presence within. To the right of the photo was a large chamber, apparently screened by a partition, where the Sibyl would have rested before and after her prophesying sessions. At the foot of this photo was a reception chamber for guests. The door in this outer opening would have been one of the many flung open dramatically at the moment of the Sibyl's seizure by the spirit of the goddess (later by Apollo when he replaced the goddess) as she uttered her prophecies in a state of trance. Local crowds waiting outside could thus hear her cries as she prophesised. (*Michael Baigent*)

PLATE 22: A close up of one of the tetherings carved in the rock of the Sibyl's Chamber at Cuma. They are to either side of where she sat, and must have been intended for savage hounds who flanked her during her prophesying. (*Michael Baigent*)

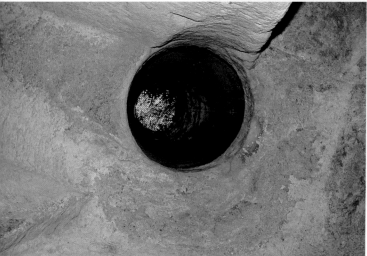

PLATE 23: The round shaft, now covered with wire mesh, carved into the roof of a side chamber of the Sibyl's Grotto at Cuma. This was a chute down which someone could be lowered into a large pit in the Grotto complex. According to Pausanius, he descended down such a chute at the underground Oracle of Trophonios at Lebadaea (now Livadia) in Greece, which has not yet been unearthed. In his case, he landed in a pit full of snakes, scaring him out of his wits. It was common for enquirers there to die of shock, whereby their relatives were told they had been 'claimed by the underworld gods'. (*Michael Baigent*)

PLATE 24: Olivia is standing where the Sibyl of Cuma sat to deliver her prophecies – a recess of the side chamber at the end of the corridor seen in plate 20. Beyond the recess, on either side, are the tetherings for the hounds (see plate 22). (*Robert Temple*)

PLATE 25: Olivia ascending from the Underworld. This is the entrance to the underground séance chamber, or crypt, of the Greek Oracle of the Dead. (*Robert Temple*)

PLATE 26: The author in the entrance from the labyrinth into the interior of the Greek Oracle of the Dead. (*Olivia Temple*)

PLATE 27 (*left*): The stairway descending into the underground séance chamber, or crypt, at the Greek Oracle of the Dead. (*Robert Temple*)

PLATE 29 (*opposite right*): This beautiful mosaic from the villa of the Emperor Hadrian is a copy of a painting by Sosos at Pergamon (3rd to 2nd centuries AD), and is one of the few examples of the skill of the ancient classical painters to survive. These doves, drinking from a luxurious bronze or gold basin, are probably the pampered and expensive carrier-pigeons of a Roman aristocrat such as Lucius Axius, mentioned by Pliny. They sold for 400 denarii a pair. (*Capitoline Museum, Rome*)

PLATE 30 (*opposite bottom left*): Ancient Minoan clay models from the Old Palace at Knossos showing sacred doves or carrier-pigeons resting on their perches in a sacred precinct. (*National Archaeological Museum, Athens; photo: Dimitrios Harissiadis*)

PLATE 31 (*opposite bottom right*): A statue of a goddess or priestess from Gazi, Crete, c. 1400–1200 BC. Opium was used in Minoan religious rites; the poppy pods in the headdress are incised as in the collection of opium. The pods exude a milky white juice through the incisions, which then hardens to a sticky resin. (*Heraklion Museum, Crete; photo: Dimitrios Harissiadis*)

PLATE 28 (*left*): The far end of the underground séance chamber, or crypt, at the Greek Oracle of the Dead. The rough state of the floor may be seen here. (*Robert Temple*)

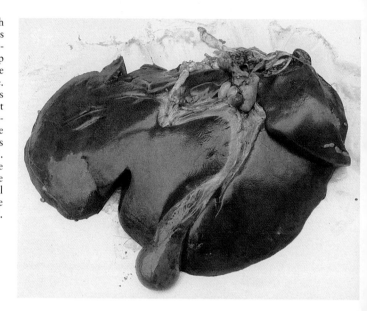

PLATE 32: A lamb's liver with the gall bladder lying across it. At top right is the *processus pyramidalis*, at the tip of which are some white abscesses, a sign of disease. The left lobe of the liver is much smaller than the right and the pronounced indentation at the bottom of the liver is what the Babylonians called the 'Palace Gate'. Several divinatory fissures are missing, for example the 'Path to the Left of the Gall Bladder' and the 'Path to the Right of the Gall Bladder'. (*Robert Temple*)

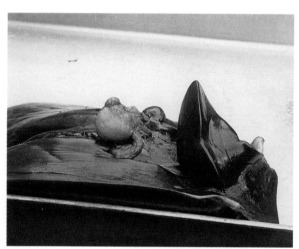

PLATE 33: The *processus pyramidalis*, the most important single feature of the liver in extispicy in Greek, Roman, Etruscan and Babylonian cultures. The feature is not a pyramid, but a tetrahedron, having three sides in addition to the (attached) base. It was probably associated with fire by the Pythagoreans and Platonists, who believed fire to be constituted out of tetrahedronal particles. The Romans called this feature the 'Head' (*caput*) and the Greeks called it the 'Lobe' (*ho lobos*). (*Robert Temple*)

PLATE 34: Babylonian clay model of a sheep's liver, c. 2000 BC. It is divided into fifty-five sections and is covered in cuneiform texts relating to liver divination. The model is pierced by many holes. The gall bladder and *processus pyramidalis* are clearly shown. The smaller protuberance on the left is the *processus papillaris*. Models such as this were used for instructing diviners and as permanent records of the traditional lore. (*British Museum, London; object 92668*)

PLATE 35 (*above left*): The Huwawa-Humbaba mask, c. 650 BC, found at Sippar. The object measures 9 × 9.5 cm and is made of clay. The inscription on the back reads: 'If the entrails resemble the face of Huwawa, it is an omen of Sargon, who ruled the land. If . . . the house of a man will extend. Hand of Ardi-Hannar, the seer, the son of Lubburum, the seer.' Sargon was king of Agade and the mask was either made for or by the seer Ardi-Hannar. The name 'Huwawa' is written in the old Babylonian form, the rest of the inscription being written in Neo-Babylonian form. This and other features point to an extremely ancient tradition, which goes back to at least 2750 BC. (*British Museum, London; object BM 116624*)

PLATE 36 (*above right*): Babylonian clay model, c. 600 BC, of a spiral colon of a lamb laid flat on the diviner's table (see Appendix 3). The 'count' is 14, a good omen. (*Yale University Babylonian Collection; object YBC 3000*)

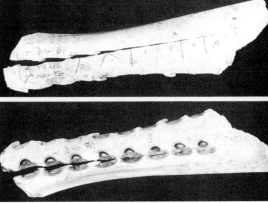

PLATE 38 (*above right*): Front and back views of an oracular shoulder bone from the Shang Dynasty period in China. (*British Library*)

PLATE 37 (*above left*): The spiral colon of an unhealthy lamb. One of the arcs is severely swollen by enteritis and appears white, like the fat. In making a divinatory 'count', this portion would be omitted, resulting in an unfavourable odd number (see Appendix 3). (*Robert Temple*)

PLATE 40 (*below*): Photograph taken through an electron microscope (magnification × 3000) showing that clay (in this case kaolinite) consists of microscopic hexagons, which slip and slide over each other, causing clay to feel slimy. (*W. D. Keller*)

PLATE 39 (*above*): The first photograph ever taken of *Achillea sibirica*. This plant is grown at Kew Gardens, London, apparently the only place where this species of yarrow is to be found outside the Orient. The 30° angle of the branches from the main stem can be clearly seen. (*Sylvia Cave*)

PLATE 41: My two sets of yarrow stalks used for consulting the *I Ching*. In my right hand are my short everyday ones. In my left hand are the five foot-long ones which, according to Chinese tradition, were the correct length for use by 'high officers of the realm', such as prime ministers. These stalks are rather cumbersome and you require a large, clear table, which of course makes the whole procedure more impressive. (*Olivia Temple*)

This may sound like high praise of Goldschmidt from J. D. Bernal, but in fact Bernal does not even mention whole areas of Goldschmidt's work, for so wide-ranging was the genius of Goldschmidt that it is difficult to list all the many disparate areas of human knowledge to which he made significant contributions. I have a splendid little book he published in 1932 on the origin of numerical systems in antiquity.[22] In it, he shows himself equally at home amongst Egyptian hieroglyphs and Chinese characters. He published another on the alphabet, another on the planet Pluto, another on colour, and wrote about philosophy. He published several volumes on the subject of musical and harmonic theory, the most important being *On Harmony and Complication* (*Über Harmonie und Complication*),[23] the latter part of the title referring to a new 'Law of Complication' which he had discovered in Nature. I first came across him because of his work in harmonic theory, since he is repeatedly cited by Hans Kayser, whose rare works on that subject I collect and study, and some portions of which I have translated, as indeed I have of Goldschmidt's. It was one of Goldschmidt's most profound and important discoveries that some harmonical numerical series which he found operative in crystal structures are identical with those in harmonic theory. These are matters I hope to deal with in a future book; I have published some remarks about harmonic theory in my book *The Crystal Sun*,[24] where I also show some of the extensions of that subject as they apply to cosmology and the natural constants.

An extremely rare pamphlet in English by Goldschmidt, of which there seems to be no copy in any British library, is entitled 'From the Borderland between Crystallography and Chemistry', published in 1904 as the text of an address he delivered in Wisconsin, USA, in 1903.[25] It was my stroke of good luck to obtain a copy of this invaluable pamphlet for only a few dollars from a bookseller in Oregon, who had no idea of its importance. For this is the pamphlet in which Goldschmidt reveals his *theory of voids*. In it, he points out that an Austrian scientist named Widmannstätten (of whom I can find no other trace, so that I do not know his full name) originated the theory of voids as far back

as 1808 – a fact surely forgotten by everyone else on Earth!
Goldschmidt says:

> Now let us first briefly examine the *etch-figures*. These are
> small elevations and excavations – hills and hollows – which
> are brought out when a crystal face is acted upon for a time
> by a solvent; for example, calcite ($CaCO_3$) treated with
> hydrochloric acid (HCı). Widmannstätten in Vienna in 1808
> was the first to call attention to this. He etched the surfaces of
> meteoric iron and showed that the structure of these
> wonderful visitors to earth from the sky can be recognized by
> means of the etch-figures, and distinguished from telluric
> iron. At present a development of this method of research is
> technically employed in the study of the composition and
> structure of the many varieties of iron and steel, as well as of
> alloys which the metal industry furnishes.[26]

All the scientists I have mentioned previously, and their
colleagues, are probably wholly ignorant of the birth of their
ideas in 1808 in Vienna, and doubtless they are equally ignorant
of the work of Victor Goldschmidt on voids, if they have even
heard of him at all. But fortunately my acquisition of the rare
pamphlet enables me to record his astounding insights on that
subject here. And his ideas are by no means exhausted, but
should be revisited and investigated further.

Goldschmidt was the first person to invent a means of
measuring crystal surfaces which curved; his device, which was
adopted by everyone in the world at the time, was called the
'two-circle goniometer'. He says: 'A curved face, the direction of
which varies at every point, gives as a reflection on the
instrument, a streak of light – a *light-path*.' This leads to a means
of 'representation of the position and curvature of the face' of the
crystal. By doing this, Goldschmidt established that the plane
faces of crystals, which were the only faces which could be
studied before his time, were only 'special cases', and that
'crystal-faces in general are curved, and that in these curves a
wonderful regularity and obedience to law are seen. This opens

up a wide field of research and shows the paths of creative Nature. But this is just what we want to know. We try to follow Nature on her creative pathways.'

Goldschmidt discovered that the light-paths always extend from one 'chief-knot' (chief-faces) to another, and this leads to a recognition of differentiated and undifferentiated zones in the crystals (areas of growth or dissolution). This led him to a variety of observations and conclusions upon which 'a cooperation of crystallography and chemistry can be inaugurated'.

Because Goldschmidt was the first person to be able to study the curved surfaces of crystals, he was therefore the first person to be able to lay the groundwork for a true theory of voids. Here are his remarks about the basic ideas:

Two sorts of curved faces of crystals engage our special attention; the first due to the growth of the crystal, the second due to dissolution. In the first case we speak of crystal faces and growth figures; in the second case of etch-figures, dissolution-faces, and dissolution-forms. We may as well call the latter *decreasing forms* or *forms of decretion*. On the one hand, we have to do with the forms of construction, on the other with those of destruction.

In the case of the forms due to the constructive action of the particles, we can trace in their curved reflections, the light-paths – the action of the particle-forces when the crystal is being built. Those curved faces with their most characteristic features are historical monuments in the history of crystal-building. Nature has preserved them for us in millions. In comparison the monuments of human history are few in number.

The *etch-figures* and *dissolution-forms*, on the contrary, show in their curved light-paths determined by measurement, the historical method followed by the process of dissolution. They show the direction and the manner of co-operation of the aggressive and defensive forces in the act of destruction. In this manner they give us a foundation for a theory of the *mechanics* of the dissolution process.

This theory of dissolution, just as well as the mechanical theory of crystal growth, interests the physicist and chemist, as much as it does the crystallographer. It also interests the biologist and geologist. For all creation and decay in Nature is a process of construction and destruction, and we can say that the solution of this problem in its most elementary form belongs to the domain of crystallography; and this task, with all that pertains to it, assigns crystallography to a central place among the sciences, whose task it is to give to the human mind an insight into creative Nature's working.'[27]

Goldschmidt then extends the general concepts of form-dissolution to a consideration of patterns of void formation. He calls the voids 'dissolution-forms', and gives his German term for them: *Lösungskörper*. He makes clear that these void-patterns have a life of their own. He liked to study them under the microscope, and his measuring device made their systematic study possible for the first time. Here are some of his further observations:

A still deeper insight into the nature of the process of dissolution is given by those bodies which we have called *dissolution-forms* (*Lösungskörper*). These are bodies (residual forms) produced when a sphere ground from a crystal, for instance, of calcite, is etched and further subjected to solvent action. . . . It is difficult to give an idea of these wonderful forms without presenting them to your view, but you can easily prepare similar ones for yourselves, therefore a few hints may perhaps suffice to induce some of you to undertake the study of them.

He then describes what happens when calcite is eaten away by the solvent, when 'a great many etchings are formed upon it' in patterns aligned with the crystal structure. But then comes the really interesting part:

If we continue the process of dissolution, something quite unexpected occurs. Exactly where the rows of etch-holes were first excavated, there arise prominent, sharp edges, which intersect forming pointed corners just on the spots where the chief-knots are located. We have thus once more the form-system of calcite before us, but in a new guise.

We will call the so formed bodies derived from the sphere by dissolution by preference, *dissolution-bodies*. They show the forms of the crystal in the course of its destruction; when in a state of *disappearance*, or of *dissolution* just as what we usually call crystal forms are the forms of the crystal in its course of construction, or of growth. To the study of the domain of crystal forms, which illustrates the process of growth, is added therefore as a new field of research that of the solution bodies, which illustrate the process of dissolution. In the study of crystals and of dissolution-bodies, we find chiselled on their surface by Nature's hand the history of their growth and decay; just as the historian, from monuments and documents, reads of the rise and fall of the Roman Empire. We must, however, learn to read Nature's handwriting. But Nature is patient and kind to us. As soon as we cause a crystal to grow, or a crystal sphere to be dissolved, she writes down for us her story, truly and fully, as often as we wish, and then leaves the documents in our hands to read them over and over and study them out in detail.

Solution bodies and crystal forms present this remarkable reciprocal relation – where the dissolution-body presents an edge, the grown crystal shows a zone, and vice versa . . . eroding whirlpools arise which engrave the etch-depressions, until the face becomes covered as though with pock marks. . . . In the case of amorphous substances, the little depressions have the form of skull-caps: they resemble microscopic fingerprints in plastic clay. In the case of crystals they have a style of their own – that is, they are bordered by regularly curved facets . . . the most perfect analogy exists between dissolution and erosion and vice versa. Similarly, the whirls of air bore holes into the stones of the desert and into the meteorites during their furious rush through the atmosphere and engrave on their surface erosion-figures of the same shapes, which are characteristic of the dissolution process. We see here several wide fields of investigation interconnected in such a way that the one throws rays of light upon the other. ... Finally a state of equilibrium is reached [with solvents acting on crystals] in which corners and edges cease migrating. A form is obtained which we call an *end-body*. This body subjected to continued solvent action becomes smaller and smaller without altering its shape until it completely disappears.

In other words, with the *end-body* one reaches the final form of the void lattice, and further action by the solvent merely reduces it in size but no longer alters its conformation. One has attained the *pure void form*, or we could call it *the substance lattice*, traced and outlined by some remaining residues of matter, and which is the *yin* corresponding to the *yang* of the *material shape*.

We can see clearly that Victor Goldschmidt was the true founding father of the entire discipline of void studies, and as he was a founder of modern alloy chemistry and metal chemistry, the scientists whom we have seen considering void lattices in metals are drawing upon foundations laid down by Goldschmidt, whether they know his name or not. Perhaps the highest tribute which can be paid to a founding father is to say that his contributions are so all-pervasive that everyone now takes them for granted without thinking about where they came from. But nevertheless, Goldschmidt's name should be resurrected, because not all of his insights have been fully explored, even while they continue to be built upon by his lineal descendants in many fields. As for myself, I came upon all the previously reported work and formulated my own views before I knew anything of this work by Victor Goldschmidt, and I have added an account of it not long before going to press, because the excitement of encountering such genius so unexpectedly, and so harmoniously to our concerns here, was one of those rewards which intellectual labour occasionally brings, and I wished to share it.

We return now to hexagonal arrays, which we saw were so widespread in the Earth's atmosphere that, as I said earlier, 'the entire atmosphere of the Earth may be structured in an array of hexagonal cells'. This is a most extraordinary conclusion, but it is by no means the only such shock we shall encounter with hexagonal arrays. We shall now see that they are even more widespread, and even closer to us than that.

Let us therefore turn our attention to cells in living bodies. We will now see that most of the cells in all the living creatures on the Earth are connected to their neighbours by hexagonal links which have an 'on' and an 'off' configuration, or a 'stagnant' or 'flow' mode.

Robert Hooke (1635–1703) coined the word 'cell' after viewing cells through microscopes, because they reminded him of a monk's cell. A modern definition of a cell is 'the smallest unit of living matter capable of assimilation, respiration, growth, and reproduction'. But it was Matthias Jakob Schleiden (1804–1881) who, in 1838, published the first real theory of plant and animal cells, in which he stressed their independence rather than their interrelationships. The concept of cell independence became so firmly embedded in our minds that it was to blind us to certain facts about cells until about 1963 – 'so persistent has been Schleiden's cell theory of 1838 emphasizing that cells are self-contained independent units'.[28] But the new discoveries tell us that cells are *not* self-contained independent units. And it is the connections between them which are hexagonal in nature, as we shall see. So in exploring this, we need to keep in mind that a change has come about in our concepts of what living cells are and how they relate to one another, which has made for a drastic revision of Schleiden's early ideas of 1838.

The central problem about cells being in communication with each other is that the communication must be very strictly controlled. As one scientist puts it: '... individuality of the cooperating cells is maintained while the sharing of simple ions and molecules is permitted. The arrangement can appear as a sort of compromise between ... independence ... and the wholesale fusion of cells . . .'[29]

Cells do draw the line at some things in their communicating. If we compare them to people, we could say that they share their tea and coffee but not their wives and their fortunes. A cell might say to another cell: 'You can come to dinner, but don't leave with the silver.' In short, cells are well-behaved and have the most impeccable manners. They very rarely take liberties with one another.

But we now know that cells do not sit singly, immersed in their melancholy contemplations, lonely and pining for company. They are continually sending each other little emails, and are constantly in touch. Every cell is surrounded on the outside by a kind of skin, called a plasma membrane. Since cells are so tiny, microscopic in fact, we could not call this a skin. Skin itself is composed of countless cells. So we have to use the word 'membrane' instead.

Cells are watery inside, and containing or bounding one with a membrane is a bit of a puzzle. It is rather like being presented with a swimming pool and told to construct its bottom and sides entirely out of a pile of live fish, with the condition that the fish must still be alive by the time you have finished!

The first idea that comes to mind is that you can arrange the fish in rows with their heads and gills facing inwards, so that when they form the wall of the pool, they can stay alive by taking the water into their gills. It doesn't matter if they have their tails sticking out and flopping about in the air, because they won't die if only their tails are exposed to the air. Cell membranes are very similar to this: they are composed of endless rows of things with 'water-loving' heads and 'water-hating' tails. Cell biologists call these respectively *hydrophilic* (which means 'water-loving') and *hydrophobic* (which means 'water-hating'). The hydrophilic heads face inwards towards the watery interiors, and the water-hating tails point outwards, consisting of long, floppy hydrocarbon chains. Then to seal themselves off really well, an identical layer forms facing outwards – the two stick together as

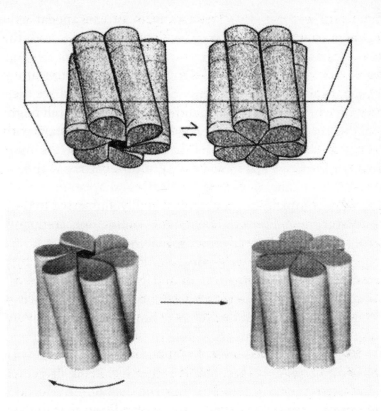

Figure 62: A drawing of a model of a gap junction; left, the six elements have twisted so that the central channel is open, and, right, the gap junction has snapped shut. (Courtesy of Dr Nigel Unwin)

a kind of double-layer, like two rows of fish tails pressed up against one another. Cell biologists call them 'bilayers'.

It was not until the year 1980 that the structure was actually worked out for the tunnels which exist through the bilayers between cells, the first trace of which was found about 1963 but not then fully understood. And these tunnels are the most extraordinary 'hexagonal switches'. They have the somewhat uninspiring name of 'gap junctions', which sounds rather like something to do with railway tracks coming together in the mountains.[30]

In Figure 62 we may see a drawing of a wooden model of a typical gap junction. A photo of a real wooden model is shown also in Figure 63. In both cases, we see this model in both closed and open positions. I am grateful to Dr Nigel Unwin of Stanford University for supplying me with offprints and illustrations of gap junctions, on which he did so much important work over the years.

When the six rods have twisted slightly, a narrow channel opens in the middle, and water and various small molecules can flow through from one cell to another. But then the six cylinders twist back and – as the model shows clearly – snap shut, cutting off all flow. A complete gap junction actually consists of two of these units stuck together end to end; these units singly are called 'connexons', and are embedded in the cell membrane.

Before gap junctions were discovered, such connections between cells were not imagined or recognized. Now that we know that cells can be joined in this way, the concept of the cell has undergone the very profound change hinted at earlier. For we can now think of large numbers of cells acting as a unit, and one scientist has gone so far as to say that the single cell is not the prime element of living bodies, but instead it is the double-cell as linked by a gap junction which is the true prime element. He wrote as long ago as 1975: 'Small molecules pass freely from one cell to another through these channels, which implies that the coupled cell system rather than the single cell is the unit in many functional respects.'[31]

This was an enormous conceptual leap in biology, which could still have many unforeseen implications. Many scientists have still not realized today what this might eventually mean for biology and science in general.[32]

It is important to realize that gap junctions are not exceptional or rare; they are so widespread that we can speak of them as a universal feature of all living things on Earth.[33] Not only do the gap junctions consist of hexagonal rods which twist open and shut, but these junctions themselves pack together in vast masses in enormous hexagonal arrays, along sheets of cell membrane. This may be clearly seen in Figure 64, an artist's conception of how two cell membranes lie on top of each other, the hexagonal

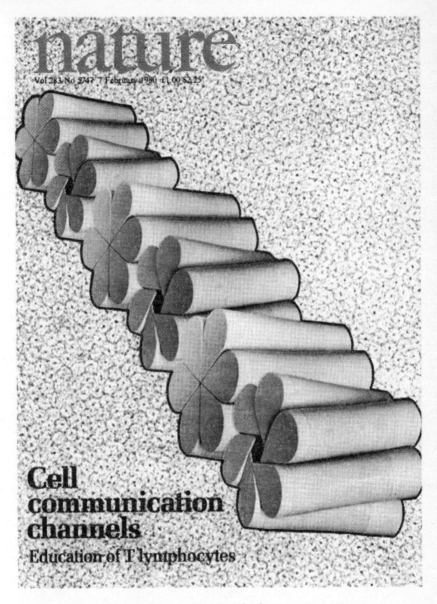

Figure 63: A photo of a wooden model of six gap junctions in a row, each composed of six elements. Alternatively, the gap junctions are 'open' and 'shut', depending on whether the six elements have twisted to allow the central channel to open, or have snapped shut. This photo appeared on the cover of Nature Magazine, 7 February 1980 *(Vol. 283, No. 5747). (Courtesy of Dr Nigel Unwin)*

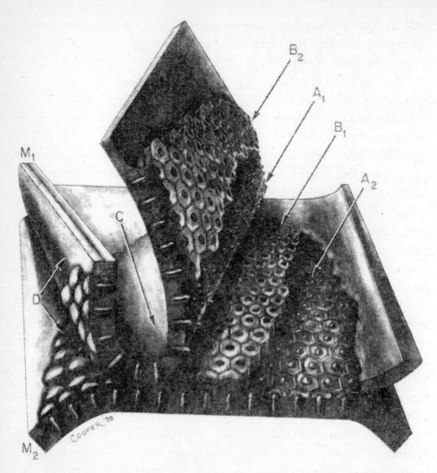

Figure 64: Gap junctions are arrayed in hexagonal double-sheets like this, and are very much 'plug-and-play', the same for any animal species. It is as if some cosmic engineer had designed a very simple all-purpose electric plug for tissues, and it had been universally adopted. Imagine a world where your electric razor or your hair-dryer could be plugged into any electric power supply in any country and you didn't need adapters!
M1 and M2 are the two plasma membranes in this artist's drawing reproduced from The Journal of Cell Biology *(Volume 47, 1970) in an article by N. Scott McNutt and Ronald S. Weinstein*

array of one fitting precisely into the hexagonal array of the other like so many electric plugs. And, as we have just noted, channels form between these membranes, through the hexagons, within as little as four minutes of being pressed into contact – even if the tissues are from different creatures. The gap junctions are therefore a kind of standardized 'kit assembly system' of Nature, for the construction of channels of communication between living cells, whether those cells which are pressed together are from the same species or not.

Lest we form a wrong idea about the size of a gap junction, it should be stressed that the narrow channel through the centre of a gap junction is only twenty millionths of a centimetre across. Naturally, one reason for gap junctions remaining unknown for so long was because it took electron microscopy to see them, and even that is not easy. It is absolutely impossible to see a gap junction through any optical microscope.

Gap junctions are responsible for a number of hitherto puzzling phenomena. Have you ever wondered how a woman's abdominal muscles know just when to contract for giving birth to her baby? Studies on rats have now revealed the secret. The smooth abdominal muscles were examined during pregnancy and it was discovered that there were no gap junctions between the cells. However, sheets of gap junctions suddenly appeared in the smooth muscles immediately before giving birth. They just suddenly formed, as if out of nowhere, and they made long-range communication possible across the muscles, to enable co-ordinated muscle contractions to take place. It appears that pregnancy is impossible without the *absence* of gap junctions in the muscles, and giving birth is impossible without the *presence* of gap junctions in those same muscles. The sudden appearance of the sheets of gap junctions is associated with the instantaneous manifestation of what modern complexity theorists call 'long-range order', where a vast region of entities undergoes a sudden unexpected coordination.

The three Canadian scientists who did the study revealing the appearance and disappearance of gap junctions in connection with pregnancy pointed out that a shortage of the hormone progesterone seems to have been responsible for the gap junctions suddenly forming. And as soon as they had formed, electrical charges passed in the watery fluids between the cells, through the junctions, for, as they say, it had already been determined with rabbits that 'propagation of electrical activity is greatest during parturition'.[34]

These scientists concluded:

That gap junctions are visible in thin sections between smooth muscle cells exclusively at term and during or following parturition has important implications for the maintenance and termination of pregnancy. Throughout the gestation period, the absence of gap junctions between contractile cells may be a major factor in the maintenance of pregnancy by preventing electrical communication between cells and coordinated contractions. The appearance of gap junctions between smooth muscle cells immediately prior to parturition may provide a large membrane area of low resistance allowing spread of electrical information between cells and terminating pregnancy by synchronizing uterine contractility for effective expulsion of the foetus.

We believe that gap junctions are present in tissues at term only when the animals have entered the final stages of gestation, that is, are ready to deliver. ... Our studies ... show conclusively the rapid formation of large gap junctions either just prior to or during parturition. We suggest that this formation is essential prior to normal labor and if it occurs prematurely it may lead to irreversible premature labor. ... We propose that gap junction formation is a necessary precondition for the coordinated contractions of labor and is controlled by a signal such as progesterone withdrawal.[35]

Before we knew of the existence of the gap junctions, we had a pretty static conception of the supposed unit of life, the cell. Now we see the new dynamic, coordinated view of cells acting together and the onset of long-range order over wide areas of tissue. The isolated cell of the earlier theories is replaced now by cells in flux, acting in coordinated and purposeful manner to bring about *change*. This shift in our view takes us from a particulate, or 'breaking-things-down-into-bits' attitude towards an attitude of wholes, of larger systems, and an ascending hierarchy of entities within the organism. The lonely cell, which once had just the status of *position*, has now taken on relations with its neighbours, and has acquired the enhanced and more accurate status of being part of an *event*.

This brings us back to events and their proposed structure. We have seen how smooth muscles without connecting gap junctions suddenly formed connections and underwent a kind of 'phase transition' where long-range activity was possible over distances enormous compared to the size of a single cell. It was as if tens of thousands of scattered people had spontaneously turned on their radios to listen to a single message, whereas a moment before they had each been lost in their own separate thoughts. And then those tens of thousands of people had all followed an instruction given over the radio to cooperate in some large enterprise even though most of them had never met and never would meet. This sudden onset of long-range order was made possible by the appearance of huge hexagonal sheets of connecting elements which had previously been absent. It was like a sudden massive crystallization, a bit like the previously described 'half-melting'.

What I propose is that events which are in the process of changing drastically, of coming to fruition – of giving birth, as it were – manifest similar connecting links with 'event-cells' far distant as well as near, and that some geometrical or structural 'crystallizations' occur when this happens. Such forces may possibly affect material objects within the 'event-fields' in which they are operating, leading to cracking or other phenomena of that kind. And I believe we cannot rule out that 'event-fields' may influence physical processes or material objects such as the sorting of yarrow stalks or the cracking of bones and shells by heat. In other words, there may well be a thoroughly respectable and scientific basis for the occasional or even frequent accuracy of traditional Chinese divinatory techniques.

The 'off' and 'on' configurations of the cell gap junctions remind us of the 'off' and 'on' results in Chinese divination. The ancient Chinese were close and attentive enough to Nature to observe a universal phenomenon in some of its manifestations, and to appreciate the importance of these in a way which was missed in Western antiquity. This was a triumph of proto-science in China. But it should not surprise anyone who knows anything about the history of Chinese science. As I explained in my book *The Genius of China* (written in association with my friend Joseph Needham),[36] more than half of the basic inventions and discoveries which led to the existence of the modern world are Chinese in origin. These include such unlikely inventions as the suspension bridge, deep drilling for natural gas, the first use of petroleum as fuel, the helicopter rotor and the propellor, the first manned flight, and so on – all of which are thoroughly and conclusively documented and are not mere speculation. The Chinese have an obvious and proven natural genius for scientific thought, and it is therefore only to be expected that at some very early date indeed they noticed the natural phenomena which demonstrate the two basic kinds of cracking, and then they made the mental leap to assume that such basic patterns related also to the 'shapes' of events, and the ways in which these change.

But events do not only change, they first must grow. An event is like a creature which must be mature before it can give birth, or before it can join with others in some great endeavour. Let us look again at cells: How do bodies grow? How do cells coordinate themselves, to enable the growth of the tissues? We have now learned that it is the gap junctions which are involved in regulating these things. And these are sheets of hexagonal connections.

An important step forward was made when a team of scientists proposed the following: '... an important function of gap junctions is to allow the synchronized movement of small regulatory molecules between functionally related cells during growth and differentiation.'[37]

Their work showed that the formation of eggs in animals involves essential communication through gap junctions. The developing egg (oocyte) forms gap junctions from its cell membrane to the membranes of the follicle cells which surround

it. Hormones regulate the processes involved. The formation of
the gap junctions makes possible the development without which
there would be no eggs:

> Gap junctions, through their structural modifications of the
> membranes of the adjointed cells allow for cell to cell
> communication by the passage of ions and of molecules of
> low molecular weight. . . . It is significant not only that the
> gap junctions between the . . . oocyte and its follicle cells
> may serve to transmit a hormonal stimulus, but also that the
> means of communication, a permeable gap junction, is
> hormonally regulated . . . [such] gap junctions may allow
> the passage of secondary messages from the follicle cells to
> the oocyte . . .'[38]

Yet another scientific team did research on embryos of various
animals and found that:

> All stages and species showed similar electrical properties.
> . . . Intact cell pairs were always electronically coupled. . . .
> The degree to which ionic current spreads from cell to cell is
> readily measured electrophysiologically. . . . Substances that
> can permeate gap junctions conceivably serve regulatory or
> signalling functions, and control of intercellular flow of
> small molecules may play an important role in tissue
> differentiation. . . . One of the major questions about early
> development is how coupled [embryo cells] acquire and
> maintain individual developmental programs. In several
> instances specific cells or cell groups are known to uncouple
> or lose their gap junctions at specific times, and a large
> difference in resting potential can develop between different
> regions of an embryo.
>   The phenomena described here would allow a cell to
> determine the extent to which its cytoplasm [its internal
> fluid] communicates with that of its neighbours by making
> small changes in its membrane potential . . . the relatively
> rapid changes reported here provide a possible mechanism

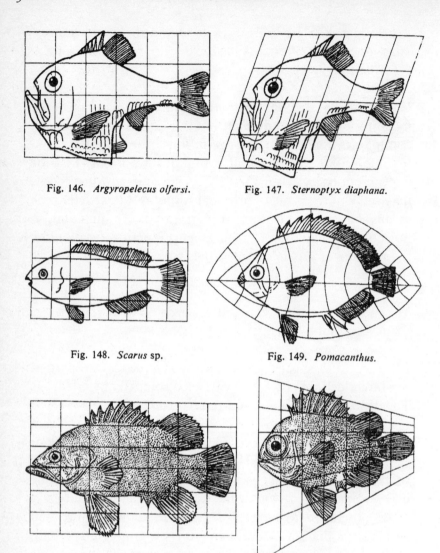

Fig. 146. *Argyropelecus olfersi.*   Fig. 147. *Sternoptyx diaphana.*

Fig. 148. *Scarus* sp.   Fig. 149. *Pomacanthus.*

Fig. 150. *Polyprion.*   Fig. 151. *Pseudopriacanthus altus.*

Figure 65: D'Arcy Thompson's famous drawings from his book On Growth and Form, *showing how different-shaped fish start out similar but in the process of their growth, their differences in shape result from spatial distortions caused by varying growth-rates of their different parts, portrayed here as distorted or bulging geometrical coordinate lines. It is as if the fish bodies were squashed or squeezed, and it is the varying growth rates of the body-parts which causes this. We now know that*

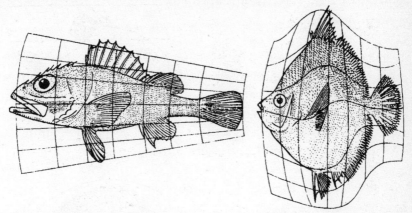

Fig. 152. *Scorpaena* sp.   Fig. 153. *Antigonia capros.*

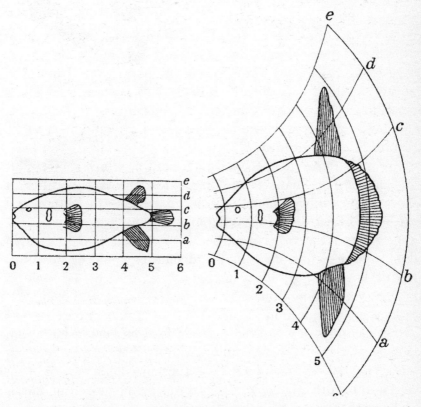

these varying rates are caused by electrical signals regulated by the
hexagonal gap-junction arrays

for short-term regulation of cellular communication during development.[39]

What all this means is that these gap junctions may be the 'missing link' in our attempts to understand how creatures grow from little, round eggs to great, hulking beasts or humans, with different sizes and shapes of different limbs. After all, why should a round egg grow two arms and two legs? Or, if it were going to grow limbs, why should it grow two different kinds – arms and legs? Why don't we just have four legs, like dogs? And why is the neck shorter than the leg? These questions are endless.

If we look back to the early stages of growth of the embryo, we see that different regions grow at different rates. D'Arcy Thompson showed that by varying the rates of growth, shapes could distort, and that various creatures have shapes which would be the same if not viewed as distorted by different rates of growth of their parts.[40] In Figure 65, we see some of his suggestive drawings showing this in dramatic form. Thompson wrote: 'In short it is obvious that the *form* of an organism is determined by its rate of *growth* in various directions; hence rate of growth deserves to be studied as a necessary preliminary to the theoretical study of form . . .'[41]

At last we have the mechanism to hand by which shutting off and opening up channels of communication between different parts of the embryo may control and regulate the differential rates of growth of the different regions, resulting in the appearance of the forms of the bodies of animals, and people. No doubt the sequence of opening and shutting could be 'read off' from a linear 'programme' such as DNA. As far as I know, no one has yet proposed this.

The general question of 'links' and communication channels between entities of whatever kind merits careful reconsideration. Let us take stock, then: communication channels manifesting hexagonal lattices link all but a tiny specialized minority of living cells in the world. These links appear to be the mediating factor in how entities grow into differing shapes. That is a pretty important stage of insight for us to have reached, for we have elucidated a basic principle which underlies the connections between all living things.

If we extend such ideas to our postulated event-structures, we may conceive of geometrical cracking patterns as mediating event-cells in higher space, which we could call 'event-space'. And these patterns are involved with the differential growth and shapes of events – why some enterprises fail and die, while others thrive and mushroom with profuse growth.[42]

When considering body cells as we have done, we must not make the mistake of assuming that only cells represent the empty spaces inside bodies. A physiologist has aptly written:

> Our bodies are catacombs of spaces connected to the outside world and filled with fluid. . . . Separating these spaces from the bloodstream are cell sheets called epithelia, which secrete or absorb fluids by pumping ions from the blood into the spaces or vice versa. . . . Epithelia are not merely polarized cells arranged in a sheet. Each cell in the sheet is joined to its neighbours by junctions, which in principle offer a path across the epithelium that by-passes the cells.[43]

We do not normally hear of this view of the body. It is rather like the new view of the universe mentioned earlier, where the universe is full of 'giant voids . . . a cellular structure of high density sheets . . .' Now we have a physiologist telling us that the body is composed of 'catacombs of spaces. . . . Separating these spaces . . . are cell sheets . . .' (By a curious coincidence of how ideas sometimes take shape in different disciplines along parallel lines, both remarks just quoted were published in the same month of the same year.)

The new general view in biology seems to be the conception of cells of space and sheets of 'skin', and geometrical patterns and lattices in that 'skin' which regulate communication between the cells. And it seems inescapable to me to believe that this is relevant whether we are talking about galaxies or organic cells – and it all seems to have to do with 'getting something out of nothing', or the manifestation of entities where there had apparently been none before. Just as, above a certain critical level of flow, a stream gives rise to eddies (and see footnote 4 for a possible, similar process in metals), so out of that flow of what appears to be nothingness, entities suddenly appear – and they appear along the cracks and skin of 'cells' which form as the nothingness differentiates along the spatial lattice patterns of an emerging and fundamental geometry of change.

Part of the emerging theory of universal phenomena must involve a recognition of the two kinds of structure: internal and external. This will be akin to Lord Todd's observations on the difference between structure and conformation, or Gauss's observations on the intrinsic and extrinsic curvatures of surfaces.[44]

Just as we have seen that the cell has been dethroned as the ultimate unit of living matter, it may surprise us to learn that the atom is not always the true unit of inanimate materials. As with the cells which are shared or joined, atoms have recently been discovered which are shared by larger entities which are the real units. This happens in a special kind of matter called *quasicrystals*. These strange substances were only discovered in 1984, but an understanding of their true nature was not achieved until 1998. Quasicrystals are solids with long-range order made out of single repeating units, and thus they resemble crystals. But in the case of quasicrystals, the single repeating units are *not atoms*. The units are called 'quasi-unit cells'. And these 'overlap their neighbours, in the sense that they share atoms'.[45]

Quasicrystals 'occur in a great number of alloys, most of which consist of aluminium and transition metals . . . quasicrystals represent a packing of a single type of atom cluster. This cluster can share atoms with its neighbours, . . . this cluster corresponds to a minimum-energy atom configuration . . .'[46] So we have here materials composed of 'atom clusters' which are not mutually exclusive but which share atoms, just as we have brain cell clusters which steal neurons from one another (as explained in footnote 32), and sheets of cells and pairs of cells in tissues. It seems somehow that the reductionist dream of simple units is falling apart wherever one looks. It is groups of cells or atoms which are seen in these instances to be important, not the cells or atoms themselves. And this is all connected with a *systems* view of how things work rather than the overly simplistic *reductionist* view which tries to reduce every process in the world to simple units and explain everything which happens by breaking it down into bits. Many of us have known all along that things are more than the sums of their parts, but the prevailing scientific dogma has been a reductionist one until now, with all the intolerance and scorn for systems viewpoints that always comes from any Establishment. But reductionism is being dismantled on every side, and not a minute too soon in my opinion.

Returning to the subject of hexagonal patterns, it is essential for us to realize that not all sheets of material will manifest these in the way that tissues with gap junctions do, for instance. We have already noted that when there is a 'direction' and 'flow', the cracking which we can expect will be right-angled. But are there biological sheets of cells which show this? The answer is yes.

We have already seen that hexagonal gap junctions are sometimes or always absent from muscles, and only appear for particular and unusual purposes. Let us see what one textbook tells us about muscles: 'One of the basic attributes of muscle cells and fibers is that they are able to exert force in only one direction. Another is that they contract actively and relax passively . . .'[47]

Clearly, if we were to find right-angled patterns appearing in tissue sheets, it must be expected in muscles, since muscles are the perfect example of directional bias in tissues! And we are not disappointed. One of the two proteins out of which muscle is made is actin. And in the 1980s, its crystalline lattice structure was finally discovered, and turned out to be – you guessed it! – essentially rectangular.[48]

If the scientists hadn't already discovered this, we could have predicted it. So perhaps I had better get in quick with a little prediction of a similar kind: myosin, the other muscle protein, should be found to have a structure involving squares or rectangles, or at least displaying some configuration approaching a right-angled array. It cannot have a hexagonal pattern.

Also during the 1980s, the first three-dimensional structures of photosynthetic membranes were published. Photosynthesis, the reader will well know, is the process by which plants gather sunlight and turn it into the energy needed to grow and survive. Using electron microscopes, it has now been discovered that photosynthetic membranes are large sheets of hexagonal units. Just as animal gap junctions have six rods and a central channel, so the plant units have six 'light-harvesters' arrayed in hexagons for collecting sunlight, but instead of having a channel in the middle, they have a large central protrusion which is thought to house the reaction-centre for converting the energy gathered by the surrounding light-harvesters. The scientist who discovered all this believes each hexagon is like a separate little entity: 'I therefore suggest that each subunit of the membrane contains a complete set (but only one) of reaction centre, electron transport and light-collecting components.'[49]

He has also published photos of the hexagonal lattices, which look just like photos of honeycombs, as do the photos of gap junction sheets.[50]

The similarity of photosynthetic membrane sheets and gap junction sheets leads one to suspect not only that simple basic forms are being used by all classes of living things, but possibly that the one is an evolutionary variation of the other. Could gap junction structures actually have evolved from photosynthetic membranes in the transition from plant to animal life? It is certainly a suggestive possibility.

The idea that each hexagonal unit in the photosynthetic membrane is in a curious way independent, almost an entity to itself, is rather attractive. If we compare such a unit to an event in 'event-space', we may not go far astray. We like to think of events as relatively independent, or at least as being self-contained to a certain extent, even though we realize that every event is thoroughly interlocked with surrounding events, and cannot free itself from them.[51]

For comfort and sanity, space is needed between people. Overcrowding results in deteriorating mental and physical health and disgruntled or hysterical behaviour. Voids are positively required between ourselves if we are to 'keep our cool', as the phrase goes. But I believe there is a more general principle of empty spaces or voids occurring between things at all levels and in all contexts. The fact is that empty regions are always necessary between regions of high activity, at whatever level of process in the Universe.

A close inspection of human life will reveal that the densest and most closely packed 'event-spaces' – namely, enormous cities – inconspicuously and largely unnoticed manage to create desert areas in close proximity to themselves and also riddling themselves like void intrusions. We overlook these, but they are there. There are always areas of decay in cities, where few people live. Sometimes 'empty' areas are dismissed as factory areas. In London, a huge empty area (a 'free volume' at night) is the City of London. Essentially no one lives in it, and at night perhaps a few dozen or a few hundred souls take their rest in this huge city void. And yet, one always hears of such over-crowding in London. Any city one cares to inspect will be found to contain vast voids which, when recognized, go far to contradict the popular myth that cities are densely populated. In fact, all densely populated areas will, according to a principle that I now wish to enunciate, create voids, but those voids will be largely disguised, for the existence of the voids will appear logically incomprehensible if admitted.

One of the most overcrowded cities I have ever seen is Cairo. No one knows what its true population is, though an informed Egyptian told me in 2000 that it was reliably thought to contain 30 million people! I believe an official figure might be 15 to 20 million. But possibly it doesn't matter. Life in Cairo is so difficult that one might think there is not an inch of space anywhere. And yet upon close examination, this city bursting at the seams will be found to have vast areas of voids riddling it, the largest being the so-called City of the Dead, which is a gigantic area of houses-as-tombs. It is true that two to three million migrants from the countryside have now spilled into these voids and live in the tombs, but it is obvious to any passer-by that they do not by any means fill the voids. In other words, despite spillage, the principle stands. But the vast voids to be found in all densely populated cities are always 'invisible' through consensus blindness, where we all tacitly agree not to 'see' them. For some strange psychological reason, people are 'in denial' about them and will not acknowledge their existence. This is analogous to the true patterns of daily living to be found in large private houses: how often one finds that affluent people in houses with lots of rooms really tend to spend most of their time in only one or two of the many rooms, the women who are housewives essentially living in the kitchen-dining room, and the men when they are at home living in the study. Even lower-middle-class families are noted for having one empty 'show room' with sofas in their small houses, which are never entered except on 'ceremonial' occasions when visitors arrive. These so-called 'living rooms' are not really for living at all, but have a wholly ritualistic purpose for the receiving of guests. All but the smallest private houses thus have substantial voids left in them by their inhabitants, although the people who do this are all in denial and will never admit what they are doing.

What could be the reason for this strange behaviour? I believe it is connected with the discovery made by the psychologist Carl Jung that dreams of houses are generally symbolic of the mind or the psyche. He found that when one dreams of wandering through vast empty rooms in a dream-house, one is experiencing one's hidden and undeveloped mental potential. Therefore, it seems not unreasonable to assume that people associate unused rooms in their houses with their own unused capacities, which perhaps they hope one day to develop. This could also explain the uncontrollable hysterical behaviour of some people which one sometimes encounters when the cushions on the sofas of the unused so-called 'living rooms' are disturbed by heedless intruders, or worst of all, by the children, who do not understand the true subconscious reasons for the sanctity of the unentered rooms. To enter an unentered room and disturb its cushions is really equivalent to a rape of the psyche of the person whose undeveloped mental potential is symbolized by the empty room. City-voids fall into the same category of taboo subjects, though shared by whole societies.

We have seen that 'event-space' in human life seems to take place in sheets, or skins. It may thus even be that people have sited their cities beside rivers in order to have a void ready to hand, just in case a void on land might be awkward to create and maintain. That densely packed vertical membrane known as Manhattan has slices of void all around it, enabling it to remain a skin. As the skin thickened, the Bronx became more void-like to accommodate its growth by the provision of a compensating hole.

Psychologists have shown by experiments with rats that the rats 'go insane' if kept too closely confined with too many other rats. What the psychologists have done is to deprive the rats of voids, so that their functioning in 'event-space' is obstructed. The same may be said of the poor unfortunate animals and fowl which are intensively reared in modern farming: the pigs bite each others' tails off, and the hens peck each others' eyes out because they are excessively confined and driven insane.

It would be interesting to learn from demographic surveys just what patterns, if any, are formed by the void-spaces in and around cities. Is it possible that they form geometrical patterns such as honeycomb-weathering? Do they even have a life of their own, like void lattices? I have no idea, but these are possibilities worth examining if one could get the right kind of maps and plotted data.

It would also be highly revealing to establish percentages of void spaces versus 'full' spaces for cities, and see whether there is some constant ratio from city to city. I would expect that even the most densely populated cities would by such a survey be shown to have enormous percentages of void-space; it is even possible that more than 50 per cent of the areas of greater metropolitan districts may be devoid of occupation, and hence genuinely empty. In doing such a survey one would have to disregard all rationalizations and 'excuses' made for the non-occupation or emptiness of land. If someone said, 'You can't count this site as empty because it's waste ground', or 'this is the site of a disused factory,' or 'the site of old docks', or 'a former railway yard', the excuses would have to be ignored. The fact is that such voids do occur in and around every major city in the world, but we generally ignore them and shut our eyes just as we have contempt for cracks and creases. These are all subjects labouring under a kind of taboo. But the fact that we refuse to recognize or acknowledge them does not mean that they do not exist! Being in denial does not erase the things denied.

Such issues have great relevance to town planning, urban renewal, and so forth. If there are dynamics at work which are more fundamental than those we commonly recognize, our plans will be undermined. This is especially relevant in America, where towns throughout the entire nation are now like ghost-towns compared to what they were as recently as the 1970s. Everything has moved to the malls, which surround the towns in rings or extend from them like spokes, because of the car. In computing the percentage of voids in settled areas, one should do a mathematical transformation on the figures, treating historic towns and cities as functions of foot-power and suburbs as functions of car-power. By shrinking the latter figures at the same rate as that from foot to car, one would probably arrive back at the same ratios.

Before leaving this subject I wish to point out also the need for psychological space. Individuals should not be in a state approaching that of *total contact*. I am alarmed at the deleterious effect on people's psyches by their weird desire today to be constantly in touch. Everywhere I go in London I am surrounded on the street, in buses, and in shops by oblivious, apparently deranged, ranters who notice nothing of their surroundings but are instead 'speaking to themselves'. Of course, this is merely what it looks like. What they are really doing is clutching mobile phones and braying into empty space such useless things as: 'OK. See you in about three minutes.' It is very frequent to see two such people slowly come towards one another, make eye contact, and only then simultaneously shut off their mobile phones through which they had been speaking to one another in an act of foreplay leading up to this great climax of meeting for lunch or a drink. There seem to be no spaces between such people. They appear to wish to remain in a state of *permanent communication*. It is more than mobile-mania, it is a serious psychological affliction of being unable to be alone even for one second. As they exchange their continual flows of what is often senseless drivel through their mobiles, they achieve a kind of apotheosis of that sublime ideal of our time: continuous instant gratification, like a baby which never has to remove the teat from its mouth at all.

But this condition of compulsive uninterrupted proximity means that these psyches have no space remaining, are sealed in from all sides, are welded to a continuum of humanity, and thus cannot individuate. This is one reason why most people in the modern Western world are becoming just like each other, because increasingly they *are* each other, and they might as well be identical silicon chips in a group mind, so little do they care to differ.

Mental reflection is necessary for a sane mind, but reflection is impossible when there is unremitting contact, relentless inflow and outflow of information, or feedback-by-avalanche. And so individuals are no longer coming into being, only clones are being produced, as people become more and more like bees and ants. And if a child happens to have any individual differences, they are soon ironed out by peer pressure or information-saturation. Total contact with others or with screens will see to that. And anyone who tries to be alone, tries to have a moment to reflect, has little chance of success. For this is seen as a threat to the uniformity of the mass. And as if the manic need to be constantly in touch were not enough, we are now hounded and harried on all sides by endless new penalties, fines, official threats and sanctions, court orders, bullying and harassment by all authorities, whether public or private. For now no one can escape; if you drive a car one mile an hour over the speed limit, you are photographed and a computer fines you; if your parking meter (the clocks of most of which run fast) runs out, the men are waiting there in advance and tow you away in thirty seconds. If you are a week late with your phone bill, you are cut off before you can return from your holiday. If you are one day late with your tax return, the fine is automatic and another computer bills you. And I have even had my American Express card deactivated *before I received the bill* which they claimed was unpaid; when I complained on the phone that I couldn't pay a bill which I had not yet received, I was told that was no excuse, because I owed the bill whether I had received it or not, and I had disregarded my debt. I recently had a big dispute with Companies House who fined me because my company accountant died before he could get to the post office to file my returns, and they said death was no excuse. Recently a bank sued a girl who was dying of leukaemia because she was not repaying her student loan, even though they knew of her terminal condition. We thus live today in a *total penalty culture*, where everything is monitored and no one is allowed any excuse for anything, but must be penalized continually in a relentless blizzard of *imposed submission*.

So there are no voids left, there is nowhere to hide, reflection is becoming impossible because the emails keep coming in, the fines keep being imposed, other people and all organizations *demand* that you give them your attention. In order to preserve some semblance of sanity, I refuse to use a mobile phone in Europe, and only use one in Asia, where it is absolutely necessary. If people can't reach me when I am walking or driving, then thank God! But I have seen this all in another culture without modern communications: Egypt. I have spent a fair amount of time there and have begun to know the modern Egyptians both in Cairo and in the villages. I have been horrified to discover that few Egyptians have any time alone. They are in *total contact* with friends, family, neighbours, and Islam. And just in case they thought they might escape into the privacy of their own dreams, these too are shattered by the loudspeaker-assisted 4 a.m. call to prayer. I believe that the lack of voids between people in Egypt is a major cause for the country's economic backwardness. It is simply impossible to be innovative and dynamic in a culture which will not allow you a moment alone to think. And this is what we in the West are now imposing upon ourselves. But what will become of us? If ever there were a need for social voids, it is now! If the Universe can be 90 per cent empty, then why must our waking time be 100 per cent full? But let us turn back to Nature, for our societies are largely unnatural.

We have discussed skin so often, perhaps we should now look at just what skin really is. Upon closer examination, skin is seen to consist of arrays of hexagons!

This was first properly recognized about the middle of the 1960s, and a theory to accommodate it had taken shape by the early 1980s. But why was the hexagonal structure of skin not known previously? Obviously, technology had not evolved sufficiently for it to be possible until recent decades. And a scientist writing in 1969 gave this answer:

> Mammalian skin usually appears in histological preparations as a loosely arranged layer of squames with little organisation. The absence of organisation is incompatible with the important barrier function of this layer and it has been suggested that histological [i.e. tissue] processing severely distorts the true structure.[52] [Histology is the branch of microscope investigation dealing with the structures and properties of tissues. Squames are the skin cells which we shall consider in a moment.]

When better techniques for studying skin were developed, it was found that skin cells 'possessed a roughly hexagonal outline when observed from the surface'.[53] The scientific name for skin is *epidermis*. We all shed skin at a rapid rate, so there must be a steady growth of new skin to take its place. Where does it come from? Modern research has shown that skin, or epidermal cells, work their way up in stacked columns of hexagons! These are called 'epidermal columns'. They tend to be about ten cells deep. Each column loses about one cell per day resulting in new cells being created underneath and moving into the columns at the base: 'an entry of one cell per day into each column, which must equal the cell loss rate'.[54]

Now that this hitherto concealed structure of skin has been discovered, biologists can speak of 'ordered epidermis', and describe it as 'presenting a characteristic hexagonal patterning'.[55]

But the hexagons are only apparent looking face-down on the adjoining columns. The actual squames, or skin cells, are

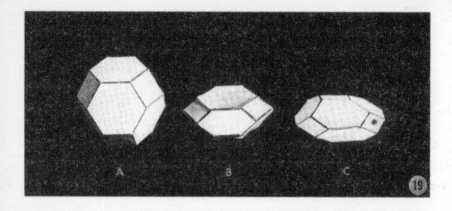

Figure 66: A photo of paper models made by Dr David Menton showing the Volume-Packer ('orthic tetrakaidecahedron'), in its full state (A), and in successively flattened states (B and C). Skin cells are shaped like this, with hexagonal tops, but are usually more or less flattened.
(Courtesy of Dr David Menton)

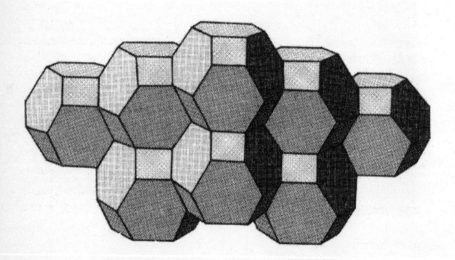

Figure 67: Volume-Packers (14-faces, or tetrakaidecahedra) close-packed together, as drawn by the mathematically inclined biologist F. T. Lewis in the 1920s, and reproduced by D'Arcy Thompson in the various editions of his book On Growth and Form *(original edition, 1942)*

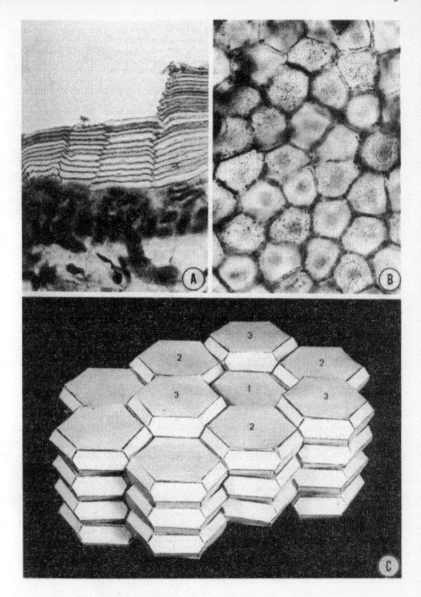

Figure 68: The artist's drawing below (C) shows cell columns in the skin, and indicates how the Volume-Packers have hexagonal tops and bottoms and in turn fit together to form a hexagonal array around a seventh column. The photos A and B are of frozen sections of mouse ear skin. A shows the epidermal columns from the side. B shows a whole mounted sheet of skin from the top, where the hexagonal shapes of the cells at the tops of the columns may be seen. (Courtesy of Dr David Menton)

ingeniously shaped as in Figure 66. These geometrical shapes
have the appalling name of (don't even try to pronounce it!)
tetrakaidecahedra. (It may help to realize that the word *kai*
means 'and' in ancient Greek. The name of the shape in Greek
means 'fourteen faces'.)

Obviously, it is clumsy to use such a terrible name as this to
talk about something, or indeed to talk about anything. So I have
coined a nickname for the shape. I call it the Volume-Packer. It
is a solid which was known to Archimedes in the fourth century
BC. It has fourteen sides consisting of six square faces and eight
regular hexagons, and another name for it is the truncated
octahedron.

Dame Kathleen Ollerenshaw the mathematician says it is
her 'favourite' solid. She says of what I call the Volume-Packers
that 'They fit together to fill space in a manner [which is]
fascinating . . .'[56]

We can look upon the Volume-Packer as a three-dimensional
version of the hexagon. I promised at the beginning of the
chapter that I would introduce this shape, and here it is. In actual

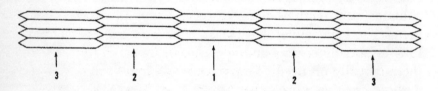

*Figure 69: A drawing from the side showing how the skin columns
interlock in their cell-stacking. Each cell is a flattened Volume-Packer.
To avoid leaving unfillable gaps, new cells have to be added first at
position 1, then at positions 2, followed by positions 3. The cells then
move up the columns and are shed at the top. (Drawing courtesy
of Dr. David Menton)*

skin, the Volume-Packer gets squeezed pretty flat, so that it
becomes like a disc, its most prominent remaining feature being
that its top and its bottom are hexagons. But the sides, nicely
compressed, now form a very handy 'biting edge' with which to

grip the cells next door. The edges thus produced make possible a high degree of order in the regulation of the columns, and a cell can only be shed from the skin when all six of its side edges are free by each being slightly elevated above its neighbours.[57]

The skin cell columns are similar to the photosynthetic units and the gap junctions, in that they form hexagonal arrays of six columns (like the six cylindrical rods of the gap junctions) with a central column (like the gap junction).

The skin cell column even seems to take on a kind of life of its own, as an individual entity. This even led some scientists to misinterpret the columns. Two of the best known in the field, Allen and Potten, decided in the 1970s that the cell columns should be called EPUs, for 'epidermal proliferative units', as if they were chimneys spewing out cells at the top from some furnace underneath. They wrote: 'In stacked epidermis it therefore seems reasonable to view each column as an individually controlled entity, with cell replacement occurring in the group of basal cells directly beneath the column, that is, an epidermal proliferative unit.'[58]

However, this was a bit too hasty in invoking a kind of a 'ghost in the machine'. Although the columns are truly remarkable, it is not necessary to imagine them being 'alive' in this way, as if the columns were entities in themselves (in addition to the cells themselves being alive, as we know they are). The concept of the EPU essentially creates another level of living entity for which there is really no need. We have enough living entities already without creating more unnecessarily.

The scientist who came to a true understanding of what was really going on with the skin cell columns is David N. Menton of the Department of Anatomy, Washington University School of Medicine in St Louis, Missouri, in the USA. He set about making artificial models of cell columns. He used randomly produced soap bubbles and let them organize into a 'stable froth'. He discovered that the soap bubbles produced columns of Volume-Packers:

Upon floating to the surface of a liquid, soap bubbles have been found to spontaneously assemble into precise columns of interdigitating bubbles. The tetrakaidecahedral [Volume-Packer] shape and the spatial configuration of these bubbles closely resemble those of stacked epidermal cells, although the columns of a froth were oriented at 60° angles to their substratum rather than at right angles as occurs in the epidermal cell columns.[59]

Menton discovered that the stacking pattern of the cell columns of skin was found also in cork and in the pith of woody plant stems.

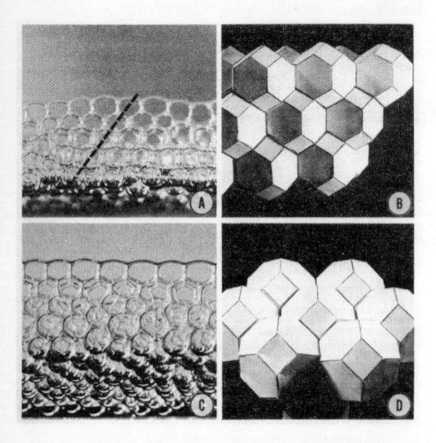

Figure 70: David Menton's photos of his soap bubble experiments set side-by-side with drawings of the geometrical shapes represented. A shows stacked bubble columns, with the bubbles shaped as Volume-Packers (drawn in B), with the columns leaning at an angle of 60°. C is an oblique photo showing a uniform layer of bubbles resting on the surface of a stable froth, and D shows a drawing of how the units of each layer are structured. (Courtesy of Dr David Menton)

In order to study this more carefully still, Menton constructed paper models of flattened Volume-Packers, and by stacking these he discovered clearly that 'only polygons of this type are capable

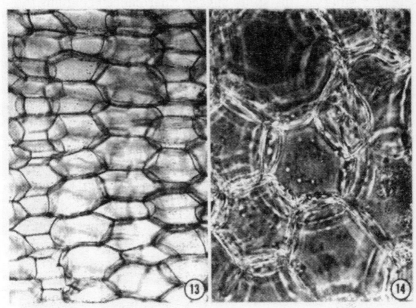

Figure 71: These plant pith cells in photos of a section of elder stem show the same structure as the columns of skin cells in animal and human skin. Left, we see the stacked columns from the side and right, we see the hexagonal tops of the cells from above. (Courtesy of Dr David Menton)

of aggregating without interstices [i.e. without leaving gaps] in the manner of the stacked cells. A study of stacked arrays of these models has revealed a mechanism by which epidermis might become organized in columns of stacked and interdigitating cells. The proposed mechanism assumes that cells within an array seek the smallest possible surface-to-volume ratio . . .'[60]

What Menton discovered, as a result of 'getting his hands dirty' and making real models and simulations of skin columns in this way and also with the soap bubbles, was that Volume-Packers form columns and act spontaneously because of natural physical constraints. It is not necessary, therefore, to postulate EPUs as real and mysterious 'entities'. The whole thing happens because of the simplest physical laws, in a wholly natural manner. He summed it up by saying:

> The results of this study suggest that cell stacking in the epidermis may be the result of a mechanism involving the close packing of cells, surface tension and topological principles, concerning the division of space with minimal partitional area. Living cells are physically similar to drops of water or soap bubbles in the sense that they exhibit surface tension and typically assume a shape with minimum surface (spherical) when not in contact with a solid substratum. There is considerable evidence, moreover, that cells, like soap bubbles, also tend to approach a minimum surface-to-volume ratio when packed in an array. . . . The polygon having the smallest surface-to-volume ratio, while retaining the capacity to assemble in an array without interstices, is the . . . tetrakaidecahedron [i.e. the Volume-Packer]. . . . This study has shown that cells of some tissues which are organized as stacked columns bear a remarkable similarity, whether they be plant or animal, and that such cells appear to be fundamentally of tetrakaidecahedral shape. In the case of epidermal cells, other intrinsic forces have modified this shape to produce a flattened form. . . . A study of models indicates that flattening . . . does not interfere with its stacking pattern. . . . The tetrakaidecahedron is the only geometric form that can stack in regular columns having all units interdigitated with adjacent units in six surrounding columns.[61]

Naturally, Menton goes into full details, which need not concern us here. But his case is overwhelmingly convincing. He has discovered nothing less than the simplest possible principles to explain the hexagonal arrays of skin, principles which do not require mysterious entities governing the process, but which derive from natural configurations in space, and the equally natural propensity of forms to find minimum stress when they come together.

The last publication on this subject by David Menton was in 1976, so I contacted him by phone in 2000 to ask him if I had missed some of his later publications, because I was intrigued about where he had taken his exciting ideas and insights in further development. He was about to retire, and he told me a sad story. Apparently, his work in this field had not been recognized or accepted by other colleagues, who continued to invoke the unnecessary EPUs as mysterious forces to create the skin columns. All of his applications for grants to continue his work had been rejected. I was the first person in a quarter of a century to contact him and praise his work and ask about his further thoughts on the subject. It is understandable that he was somewhat disheartened between 1976 and 2000. He was forced to turn to other areas of research and drop his work on skin columns completely. This was a great loss for science, because Menton had profound insight, used superb methods, and formulated broad conclusions with relevance far beyond the area of his immediate research. I am grateful to him for sending me his offprints and allowing me to reproduce his illustrations. He told me if I had been three months later, I would have been too late, for in cleaning out his office upon retirement he would have thrown them all away. It is extremely upsetting that Menton's work could not continue due to the lack of comprehension by colleagues and that twenty-five years of brilliant research was aborted so that it never happened. Imagine what Menton would have done if he had been able to continue. There can be no doubt whatsoever that he was right and the others are wrong. But it seems I am the only person interested in salvaging his work from the scrapheap of wasted science. I hope for his sake that through my book his own excellent work will be rediscovered by readers and receive the attention and recognition which it so richly deserves.

When I first mentioned Menton's work, I referred to his experiments with soap bubbles. He noticed that the soap bubbles instead of being oriented at right angles to their base were oriented at 60°. This is an interesting finding. Let us just consider this difference in angle between the 60° angle at which the soap bubbles shot upwards, along a hexagonal trail, and the 90° angle at which the real skin cells grow upwards.

In considering this we should recognize that the real skin cells are genuine, and have a real job to do. They are engaged in a distinct and purposeful movement in a single direction; they have a 'flow'. We have seen previously that in such situations, a 90° angle will appear. But the soap bubble simulation by Menton was lacking this purposeful directive thrust – the soap bubbles weren't really growing, they were mimicking the skin cells in an idle way. Soap bubbles are notoriously flighty, and, like some people, not to be trusted! Being mere amateurs and not in earnest, they followed the easiest path, a hexagonal one. They were not, as the skin cells are, subjected to a relentless directional imperative; hence, the angle was different.

Although the Volume-Packer, particularly when squashed, is a kind of three-dimensional hexagon, there is one other solid figure – and a very subtle and mysterious one – which really represents the ultimate in solids. I have given it the name of the Space-Packer. Its technical name is the cubo-octahedron, or cuboctahedron. Its faces appear to consist of squares and triangles, but in reality if you conceive of the faces having been bent or folded round, all the faces are actually irregular hexagons with the triangular tips folded down and multiply-overlapping. It thus really consists of six incestuous, overlapping irregular hexagons, the shared triangular tips of which are all bent in space at an angle of 60°.

Buckminster Fuller, the inventor of the geodesic dome and one of the great twentieth century geniuses of geometry, recognized the importance of the Space-Packer. He gave it a special name of his own, calling it the Vector Equilibrium. However, I think everyone will agree that Space-Packer is a much simpler and handier name. Bucky (as everyone called him, whether they knew him or not, and I was fortunate to know him) came across the Space-Packer when he was looking into the 'closest-packing of spheres'. He found that if you take a ping-pong ball and see how many other ping-pong balls you can pack around it, you can only pack twelve. These twelve will all touch each other and the central ball equally. This is called 'closest-packing'. Now imagine that the ping-pong balls dissolve away in front of your very eyes, leaving only some lines joining their centres to each other (ignoring the central ball). The resulting figure will be the Space-Packer. The balls and the figure are both represented in Figure 72 below.

This strange solid has many peculiar properties, apart from being a kind of 'meta-hexagon'. A mathematics reference book

Figure 72: The 'closest-packing of spheres' – twelve ping pong-balls glued together in tightest formation round a central one form, by the lines connecting their centres, a mysterious solid known as the cubo-octahedron, or, as I call it, the Space-Packer

explains why Fuller gave it the name of the Vector Equilibrium: 'The name is derived from the fact that the radial vectors of this figure have the same value as the circumferential vectors. In terms of dynamics, the outwards thrust of the figure is exactly balanced by the restraining, chordal force; thus the figure is an equilibrium of vectors.'[62]

We have already seen in many examples how equal forces in every direction result in hexagonal cracking patterns. Now we have a higher-dimensional version of the same situation: a solid in unique equilibrium composed of interlocking hexagons. (They are irregular hexagons which consist of a central square with equilateral triangles for tips.) And these interlocking hexagons represent the ultimate in 60° angles – every three-dimensional angle in the entire solid figure is one of 60° – carrying the central concept of 'hexagon-ness' to its ultimate three-dimensional realization. The Space-Packer is truly a *hyper-hexagon*.

What else is unusual about this solid? Fuller did a lot of research on it (though he never seems to have discovered the interlocking hexagon aspect of the figure, or at any event he never commented on it). He found that if he constructed a Space-Packer out of metal rods connected by flexible joints, by a slight push, the figure would actually collapse successively into an icosahedron, an octahedron, and finally a tetrahedron! It thus encompassed these regular polyhedra (geometrical solids) as alternative versions of itself! Fuller discovered this in 1948, and from the way in which the structure moved, he was led to refer to it by the name of a dance popular at that time called 'the jitterbug', so that the collapsing and transforming process was named by him 'the jitterbug transformation'. As the mathematics reference book just quoted comments of this transformation: 'It follows that, in the dynamics of energy transformations, the vector equilibrium [Space-Packer], icosahedron, octahedron, and tetrahedron, are simply different phases of the same configuration of forces.'[63]

So we see that the hyper-hexagon known as the Space-Packer not only represents the ultimate equilibrium of energy forces, but it can also transform itself directly into the standard solid configurations known for thousands of years as the Platonic solids. (There are two other Platonic solids, the cube, which as it is formed entirely of 90° angles represents a different energy concept altogether, and the twelve-faced dodecahedron, which lives a life of its own, which we cannot go into here.)

We now come to the most interesting aspect of the Space-Packer of all. Apart from the cube (or its 'bent' variants composed of quadrilaterals), the only other solid figure which can fill all of space completely leaving no gaps is the (now we understand why!) aptly-named Space Packer. Clearly, a space filled with cubes is a space with a directional force operating, and a space filled with Space-Packers is a space at equilibrium. This is bringing us closer to a true comprehension of what event-structures would have to be like. But let us look even closer.

Space filled with cubes is called a *regular honeycomb*. Space filled with Space-Packers is called a *quasi-regular honeycomb*. These are the only two essential configurations to fill all of space

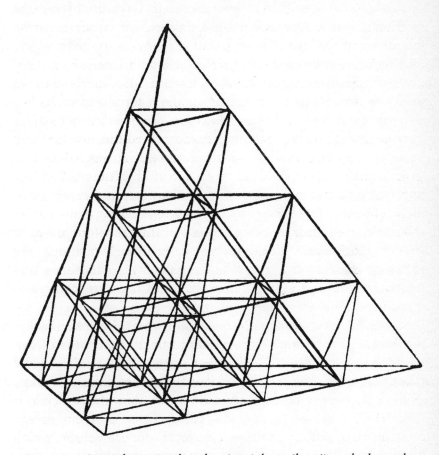

Figure 73: Apart from simple cubes (straight or 'bent') packed together, this configuration of packed 'Vector Equilibria' is the only regular honeycomb which fills all of space without leaving any gaps. Officially known as 'the solid tessellation [3⁴]', this configuration was illustrated in one of the later editions of Mathematical Recreations and Essays *by W. W. Rouse Ball and H. S. M. Coxeter, in the section on polyhedra. One tetrahedron is inscribed in each cube and one octahedron surrounds each omitted vertex. There are other solid tessellations, but this is the most elegant*

completely without leaving holes, or voids. The fact that space filled with cubes is known as *regular* may mean that we have got our priorities upside-down. Since it is the Space-Packers which are really at equilibrium, we would be better justified in describing Space-Packer-filled space as 'regular' – but it is too late to alter conventional mathematical language. I merely mention this as a corrective to our thinking, but the terminology will have to be accepted as it stands.

Fuller has shown that a Space-Packer is a variant of a cube, in a way. He discovered that if you take a cube and bisect its edges, and then at those points truncate the eight corners of the cube, you will get a Space-Packer. I have no doubt whatsoever that there is an extremely profound significance to this discovery, if we could think it through. What this really means is that a geometrical model has been found for the transition from anisotropy to isotropy, or from 'flow' to stagnation, or from motion to rest.

What actually is happening when we cut a cube and make it into a Space-Packer? We are slicing a cube in eight places at 60° angles, to truncate its corners. That means we are imposing 60-degree-ness upon a configuration which is the essence of 90-degree-ness. We are going from the right-angled crack to the hexagonal crack. And to go back again, we rectify the truncation by restoring the missing eight corners, 'giving back the missing angles'.

But I prefer to look at it the other way around – from the point of view of systems at rest, 60° is the norm, and it is only when directionality sets in that 60° adds half of itself to itself to arrive at the new and daring directional angle of 90°. With this onset of directionality, of an arrow of process, irreversible events can begin to occur. And thus we get *history*, in the physical sense, *a direction to time* in the temporal sense, and entropy as a result. However, to discuss those issues would take us far afield, so we must avoid the temptation.

I did not take Fuller's word for it about slicing a cube to get a Space-Packer. I actually carried out the operation, and finding nothing suitable to hand besides a boiled ham (off the bone), I first cut it to a perfect large cube, and then set about carving it into a Space-Packer. I could not resist making a jocular observation to my wife that I might very well be the first man in the history of the world who had cut a ham into a perfect cubooctahedron. It looked exceedingly strange, but eerily impressive. We ate it the next day, sliced, with parsley sauce, which seemed somehow an ignominious end to such a paragon of the art of culinary sculpture. I felt the same sense of betrayal that I might have felt if I had made a beautiful snowman and then gone outside and hacked its arms off to provide ice for some drinks.

I did notice in carving my ham Space-Packer that the top and bottom of the cube were transformed into smaller squares at sixty degrees' rotation from the positions of the original square faces of the cube. In short, everything about the Space-Packer seems to manifest a 60° twist or bend – the true apotheosis of 60-degree-ness in three dimensions.

But we must not stop at three dimensions. The Space-Packer has a peculiar connection with higher dimensions, and in saying this I am not indulging in mere speculation, but in thoroughly established and wholly orthodox geometry. The famous mathematician David Hilbert informs us of this. He says that the Space-Packer is the three-dimensional result of the intersection in ordinary space of the twelve three-dimensional spaces of a four-dimensional figure known as the 24-cell![64]

This may sound weird, but it is how geometricians talk. God knows what it really means, but it sounds impressive. However, it clearly indicates that the Space-Packer can therefore be seen as the three-dimensional product of configurations of a higher dimensionality, from another and more complex level of reality than the ordinary space in which we believe ourselves to be living. And who knows? – Maybe it is at this level that 'event-space' exists.

Space-Packers are found in nature as constituents of some important substances known as zeolites. Zeolites are noted for their regular *voids*, which are so important that some industrial chemical reactions take place in zeolites because the voids are of a precise size, enabling the reactions to be possible, since they must take place at that precise size provided by the void. But it is interesting, in the light of the void-formations we have considered previously, that zeolite voids are often surrounded by networks of Space-Packers. What no one seems to have realized is that, if the solid portions of the zeolites are composed of Space-Packers, then the *voids are also composed of Void-Packers, or in other words Negative Space-Packers, where space takes the place of substance, but the shape remains the same.*

So we have seen that the so-called '24-cell four dimensional solid' gives us the Space-Packer as its by-product in three-

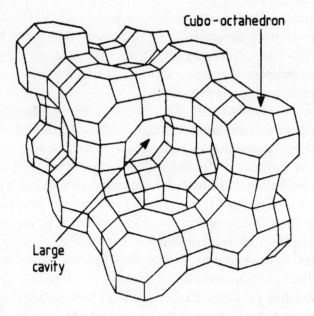

Figure 74: A drawing showing the natural occurrence of Space-Packers (cubo-octahedra) as the constituents of the alumino-silicate framework of materials known as zeolites, as detected through high-resolution photography by electron microscopes[65]

dimensional space. But what do we know about this '24-cell'? We know that it is a four-dimensional Space-Packer, with which 'four-dimensional space can be filled', according to the man who is probably the world's leading authority on geometrical figures,

H. S. M. Coxeter.[66] He adds, suggestively: 'Another peculiarity of four-dimensional space is the occurrence of the 24-cell ... which stands quite alone, having no analogue above or below.'[67]

But does Coxeter mean all of this seriously? He writes further:

> Only one or two people have ever attained the ability to visualize hyper-solids as simply and naturally as we ordinary mortals visualize solids; but a certain facility in that direction may be acquired by contemplating the analogy between one and two dimensions, then two and three, and so (by a kind of extrapolation) three and four. This intuitive approach is very fruitful. . . . As for . . . figures in four or more dimensions, we can never fully comprehend them by direct observation. In attempting to do so, however, we seem to peep through a chink in the wall of our physical limitations, into a new world of dazzling beauty.[68]

In 2000, two fascinating and more or less authoritative books were published dealing with the geometry of foams. The more popular of the two is *Universal Foam: from Cappuccino to the Cosmos* by Sidney Perkowitz.[69] The more technical book is *The Physics of Foams* by Denis Weaire and Stefan Hutzler.[70] Both make excellent reading, and the former is very amusing for the average reader. However, I was disappointed that in neither book was any awareness shown even of the existence of the *cuboctahedron* (Space-Packer). Both books mention the *tetra-kaidecahedron* (Volume-Packer) cursorily, but largely because Lord Kelvin talked about it in the nineteenth century, and the three authors all seem inclined now to disregard it. They refer to a soap bubble experiment undertaken in the 1940s by a botanist named Edwin Matzke, involving 25,000 bubbles (!), where not a single Volume-Packer was observed. They believe this indicated that the Volume-Packer is an ideal form which in real soap bubble situations does not occur because of slipperiness and the fact that real bubbles cannot be fixed exactly in place for such perfect packing. However, the subsequent experiments with soap bubbles by David Menton give a wholly different picture, but are unknown to Perkowitz, Weaire, and Hutzler. Since these authors also limit themselves to foams, not dealing with skin or the other matters we have considered, their conclusions are restricted to far too narrow a base of information to be acceptable for any general conclusions about Volume-Packers, and of course say nothing at all about Space-Packers. Perhaps their otherwise excellent books can be revised in due course to rectify this inadequacy, as it is pretty crucial and should be dealt with by them in subsequent editions.

There is another promising way of looking at the alternatives of 'stagnant' and 'flow' situations for events, with their hexagonal versus right-angled structures. And this approach gives a possible means of envisaging the 'truncating' of a cubic spatial formation to render it 'hexagonal', by turning a cube into a Space-Packer. This comes from a rather unusual source. The religious leader, philosopher and visionary Rudolf Steiner had an interest in unusual aspects of geometry. His interest was continued by a disciple named Olive Whicher, whose fascinating book *Projective Geometry: Creative Polarities in Space and Time* was actually published by the Rudolf Steiner Press.[71]

Whicher's book might have appeared upon casual inspection to be a tract representing some curious geometrical teachings of a sect. But it is a serious work drawing upon many previous works in the field by various German scholars, and it appeared in a German edition the previous year, although it seems to have been written in both languages by the author rather than actually translated.

Without having mastered the principles of Whicher's unusual type of geometry which she calls 'projective geometry' – although impressed that it partially derives from the work of the great mathematician Arthur Cayley (co-inventor of an important higher algebra) – I discovered a fascinating way of looking at the matters we have just discussed in our preceding pages.

Olive Whicher gives a wholly different way of generating both hexagonal tessellations and those of quadrangles. She does this by the emanation of straight lines which intersect. This may sound very simple, or indeed unlikely, but it actually works, as may be seen in Figures 74 and 75, taken from her book. She obviously thinks in her own original manner, and it is refreshing to come across this wonderful novelty.

She takes a straight line – a kind of 'horizon' in the distance – and from it she lets rays shoot out from three points. These rays cross and the points where they cross form the basis for an amazing tessellation of irregular hexagons, seen in Figure 76. As she says: '. . . a whole field of hexagons arises in the plane. . . . No one hexagon is similar to another, and they lie side by side in never-ending sequence . . . order is maintained . . . [as if] by some hidden law.'[72]

By a slight variation in the initial conditions, Ms Whicher is able by her rays to generate the amazing tessellation of

Figure 75: Olive Whicher's drawing of an array of quadrangles generated by intersecting rays from four points on a 'horizon'. The changing of the initial conditions of the emission of intersecting 'rays' from distant points determines whether six-sided or four-sided patterns will emerge in what Ms Whicher calls the resulting 'net' on the plane

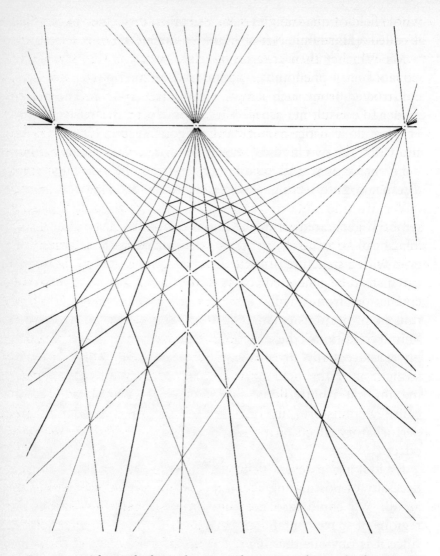

*Figure 76: Olive Whicher's drawing of an array of irregular hexagons
generated by intersecting rays emitted from three points on a 'horizon'.
As she says: 'a whole field of hexagons arises in the plane'*

quadrangles seen in Figure 74 instead of a tessellation of
hexagons. As she then says: 'In the hexagon net, each line served
alternately as side and then as diagonal. In the quadrangle net,
two points must be different from the start . . . [resulting in] a

whole field of quadrangles to be drawn side by side. Such a field is called a Harmonic Net or Moebius Net.'[73]

Ms Whicher then goes on to demonstrate a whole range of extraordinary phenomena which arise from these nets of hers, constructed from such simple elements. I leave the interested reader to consult her astonishing book for himself or herself, as I cannot do it justice in a brief summary. But the main point is to show that the two kinds of 'event-space', stagnant and changing, – i.e. hexagonal and quadrangular – can be generated at a distance by intersecting emanations from simple sources.

We are thus able to conceive of the 'event-spaces' as being remotely generated arrays rather than as inherent standing fields. Space can be neutral, not inherently structured or patterned or even with a structure of pattern imposed upon it, and the arrays can instead be generated across it from a distance by intersecting emanations from singular events or sources. The emanations can thus be projections emanating from what physicists love to call 'initial conditions', the variations in which can be caused by what physicists equally love calling 'perturbations'. This brings us straight into the field of chaos theory and the now-famous maxim that a butterfly beating its wings in South America can cause a rainstorm in England by the magnification of its perturbatory effects on a system, what is now called 'the butterfly effect'.

By looking at 'event-fields' in this way, we might avoid the necessity of postulating actual large-scale standing 'event-fields' at all. We could also accommodate the evident necessity of regions of space containing more than one field simultaneously, since it is obvious that many events can take place at the same time and place. As a simplistic instance of this, we need only to think of two people standing side by side but doing and thinking different things. There are also smaller 'event-fields' nested within larger ones, so that if I am tying my shoelaces that is one thing, whilst I am also threatened by an oncoming car headed straight for me, which is another.

Certainly a nagging problem about the very concept of 'event-fields' is how can they all co-exist? By adopting the projective geometry approach, we might be able to accommodate countless simultaneous 'event-fields' in the same region of space practically without limit, all generated by harmonically resonant frequencies of intersecting world-lines of initiated events. Those 'event-rays' harmonic with one another would not cause destructive interference patterns or action-dissonance.

Some 'event-rays' would interfere, some would be too high a frequency or too low a frequency to effect one another at all, some would generate overtones, and so on. Since sound automatically generates overtones for many, many octaves, lower-frequency events by analogy can be assumed to resonate and be perceptible at higher levels, but higher-frequency events would be imperceptible at lower levels because of the fact that undertones in music and sound, unlike overtones, are not generated. One can compare this to my dog's inability to understand me if I talked to her about algebra, but my ability to hear her when she barked. Thus it is that two people can be in love, standing in a bus, next to a murderer. The murderer is not softened by the presence next to him of all this goodness and sweetness, but the two people feel an intuitive unease about his evil emanations. The higher senses the lower, but the lower cannot perceive the higher. That is because vibrations give off countless overtones but they do not give off undertones.

It is such higher-order events which I envisage taking place all around us, and the intersections of these events with one another yield geometrical forms which puzzle us as they recur over and over again. At every turning of the way we encounter the same configurations in different contexts. They are more than the lineaments of space and time. They are the 'something out of nothing', the emergence along the cracks and seams of the Universe of what precipitates from the Beyond, and melts back into it again.

Hidden influences are stronger than those which are evident.

Heraclitus, *Fragment* 54[74]

APPENDIX I

A Hitherto Unpublished Seventeenth-Century
Account of the Area of the Baian Oracle

*In the collection of Count Nikolai Tolstoy is an unpublished
manuscript – written by an officer of Admiral Killigrew's Naval
Squadron in the Mediterranean in the year 1690. I am grateful to
Count Tolstoy for allowing me to extract and publish a section
which offers interesting descriptions of the area of the Baian
Oracle:*

... Being got over ye bay we went to see the Lacus Avernos soe
much spoken off [of] by ye poetts tis now a pretty Large Lake
surrounded with hills ye watter is about fifteen fathom deepe
cleare and sweete though formerly it was salt there being a way
out of ye Bay into it and here was their Station for their Ships and
Galleyes this passage is now stopped up for in the yeare 1530
there hapned a violent earthquake and grate eruptions of fire
issued forth as usall at The Sulfatirerra as afore mentioned at ye
same time rose out of ye Sea Mounte Nove or ye new Mountaine
which hath cute of [cut off] all intercourse betwene ye sea and
Lacus Avernos And wch was formerly ye sea is now become a
Loftey hill planted with vines is not stoney or rockey but a
spungey earth in ye side of one of ye mountaines wch surround
ye Lake is an entrance into Sibbles groate [Sibyl's Grotto]
Sibbilas Groate or cave cut into a hard rocke the people tell it
went formerly to Cumea wch is on ye other side ye Lake whence

she was called ye Cumean Sybbell ye entrance into it is a Little inconvenient becase tis darke soe each of us had a torch into our hands we went far strait forward into ye Cave it is verry Lofty and broad enough for Six to go abrest to ye end we went about 350 paces where found it filled up with rubbish about 14 paces short of ye end we found a small passage, so meting steepe at ye end there was a roome 14 foote Long and halfe as broade in wch is a Sesterne of watter in wch She [the Sibyl] was want to bath and alsoe a Stone cut out of ye Rock Like a bead [bed] whence ye Sibbles used to deliver their ouracles from hence we returned to or [our] faluca and rowing a Long [along] ye Shower [shore] we came to the Sudatore de Tritone wch are bannios all cut out a rocke by ye Sea Side [he is here referring to the Baths] we went into ym [them] by Stone Stepes [steps] and thorrow [through] Long Passages togethr ye further we went ye hotter it was we were forced to keepe stoppeing ye heat assending to avoyde ye heat but before we came to ye end those passages we were all over in a baneo Sweatt there are in all about 50 one is 166 paces this was a placc of great esteeme in ye Roman times at ye entrance each Bath was a Statue with inscriptiones around what each Bannieo was usefull for for ye directiones of those wch came thither as greate resort was had to ym [them] find vast bennifitts arriseing from ym [them] wch soe allarmed the world that thay tell you ye Phesitiones [physicians] agreed to distroy ym wch accordingly thay did heyring [hiring] a Ship and people who came by night pooling [pulling] down ye Statues as likewise damaging ye apartmts soe that since they have not benn able to distinguish it againe soe as to set it aright thay tell you as soone as thay had done and returned to their Ship their arrose a Storme & thay were cast away and not a Sole of ym saved splitting against ye rockes there are three Apartments wch are made used standing one for Women a 2d for Religious Persons a 3d for People sent from ye Anatima (?) Convent or Scooles in Naples the time of useing ym is in June or July hence we went with our falucaes and as we rowed a Long ye Cost we saw three considerall ruinated Buildings wch thay say were Venus Deana Apollo and Backusest [Bacchus's] Temples with other Banioes and Sudatores Supposed to be made by Nero where was writ or engraved on Stone ye following Saying of Marshall [Martial], quid Nero pejus, quid Thermes Melious Neronianis we continued rowing a Long till we came to ye Antient Citty of Bowles as likewise the plasant Bajom [Baia] under watter wch was over whelmed with ye mountaines that rose out of ye sea. here we saw Agreppina [Agrippina's] Tomb tis cut in a rock ye entrance is soe strate [strait, i.e. narrow] you can but goe in one at a time to goe downe into it tis cut cuparla fashion it has benn very anxiously painted but with ye torches people carrey in there hands when they goe to see it hath Blackned ye figures wch one may perceive hath binn of Ancient history recording Nero haveing binn frustrated in his desegnes of taking away ye life of his Mother Agreppina sent Annicitus a Capt [Captain] of his Navey with a Senturion [centurion] Soldier to despatch her who brakeing into her Chamber and finding her abed she seeing ym presented her Belly to ye pointe of there [their] swords saying perce [pierce] this belly that brought forth Such a Monster as Nero who seeing her said he little thought he had had such a butefull woman to his Mother ye same night she was buried obscurely but her bones being preserved thay were here entered after the Death of her sone [son]

Piscine Merabilis into which we descended by forty Stone Steps it is an oblong Squareplace diged into a mountaine about one hundred Paces Long and fifty broad the roofe is supported by 48 pillars of great Magnitude ye toope [top] is part broake downe which afords light enough for People that goe into it to see it is plastered over ye better to preserve the watter this Sisterne was made by Agrepena to preserve watter for his Armey [he means Agrippa, not Agrippina] that was encamped near this place whence we went to see the Centum Camerelle or hundred Chambers soe called from their numbers you come first into a large spacious place supported by severall Large pillers like ye Pesina Marabiles on ye walls are abundance of travellers names English that have binn there to see it amongst I cut mine out of this is a narrow passage downe into ye other apartmts [apartments] that are properly called ye Hundred Chambers thay have noe Light comes into them soe you carry torches in your hands to see ym thay are cutt severall ways into ye rocke each apartment is about three yards Long and halfe ye bredth separated from ye rest by a strong pertition [partition] and a very Narrow passage from one to ye other some say Nero kept his his [sic] Slave and prisoners there from hence wee returned to The Temple of Bacchus which is now turned into an ostaria where we refreshed our Selves with extrardonery good Wine – and soe we returned to Putzoly [Pozzuoli] in ye evening to Naples where we saw the Catacombs being a place adjoyning to ye Hospitall and Church of St. Genaro wch we found to be a Long place and of each side in ye Rock nitches to Lay ye Dead bodies 3 or 4 not bigg enough for a Coffinn but only for ye body with matts underneath to put ye boanes wch ye nitches were full thay say tis five or six miles Long there were several inscriptiones engraved on ye nitches with Effigies of persones on ye Walls one inscription was plain – *Hic Iacet Proculus* –

End of the Account

Note: It is obvious from this account that three hundred years ago the site of the Oracle of Cuma was well known and frequently visited. Thus, Professor Amadeo Maiuri's 'discovery' of it in 1932 was a rediscovery of a site which had been lost for only two and a half centuries at the most. This is a fact previously unknown to archaeologists, and for this we are indebted to the survival of the naval officer's manuscript. But the other details of various ruins preserved in the account should also be of interest to archaeologists, and may yield information about ruins since destroyed. Unfortunately, the naval officer rowed past the entrance to the Oracle of the Dead, which was evidently still unknown.

APPENDIX 2

FABLES, RIDDLES, AND
MYSTERIES OF DELPHI

The following talk was delivered by me at the International Delphic Conference, at Delphi in Greece, on 21 March 1998. It has been published in the Proceedings of that Conference:

Seira: Delphikē Idea, Archaioellēnikos Logos kai Synchronos Kosmos, Akadēmia Delphikōn Meletōn, Delphikos Logos, No. 4, Athens, 1999, pp. 64–72.

What is it which swallows what is before it and what is behind it, as well as anyone who is watching?

The answer is: TIME. It devours the past and the future, as well as all observers.

What I have just asked you is a *riddle*. And we are today at Delphi, which is the most famous place in the world for riddles. Probably more of the world's riddles were written here than anywhere else on earth. For many of the answers given by the Delphic Oracle were given in the form of riddles, many of which became famous because they were so difficult. And a great many of these riddles have been recorded and preserved, so that we may still read them and try and solve them. In fact, many of the Delphic riddles had a profound influence upon Greek history and culture, as historians have pointed out for two and a half millennia.

At Delphi also there is an association with fables. For it was here that the most famous of all writers of fables was said to have died – I refer to the story, which in fact was greatly distorted and is probably untrue, that Aesop was thrown from the cliff Hyampeia here at Delphi as he was reciting his fable about 'The Eagle and the Scarab Beetle' (Fable 4 in *The Complete Fables* as recently published in English by myself and my wife Olivia). Apart from the fact that a man would not necessarily recite a fable as he was being thrown from a cliff – surely he would interrupt the tale to protest! – the story of Aesop being murdered by the Delphians appears to be as false as many of the other stories which clustered around the name of Aesop in popular tradition. For instance, it was said that Aesop knew King Croesus, but their dates do not match and he could not have done so. It is indeed highly likely that Aesop came to Delphi, and there may have been some political tension connected with his visit. But I doubt the truth of the story that the Delphians concealed a valuable object in his baggage and then seized him and pretended to discover it, thereby accusing him of stealing from Apollo, so that they could execute him. This seems to me mere folklore. And if more of the writings of Aristotle had survived, we would probably know the full story of the real Aesop. Aristotle did say in surviving fragments of his lost *Constitution of Samos* that he had discovered that Aesop was not a Phrygian from what is now the Turkish coast – which most people of his day believed – but that in fact he came from the obscure town of Mesembria on the Black Sea coast of Thrace very far north of Byzantium (in what is today Bulgaria) and had been seized there either by pirates or in a military campaign and along with the other inhabitants sold into slavery. But Aesop was not a slave who laboured in the fields. He was a secretary and even practised as a lawyer on the island of Samos, where he lived much of his life. He probably came to Delphi on an important mission and even told some fables, but I believe we can ignore the probably false tale of his murder here.

It is very appropriate to discuss Aesop and his animal fables here today because animals were so important in the poetry of Angelos Sikelianos, the man who tried to revive the Olympic and

Delphic Ideals. Sikelianos was brilliantly successful with the
Olympics, and we are here today trying to relive the Delphic
Ideal of culture, but unfortunately culture has less world appeal
than sport.

Animals are constantly mentioned by Sikelianos, especially
horses. I presume he liked riding. Sometimes he mentions
Pegasus, the horse with wings. And of course sometimes he was
thinking of the suicide of Pericles Yannopoulos, who rode his
horse into the sea near Eleusis. In Sikelianos's poem 'The Sacred
Way', about the road from Athens to Eleusis, he gives a very
touching description of two chained performing bears belonging
to a gypsy whom he met on the road. The pathos of this poem
reminds me of the fables of Aesop, for in both the animals are
suffering and are representative of ourselves, for we too are so
often chained, and each of us is one of those chained bears, but
also each of us is a Prometheus in his own way. Sikelianos says
near the end: 'And as I walked my heart asked in anguish: "Will
the time, the moment ever come when the bear's soul and the
gypsy's and my own . . . will feast together?"' In Sikelianos, as in
Aesop, we wonder if peace will ever come, if the animals will be
freed – if *we* will be freed. Sikelianos speaks of 'all the primaeval
suffering for which, throughout the human centuries, the soul's
tax has still not been paid. Because the soul has been and still is
in hell.' But he sees hope and the poem ends by saying of the time
when all shall be freed: 'a murmur spread through all the air
above me, a murmur, and it seemed to say: "It will come."'

Here in Greece you have human suffering imprinted onto
every inch of the soil. At every site struggles and deaths have
taken place, and souls have cried out in despair. But also glory
has been felt, transcendent experiences have elevated the human
spirit, beautiful locations like this one at Delphi have inspired
and given hope. You are drenched in tradition here – the hands
of all the dead are about your throats at every moment, but also
the wings of countless angels flutter about your heads and you
can walk in the light and breathe the good fresh air – everywhere
except in Athens, that is.

The oldest recorded Greek riddle is the famous riddle of the

Sphinx of Thebes, which was solved by Oedipus: *What walks on four legs in the morning, on two in the afternoon, and on three in the evening?*

The answer is: MAN. For man crawls on all fours as a baby in the morning of his life, walks on his two legs in the afternoon of his life, and in the evening of his life hobbles with a stick, so that he then could be said to have three legs.

Why were such riddles so important in ancient times? For one thing, they did not have television and they were not confronted with the nightly riddle of all that nonsense.

But seriously, it was Aristotle who made the first real study of the cultural importance of riddles in ancient Greek culture, and it can be said with certainty that riddles were one of the great secrets of the Greek genius, especially the ones which emanated from here, Delphi.

The Greeks in ancient times were very conservative about their traditions and their religion. So the oracular statements of Delphi and the other official oracles such as Dodona and – prior to the seventh century BC when it was still functioning as an active oracle, Delos – tended to combine the conservative and the radical in a marvellous way. In terms of tradition the oracular statements were always extremely conservative, so that they never threatened established rituals, but reinforced them, like a strengthening of the bones. But while bones need strengthening, muscles need exercising. So the oracular statements also provided extreme examples of mental agility and challenged the best brains of Greece to try and figure out their meanings by solving the riddles which they stated. This, I believe, is one of the secrets of Greece's greatness.

It was that greatest of Greek philosophers, Aristotle, who first figured this out and stated it explicitly. In his book on *Rhetoric* he wrote: 'Well-constructed riddles are attractive [because] a new idea is conveyed. . . . The thought is startling, and . . . does not fit in with the ideas you already have. . . . The effect produced . . . is a surprise.' [III, 1405/1412]

I believe that the ancient Greeks achieved intellectual greatness because they mastered the art of making statements by unexpected and novel means. Fables and riddles were essential in this, for they conveyed meanings indirectly, with the suddenness and glaring nature of lightning flashes. Since Delphi produced more such riddles than anywhere else, Delphi thus became *a centre of new thinking*. Fresh ideas were stimulated by this means. The classic example of this is the famous Delphic riddle reputed to have been solved by Plato: the inhabitants of Delos were told that Greece would be at peace if they could double the altar at Delos. But when they tried doubling the lengths of all the sides, they got an altar eight times larger, not double. They then realized that sophisticated geometrical principles had to be taken into consideration, and the task was not at all simple. Plato was consulted, as he was a noted geometer, and he explained to the Delians that they should study geometry, which was the true message of Apollo. This is a particularly clear example of the kind of fresh thinking which was being continually stimulated by the Delphic oracular riddles.

A more typical example of a Delphic riddle was the one given to the Spartans, and preserved by Herodotus. Delphi told them that they would defeat the Tegeans only when they had brought back the bones of Orestes the son of Agamemnon. [I, 67] But no one knew where this Orestes had been buried. So the Spartans again enquired of Delphi and were told that Orestes was buried somewhere at Tegea, 'where two winds by hard compulsion blow, and blow answers to blow, and woe lies upon woe'. But the Spartans, not noted for their intellectual agility, had a great deal of trouble figuring this out, and a large proportion of their leading citizens applied their brains to this matter of state for a long time, as the future of Sparta seemed to be at stake. It was by forcing people to think like this that Delphi encouraged the habits of deep thought and analysis, engendering a mode of creative genius which was to raise Greece to the highest level of all Western cultures for philosophy. Note that the riddles of Delphi were generally phrased within an arch-conservative tradition: legendary personages were treated as real, and the Orestes who may or may not actually have existed was in the case of the riddle assumed to have been real. This meant that no resistance to the fresh thinking would be encountered by the most reactionary members of the society, for the most conservative ritualistic views appeared to be supported by the riddles. No doubt was ever thrown upon tradition, but tradition was ingeniously turned to the use of innovation. This was simply brilliant, and resolved the problem of constructive cultural growth in a manner which has not, in my opinion, been excelled since that time anywhere in the world.

The Christian historian of the fifth century AD, Hermias Sozomen, said of the oracular riddles that they 'were intelligible only to the few who by their erudition were able to understand more important truths than those commonly taught to the people'. Even if this elitist view were true, those erudite few learned a great deal in the process. But I maintain that the riddles percolated down to the lowest levels of society, and that in many famous cases, whole populations chattered about the riddles in the marketplace and at dinner parties for months on end. This must have had a profound effect upon society.

Fables are another, less drastic, example of saying things by indirect means. Instead of describing interactions between people, fables generally describe interactions between animals. But everyone knows that the animals represent people. A fable is thus a riddle in milder form. When we hear the fable of the Raven and the Fox, the riddle associated with it is: who is really the raven and who is really the fox?

It is the use of unfamiliar ways of expressing the familiar that stimulates the imagination and causes us to grow mentally. This is what riddles and fables always did. But it should be obvious that the other chief method of stimulating us in this fashion is poetry. For the essence of poetry is the juxtaposition of astonishing and unexpected images. And this brings us back to a great poet like Angelos Sikelianos. What could be more unexpected than this:

Breath like a lily that the north wind has frozen.

It is true that one's breath in winter emerges sometimes almost in the shape of a lily, which can be seen in the cold. And if lilies were blooming in winter, the north wind might freeze them. But who would normally think of such an association? And yet, that is the job of the poet. The unexpected image shocks us, stimulates our imagination, and thrills us. Then we are free to grow, for we have broken out of another layer of the chrysalis of conformity.

I have already mentioned that Sikelianos often uses animals in his imagery, in the tradition if not in the same manner as Aesop. Here is a classic example from his poem 'The Consciousness of Faith':

> *Like a peasant*
> *who assists the birth of his cow –*
> *and she from the pain groans like a wild beast –*
> *plunging the hand into her bowels*
> *until the calf slips*
> *in one movement*
> *to the floor of the shed . . .*
> *thus was I covered with blood*
> *assisting with all my soul the birth of the gods,*
> *mysteriously!*

> *Red still,*
> *like the moon in its rising,*
> *I held in my embrace*
> *the holy children*
> *from the womb of the goddesses!*

This marvellous translation is by Philip Sherrard, whom I was fortunate to know slightly. Sikelianos's poetic imagery is as authentic to the life of a farmer as most of the fables of Aesop, and just as timeless. Speaking as one who has witnessed such animal births in sheds, and who has lived much of his life in the countryside surrounded by farmers, I can appreciate the full impact of what Sikelianos wishes to say. Whether a pure city-dweller could do so I do not know, as I am not one, and I cannot imagine being one. My wife and I frequently watch unassisted births of calves from our windows, in the pasture opposite our country house. And each time it is a miracle, which moves us deeply, as it moved Sikelianos.

But let us turn now from such subtleties to much more astonishing and drastic matters – to things which are certainly very different indeed from what they seem, and which concern not only Delphi but potentially the whole of human civilization and its origins. I refer to the mysterious foundation of Delphi, of its location, of the myths of its origins, and of the true significance of these things which superficially may seem obscure and of little relevance, since they are largely unknown.

No one knows when Delphi was really founded. Traces of Minoan occupation at Delphi have been found by archaeologists, and go back to at least 1500 BC. But this appears by no means to have been the true beginning of the sacredness of this site. Before all of this, there was apparently an earlier phase, higher up the mountain.

For the original site of the oracle was not here at Pytho at all, but was much higher up at an obscure location known as Lykoreia. This information is preserved by the ancient geographer Strabo, as well as by scholiasts of both Pindar and Apollonius of Rhodes. There seems to be no doubt of its truth. Lykoreia is where the ark of Deucalion was said to have landed after the Great Flood. An alternative Greek tradition is that the ark of Deucalion landed on Mount Tomaros at Dodona. As all Christians know, the ark of Noah landed on Mount Ararat, according to the Bible.

What is the significance of these three 'ark landing' sites? Do they have any connection with one another? – Indeed they do! Mount Tomaros and Mount Ararat are on precisely the same line of latitude, despite being thousands of miles apart. It seems incredible that the Greek ark and the Hebrew ark could have come to rest on mountains which shared the same latitude line. – What have the Greek and Hebrew traditions to do with one another?

But the mystery deepens when you realize that Delphi is precisely one degree of latitude south of both Mount Tomaros and Mount Ararat. And the other great archaic oracle centre of Greece, the island of Delos, is precisely one degree of latitude further south again.

Surely there must be some strange tradition behind all of this? The division of the circle into 360° goes back to the Babylonians, and so degrees of latitude are not modern at all, but are of indeterminate antiquity. Thus the integral degree separations are not arbitrary and are not artefacts of a modern system of measurement which have arisen by coincidence. The conclusion which thus seems inescapable is that *they were planned*.

But planned when and by whom?

The story of the ark and the Great Flood goes back to Sumerian times, long prior to 2500 BC. I have myself translated the *Epic of Gilgamesh*, which preserves these traditions. My translation was produced on stage at the Royal National Theatre in London. The *Epic* was originally written for dramatic presentation, 2000 years before Aeschylus. Greek drama thus began at Sumer.

And it was not only Greek drama which began there, but the Greek story of the ark, and of the legendary figure who was called Deucalion by the Greeks but Ziusudra by the Sumerians, Utnapishtim by the Babylonians, and Noah by the Hebrews.

The question obviously arises: how was it that at the earliest stages of Greek culture, or of whatever it was which preceded Greek culture in Greece, even before the Minoans, obscure mountain locations were found, and apparently scientifically surveyed with precision, which could correspond with other geodetic points thousands of miles away? Herodotus records that Dodona was founded from Egyptian Thebes. [II, 54–7] Perhaps we should take him seriously and not dismiss his claim. Such extremely ancient origins can no longer be dismissed; scientific evidence is accumulating which indicates that things are not necessarily what they seem. History may actually be a fable, and what we thought were fables may be truths. Research continually pushes back the frontiers of civilization's known origins. Even in the case of Aesop, whom I was discussing a moment ago, we can now demonstrate that at least one of his fables was Sumerian in origin and existed an incredible 2000 years before Aesop! If we can prove that one of Aesop's fables is that old, why not the story of Deucalion as well? And why not also the founding of Delphi? Not of the classical site where we are meeting today, of course, but the older one at Lykoreia, where scientific excavations are obviously urgently required. At the moment we have little idea of what an advanced state of early science must have been required to survey mountain tops so accurately over thousands of miles that sacred sites thousands of miles distant from one another could nevertheless be precisely correlated on a large-scale map.

Who would do such a thing? And why?

In our perplexity, and lacking answers as we do at present, perhaps we should feel that we are brothers with Sikelianos, who in his poem 'Rehearsing for Death', expresses his own certainty that 'Memory has no end here and no beginning . . .', and who experiences his own psychological plunge into the abyss of uncertainty by saying:

> *I held the great pearl in my hand, took spring*
> *into my heart, and felt the scarlet roses*
> *of my fever suddenly become*
> *a crown, felt my black bed become a ship,*
> *the unhurried ship of God, and my struggle*
> *the navigator of my mind among the stars.*

> *. . . the earth sailed among*
> *the stars, the earth sang psalms, and my bed's prow*
> *climbed toward the pole, crushing the waves of time,*
> *and beginning, voyage, end were all*
> *a cataclysm of celestial light before me.*
> [translated by Philip Sherrard and Edward Keeley]

When truly great enigmas confront us, when riddles too great for us to solve taunt us with their impenetrable mystery, we must first, like the citizens of Sparta, try our best to work out the answer. But sometimes the ultimate truth, surpassing even the highest science, is the poetic truth, and the beginning, the voyage and the end become all, as we perilously steer our ship towards that 'cataclysm of celestial light' which may, if we are lucky, grant us one day some true illumination.

Appendix 3

An Anatomical Verification of the Reading of a Term in Extispicy

(article by Robert K. G. Temple, reprinted from the
Journal of Cuneiform Studies, *Vol. 34, 1982)*

The technical term in extispicy, *tirānu,* was originally translated as 'marks' or 'signs'.[1] Lutz amended this to 'zones'.[2] But as knowledge of the terminology advanced, the term came to be recognized as meaning 'convolutions of the intestines'.[3] No report seems to have been published in which an attempt has been made to verify this translation by anatomical investigation of the intestines of a sheep or lamb. I shall here report such a verification, together with an anatomical explanation for the traditional 'numerology' of the *tirānu.*

I have been fortunate to know the owner of a small private abattoir, who has allowed me to have access to freshly slaughtered lambs, and has cooperated in altering his slaughtering practices to conform with the requirements of study of ancient Babylonian and Assyrian extispicy. This would pose insuperable inconvenience to a large modern abattoir of the kind usually found today, where numbers of animals are slaughtered in rapid succession on a scale where leisurely inspections would be impossible, and experimental cutting of carcasses unthinkable.

In my examinations of the entrails of a number of lambs several interesting facts emerged relating to the livers, which were after all the main objects of extispicy of ancient times. But

two specific points which I especially wished to establish related
to the intestines, and the curious final remarks about them
commonly found at the end of extispicy texts. We are continually
informed in these texts that a certain number of *tirānu* have been
observed. The number given is almost always an even number
between 10 and 16. We also know that in the rare instances
where an odd number, such as 15, is given, it is considered to be
an extremely unfavourable omen.[4] No reason ever seems to have
been advanced in modern times to account for this, apart from
the obvious guess that perhaps odd numbers were thought
unlucky, which hardly seems sufficient or satisfactory. It was
therefore my intention to discover, *first*, whether the intestines of
a lamb could be examined in any way at all in which numbers of
'convolutions' between 10 and 16 could be observed, thereby
confirming the now accepted reading of the term *tirānu*, and
secondly, whether any explanation could be found to account
for the unfavourable omen implied by an odd number of convolutions.

Neither task presented an immediate or obvious solution. The
small and large intestines of a lamb, which together form a
voluminous and unwieldy mass of soft and undulating, wet and
slippery material of light weight, are not easy to inspect. It is
difficult to get hold of them, and too firm a pressure can result in
malodorous consequences. They form an impediment to the
examination of the liver and gall bladder and are best removed
and set aside so that the liver can be properly and carefully lifted
out of the carcass without suffering damage.

When confronted initially with the vast mass of the intestines,
one's first reaction is inevitably confusion and a feeling of
hopelessness that any 'convolutions' from the amorphous mass
can possibly be observed with any meaning or rigour at all. The
small intestines present a large number of convolutions – 'which
form a sort of festoon', in the words of the anatomist Sisson[5] –
but they slip and slide and have no permanence, and no number
as low as 10 to 16 can possibly apply to them in any meaningful
way. However, according to Hussey, *tirānu* applies specifically
to 'the large colon'.[6] By this, Hussey evidently means that part of

the large intestines known as the colon. So an attempt was then made to study the colon, which appeared hopeless as well, until I hit upon the expedient of spreading the intestines out as flat as possible over as great an extent as they would cover.

From a young lamb one thus gets a circular spread about two feet across, when laid out on a slab or table, after having been removed from the lamb. When this is done, that part of the large intestines, the colon, which is posterior to the caecum, naturally resolves itself within this mass into an extraordinary spiralling configuration which is very striking. Veterinarians whom I have consulted have told me that their term for this part of the intestines inside a farm animal is 'the spiral colon'. This configuration is dramatically shown in a projection of its three-dimensional position in the body in a diagram of the colon of a pig in Sisson's *Anatomy*.[7] The spiralling pattern is actually a double helix when seen in this way. From the caecum, the colon descends in what are called the centripetal coils until it reaches its lowest point, where it runs in a tight S-bend and spirals up again in what are called the centrifugal coils, and then leads off to the rectum. Nothing of this kind occurs in the human body: our colons simply rise, cross over, and descend to the rectum without forming a spiral configuration.

It is immediately obvious to anyone familiar with the well-known terracotta Humbaba-mask of intestines in the British Museum (BM.116.624)[8] that this natural spiralling pattern is the inspiration for it, though it might take the colons of two separate lambs to be arranged into an actual Humbaba-mask, which could probably be done. I have not undertaken this task, which would be exceedingly tedious and necessitate skilled cutting with a scalpel to free and uncoil the colon prior to rearranging it. Smith has pointed out that the Humbaba-mask is formed by 'a long strip of clay, turned and twisted about in such a way as to represent all the important features'.[9] In a later article, Smith reports another Humbaba-mask in the British Museum (B.M.116.737) and seems to have had second thoughts as to whether the twisting single line was actually laid on rather than moulded in some other way, but stresses that what distinguishes the Humbaba-face from the faces of all other demons is the single line.[10] And this single line is, of course, the intestinal tract. A perfect and straightforward ancient depiction of the spiral colon of a lamb may be seen on a small object (YBC 3000) which is shown in Figure 274 of Van Buren.[11]

The spiral colon of the lamb, laid flat, forms not only a spiralling pattern, but one closely resembling the classic spiral maze. If one follows the path of the colon along, when one comes to the centre, the colon turns and spirals out again the other way. It is to be suspected that at least part of the inspiration for spiralling maze patterns in a variety of separate cultures in antiquity must have come from the observation of the intestines of sacrificial animals. Many of the ancient representations of spiralling mazes from different cultures, such as the ancient British, are perfect representations of the spiral colons of lambs or pigs. It seems safe to assume that observations of the animal colons were extremely widespread and influenced art and religion in many parts of the world.

The 'numerology' of the observations of the *tirānu* in the ancient extispicy texts of the Near East now comes to be immediately evident, and fully explained: If one imagines a diameter of the roughly circular spread of the spiral colon when laid flat, and counts the number of stretches of colon crossed in descending from the top to the bottom (disregarding entirely whether they 'connect' with one another and are in fact only half a convolution each), the number will in the case of all healthy sheep be an even number. So far, since I was examining young lambs less than a year old, I have only encountered 'counts' of 10 or 12. But as lambs in ancient times would often have been slaughtered when older, and their colons would have been longer, presumably 'counts' of 14 and 16 would be encountered in them. A 'count' of 14 is found in the object shown in Figure 274 of Van Buren.[12]

These facts confirm with remarkable precision the evidence of the ancient texts. We can thus be assured that the translation of *tirānu* as the large intestines is justified, though we should specify that it refers actually to the spiral colon without the caecum, and not 'the large colon' as stated by Hussey,[13] who seems to have confused Goetze's clearer account to which she gives a reference. Goetze's translation as, simply, 'colon', is more precise anatomically. *Surummum* is obviously the very posterior end of the colon which emerges from the spiral and becomes the rectum.[14]

However, the word 'convolutions' is slightly misleading. The 'count' was quite obviously of the number of stretches of colon crossed in a straight line, and it disregarded the connectivity of those stretches entirely. One cannot thus say with equanimity that it was specifically the convolutions which were being counted. What was being counted was the stretches of colon produced by or constituting the convolutions, which is a different thing. Strict precision thus suggests a very slight alteration in the translation. We would be quite safe in speaking of the ancient *tirānu* observations as being the counting of 'the arcs of convolution of the intestines', so that we avoid the implication that each count was an entire convolution, and thus represented some sort of circular or convoluted form which had a complete shape of its own.

Finally we come to the omen value of the *tirānu* counts. It has been explained how the counts must in all normal cases yield an even number. But how can an odd number occasionally be produced? For we know that the colon must be continuous, and an animal could not live if the spiral were not intact. What sort of abnormality could possibly bring about an odd count in the spiral? It cannot have been too common an occurrence, but fortunately for the sake of this study, I have actually encountered an example, and can offer an explanation. One lamb which I examined showed internal signs of being seriously diseased. Its liver was pale, with a greyish cast, washed-out looking (this often indicates anaemia), and with various anatomical abnormalities. The *ubānu (processus pyramidalis)* was covered in white abscesses. The liver was also abnormally small. When the intestines were laid out flat for inspection they too presented abnormalities which altered the count.

In order to explain this, it must be mentioned that the spiral colon is surrounded by and enmeshed in a good deal of whitish internal fat. Butchers call this 'caul fat', and in the days when purified lard was still used for medicinal purposes as an ointment base, it was obtained from the corresponding fat in the pig, which was then called 'the finest "leaf" lard', so-called from the appearance of sections of the fat, which has a veined structure like an autumn leaf held up to the light. This intestinal fat in lambs considerably obscures observations of the colon when it is fresh and warm from the body of the lamb. One reason why the *tirānu* observations may have been left until last in all the extispicy inspections by the ancients may be that from experience the priests must have learned that twenty minutes to half an hour after being spread out in the air, the intestinal 'caul fat' of the lamb ceases to be such an obstacle to making a count of the *tirānu*. For the fat congeals and hardens to the consistency of lard after about that length of time and then, far from hampering a *tirānu* count, it actually enhances it by making the colon stand out plainly in relief against it both in terms of colour and texture. I have taken several photos demonstrating this. Prior to the congealing of this intestinal fat, no amount of probing and peering can yield an entirely reliable estimate of the count, for the colon cannot easily be made out in its outer coils. As Goetze has said, the order of inspection in extispicy 'remained virtually unchanged through the centuries'.[15] We see here that in the case of the *tirānu* at least, there was a good physical reason for always leaving it till last. And since it was the custom to do a second inspection of the extispicy victim, known as the *piqittum*, 'check',[16] by which time the intestinal fat would definitely have congealed, the earliest extispicy inspections must have been proved wrong in their *tirānu*-counts so frequently that very quickly the priests would have fallen into the habit of leaving the intestines spread out in the air until the end of their liver examinations to avoid the embarrassment of being found wrong during the *piqittum*, with its built-in advantage of a guaranteed period of exposure to the air and hence a congealing of the fat.

However, there is one case where even the congealing of the intestinal fat is not sufficient to make the colon quite plain for the

count. This is in the case of a diseased lamb. The diseased lamb
mentioned above had a section of its colon badly distended and
swollen, and also discoloured, so that it was quite white – just the
colour of the uncongealed intestinal fat. In the spiralling maze,
this whole arc-section of an intestinal convolution was effectively
obscured for these reasons. It was of course possible by following
the course of the colon with my fingers to trace its full course,
and realize that this obscured portion was an abnormality of
appearance due to inflammation in the interior, presumably
caused by enteritis. But there is no way this stretch of colon could
legitimately be thought to qualify for the count of the *tirānu*,
since it was all but invisible. And to the ancient priests, appearance was everything The fact that the colon was anatomically
intact and was not disconnected was not the point. The practice
of extispicy was avowedly to study the *appearance* of the
entrails. In the case of the diseased lamb, then, an odd count of
the *tirānu* resulted, for although anatomically there were 12 arcs
of convolution present, to a visual inspection only 11 could really
be seen. This bad omen fully confirms what we know of most
abnormalities observed in extispicy: abnormal configurations
and appearance of entrails resulting from disease were largely
unfavourable. This makes sense, whether to an ancient or a
modern. Disease itself is an evil, and hence its results must be bad
omens except in special cases. Veterinarians have assured me that
animals may appear perfectly healthy on the outside, but
examination of their entrails will reveal that they were often
quite ill. To ancient man, this must have seemed a deep mystery,
with profound implications. Modern man still seeks the answers
to mysterious questions in the entrails of dead bodies: in
autopsies! The medical aspect of ancient extispicy may have been
underestimated by modern scholars, though Jastrow appreciated
it from the point of view of anatomical knowledge.[17]

There is a very striking example in ancient Greek extispicy of
an abnormality of the entrails being interpreted as a good omen
rather than as a bad omen. But this abnormality was one of
inheritance rather than of disease. Plutarch records in his *Life of
Aratus*[18] the following incident: 'Thus was the sign which the god

had given him in the sacrifice brought to pass: for it is said that a short time before this, Aratus was offering sacrifice and that there appeared in the liver of the victim two gall bladders enclosed in one caul. The soothsayer explained this to portend that Aratus would shortly form an intimate friendship with his greatest enemy.'[19] This actually came to pass.[20] This abnormality was a congenital freak of nature, rather than a product of disease, and therefore was not necessarily an unfavourable omen.

NOTES

Note: these notes are given in the abbreviated style of the *Journal of Cuneiform Studies*

1. Lutz, JAOS, 38 (1918) p. 77.
2. *Ibid.,* p. 79.
3. Goetze, Old Babylonian Omen Texts, YOS 10, pp. 8–9, 11.
4. Starr, HUCA 45 (1974) p. 23.
5. Sisson, Septimus, *The Anatomy of the Domestic Animals,* 4th ed., p. 470.
6. JCS 2 (1948) p. 30.
7. Sisson, *op. cit.,* p. 493.
8. An excellent photograph of this object (BM. 116.624) may be seen in Plate XIII, AAA XI (1924).
9. *Ibid.,* pp. 107ff.
10. JRAS (1926) pp. 440ff.
11. Van Buren, Clay Figurines, YOSR 16 (1930).
12. *Ibid.*
13. Hussey, *op. cit.,* p. 30.
14. Goetze, *op. cit.,* p. 9.
15. *Ibid.,* p. 4.
16. See Starr in Essays Finkelstein, *Conn. Acad. Arts and Sciences, Memoir 19* (1977) p. 203.
17. Jastrow, *Trans. College Physicians of Philadelphia* 29 (1907) pp. 118ff.
18. In *Plutarch's Lives,* IV, trans. A. Stewart and G. Long, Bohn's Library, London, 1892.
19. *Ibid.,* p. 521. (Life of Aratus, 43.)
20. See Jastrow in *Studies in the History of Religions,* ed. by O. G. Lyon and G. F. Moore (1912) p. 163.

APPENDIX 4

I reprint below the table of binary numbers converted into decimal numbers which appeared at the end of Immanuel Olsvanger's rare pamphlet *Fu Hsi: The Sage of Ancient China*, Jerusalem, 1948 (16 pp.), of which no copy is to be found in the British Library. It is a pity that Olsvanger's brilliant pamphlet is so little known and essentially unavailable. I have been fortunate enough to purchase a copy of it for my own use through the serendipity of scholarly book-browsing. The diagram in Figure 44 is also reproduced from Olsvanger's pamphlet, and his ideas are discussed in the main text.

The numbers from 0 to 63 written a) in the binary and b) in our decimal system:

a) binary	b) decimal	a) binary	b) decimal
000000	00	001000	08
000001	01	001001	09
000010	02	001010	10
000011	03	001011	11
000100	04	001100	12
000101	05	001101	13
000110	06	001110	14
000111	07	001111	15

a) binary	b) decimal		a) binary	b) decimal
010000	16		101000	40
010001	17		101001	41
010010	18		101010	42
010011	19		101011	43
010100	20		101100	44
010101	21		101101	45
010110	22		101110	46
010111	23		101111	47
011000	24		110000	48
011001	25		110001	49
011010	26		110010	50
011011	27		110011	51
011100	28		110100	52
011101	29		110101	53
011110	30		110110	54
011111	31		110111	55
100000	32		111000	56
100001	33		111001	57
100010	34		111010	58
100011	35		111011	59
100100	36		111100	60
100101	37		111101	61
100110	38		111110	62
100111	39		111111	63

Note the different values of the following numbers written in the two systems:

a) binary
$$10 = 2^1 = 2$$
$$100 = 2^2 = 4$$
$$1000 = 2^3 = 8$$
$$10000 = 2^4 = 16$$
$$100000 = 2^5 = 32$$

b) decimal
$$10 = 10^1$$
$$100 = 10^2$$
$$1000 = 10^3$$
$$10000 = 10^4$$
$$100000 = 10^5$$

The number of zeros to the right of the 1 indicates in either system the power of its base: of 2 in the binary, and of 10 in the decimal.

NOTES

CHAPTER ONE

1. Faber and Faber, London, 1973.
2. Paget, Robert F., *In the Footsteps of Orpheus: The Discovery of the Ancient Greek Underworld,* Robert Hale, London, 1967, p. 17.
3. *Ibid., pp.* 90–1.
4. Vergil, 'Fourth Eclogue', from *Virgil: The Pastoral Poems,* trans. E. V. Rieu, Penguin Books, Harmondsworth, 1967, pp. 53–7.
5. Rieu, *op. cit.,* p. 142 (Essay on the 'Fourth Eclogue' entitled 'The Golden Age Returns').
6. Monteiro, Mariana, *'As David and the Sybils Say': A Sketch of the Sibyls and the Sibylline Oracles,* Sands & Co., Edinburgh and London, 1905, pp. 13–14.
7. Vives, Juan Luis (Io. Lodovicus), *Commentary on Augustine's 'The City of God'*, translated into English only in 1620 and published along with Augustine's text in the volume *Saint Augustine, Of the Citie of God: with the Learned Comments of Io. Lodovicus Vives,* trans. 'J.H.', G. Eld & M. Flesher, London, 1620. The passage quoted is from pp. 662–3 of this volume. Readers wishing to consult the Latin original of Vives's *Commentary* will find the passage in the commentary on Augustine's Book 18, Chapter 23.
8. Monteiro, *op. cit.,* p. 14.
9. Augustine, *Citie of God,* p. 661, Book 18, Chapter 23.
10. Cicero, Marcus Tullius, *De Divinatione (On Divination),* II, 54, trans. C. D. Yonge in *The Treatises of M. T. Cicero On the Nature of the Gods; On Divination* ... Bohn's Classical Library, London, 1878, pp. 246–7. (This translation is superior at this point to the one by William A. Falconer in the Loeb Library, who, however, adds in his translation that the Sibyl's writing 'surely is the work of concentrated thought and not of a frenzied brain'. See p. 497 of Cicero, *De Senectute, De Amicitia, De Divinatione,* Loeb Library Series, Heinemann, London, and Harvard University Press, 1964.)
11. Diogenes Laertius, *Lives of Eminent Philosophers,* Book VIII, 78 (in Chapter 3, on Epicharmus). Unfortunately, the standard English translation of this work, by R. D. Hicks, obscures the true meaning of this important passage

by mistranslating the crucial word *parastichida* as 'marginal notes', whereas *parastichidos* is a technical term turning the simpler meaning of 'something written at the side' to the quite specific meaning of 'acrostic formed by letters at the side'. The word is used again by Diogenes Laertius in Book V, 93 (in Chapter 6, on Heraclides), at which point in his translation Hicks correctly translates *parastichida* as 'acrostic', demonstrating that he was in fact aware of the true meaning. His misrepresentation in the other instance serves to highlight the dilemma of the Loeb translators, who constantly have to do a balancing act between accuracy and 'readability'. For the Hicks translations see Vol. I, p. 547, and Vol. II, p. 393, of the Loeb Classical Library volumes of Diogenes Laertius, Heinemann, London, and Harvard University Press, 1965–6.

12. Margoliouth, D. S., *The Homer of Aristotle,* Blackwell, Oxford, 1923, p. 38.

13. Aeschylus, *Seven Against Thebes,* trans. Philip Vellacott, Penguin Books, Harmondsworth, 1961, p. 88.

14. Cicero, Marcus Tullius, *De Divinatione,* II, 54; p. 247 of Yonge's translation for Bohn's Library, *op. cit.*

15. These verses are preserved by Eusebius, but Vives does not give the reference. However, the Greek text is reproduced along with the 1620 English translation (and presumably by Vives in his Latin *Commentary,* though I have not consulted it). The reference for this, therefore, is p. 664 (and p. 663 for the Greek text) of the volume listed in Footnote 8.

16. Monteiro, *op. cit.,* pp. 41–2.

17. *Ibid.,* p. 38.

18. *Ibid.,* p. 165.

19. Paget, *op. cit.,* p. 91.

20. *The Aeneid*, in *The Works of Virgil,* literally translated by Davidson, William Clowes [Bohn's Classical Library], London, 1873, pp. 223–4.

21. G. Consoli Fiego, *Cumae and the Phlegraean Fields*, translated and edited by Alam Reed, American and British Club, Naples, 1927. Figure 46 on page 224 shows a coin with the Sibyl's head on the obverse and a three-headed Cerberus hound on the reverse, over the name of the city.

22. *Ibid.,* p. 159.

23. Strabo, *Geography,* Book V, Chapter 4, Section 4, trans. H. C. Hamilton, Vol. I, p. 361, Bohn's Library, 3 vols., London, 1881–7.

24. *Ibid.,* Book V, Chapter 4, Section 5, and the last sentence of the quotation is from Section 6; pp. 362–4 of Bohn translation.

25. Paget, *op. cit.,* p. 114.

26. *Ibid.,* pp. 113–14.

27. *Ibid.,* pp. 129 and 135.

28. *Ibid.,* p. 135.

29. *Ibid.*

30. *Ibid.,* p. 136.

31. *Ibid.*

32. Tacitus, Cornelius, *The Annals of Imperial Rome,* trans. Michael Grant, Penguin Books, Harmondsworth, 1956, p. 30. (Book I, Chapter 1.)

33. Suetonius (Gaius Suetonius Tranquillus), *The Twelve Caesars,* 'Life of

Augustus', 66, trans. Robert Graves, Penguin Books, Harmondsworth, 1962, p. 87.

34. Paget, *op. cit.*, p. 128.

35. *Ibid.*, p. 103.

36. *Ibid.*

37. Strabo, *op.cit.*, Book V, Chapter 4, Section 6; Vol. I, p. 364.

38. Dakaris, Sotirios I., 'The Dark Palace of Hades', in *Archaeology*, USA, Vol. 15, No. 2, Summer 1962, pp. 85–93. The passage quoted is from pp. 88–90.

39. *Ibid.*, p. 93.

40. Dakaris, Sotirios I., *The Nekyomanteion of the Acheron*, 3rd edition, Ministry of Culture, Athens, 1998, pp. 14–21.

41. *Ibid.*, pp. 13–14.

42. Herodotus, *Histories*, Book V, 92 . . .

43. Strabo, *The Geography*, Book IV, Chapter 5, translated by H. C. Hamilton, 3 vols., George Bell & Sons (later Bohn's Library), London, 1887, Vol. I, p. 363.

44. *Ibid.*

Chapter Two

1. Paget, *op. cit.*, p. 163. Vergil, *Aeneid*, Book VI, in Davidson, trans., *The Works of Virgil*, Bohn's Classical Library, London, 1873, p. 231.

2. Watson, Peter, *War on the Mind: The Military Uses and Abuses of Psychology*, Hutchinson, London, and Basic Books, New York, 1978, p. 253.

3. *Ibid.*, p. 254.

4. *Ibid.*, p. 269.

5. *Ibid.*, p. 270.

6. Paget, *op. cit.*, p. 163.

7. *Ibid.*, p. 160.

8. *Ibid.*, p. 163.

9. *Ibid.*, p. 122.

10. *Ibid.*, p. 164.

11. *Ibid.*

12. *Ibid.*

13. *Ibid.*, p. 160. (Paget quotes the Penguin translation, which is far clearer than that by Davidson, *op. cit.*, pp. 231 and 239–40.)

14. *Ibid.*, p. 165.

15. *Ibid.*, p. 127.

16. *Ibid.*, p. 130.

17. *Ibid.*, p. 161.

18. *Ibid.*, p. 43.

19. *Ibid.*, p. 43.

20. Frazer, Sir James, *The Golden Bough*, London, 1923–7.

21. Graves, Robert, *The White Goddess*, Faber & Faber, London, 1977, p. 250.

22. Paget, *op. cit.*, p. 165.

23. *Ibid.*, pp. 114–15.

24. Dyer, Louis, *The Gods in Greece*, Macmillan, London, 1891, p. 48.

25. Paget, *op. cit.*, p. 165.
26. *Ibid.*, p. 75.
27. *Ibid.*
28. *Ibid.*, pp. 74–5.
29. *Ibid.*, p. 76.
30. *Ibid.*, pp. 75–6.
31. *Ibid.*, p. 76.
32. *Ibid.*
33. *Ibid.*, and *Aeneid, op. cit.*, p. 245.
34. Paget, *op. cit.*, p. 123.
35. *Ibid.*, p. 165.
36. *Ibid.*, p. 77., and *Aeneid, op. cit.*, p. 251.
37. Paget, *op. cit.*, pp. 165–6.
38. *Ibid.*, p. 166.
39. Pausanius, *Guide to Greece*, Book I, 17, 5, trans. Peter Levi, Penguin Books, Harmondsworth, 1971, Vol. I, p. 49.
40. Homer, *The Odyssey*, trans. S. H. Butcher and A. Lang, Macmillan, London, 1900, p. 177.
41. Denys Page, *The Homeric Odyssey*, Oxford University Press, 1955, pp. 21–51.
42. *Ibid.*, p. 46.

CHAPTER THREE

1. Artemidorus, *The Interpretation of Dreams: The Oneirocritica of Artemidorus*, translated from the Greek by Robert White, Noyes Classical Studies, Noyes Press, Park Ridge, New Jersey, USA, 1975.
2. Temple, Robert, *He Who Saw Everything: A Verse Translation of the Epic of Gilgamesh*, Rider, London, 1991 (see in particular p. 124 and Footnotes 18 and 19 on pp. 135–6; the geodetic point at Mount Ararat is associated with an ancient religious site and oracle centre called Metsamor, all the archaeological publications concerning which are in either Russian or Armenian); *The Sirius Mystery*, revised and expanded edition, Century, London, 1998 (see Chapter 6 and Supplement (1997) to Chapter 6).
3. Temple, Robert K. G., *The Sirius Mystery*, Sidgwick & Jackson, London, 1976, Chapter 5. (This chapter was entirely omitted from the British paperback edition, and from many foreign editions.)
4. Pliny, *Natural History*, Book X, 53, 110, trans. H. Rackham, Loeb Classical Library, Heinemann, London, and Harvard University Press, 1967, Vol.III, p. 363.
5. *Ibid.*, Book X, 34–5, 71–3, Vol. III, p. 339.
6. Pritchard, James B., ed., *Ancient Near Eastern Texts Relating to the Old Testament*, 2nd ed., Princeton University Press, 1955, pp. 94–5.
7. *The Sirius Mystery* (1976), Chapter 5, and some discussion in Chapter 4.
8. Hutchinson, R. W., *Prehistoric Crete*, Penguin Books, Harmondsworth, 1968 (revised edition), p. 101.
9. *Ibid.*, pp. 101–2.
10. Pliny, *Natural History*, Book VII, 22, 86, trans. H. Rackham, Loeb Classical

Library, Heinemann, London, and Harvard University Press, 1969, Vol. II,
p. 563.

11. Cicero, Marcus Tullius, *De Natura Deorum (On the Nature of the Gods)*,
Book II, 2, 6, trans. H. Rackham, Loeb Classical Library, Heinemann,
London, and Harvard University Press, 1967, p. 129.

12. Parke, H. W., 'The Oracles of Zeus: Dodona, Olympia, Ammon', Blackwell,
Oxford, 1967, p. 34.

13. Herodotus, *History*, Book I, 159–60, trans. A. D. Godley, Loeb Classical
Library, Vol. I, pp. 199–201.

14. *Ibid.*, Book I, 20, trans. Vol. I, pp. 23–5.

15. *Ibid.*, Book II, 55, trans. Henry Cary, Bohn's Classical Library, London,
1861, pp. 116–17.

16. *Ibid.*, Book II, 57, trans. p. 117.

17. Philostratus, *The Life of Apollonius of Tyana*, Book II, x, trans F. C.
Conybeare, Loeb Classical Library, Vol. I, pp. 139–41.

18. Fontenrose, Joseph, *Python: A Study of Delphic Myth and Its Origins*,
University of California Press, 1980 (paperback), pp. 408 and 416.

19. See *The Sirius Mystery*, Chapter 5, and maps and charts of oracle centres.

20. Wide, Sam, 'Eine Lokale Gattung Boiotischer Gefässe', *Mitteilungen des
Deutschen Archaeologischen Instituts*, XXVI (1901), p. 150.

21. *The Sirius Mystery*, p. 139.

22. Parke, *op. cit.*, p. 43.

23. *Ibid.*, p. 43.

24. Chamberlain, Edgar, *The Homing Pigeon*, The Homing Pigeon Publishing
Co., Manchester, 1907.

25. *Ibid.*, p. 14.

26. Feynman, Richard P., *Surely You're Joking Mr. Feynman!*, Vintage, London,
1992, p. 17.

27. Pausanius, *Description of Greece*, Book IX, 39–40, trans. Peter Levi, *Guide
to Greece*, Penguin Books, Harmondsworth, 1971, Vol. I, pp. 392–7.

28. Plutarch, 'On the Sign of Socrates', 590–3, trans. Philip H. de Lacy and
Benedict Einarson in *Plutarch's Moralia*, Vol. VII, Loeb Classical Library,
Heinemann, London and Harvard University Press, 1968, pp. 461–77.

29. Philostratus, *The Life of Apollonius of Tyana*, Book VIII, xix–xx, trans. F.
C. Conybeare, Loeb Classical Library, Vol. II, pp. 379–83.

30. Cicero, Marcus Tullius, *Tusculan Disputations*, Book I, 47, 114, trans. J. E.
King, Loeb Classical Library, Heinemann, London and Harvard University
Press, 1966, p. 137.

31. Cicero, Marcus Tullius, *De Natura Deorum (On the Nature of the Gods)*,
Book III, 22, 56, trans. p. 341.

32. *Ibid.*, Book III, 19, 49, trans. p. 333.

33. *Ibid.*

34. Lucian, *The Dialogues of the Dead*, Number 10 (338–40), trans. M. D.
Macleod, *Lucian*, Loeb Classical Library, Heinemann, London, and Harvard
University Press, Vol. VII, pp. 51–3.

35. Lucian, *Menippus, or the Descent into Hades*, 22, trans. A. M. Harmon,
Lucian, Loeb Classical Library, Vol. IV, p. 109.

36. Pausanius, *op. cit.,* Book IX, 39, trans. pp. 393–5.

37. Philostratus, *op. cit.* Book VIII, xix, trans. p. 381.

38. Pausanius, *op. cit.,* Book IX, 39, trans. pp. 392–4, footnotes by translator.

39. *Ibid.,* footnote, p. 394, by translator.

40. Philostratus, *op. cit.,* Book VIII, 19, trans. p. 381.

41. Cicero, Marcus Tullius, *Letters to Atticus,* Book VI, Number 2, trans. E. O. Winstedt, Loeb Classical Library, Heinemann, London, and Harvard University Press, 1962, Vol. I, p. 445.

42. Cicero, Marcus Tullius, *De Divinatione (On Divination),* Book I, 34, trans. C. D. Yonge, Bohn's Classical Library, London, 1878, p. 176.

43. Plutarch, *op. cit.,* 590, trans. p. 461.

44. Philostratus, *op. cit.,* Book VIII, xix, trans. p. 383.

45. Plutarch, *op. cit.,* 590B–592F, trans. pp. 461–77.

46. Harrison, Jane, *Prolegomena to the Study of Greek Religion,* Cambridge, 1903, p. 581.

47. Salverte, Eusebe, *The Occult Sciences: The Philosophy of Magic, Prodigies and Apparent Miracles;* trans. with notes by Anthony Todd Thomson, London, 1846, Vol. I, p. xi, Biographical Sketch of Salverte by Francois Arago.

48. *Ibid.,* p. v, from author's preface.

49. *Ibid.,* pp. v–vi.

50. *Ibid.,* p. vii.

51. *Ibid.* Salverte politely mentions the matter without giving the name of Clavier; but the reference is obvious to anyone acquainted with Clavier's book. Salverte was concerned lest people think that he was copying Clavier.

52. *Ibid.,* p. xvii.

53. *Ibid.,* p. 3.

54. *Ibid.,* p. 2.

55. *Ibid.*

56. *Ibid.,* pp. 15–16.

57. *Ibid.,* p. 8.

58. Saint-Martin's own works may be consulted, but for a biography of him see Arthur Edward Waite, *The Life of Louis Claude de Saint-Martin,* London, 1901, where Saint-Martin's ideas are expounded at length.

59. Salverte, *op. cit.,* pp. 3, 5 and 40.

60. Athenaeus, *Deipnosophistae,* XIV, 614, trans. Charles Burton Gulick, Loeb Classical Library, 1937, Vol. VI, pp. 307–9.

61. *Ibid.* (p. 308 of translation).

62. Salverte, *op. cit.,* Vol. I, p. 32.

63. Fernie, W. T., *Herbal Simples,* Bristol, 2nd edition, 1897, p. 253.

64. Salverte, *op. cit.,* Vol. II, p. 38.

65. Fernie, *op. cit.,* p. 389.

66. Grieve, Mrs M. (ed. Mrs C. F. Leyel), *A Modern Herbal,* Penguin Books, Harmondsworth, 1976, p. 399.

67. Fernie, *op. cit.,* p. 255.

68. Pliny, *Natural History,* Book XXV, 17, 35–7, trans. W. H. S. Jones, Loeb Classical Library, Heinemann, London, and Harvard University Press, Vol.

VII, pp. 161–3.

69. *Ibid.*, Book 25, 20, 47, trans. p. 171.

70. Dioscorides, Pedanius, of Anabarzus, *Materia Medica,* trans. John Goodyear, London, 1655, p. 47.

71. Theophrastus, *Peri Phytōn Historias (Enquiry into Plants)*, Book IX, xi, 6, trans. A. F. Hort, Loeb Classical Library, Heinemann, London, and Harvard University Press, 1961, Vol. II, p. 273.

72. Philostratus, *op. cit.,* Book III, xvii, trans. Vol. I, p. 265.

73. Pliny, *Natural History,* Book XXV, 59, 106, trans. Vol. VII, p. 215.

74. Philostratus, *op. cit.,* Book III, xliv, trans. Vol. I, p. 327.

75. Iamblichus, *De Mysteriis* (in the translation cited, given the title: *Theurgia or the Egyptian Mysteries),* trans. Alexander Wilder, Rider, London, 1911, p. 127.

76. Pliny, *Natural History,* Book II, 106, 232, trans. H. Rackham, Loeb Classical Library, 1967, Vol. I, p. 359.

77. Iamblichus, *op. cit.,* p. 124.

78. 'Was the Oracle of Delphi a Gasbag?' by Roger Highfield, *Daily Telegraph*, London, 15 August 2001.

79. De Boer, J. Z., and Hale, J. R., 'The Geological Origins of the Oracle at Delphi, Greece', in McGuire, W. J., Griffiths, D. R., Hancock, P. L., and Stewart, I. S., eds, *The Archaeology of Geological Catastrophes*, The Geological Society, London, 2000, p. 408.

80. De Boer, J. Z., Hale, J. R., and Chanton, J., 'New Evidence for the Geological Origins of the Ancient Delphic Oracle (Greece)', in *Geology*, Geological Society of America, pp. 709–10.

81. Parke, H. W., and Wormell, D. E. W., *The Delphic Oracle*, Blackwell, Oxford, 1956, Vol. I, p. 21.

82. Oesterreich, T. K., *Possession: Demoniacal and Other among Primitive Races, in Antiquity, the Middle Ages, and Modern Times,* Kegan Paul, London, 1930.

83. *Ibid.,* pp. 320–1.

84. Iamblichus, *op. cit.,* p. 95.

85. Theodoret (Bishop of Cyprus), *Ecclesiastical History,* Book V, Chapter 22, trans. anonymously, Samuel Bagster & Sons, London, 1843, pp. 318–19.

86. Pillement, Georges, *Unknown Greece, Athens and the Peloponnesus,* Johnson, London, 1973, p. 101.

87. Pliny, *Natural History,* Book XVI, 6, 15, trans. H. Rackham, Loeb Classical Library, 1968, Vol. IV, p. 397.

88. *Ibid.,* Book XVI, 1, 1, trans. p. 387.

89. Densmore, Frances, *How Indians Use Wild Plants for Food, Medicine and Crafts,* Dover, New York, 1974, p. 320. (A reprint of 'Uses of Plants by the Chippewa Indians' from *Forty-fourth Annual Report of the Bureau of American Ethnology to the Secretary of the Smithsonian Institution, 1926–1927*, US Government Printing Office, Washington, 1928.)

90. Herodotus, *op. cit.,* Book I, 66–8, Bohn trans., pp. 27–9; Loeb trans., Vol. I, pp. 77–83.

91. Pliny, *Natural History,* Book VII, 16, 73–4, trans. H. Rackham, Loeb

Classical Library, 1942, Vol. 11, pp. 553–5.

92. Plutarch, 'Life of Theseus', xxxvi, in *Lives*, trans. Aubrey Stewart and George Long, Bohn's Library, London, 1892, Vol. I, p. 28.

93. Parke, H. W., *A History of the Delphic Oracle*, Blackwell, Oxford, 1939. This work, in one volume, was heavily revised and issued in two volumes, with D. E. W. Wormell as co-author, as *The Delphic Oracle*, 1956. The original volume (which was largely ignored because of the outbreak of war at the time of publication) is preferable for reading for pure interest and enjoyment. The latter version of the book is the one used for purposes of scholarly reference, but it is far more cumbersome and too long for ordinary reading. Unfortunately some of the charm, balance, and liveliness of the original work were lost by revision and expansion, especially since so few copies seem to survive and so few people have ever seen it. Joseph Fontenrose has written *Python: A Study of Delphic Myth and Its Origins*, University of California Press, 1959, and reprinted in paperback, 1980. More recently, Fontenrose has brought out a lengthy volume, *The Delphic Oracle* (see note 94 below), with a complete collection of its surviving responses to enquirers.

94. Fontenrose, Joseph, *The Delphic Oracle*, University of California Press, 1978, pp. 79–83.

95. Cicero, Marcus Tullius, *De Divinatione*, Book II, lvi. Bohn trans. p. 248.

96. Aristotle, *Rhetoric*, 1407a–b, Book III, 5, trans. W. Rhys Roberts in Sir David Ross, ed., *The Works of Aristotle* (in English), Oxford University Press, 1966, Vol. XI, 1407a–b.

97. Sozomen, Hermias, *Ecclesiastical History*, trans. Edward Walford, Bohn's Ecclesiastical Library, London, 1855, p. 9.

98. See footnote 93.

99. Ohlert, Konrad, *Rätsel und Rätselspiele der Alten Griechen*, 2nd edition, Berlin, 1912. Schultz, Wolfgang, *Rätsel aus dem Hellenischen Kulturkreise*, 2 volumes, Leipzig, 1909–12.

100. Taylor, Archer, *The Literary Riddle before 1600*, University of California Press, 1948. Taylor wrote two books with Vernam E. Hull: *A Collection of Welsh Riddles*, 1942, which appeared in University of California Publications in Modern Philology, Vol. 26; and *A Collection of Irish Riddles*, Folklore Studies Number 6, University of California Press, 1955 (and see note 113).

101. Ohl, Raymond Theodore, *The Enigmas of Symphosius*, Ph.D. thesis submitted to the University of Pennsylvania at Philadelphia, 1928.

102. Plutarch, 'Life of Numa', xv, in *Lives*, trans. Aubrey Stewart and George Long, Bohn's Library, London, 1892, Vol. I, pp. 115–16.

103. Riddle Number 22 in Book XIV ('Arithmetical Problems, Riddles, Oracles') of the Palatine *Greek Anthology*, trans. W. R. Paton, *The Greek Anthology*, Loeb Classical Library, Heinemann, London, and Harvard University Press, 1918, Vol. V, pp. 36–7.

104. Riddle Number 56 of *ibid*. The translation used here is by E. S. Forster, from his article 'Riddles and Problems from the Greek Anthology', in *Greece and Rome*, Vol. XIV, Nos 41–2, June 1945, p. 44.

105. Riddle Number 5 from *ibid*., Forster trans., p. 44.

106. Riddles Numbers 40 and 41 from *ibid.* Forster trans., pp. 43–4.

107. Riddle Number 110 from *ibid.,* Paton trans., pp. 82–3.

108. Riddle Number 103 from *ibid.,* Paton trans., pp. 78–9.

109. Riddle Number 35 from *ibid.,* Paton trans., pp. 44–5.

110. Fontenrose, *op cit.,* p. 79.

111. Taylor, *op cit.,* p. 42.

112. *Ibid.,* pp. 1–2.

113. Taylor, Archer, *English Riddles from Oral Tradition,* University of California Press, 1951, p. 83.

114. Forster, E. S., 'Riddles and Problems from the Greek Anthology', in *Greece and Rome,* Vol. XIV, Nos 41–2, June 1945, pp. 42–3.

115. Aristotle, *De Poetica (On Poetry),* trans. Ingram Bywater, Chapter 21, 1458, in Sir David Ross, ed., *The Works of Aristotle* (in English), Vol. XI, Oxford University Press, 1966.

116. Aristotle, *Rhetoric,* Book III, 1405a-b, and 1412a, Roberts trans., *op. cit.*

117. See Chapter 9 of my book *Götter, Orakel und Visionen,* Umschau Verlag, Frankfurt am Main, 1982.

118. This is described in Chapter 7 of the above book. The 'hidden observer' is a term originated by Professor Ernest Hilgard, though he tells me he is doubtful of the literal existence of this level of the mind which he was the first psychologist to uncover. But the phenomena attributed to the 'hidden observer', to whatever level of the mind they are finally assigned, remain demonstrable. And they include the capacity in very deep trance to 'stand outside time' altogether in experiments described in my book just mentioned.

CHAPTER FOUR

1. Pliny, *Natural History,* Book XVIII, 69; translated by H. Rackham, Loeb Classical Library, Harvard University Press, USA, Vol. 5, 1971, p. 369.

2. Thorndike, Lynn, *A History of Magic and Experimental Science,* Columbia University Press, New York, Vol. I, 1929, pp. 42–3.

3. Hesiod, *Works and Days,* translated by Dorothea Wender, in *Hesiod. Theogony; Works and Days; Theogonis. Elegies,* Penguin Books, Harmondsworth, England, 1973, pp. 72–3.

4. *Ibid.,* p. 72.

5. *Ibid.,* p. 73.

6. *Ibid.,* p. 80.

7. *Ibid.,* p. 74.

8. *Ibid.,* pp. 74–5, 76.

9. Pliny, *op. cit.,* Vol. 5, p. 347.

10. Blum, Richard and Eva, *The Dangerous Hour: The Lore of Crisis and Mystery in Rural Greece,* Chatto & Windus, London, 1970, p. 115.

11. *Ibid.*

12. *Ibid.,* p. 116.

13. Apollonius Rhodius (Apollonius of Rhodes), *Argonautica; The Voyage of the Argo,* translated by E. V. Rieu, Penguin Books, Harmondsworth, England, 1969, pp. 65–7.

14. *Ibid.,* pp. 68–9.

15. Pliny, *op. cit.*, Vol. 5, p. 417.

16. Sir James Frazer, *The Golden Bough*, Macmillan and Company, London, third edition, Part I, Vol. I, p. 52.

17. Cicero, Marcus Tullius, *On Divination (De Divinatione)*, translated by C. D. Yonge, George Bell and Sons, London, 1878, p. 261.

18. Pliny, *op. cit.*, Vol. 5, p. 415.

19. Jermyn, L. A. S., 'Weather-Signs in Virgil', in *Greece & Rome*, Oxford, Part I in Vol. XX, No. 58, January 1951, pp. 26–37, and Part II in Vol. XX, No. 59, June 1951, pp. 49–59.

20. Theophrastus, 'Concerning Weather Signs', in *Enquiry into Plants and Minor Works on Odours and Weather Signs*, translated by Sir Arthur Hort, Loeb Classical Library, Harvard University Press, USA, Vol. 2, 1980, p. 403.

21. Spence, Jonathan D., *Emperor of China: Self-Portrait of K'ang-Hsi*, Vintage Books, Random House, New York, 1988, pp. 15–16.

22. Theophrastus, 'Concerning Weather Signs', Sections 14, 25, 42, and 54, in *Enquiry into Plants and Minor Works on Odours and Weather Signs*, translated by Sir Arthur Hort, Loeb Classical Library, Harvard University Press, USA, Vol. 2, 1980, pp. 399–431.

23. Pliny, *op. cit.*, translated by H. Rackham, Vol. 5, p. 417.

24. An Edwardian naturalist, R. Bosworth Smith, in a book about birds has left an account of an extremely strange episode in the natural history not of birds but of rats, which indicates in an uncanny way the ability of these creatures to sense future events. After a long passage in which he demonstrates that owls do not eat young pigeons and therefore should be allowed to live unmolested in their favourite habitations, dovecotes, Smith says: 'From the arch enemy of the rat (the owl), I pass, once more, to the rats themselves, that I may relate a curious experience of my own, of a few years ago, near my present home. . . . I was tricycling homeward, one evening, from the village of Puddletown, near Dorchester [in Dorset, England], when I saw passing slowly across the lane in front of me, down one steep bank and up another, a creature which at first completely puzzled me. It had long shaggy, grizzled hair, and everything about it betokened extreme old age. Its long hair, it may well be, made it appear at the time to be bigger than it really was, and, for the moment, I thought it must be a species of pole-cat. I now believe it to have been a rat, but a Nestor among rats – a Nestor [wise old man mentioned by Homer] who had lived (like the Homeric Nestor) through some three generations of its kind. I stopped my tricycle short, wondering what this strange creature could be. It was closely followed by an ordinary rat, and then, as though it were a second Pied Piper of Hamelin, by another and another, and yet another, sometimes singly, sometimes in twos or threes, and of all ages. I watched, for some time, the ragged regiment till there was a pause in it, and then, dismounting, gently stirred the tufts of long grass or clumps of nettles on the bank whence it came. They concealed, nearly every one of them, a rat or a mouse. The bank was alive with them. With a stick, I could have killed a dozen or more. They were evidently migrating in a body, as it is known that they sometimes do, and as their congener, the lemming, does on an enormous scale and under the most mysterious circumstances in

Norway, till they plunge into the sea by thousands, and so, of their own free motion, redress the balance of Nature. But what was the explanation of their uncanny leader? . . . I looked over the hedge into the field from which a procession had descended, and saw there a lot of cornstalks, with a threshing-engine, which, with all its paraphernalia, ready for use on the next morning, had apparently just arrived. My theory is that the uncanny creature was a 'king of the rats'; that the 'eye of old experience' had taught him that the appearance of a threshing-engine was the prelude to disaster and massacre on the morrow, and that he gave, in the right of his office, and, as in duty bound, the signal to be off. If, as is well known, rats instinctively quit, in a body, an unseaworthy vessel before she puts out on her last voyage; if they quit a crazy tenement which is about to fall from lapse of time . . . why should they not quit a rick, under the guidance of, perhaps, the one survivor, or the oldest of the survivors, of a previous massacre, and make off for the next group of ricks? . . . I put this forward only as an hypothesis, in the hope that some of those who read the story, and are interested in it, may be able, from their own experience, to throw some light upon it, whether by way of confirmation or of refutation.' (From Bosworth Smith, R., *Bird Life & Bird Lore*, John Murray, London, 1905, pp. 33–6.) Bosworth Smith attempts to explain the behaviour of rats by saying that the 'king rat' apprehends the danger which he has survived on a previous occasion. In this instance, the explanation of the animal behaviour does not involve any unusual sensory phenomena, and is probably only a result of the wisdom of the old rat. But as it is such an extraordinary example of animal behaviour with a premonitory tinge, I thought it worth recording here.

25. Yodlowski, Marilyn L., Kreithen, Melvin L., Keeton, William T., 'Detection of Atmospheric Infrasound by Homing Pigeons', *Nature*, Vol. 265, 24 February 1977, pp. 725–6.
26. *Ibid.*

Chapter Five

1. Temple, Robert, *The Genius of China*, Prion, London, 1991/8, pp. 162–6. The original title of this book in Britain was *China: Land of Discovery and Invention*, Patrick Stephens, London, 1986; the pagination was the same.
2. Adams, R. P., 'Earthquake Prediction', *Nature*, Vol. 269, No. 5623, 1 September 1977, p. 14.
3. Pliny, *Natural History*, Book II, 81, translated by H. Rackham, Loeb Classical Library, Harvard University Press, USA, Vol. I, revised edition, 1967, p. 323.
4. Schibli, H. S., *Pherekydes of Syros*, Clarendon Press, Oxford, 1990.
5. *Ibid.*, p. 5.
6. *Ibid.* pp. 145–6.
7. Cicero, Marcus Tullius, *On Divination (De Divinatione)*, Book I, 50, translated by C. D. Yonge, George Bell and Sons, London, 1878, pp. 190–1.
8. Pliny, *op. cit.*, II, 84, Vol. I, p. 327.
9. *Ibid.*, II, 82, Vol. I, p. 325.
10. *Ibid.*, II, 97, Vol. I, pp. 341–3.

11. *Ibid.*, II, 82, Vol. I, p. 327.

12. *Ibid.*, II, 84, Vol. I, p. 329.

13. Lloyd, Joel L., 'Earthquake Light', *Science*, 17 September 1976, p. 1070; Shapley, Deborah, 'Chinese Earthquakes', News and Comments Section, *Science*, 20 August 1976, p. 656.

14. Pliny, *op. cit.*, II, 83, Vol. I, p. 327.

15. Briggs, *Nature*, 24 July 1975, pp. 270–3.

16. Anderson, C. J., *Science*, Vol. 182, 1974, pp. 49–50.

17. Wakita, Hiroshi, 'Water Wells as Possible Indicators of Tectonic Strain', *Science*, Vol. 189, 15 August 1975, pp. 553–5.

18. Adams, R. P., 'Earthquake Prediction', *Nature, op. cit.*, p. 14.

19. *Ibid.*, II, 53, Vol. I, p. 277.

20. Ptolemy, Claudius, *Ptolemy's Tetrabiblos or Quadripartite being Four Books on the Influence of the Stars*, translated with commentary by J. M. Ashmand, W. Foulsham, London, 'new edition', no date. On page 51 may be found a table of the astrological affinities of various countries. I reproduce this table in Figure 25. The relevant text is Book II, Chapters 2–3; pp. 41–52.

21. *Ibid.*, p. 45.

22. Pliny, *op. cit.*, II, 23, Vol. I, p. 237.

23. *Ibid.*, II, 52, Vol. I, p. 275.

24. Cicero, *op. cit.*, Book I, 33, p. 175.

25. Cardan, Jerome (Cardano, Girolamo), *The Book of My Life (De Vita Propria Liber)*, translated by Jean Stoner, J. M. Dent & Sons, London, 1931, p. 192.

26. Pliny, *op. cit.*, II, 5, Vol. I, pp. 183–5.

27. Thorndike, Lynn, *A History of Magic and Experimental Science*, Columbia University Press, New York, Vol. I, 1923, pp. 47–8.

28. Dixon, Bernard, editorial by, *New Scientist*, London, Vol. 76, No. 1078, 17 November 1977, p. 396.

29. Hoyle, Sir Fred, and Wickramasinghe, Chandra, 'Does Epidemic Disease Come from Space?', *New Scientist*, London, Vol. 76, No. 1078, 17 November 1977, pp. 402–4.

30. Hoyle, Fred, and Wickramasinghe, Chandra (or N. C.), *Lifecloud*, J. M. Dent & Sons, London, 1978.

31. Hoyle, Sir Fred, and Wickramasinghe, Chandra, 'Lifecloud: The Origin of Life in Space', *Second Look*, Washington, DC, Vol. I, No. 4, February 1979, pp. 2–4; 'Lifecloud: Life Was Originally Brought to Earth by Comets', Vol. I, No. 5, March 1978, pp. 6–8; 'Lifecloud: The Births of the Many Worlds', Vol. I, No. 6, April 1979, pp. 5–8. These instalments were also sold separately.

32. Hoyle, Fred, and Wickramasinghe, Chandra (or N. C.), *Diseases from Space*, J. M. Dent & Sons, London, 1979.

33. Hoyle, Fred, and Wickramasinghe, Chandra, *Space Travellers: The Bringers of Life*, University College Cardiff Press, Cardiff, Wales, 1981. Wickramasinghe, Chandra, *Is Life an Astronomical Phenomenon?*, University College Cardiff Press, Cardiff, Wales, 1982. Hoyle, Sir Fred, and Wickramasinghe, Chandra, *Proofs That Life Is Cosmic*, Memoirs of the

Institute of Fundamental Studies, Sri Lanka, Number 1, Colombo, Sri Lanka, December 1982. Hoyle, Fred, and Wickramasinghe, Chandra, *Living Comets*, University College Cardiff Press, Cardiff, Wales, 1985. Hoyle, Fred, Wickramasinghe, Chandra, and Watkins, John, *Viruses from Space*, University College Cardiff Press, Cardiff, Wales, 1986, *Astronomical Origins of Life: Steps Towards Panspermia*, 2000. *Cosmic Dragons: Life and Death on Our Planet*, 2001.

34. Clark, David H., Parkinson, John H., and Stephenson, F. Richard, 'An Astronomical Re-Appraisal of the Star of Bethlehem – A Nova in 5 BC', *Quarterly Journal of the Royal Astronomical Society*, Vol. 18, No. 4, December 1977, pp. 443–9.

35. Raine, Kathleen, and Harper, George, eds, *Thomas Taylor the Platonist*, Routledge & Kegan Paul, London, 1969, p. 194.

36. Boehme, Jacob, *The Signature of All Things (Signatura Rerum)*, in *The Signature of All Things with other Writings*, no translator named, Everyman's Library, J. M. Dent & Sons, London, no date, p. 91.

37. Proclus, quoted by Thomas Taylor in his Preface to *The Hymns of Orpheus*, in Raine and Harper, *op. cit.*, pp. 195–6.

38. *Ibid.*, p. 195.

39. *Ibid.*

40. Sarton, George, *Six Wings: Men of Science in the Renaissance*, The Bodley Head, London, and Meridian Books, World Publishing Company, New York, 1957, p. 110.

41. *Ibid.*, pp. 109–110.

42. Iamblichus, *On the Mysteries of the Egyptians, Chaldaeans and Assyrians*, translated by Thomas Taylor, Stuart and Watkins, London, 1968, pp. 45–6.

43. *Ibid.*, pp. 112–3, and 146.

44. *Ibid.*, pp. 154–5.

45. Conway, David, *The Magic of Herbs*, Jonathan Cape, London, 1973, p. 31.

46. Read, John, *Prelude to Chemistry: An Outline of Alchemy*, The MIT Press, Cambridge, Massachusetts, USA, 1966, p. 96.

47. *Ibid.*, p. 97.

48. Quoted in Hartmann, Franz, *The Life of ... Paracelsus*, Kegan, Paul, Trench, Truebner & Co., London, second edition, no date, p. 55.

49. *Ibid.*, pp. 209–10.

50. Bielenstein, Hans, *The Restoration of the Han Dynasty with Prolegomena on the Historiography of the Hou Han Shu: Inaugural Dissertation ... for the degree of Filosofie Doktor ...*, Göteborg, Sweden, 1953.

51. *Ibid.*, pp. 155–6.

52. *Ibid.*, p. 157.

CHAPTER SIX

1. Jastrow, Morris, Jr, 'The Liver as the Seat of the Soul', pp. 143–68 in David Gordon Lyon and George Foot Moore, eds, *Studies in the History of Religions Presented to Crawford Howell Toy*, Macmillan, New York, 1912, p. 164.

2. *Ibid.*, p. 158.

3. Gadd, C. J., 'Ideas of Divine Rule in the Ancient East', in *The Schweich Lectures of the British Academy 1945*, British Academy, London, 1948, pp. 52–3.

4. Jastrow, Morris, Jr, 'The Liver in Antiquity and the Beginnings of Anatomy', in *Transactions of the College of Physicians of Philadelphia*, Vol. XXIX (1907), pp. 118–38.

5. Found *in* Caquot, André, and Leibovici, Marcel, *La Divination*, Tome Premier, Presses Universitaires de France, Paris, 1968.

6. Temple, Robert, 'Superstition and Science', in *Odyssey: The Glaxo-Wellcome Journal of Innovation in Healthcare*, Almere, Netherlands, Vol. 1, No. 3, 1995, pp. 60–4.

7. Plutarch, 'Life of Alexander', Chapters 73–4, in *Lives*, trans. Aubrey Stewart and George Lang, Bohn's Library, London, 1889, Vol. III, pp. 374–5.

8. Arrian (Flavius Arrianus), *Anabasis*, Book VII, 18, 2–5.

9. Plutarch, 'Life of Marcellus', Chapters 29–30, in *Lives*, 1893, Vol. II, pp. 61–2.

10. Plutarch, 'Life of Pyrrhus', Chapter 3, in *ibid.*, p. 182.

11. *Ibid.*, pp. 215–16.

12. Cicero, Marcus Tullius, *De Divinatione (On Divination)*, Book I, 25, 52, trans. William Armistead Falconer, Loeb Classical Library, Heinemann, London, and Harvard University Press, 1964, p. 281.

13. Xenophon, *Anabasis, or Expedition of Cyrus*. A translation by the Rev. J. S. Watson, with a Geographical Commentary by G. F. Ainsworth, was published by Bohn's Library, London, 1891. I have made use of it in the quotations in my text. A translation with facing Greek text is published in the Loeb Classical Library, and there are others as well.

14. Plato, *Phaedo*, 22, 118, trans. R. Hackforth, Library of Liberal Arts, Bobbs Merrill, Indianapolis and New York, 1955, p. 190.

15. *Ibid.*, footnote 2, p. 190.

16. *Ibid.*, quoting U. von Wilamowitz-Möllendorff in German from his *Platon*, II, pp. 57ff.

17. Xenophon, *Memorabilia (Recollections of Socrates)*, I, 1, trans. Anna S. Benjamin, Library of Liberal Arts, Bobbs Merrill, Indianapolis and New York, 1965, p. 3.

18. Jastrow, Morris, Jr, *The Religion of Babylonia and Assyria*, Vol. II of Handbooks on the History of Religions, Ginn and Company, Boston, New York, etc., p. 334.

19. *Ibid.*, pp. 335–6.

20. *Ibid.*, p. 336.

21. Dodds, E. R., *The Greeks and the Irrational*, University of California Press, 1951, p. 235, footnote 87.

22. Plato, *Laws*, Book X, 910–913, in *The Dialogues of Plato*, trans. Benjamin Jowett, Random House, New York, 1937, Vol. II, p. 652.

23. Jastrow, *Religion*, p. 336.

24. *Ibid.*, p. 338.

25. Dudley, D. R. and Lang, D. M., eds, *The Penguin Companion to Literature: Vol. 4, Classical and Byzantine, Oriental and African*, Penguin Books,

Harmondsworth, 1969, p. 174. (The quotation is from the entry for Vitruvius, written by D. R. Dudley.)

26. Vitruvius Pollio, Marcus, *De Architectura*, trans. Joseph Gwilt and published as *Rudimentary Architecture ... The Ten Books of Vitruvius*, Crosby Lockwood and Co., London, with a preface of 110 pp., no date, pp. 16–17 of main translated text (the preface having its own pagination).

27. Professor von Mayersbach seems not to have published this information, which is obtained from the work of another writer to whom he communicated it personally.

28. I have published two articles relating to this subject in the American magazine *Second Look* (now defunct), of which I was at that time co-editor. The first, 'Coincidence or Contact: Magnetism in the New World', appeared in Vol. I, No. 11, September 1979, pp. 8–31. The second, 'Olmec Magnetism and the Brain', appeared in Vol. 11, No. I, November–December 1979, pp. 21–3. The material presented in those articles was discussed by Stan Gooch in his book *The Secret Life of Humans*, Dent, London, 1981, though the only acknowledgement of the source was in the Bibliographical listing of the articles and no mention appeared in the text itself, so that a reader of the book would have no knowledge of the source of information.

29. Pliny, *Natural History*, Book XI, 73, 189, trans. H. Rackham, Loeb Classical Library, Heinemann, London, and Harvard University Press, Vol. III, 1967, p. 551.

30. Weinstock, Stefan, 'Martianus Capella and the Cosmic System of the Etruscans', *Journal of Roman Studies*; Vol. XXXVI, 1930, p. 122.

31. Cicero, *De Divinatione*, Book I, 52, 119, trans. p. 353.

32. Plato, *Timaeus*, 70–2, in *The Dialogues of Plato*, trans. Benjamin Jowett, Random House, New York, 1937, Vol. II, pp. 49–50.

33. Réville, Albert, *Lectures on the Origin and Growth of Religion as Illustrated by the Native Religions of Mexico and Peru* (The Hibbert Lectures for 1884), Williams and Norgate, London and Oxford, 1895, p. 63.

34. See note 1, for reference.

35. See note 4, for reference, pp. 122–3.

36. Philo Judaeus, 'On Animals Fit for Sacrifice, or On Victims', in *The Works of Philo Judaeus*, trans. C. D. Yonge, Bohn's Library, London, 1855, Vol. III, p. 221.

37. *Ibid.*, pp. 219–20.

38. See note 1 for reference.

39. Griaule, Marcel, and Dieterlen, Germaine, *Le Renard Pale*, Institut d'Ethnologie, Musée de l'Homme, Paris, 1965, pp. 294–5.

40. Plutarch, *On the Sign of Socrates (Peri tou Sōkratous Daimoniou)*, 589, in *Plutarch's Moralia*, Vol. VII, trans. De Lacy and Einarson, pp. 455–7.

41. Plutarch, *The Oracles at Delphi No Longer Given in Verse* extends from 394 to 409 in the *Moralia*.

42. *Ibid.*, trans. Frank Cole Babbitt, *Moralia*, 398D, Vol. V, Loeb Classical Library, Heinemann, London, and Harvard University Press, 1962, p. 281.

43. Plutarch, *On the Apparent Face in the Orb of the Moon*, from the *Moralia*, trans. C. W. King, in *Plutarch's Morals: Theosophical Essays*, Bohn's

Library, London, 1889, pp. 197–257.

44. *Ibid.,* pp. 254 and 256.

45. Temple, Robert, *The Crystal Sun*, Century, London, 2000, Chapter 6, pp. 243–263.

46. Thulin, Carl, *Die Götter des Martianus Capella und der Bronzleber von Piacenza,* Band III, Heft I, *Religionsgeschichtliche Versuche und Vorarbeiten,* Gieszen, 1906.

47. Deecke, W., 'Nachtrag zum Templum von Piacenza', *Etruskische Forschungen und Studien,* II, 1882.

48. Van der Meer, L. B., *The Bronze Liver of Piacenza: Analysis of a Polytheistic Structure*, Dutch monographs on Ancient History and Archaeology, Vol. II, Gieben, Amsterdam, 1987.

49. De Santillana, Giorgio, and Von Dechend, Gertha, *Hamlet's Mill, an Essay on Myth and the Frame of Time,* Macmillan, London, 1970, pp. 289, 314, 404, and the illustrations between pp. 290 and 291.

50. Temple, Robert, *The Sirius Mystery*, Sidgwick and Jackson, London, 1976, Chapter 3 and accompanying illustrations. The expanded and revised edition of this book was published by Century, London, and Inner Traditions, USA, in 1998, where the relevant section has become Chapter 4.

51. Temple, Robert, *He Who Saw Everything: A Verse Translation of the Epic of Gilgamesh*, Rider, London, 1991, pp. xxiv–xxvi, 54, 59–60, 75–77, 84–86, 91, 93–96.

52. Smith, Sidney, 'The Face of Humbaba,' *Journal of the Royal Asiatic Society,* 1926, pp. 440–2. The reconstructed drawing is in Plate V, opposite p. 440.

53. Martianus Capella, *The Marriage of Philology and Mercury,* Book I, 14, trans. William Harris Stahl and Richard Johnson with E. L. Burge, the translated text forming Vol. 11 of *Martianus Capella and the Seven Liberal Arts,* Columbia University Press, 1977. This quotation from pp. 10–11.

54. *Ibid.,* Book VIII, 857, trans. p. 333.

55. See notes 47 and 49 for reference.

56. Temple, Robert, *He Who Saw Everything, op cit.,* pp. 59–60, 75–77.

57. Thulin, *op. cit.* But far more extensive are the results of Thulin's researches embodied in his work *Die Etruskische Disciplin,* published in three parts in the Swedish journal *Göteborgs Hogskolas Arsskrift,* 1905–9. The three parts are: I. *Die Blitzlehre,* Article 5 in Band XI (1905); II. *Die Haruspicin,* Article 1 in Band XII (1906); III. *Die Ritualbücher und zur Geschichte und Organization der Haruspices,* Article 1 in Band XV (1909).

58. Deecke, *op. cit.*

59. Weinstock, *op. cit.*

CHAPTER SEVEN

1. Temple, Robert, *The Genius of China*, Prion Books, London, 1999. The original title of this book in Britain was *China: Land of Discovery and Invention*, but the original American title *The Genius of China* was adopted for the various British reprints.

2. Shih-Chuan Chen, 'How to Form a Hexagram and Consult the *I Ching*', *Journal of the American Oriental Society*, Vol. 92, No. 1, 1972, p. 238.

3. *Shu Ching (Book of History)*, modernized by Clae Waltham, from trans. by James Legge, Allen & Unwin, London, 1972, p. 123.

4. Needham, Joseph, *Science and Civilization in China*, Cambridge University Press, Vol. II, 1956, p. 304.

5. Tung Chung-Shu, 'Things of the Same Kind Animate Each Other', Chapter 57 of *Ch'un-ch'iu fan-lu (Luxuriant Gems of the Spring and Autumn Annals)*, trans. and quoted by Wing-Tsit Chan in his anthology *A Source Book in Chinese Philosophy*, Princeton University Press, 1973, p. 283.

6. Liu Ching-Shu, story from his *I-yüan*, trans. and quoted by Anna Straughair, *Chang Hua: A Statesman-Poet of the Western Chin Dynasty*, Occasional Paper 15, Faculty of Asian Studies, Australian National University, Canberra, 1973, p. 20.

7. T'ang Yung-T'ung, 'Wang Pi's New Interpretation of the *I Ching* and *Lun-yü*, trans. with notes by Walter Liebenthal, *Harvard Journal of Asiatic Studies*, Vol. 10, 1947, p. 139. The quotation seems to have been preserved in Huang K'an's subcommentary on Ho Yen's commentary on the *Lun-yü*, according to Liebenthal's footnote 34.

8. Chu Hsi and Lu Tsu-ch'ien, *Reflections on Things at Hand, The Neo-Confucian Anthology*, trans. with notes by Wing-Tsit Chan, Number 75 of the Records of Civilization Sources and Studies Series, Columbia University Press, New York and London, 1967, p. 108.

9. *Ibid.*, pp. 112–13.

10. *Ibid.*, p. 114.

11. *Ibid.*, pp. 121–2.

12. Confucius, *The Analects of Confucius*, trans. and annotated by Arthur Waley, Allen & Unwin, London, 1949, p. 193. (Book XV, Number 2.)

13. Arthur Waley, 'The Book of Changes', Bulletin Number 5: The Museum of Far Eastern Antiquities, Stockholm, 1933, pp. 121–42.

14. Arthur Waley, trans., *The Book of Songs,* Allen & Unwin, London, 1937. Ezra Pound, *The Confucian Odes: The Classic Anthology Defined by Confucius,* New Directions, New York, 1959.

15. Arthur Waley, 'The Book of Changes', p. 127.

16. *Ibid.*, p. 128.

17. Needham, *op. cit.*, Vol. 11, see index.

18. *The I Ching or Book of Changes,* trans. Richard Wilhelm and rendered into English by Cary F. Baynes, Routledge & Kegan Paul, London, 1951, Vol. I, p. 226. (Under Hexagram 54, moving line at the top place.)

19. Shih-Chuan Chen, *op. cit.*, p. 239.

20. Wilhelm, Hellmut, 'I-ching Oracles in the Tso-chuan and the *Kuo-yü*', *Journal of the American Oriental Society,* Vol. 79, 1959, pp. 275–80. Also his 'On the Oracle Recorded in Tso-chuan, Hsi 4 (656 BC)', *Journal of the American Oriental Society*, Vol. 91, 1971, pp. 504–5.

21. *The I Ching or Book of Changes,* trans. Richard Wilhelm and rendered into English by Cary F. Baynes with a foreword by Carl Jung, Routledge & Kegan Paul, London, 1951, 2 vols., and frequently reprinted, including a one-volume edition (compressed) which is probably the only version still in print. It is quite sufficient, and the 2 vols are not necessary.

22. *The Book of Change,* trans. John Blofeld, E. P. Dutton, New York, 1966; Allen & Unwin, London, 1965.

23. Wilhelm, Hellmut, *A Selective I Ching Bibliography (preliminary),* privately circulated typescript, Seattle, 1972, p. 11.

24. *The Yi King,* trans. James Legge, Part II of *The Sacred Books of China, The Texts of Confucianism,* in series of *The Sacred Books of the East,* edited by Max Müller, Oxford, 1882 (Vol. XVI of the *Sacred Books* series), second edition, 1899. The first edition has been reprinted by the Indian publishers Motilal Banarsidass, Delhi, 1968.

25. *The Oracle of Change: How to Consult the I Ching,* a 'translation' by Alfred Douglas (Douglas knows no Chinese, so this is a 'version'), Gollancz, London, 1971.

26. *The Text of Yi King (and its appendices),* edited by Z. D. Sung and apparently consisting of the translation of James Legge (according to Hellmut Wilhelm), China Modern Education Company, Shanghai, 1935, and reprinted by Paragon, New York, 1969.

27. Huang, Alfred, trans., *The Complete I Ching,* Inner Traditions International, Rochester, Vermont, USA, 1998.

28. Ritsema, Rudolf, and Karcher, Stephen, trans., *I Ching: The Classic Chinese Oracle of Change with Concordance,* Element Books, Rockport, Maine, USA, 1993–5. Unfortunately Element Books has gone out of business, and this edition has become temporarily unavailable, though Amazon offers the audio cassette of it from Spring Books. I am informed by Stephen Karcher that the book as well as his other books about the *I Ching* have been salvaged from the collapse of Element and will be reissued by Harper. Meanwhile, desperate enquirers are referred to The Eranos Foundation in Switzerland, fax number +41-91-792-2092 or email: eranos.foundation@spectraweb.ch, who can supply copies. And another edition of this same book can be obtained from Barnes & Noble's website, and bears the publisher's name of Barnes & Noble Books, New York.

29. University Press of New England, USA, 1986.

30. Karcher and Ritsema, *op. cit.,* pp. 32–3.

31. *Ibid.,* pp. 65, 83.

32. Legge's translation (footnote 22, Motilal reprint), p. xiii.

33. Carroll, Thomas D., sj, 'The Hidden Significance of the I-Ching Diagrams,' *Journal of the China Society* (Taipei, Taiwan), Vol. 2, 1962, p. 31.

34. Temple, Robert, *The Genius of China,* Prion Books, London, 1998, pp. 99–101. This book was originally entitled *China: Land of Discovery and Invention* in Britain, but its original American title is the one now adopted for use in Britain. The pagination of the many editions is the same.

35. Needham, *op. cit.,* Vol. IV, Part I, p. 325.

36. *Ibid.,* p. 324.

37. *Ibid.,* p. 326.

38. *Ibid.,* p. 326.

39. *Ibid.,* p. 327.

40. *Ibid.,* p. 316.

41. *Ibid.,* p. 317.

42. *Ibid.*
43. *Ibid.*, pp. 321-2.
44. Wilhelm, Hellmut, *Change: Eight Lectures on the I Ching,* trans. from the German by Cary F. Baynes, Bollingen Series LXII, Pantheon Books, New York, 1960, pp. 90-1. (The Bollingen Series, or what remains of it, is now distributed by Princeton University Press.)
45. Smith, Kidder, Jr, Bol, Peter K., Adler, Joseph A., and Wyatt, Don J., *Sung Dynasty Uses of the I Ching,* Princeton University Press, USA, 1990, p. 103.
46. *Ibid.*
47. *Ibid.*, p. 104.
48. Fung Yu-Lan, *A History of Chinese Philosophy*, trans. by Derk Bodde, Vol. II, Princeton University Press, USA, 1953, pp. 465-7. (The translator, Derk Bodde, is the man under whom I studied Chinese philosophy as an undergraduate student.)
49. *Ibid.*, p. 191.
50. *Ibid.*, p. 106.
51. Lévy, Pierre, *Collective Intelligence: Mankind's Emerging World in Cyberspace,* trans. by Robert Bononno, Plenum, New York and London, 1997, pp. 13-17.
52. *Sung Dynasty, op. cit.,* pp. 118-19.
53. Cammann, Schuyler, 'The Magic Square of Three in Old Chinese Philosophy and Religion', *History of Religion*, Vol. I (1961), pp. 37-80.
54. Schubert, Hermann, *Mathematical Essays and Recreations*, trans. By Thomas J. McCormack, Open Court, Chicago, 1898, pp. 40-2.
55. *Sung Dynasty, op. cit.,* p. 116.
56. *Ibid.*, pp. 111, 109-10, and 106. I have slightly simplified the quotations by removing Chinese words and substituting an English equivalent, The Supreme Ultimate.
57. Ling Hsüan, 'The Emperor and the Two Sisters', trans. by Christopher Levenson from the German trans. of Wolfgang Bauer and Herbert Franke, in the anthology *The Golden Casket,* Penguin Books, Harmondsworth, 1967, pp. 61-2.
58. Wilhelm, Hellmut, *Change,* p. 19.
59. *Shu Ching,* p. 28.
60. *Ibid.*, p. 32.
61. *Ibid.*, p. 35.
62. *Ibid.*
63. *Ibid.*, p. 71.
64. *Ibid.*, p. 81.
65. *Ibid.*, p. 80.
66. *Ibid.*, p. 71.
67. *Ibid.*, p. 78.
68. *Ibid.*, p. 79.
69. *Ibid.*, p. 100.
70. The quotation from the *Shu Ching* is from p. 204. The quotation from the *I Ching* is from Legge's trans., p. 5.
71. *Shu Ching,* p. 236.

72. Ibid., p. 224.
73. Richard Wilhelm trans., Vol. I, p. 46.
74. *Shu Ching*, p. 90.
75. *Ibid.*, p. 106.
76. *Ibid.*, p. 139.
77. *Ibid.*, p. 186.
78. Richard Wilhelm trans., Vol. I, p. 263.
79. *Shu Ching*, p. 116.
80. Wilhelm, Hellmut, *Change,* p. 19.

CHAPTER EIGHT

1. White, William Charles, *Bone Culture of Ancient China: An Archaeological Study of Bone Material from Northern Honan, Dating from about the Twelfth Century* BC, Toronto, 1945, p. 51 and see footnote 4 there, referring to M. N. Bien, 'On the Turtle Remains from the Archaeological Site of Anyang, Honan', Bulletin 17, Geological Society of China, 1937, pp. 121–33.
2. White, *op. cit.*, p. 25.
3. Shih-Chuan Chen, 'How to Form a Hexagram and Consult the *I Ching*', *Journal of the American Oriental Society,* Vol. 92, Number I, 1972, p. 238. This article is uniquely important for all *I Ching* studies, and is highly recommended. I regret that all my attempts to contact Professor Shih-Chuan Chen have failed.
4. *Ibid.*, p. 238, footnote 11.
5. Bretschneider, Emil, *Botanicon Sinicum: Notes on Chinese Botany from Native and Western Sources,* London, 1882, Vol. I, p. 245. (Call number in British Library AC. 8828/2.)
6. Shih-Chuan Chen, *op. cit.*, p. 239.
7. It should be emphasized that the manipulation of the yarrow stalks in the system currently used is not really correct, though it seems nevertheless to work. The correct yarrow stalk technique has been reconstructed by Professor Shih-Chuan Chen *(op. cit.).*
8. Lenormant, François, *Chaldean Magic, Its Origins and Development,* trans. from the French apparently by the author himself, Samuel Bagster, London, no date, but late nineteenth century (original French edition, Paris, 1874), pp. 237–8.
9. Rawlinson, George, *The Seven Great Monarchies of the Ancient Eastern World,* Hurst and Co., New York, 1872, Vol. III, pp. 588–9 (Vol. III, p. 351 of Rawlinson's second edition of 1870).
10. Herodotus, *History,* Book I, 121, trans. Henry Cary, Bohn's Classical Library, London, 1861, p. 55.
11. Diogenes Laertius, *Lives of Eminent Philosophers,* Book I, 6, trans. R. D. Hicks, Loeb Classical Library, Heinemann, London, and Harvard University Press, 1966, Vol. I, p. 9.
12. Zaehner, R. C., *The Dawn and Twilight of Zoroastrianism,* Weidenfeld & Nicolson, London, 1961, p. 169.
13. *Ibid.*

14. Strabo, *The Geography,* Book XV, 3, 14, trans. W. Falconer, George Bell and Sons, London, 1881, Vol. III, p. 137.

15. De Lacouperie, Terrien, *Western Origin of Early Chinese Civilization,* London, 1894.

16. De Lacouperie, Terrien, *The Oldest Book of the Chinese, the Yi King, and Its Authors,* London, 1892.

17. De Lacoupiere, *Western Origin,* p. 379.

18. Hung-hsiang Chou, 'Chinese Oracle Bones', *Scientific American,* April 1979.

19. *Ibid.,* pp. 102–3.

20. *Ibid.,* p. 103.

21. *Ibid.*

22. *Ibid.,* p. 105.

23. Keightley, David N., *Sources of Shang History: The Oracle-Bone Inscriptions of Bronze Age China,* University of California Press, Berkeley and London, 1978, p. 24.

Chapter Nine

1. Terada, Torahiko, and Watanabe, Tetu, 'Physical Morphology of Colour Pattern of Some Domestic Animals', *Scientific Papers of the Institute of Physical and Chemical Research, Tokyo* (call number in British Library: AC. 2697.be.), Vol. 27, April–September 1935, pp. 263–74 and Plates XVIII–XXIV.

2. *Ibid.,* p. 263.

3. *Ibid.,* pp. 263–4.

4. *Ibid.,* p. 263.

5. *Ibid.,* p. 264.

6. *Ibid.,* pp. 272–3.

7. *Ibid.,* pp. 273–4.

8. *Ibid.,* p. 274.

9. *Ibid.,* p. 273.

10. *Ibid.,* p. 274.

11. *The Yi King,* trans. James Legge, Vol. XVI, Part II, of *The Sacred Books of the East* series, and Vol. II of *The Sacred Books of China: The Texts of Confucianism;* in that series, originally published by Oxford University Press, 1882 (series edited by Max Müller), reprinted by Motilal Banarsidass, Delhi, 1968. Legge's introduction is pp. 1–55, and is full of useful information.

12. *Ibid.,* pp. 15–16.

13. *Ibid.,* p. 14.

14. *Ibid.*

15. *Shu Ching (Book of History),* modernized by Clae Waltham, from trans. by James Legge, Allen & Unwin, London, 1972, p. 213.

16. *Ibid.,* p. 211.

17. *Ibid.,* p. 213.

18. *The Yi King,* trans. Legge, p. 14.

19. Coxeter, H. S. M., *Regular Polytopes,* second edition, Macmillan, New York, and Collier-Macmillan, London, 1963, p. 58.

20. *Ibid.,* p. 59.

21. *Ibid.*, p. 73.

22. Wasianski, E. A. C., *Immanuel Kant in Seinen Letzten Lebensjahren*, Konigsberg, 1804, p. 97.

23. Dürer, Albrecht, *Underweysung der Messung*, Nuremberg, 1525 (call number in British Library: C.119. h. 7).

24. Bragg, Sir William, *Concerning the Nature of Things*, G. Bell and Sons, London, 1925, pp. 161–3.

25. *Ibid.*, pp. 169–70.

26. MacCullum, M. A. H., 'Quantum Cosmological Models', in C. J. Isham, Roger Penrose and D. W. Sciama, eds, *Quantum Gravity: An Oxford Symposium*, Oxford, 1975, p. 187.

27. *Ibid.*, p. 188.

28. Terada and Watanabe, *op. cit.*, p. 274.

29. Bragg, *op. cit.*, pp. 171–2.

30. *Ibid.*, pp. 148–50.

31. Poirier, J. P., 'Rheology of Ices: a Key to the Tectonics of the Ice Moons of Jupiter and Saturn', *Nature*, Vol. 299, No. 5885, 21–27 October 1982, p. 683.

32. Smith, Brad, *et al.*, 'The Galilean Satellites and Jupiter: Voyager 2 Imaging Science Results', *Science*, Vol. 206, No. 4421, 23 November 1979, p. 940.

33. Pieri, David C., 'Lineament and Polygon Patterns on Europa', *Nature*, Vol. 289, No. 5793, 1–8 January 1981, pp. 17–18.

34. Smalley, I. J., and Pieri, D. C., correspondence on 'Polygon Patterns on Europa', *Nature*, Vol. 291, No. 5813, 28 May–4 June 1981, p. 359.

35. Pieri, *op. cit.*, as in footnote 33, p. 18.

36. The *I Ching*, trans. Richard Wilhelm and Cary F. Baynes, Routledge & Kegan Paul, London, 1951, Vol. 11, p. 3.

37. *Ibid.*, Vol. I, p. 5.

38. *Ibid.*, Vol. I, pp. 1–5.

39. *Ibid.*, Vol. I, p. 12.

40. *Ibid.*, Vol. I, p. 10.

41. *Ibid.*, Vol. II, p. 19.

42. *Ibid.*, Vol. II, p. 21.

43. *Ibid.*, Vol. II, p. 22.

CHAPTER TEN

1. Stevens, Peter S., *Patterns in Nature*, Penguin, London, 1977, pp. 4–6.

2. Cahn, Robert W., 'The Genesis of a Void Lattice', *Nature*, Vol. 281, No. 5730, 4 October 1979, pp. 338–9. The quote continues: This is a pity, because the phenomenon is intriguing. . . . The new feature which Liou and his collaborators have now established is that voids are originally formed . . . always in a random pattern, and a void lattice is formed only later when a much higher radiation dose has been absorbed and individual voids have grown to a sufficient size. Any theory of the formation of the void lattice therefore has to be based upon the progressive ordering of an initially random dispersion of voids, and indeed such a theory must come to grips with the question of why voids have to grow to a certain size before a lattice

can form. . . . Stoneham's theory explains why such a lattice is stable once formed, but not how it is established in the first place.'

3. What scientists call 'an elastically isotropic medium' as opposed to 'an elastically anisotropic medium'; see previous reference.

4. A fluid cannot generate eddies below a certain numerical measure of its scale and flow, shown in a number called its 'Reynolds Number', named after the scientist Osborne Reynolds (1842–1912). For instance, if the number is above 2000, the flow of the fluid is turbulent, but if it is below this number, it is viscous instead. Some similar principle seems to operate in connection with metals, which might perhaps usefully be visualized as 'solid fluids'. Metals, in a manner similar to fluids, do seem to require a certain minimum 'scale and flow' in order for 'metal eddies' – i.e. void lattices – to form. I hope that one day research in these areas will progress sufficiently for a 'Reynolds number for metals' to be formulated. For I am convinced that phenomena like this are related and can be expressed by more general concepts than are yet available. But we are still at an early stage, for the first voids in steel were only discovered in 1967, and it takes some decades for people to get their minds in gear about such things. Now that we have reached the twenty-first century, a new term has entered the materials science vocabulary: *'free volume'*. This curious term is sometimes used by materials scientists today to speak of voids without implying that the voids are *actively empty*. The term seems designed to refer to voids as *spaces left free*, as if someone had not bothered to fill the attic because there was not enough junk to do so, and much of the attic space was just left unused. But because part of the attic is left unfilled by junk, one should not conclude that the empty part of the attic is sitting there brooding and plotting about how it can get some junk for itself. Or at least one presumes this is the kind of thinking behind the terminology. An example of this term occurring in a modern scientific survey article is given by Gregory Olson in *Science* Magazine:

'The present grasp of materials by [people who believe in a multi-level view of structure] is well represented by René Antoine Ferchault de Réaumur's 1722 sketch of the structure of quench-hardened steel. . . . He proposed that a single grain of steel . . . if enlarged, would reveal a set of "molecules" . . . and voids. . . . The modern view of material structure differs from Réaumur's mainly in the development of detailed morphologies characteristic at the different length scales of a material's hierarchical structure. In the case of steel, the most significant difference is the overestimation of porosity in the eighteenth-century depictions. And if Réaumur's voids are reinterpreted as "free volume", his sketch becomes a reasonable model of polymeric materials. It shows the remarkable ability of the human mind to infer necessary structure from the contemplation of properties alone.' (Olson, Gregory B., 'Designing a New Material World', *Science*, Vol. 288, No. 5730, 4 October 1979, pp. 338–9.)

5. Krishnan, K., 'Kinetics of Void-Lattice Formation in Metals', *Nature*, Vol. 287, 2 October 1980, p. 420.

6. Temple, Robert K. G., *Götter, Orakel und Visionen*, Umschau Verlag, Frankfurt, Germany, 1982; see Chapter 9, and Index. (Note that there is a

serious misprint in this book due to the publishers; the main diagram in Chapter 9 is incorrect! This vitiates the entire argument unless one realizes the error.)

7. Zeldovich, Ya. B., Einasto, J., and Shandarin, S. F., 'Giant Voids in the Universe', *Nature*, Vol. 300, No. 5891, 2–8 December 1982, pp. 407–13.

8. Smith, Peter J., 'Can Honeycomb Weathering Be ET?', *Nature*, Vol. 301, No. 5898, 27 January–2 February 1983, p. 291.

9. *Ibid.*

10. Smith, Peter J., 'Why Honeycomb Weathering?', *Nature*, Vol. 298, No. 5870, 8–14 July 1982, pp. 121–2.

11. Bell, E. T., *Men of Mathematics*, Simon and Schuster, New York, 1965, p. 266.

12. Temple, Robert, *The Crystal Sun*, Century, London, 2000; see Index.

13. Brinkman, W. F., Fisher, Daniel S., and Moncton, D. E., 'Melting of Two-Dimensional Solids', *Nature*, Vol. 217, No. 4561, 20 August 1982, p. 693.

14. *Ibid.*

15. Atkinson, Barry, 'Cracks in Rocks under Stress', *Nature*, Vol. 290, 23 April 1981, p. 632.

16. Smalley, I. J., and Pieri, D. C., correspondence of 'Polygon Patterns on Europa', *Nature*, Vol. 291, No. 5813, 28 May–4 June 1981, p. 359. Smalley is the one quoted here.

17. *Ibid.* (Smalley).

18. Briggs, John, and Peat, F. David, *Turbulent Mirror*, Harper & Row, New York, 1989, p. 137. See also the three Figures 3.1, A, B, and C, on that page.

19. *Ibid.*

20. Bernal, John Desmond, *The Goldschmidt Memorial Lecture, Reprinted from the Journal of the Chemical Society, August 1949*, Bungay, 1949. (British Library: 8897.ff.42)

21. *Ibid., passim.*

22. Goldschmidt, Victor Moritz, *Die Entstehung unserer Ziffern* (*The Origin of Our Numbers*), Heidelberg, 1932.

23. Berlin, 1901.

24. Century, London, 2000; see Chapter 9.

25. Goldschmidt, Victor Moritz, *From the Borderland between Crystallography and Chemistry*, An Address Delivered before the Science Club of the University of Wisconsin at Madison, 5 October 1903, Bulletin of the University of Wisconsin No. 108, Science Series Vol. 3, No. 2, pp. 21–38, Madison, Wisconsin, March 1904.

26. *Ibid.*, p. 30.

27. *Ibid.*, pp. 29–30.

28. Evans, W. H., 'Communication between Cells', *Nature*, Vol. 283, No. 5747, 7 February 1980, p. 521.

29. *Ibid.*

30. About 1970 there was an attempt made to name these things 'nexuses' (from *nexus*, a Latin word meaning 'connecting'), but this fell flat, thank goodness. (McNutt and Weinstein used the name *nexus* in their article of 1970: McNutt, N. Scott, and Weinstein, Ronald S., 'The Ultrastructure of the

Nexus', *Journal of Cell Biology*, Vol. 47, 1970, pp. 666–88.) It would have been far too much of a tongue-twister to have been stuck with. The connecting hexagonal switches will probably always be called instead by the dull name of 'gap junctions', which seems to have 'stuck'.

31. Loewenstein, Werner R., 'Permeable Junctions', *Cold Spring Harbor Symposia on Quantitative Biology*, Vol. 40, 1975, p. 49.

32. The implications are somewhat analogous to the realization in recent years by neurophysiologists that single brain cells ('neurons') are not the elements of the brain, but rather *groups* of brain cells are the proper elements. I explained this in my book *Open to Suggestion* in 1989, where I wrote quite clearly: '. . . what Merzenich and Edelman have proved conclusively is that . . . The individual brain cell has been found to be as dispensable as a used paper tissue. It only has importance as the member of a group, and individual cells are added to and dropped from groups as relentlessly as players are substituted in a football game. . . . Until now, the single nerve cell (neuron) was viewed as the fundamental functioning element of the brain-computer, like a fixed, wired element in a circuit. The majority of people in psychology today probably still believe this, since they do not generally keep up to date with such developments in neuroscience as the work of Merzenich and Edelman. But as I said a moment ago, the neuron is now dethroned from its place as the *ultimate working unit to which the brain could be reduced.*' (Temple, Robert K. G., *Open to Suggestion: The Uses and Abuses of Hypnosis*, Aquarian Press, Wellingborough, England, 1989, pp. 366–8.) So, it seems that individual cells of all kinds are being dethroned as ultimate units and building blocks, and groups or at least pairs of cells are taking their place.

33. 'The capacity for junctional channel formation seems to be a nearly universal feature of cells. The only exceptions among normal tissues seem to be skeletal muscle and most nerve fibers, which interestingly do not divide. In normal dividing cells, the capacity is so basic that permeable junctions are made even between cultured cells from different organs and different species. For instance, a lens cell from the rabbit eye makes perfectly viable channels with a liver cell from mouse or a fibroblast from man. . . . A wide variety of excitable and inexcitable cells [thus] make junctions containing membrane channels that connect the cell interiors with each other. . . . The channels form within minutes after establishment of cell contact. . . . When the cells are pushed together, they make permeable channels within 4–20 minutes. When the cells are pulled apart, the channels seal. New channels form when the cells are joined at different angles, and so on.' (Loewenstein, *op. cit.*, pp. 51 and 60.)

34. Garfield, R. E., Sims, S., and Daniel, E. E., 'Gap Junctions: Their Presence and Necessity in Myometrium during Parturition', *Science*, Vol. 198, 2 December 1977, pp. 958–60.

35. *Ibid.*

36. Temple, Robert K. G., *The Genius of China*, originally published in 1986 in Britain as *China: Land of Discovery and Invention*, various publication dates, London and New York.

37. Browne, Carole L., Wiley, H. Steven, and Dumont, James N., 'Oocyte-Follicle Cell Gap Junctions in *Xenopus laevis* and the Effects of Gonadotropin in Their Permeability', *Science*, Vol. 203, 12 January 1979, pp. 182–3.

38. *Ibid.*

39. Spray, D. C., Harris, A. L., and Bennett, M. V. L., 'Voltage Dependence of Junctional Conductance in Early Amphibian Embryos', *Science*, Vol. 203, 27 April 1979, pp. 432–4.

40. Thompson, D'Arcy Wentworth, *On Growth and Form*, Cambridge, new edition, 1942. See particularly Chapter 17 and its evocative diagrams, one of which is reproduced here as Figure 65.

41. *Ibid.*, p. 79.

42. But we must never make the mistake of believing that because a fecund growth spurt takes place in 'event-space', it must be perpetual. Recall the fable of the tortoise and the hare. (In fact, I recommend the translation of it by my wife and myself in our Penguin Classic volume of Aesop: Temple, Olivia and Robert, *Aesop: The Complete Fables*, Penguin Classics Series, Penguin Books, Harmondsworth, England, 1998; 'The Tortoise and the Hare' is Fable 352 on p. 257.) My studies over many years of certain English families throughout several centuries of their history has led me to suspect that too rapid a rate of growth of a family at any given period may result in a lessening of its fecundity in later epochs. A perfect example of this would appear to be the Temple family: Lady Hester Temple who died in 1656 and is buried at Burton Dassett, Warwickshire, England, set a world record by living to see seven hundred of her own descendants of her own body, as is recorded in Fuller's *Worthies* (Fuller, Thomas, *The Worthies of England*, Allen and Unwin, London, 1952, pp. 42–3, in the section dealing with Buckinghamshire, where the family seat was Stowe, now a boys' school).

One might think that from such riotous fecundity the world must now be populated entirely by Temples. But alas, if you look around to find the Temples, there are very few to be seen, as I well know, since I am or have been in touch with many branches of them, both British and American, and have a fairly expert knowledge of the genealogies. I have not been able to resist the speculation that too rapid an explosion of fecundity resulted somehow – by mysterious means which I cannot explain – in an enfeebling of the fertility of the family in later generations, as I know in some detail has often been the case. And as I have pointed out in a brief essay entitled 'The Bigger They Are the Fewer', in my book of popular science, *Strange Things* (Temple, Robert, *Strange Things: A Collection of Modern Scientific Curiosities*, Sphere Books, London, 1983), species seem to have just so much energy to go around – so why not families? If used up too quickly, does it later wither the vine?

43. Diamond, Jared M., 'Transcellular Cross-Talk between Epithelial Cell Membranes', *Nature*, Vol. 300, No. 5894, 23 December 1982–3 January 1983, p. 683.

44. Occasionally scientists are forced up against this problem. One example of this from 1980 was from the article by Alan Roberts and Ken Tregonning,

'The Robustness of Natural Systems', *Nature*, Vol. 288, No. 5788, 20 November 1980, pp. 265–6. In their study of 'natural systems' (entities which naturally exist rather than our machines which attempt to emulate them), the authors remark that they 'cannot be seen as just "externally" linked . . .'

45. Steinhardt, Paul J., Jeong, H.-C., Saitoh, K., Tanaka, M., Abe, E., and Tsai, A. P., 'Experimental Verification of the Quasi-Unit-Cell Model of Quasicrystal Structure', *Nature*, Vol. 396, No. 6706, 5 November 1998, p. 55.

46. Urban, Knut W., 'Quasicrystals: From Tilings to Coverings', *Nature*, Vol. 396, No. 6706, 5 November 1998, pp. 14–15.

47. Wilson, Edward O. and seven others, *Life on Earth*, Sinauer Associates, Sunderland, Massachusetts, USA, 2nd edition, 1978, p. 440.

48. Aebi, Ueli, Ross Smith, Phillip, Isenberg, Gerhard, and Pollard, Thomas D., 'Structure of Crystalline Actin Sheets', *Nature*, Vol. 288, No. 5788, 20 November 1980, pp. 296–8.

49. Miller, Kenneth R., 'Three-Dimensional Structure of a Photosynthetic Membrane', *Nature*, Vol. 300, No. 5887, 4–10 November 1982, pp. 53–5.

50. *Ibid.*, p. 54.

51. If we think a photosynthetic unit is unglamorous, and hardly on a par with an event in the much grander forum of human life, let us pause a moment to ponder this: most events in human life are purely vegetative or repetitive in character, and thoroughly unglamorous. The processes of eating, sleeping, digesting, foraging for food, going to the supermarket, indeed going to work to earn the salary to pay for the food, plus the processes of buying a house, keeping it in repair, paying the mortgage, plus the processes of sexual intercourse, courtship, giving birth, suckling babies, sending or taking the kids to school, etc. – all these are more or less repetitive functions of keeping life going. In 'event-space' they are generally as standardized and utilitarian as photosynthetic units, and as similar to one another in their repeating arrays across a population.'Higher activities' in which we glory, but with which we really have so little to do, are akin to *specialized regions*, or are events which are like *transformed cells*, or should we say *excited states* of cells, holding to an electric analogy. Although the majority of acts of sexual intercourse are undistinguished, there are exceptional cases which are extraordinary; courtship is generally fairly routine, but there are cases when amazing things occur. Since what distinguishes the remarkable examples of these things is the element of passion, we are encouraged to think of such instances as 'excited states' which stand out because they are more highly charged. Everything can be more highly charged and take on elements of distinction: Ezra Pound often wrote about the necessity for poets to use what he called *charged language*. One of his basic tenets, expressed in his book *ABC of Reading* is: 'Literature is language charged with meaning. Great literature is simply language charged with meaning to the utmost possible degree.' (Pound, Ezra, *ABC of Reading*, New Directions Paperbook, New York, 1960, p. 28; these statements appeared earlier in his essay 'How to Read'.) When big things really begin to happen in 'event-space', large regions

of event-cells may become charged with meaning, or activated in a manner resembling the way in which long-range order sets in in muscles just before a woman gives birth. Such long-range ordering processes may be related to the phenomena which have been observed in human crowds. Elias Canetti, a Nobel Laureate for Literature, wrote in his strange and fascinating book *Crowds and Power* a description of crowds which reminds us of what we know of the muscles before giving birth: 'The most important occurrence within the crowd is the *discharge*. Before this the crowd does not actually exist; it is the discharge which creates it. This is the moment when all who belong to the crowd get rid of their differences and feel equal. . . . During the discharge distinctions are thrown off and all feel *equal*. In that density, where there is scarcely any space between, and body presses against body, each man is as near the other as he is to himself; and an immense feeling of relief ensues. It is for the sake of this blessed moment, when no-one is greater or better than another, that people become a crowd.' (Canetti, Elias, *Crowds and Power*, Victor Gollancz, London, 1962, pp. 17–18.) In short, what Canetti is describing is a *phase transition* in the human sphere, where people are arrayed like a hexagonal sheet, and energy surges through them, rendering them all momentarily *units* in a larger configuration. Many people do indeed feel bliss at the surrender of personal identity, if only for a moment. The surrender of personal identity means also, of course, the surrender of personal responsibility, and with the responsibility goes all the anxiety which responsibility entails. For the sake of such relief, no matter how brief, large numbers of people have always been tempted to submerge themselves in mass movements, whether political, religious, or whatever kind imaginable. Surrender to a greater cause, when one becomes a unit rather than an entity, is surely a universal problem for all intelligent species. In my book about hypnosis entitled *Open to Suggestion* (*op. cit.*, pp. 290–1), I discussed crowd psychology, mass suggestion and mind control at considerable length, including the ideas of Canetti about crowds. I also recorded my eyewitness account of my only encounter with a classic Canetti mob in my teens, including these passages: 'A terrifying sight greeted our eyes. Just coming into view, having already engulfed Houston Hall and splashing along the street like a tidal wave, was a *mob*. Frothing at the edges and emitting from its core a continuous howl of anguish, power, and protest, this seething mass was headed straight towards us. It consisted of students who had one thing in common: they had all become each other. Only years later when I read Elias Canetti's *Crowds and Power* did I fully appreciate the strange phenomenon before me. It is the only genuine mob I have ever seen, and I hope never to see another. But it was alive, it was pulsating with wrath, it arrogated to itself all rights, and it sought to vent its rage upon some object in order to discharge its enormous energy. . . . The mob, consisting of aggregated individuals who on their own would never have dreamt of doing such a thing, seized on the bus as the object which would receive the discharge of energy which every mob needs for its communal orgasm. In retrospect, when I took a greater interest in physics, I came to realize that the formation and dissolution of a mob are phase transitions, rather like the sudden alignment of atoms in a piece of iron which has just been magnetized by passing through the Curie point. . . . At the height of this madness we saw other students streaming towards the mob in ecstasy, to join in the mêlée. . . . They had all gone crazy, and as they reached the mob they hurled themselves into it and onto it bodily, joining their flesh to the mob's flesh, feeding it with their bodies like corpses being hurled onto a raging funeral pyre which was burning out of control. They could not wait to merge, to become one with the mob.'

We should never lose sight of the fact that people too can become *units*. Indeed, what century proves this more dramatically than the last? The twentieth century, when dispassionate history comes to be written, may be looked upon in restrospect as the 'century when men became things'.

52. Mackenzie, J. C., 'Ordered Structure of the Stratum Corneum of Mammalian Skin', *Nature*, Vol. 222, 31 May 1969, p. 881.

53. Allen, T. D., and Potten, C. S., 'Fine-Structural Identification and Organization of the Epidermal Proliferative Unit', *Journal of Cell Science*, Vol. 15, 1974, p. 291.

54. Allen, T. D., and Potten, C. S., 'Significance of Cell Shape in Tissue Architecture', *Nature*, Vol. 264, 9 December 1976, pp. 545–7.

55. *Ibid.*, p. 545.

56. Ollenrenshaw, Dame Kathleen, 'Form and Pattern', *Proceedings of the Royal Institution*, London, Vol. 53, 1981, p. 7.

57. 'Each cell only becomes free to [shed] when it is slightly 'proud' of its six neighbours and has all its edges free. . . . Such an ordered [shedding] in relation to [the)] cell shape implies a regular alternating overlap between neighbouring columns, as observed in epidermis sections. . . . [thus] a column cannot introduce another differentiated cell into its squame pile until both neighbours have added to theirs . . . and shows that the central column must be added to before those at the periphery. The overlaps of the peripheral columns may form a vertical channel to aid this sequence, and thus provide a partial self-assembly system . . . the raised edges of the six surrounding columns may provide a physical guide to facilitate [cell] migration [upwards].' (Allen and Potten, 'Significance', *op. cit.*, p. 546.)

58. *Ibid.*

59. Menton, David N., 'A Liquid Film Model of Tetrakaidecahedral Packing to Account for the Establishment of Epidermal Cell Columns', *Journal of Investigative Dermatology*, Vol. 66, No. 5, 1976, p. 283.

60. Menton, David N., 'A Minimum-surface Mechanism to Account for the Organization of Cells into Columns in the Mammalian Epidermis', *American Journal of Anatomy*, Vol. 145, No. 1, January 1976, p. 1.

61. *Ibid.*, pp. 9–10.

62. Marks, Robert W., *The New Mathematics Dictionary and Handbook*, Bantam paperback, New York, 1967, p. 155.

63. *Ibid.*

64. Hilbert, David, and Cohn-Vossen, S., *Geometry and the Imagination* (English translation of *Anschauliche Geometrie*), Chelsea Publishing Company, New York, 1952, p. 156, note 6: '. . . the 24-cell has twelve three-dimensional spaces of symmetry that pass through its center and intersect it

in a cubo-octahedron.'

65. Illustration from Bursill, Thomas and Rao, 'Stability of Zeolites under Electron Irradiation and Imaging of Heavy Cations in Silicates', *Nature*, 15 January 1981, pp. 156–7.

66. Coxeter, H. S. M., *Regular Polytopes*, Collier-Macmillan, London, second edition, 1963, p. 154.

67. *Ibid.*, p. 289.

68. *Ibid.*, pp. 119 and ix of the preface to the first edition.

69. Perkowitz, Sidney, *Universal Foam: from Cappuccino to the Cosmos*, Walker & Company, New York, 2000.

70. Weaire, Denis, and Hutzler, Stefan, *The Physics of Foams*, Clarendon Press, Oxford, 1999 (apparently appeared in 2000).

71. Whicher, Olive, *Projective Geometry: Creative Polarities in Space and Time*, Rudolf Steiner Press, London, 1971.

72. *Ibid.*, pp. 55–6.

73. *Ibid.*, pp. 56–8.

74. Translated by the author.

INDEX